The
zkl
Programming Language
Reference Manual

Craig Durland

Feedback

Please direct comments and suggestions about this document to:
craigd@zenkinetic.com

See Also

For more on zkl, including downloads (and an electronic copy of this book), please
visit http://zenkinetic.com/

Publication history

- March 2008
- July 2008
- January 2010, updated for zkl version 1.1
- December 2010, updated for zkl version 1.3
- June 2011, updated for zkl version 1.5.2
- December 2011, updated for zkl version 1.6
- August 2012, updated for zkl version 1.7
- June 2013, updated for zkl version 1.10
- September 2013, updated for zkl version 1.12
- June 2015, updated for zkl version 1.12.21
- January 2017, updated for zkl version 1.12.38
- December 2018, updated for zkl version 1.14.1

Contents

The Young Person's Guide to zkl

zkl doesn't attempt to boil the ocean,
zkl doesn't want to warm the ocean.
zkl wants to make a nice cup of tea.
--Zander Kale

zkl[1] is a general purpose object oriented programming language. It is imperative but borrows concepts from many programming paradigms, including functional. It is curly-bracketed, dynamic, reflective, and threaded. It has built in garbage collection, strings, lists, dictionaries, threads, fibers (continuations and co-routines) and more. The syntax strongly resembles the C programming language while the data model is closer to that of Python and Smalltalk. The goal of zkl is to enable rapid prototyping, quickly developing solutions to problems and does this at the expense of the strong static checking needed for production oriented languages. On the other hand, zkl has a level of verbosity that slows development somewhat, compared, for example, to Python or (especially) Perl.

In zkl, everything is an object, even numbers. Classes and functions behave like any other object, including numbers. Classes and functions can have the same anonymity as numbers[2]. They usually don't but it is nice to be able to create them on the fly, like 123, if you need to. Even threads are objects.

The "Hello world" program looks pretty much the same as it does in most languages:
```
    println("Hello world"); or "Hello again".println();
```
There is no need for include files or main(). Even the compile step is invisible.

Another example, the ever popular factorial program:

---

1   Pronounced zee·kay·el or zee·kale (for American English speakers). Or however you like.
2   "Lambda" functions

The Young Person's Guide to zkl

```
fcn fact(x){  // Input: x   output: x!
    if (0==x) return(1);          // 0! → 1
    return( x * fact(x - 1) );    // x! → x * (x-1)!
}
```

Looks very similar to C, Java or Python. Since zkl integers are 64 bits long, it can generate big numbers:

```
fact(37)  → 10969079327018188880³
```

zkl has core support for preemptive threads. Every class is threadable, as are functions:

```
fcn thread{ println("I am running in ",vm); }
thread.launch() → "I am running in VM#543"
```

zkl includes a fair amount of threading support, such as locks, events, semaphores, waiters, timers, heartbeat timers and pipes (not to be confused with Unix pipes although they are used for interprocess communication).

The zkl core objects have been designed to try and have the same "look and feel" so they can be used interchangeably. For example, strings, lists and files have common functionality that allows them to be used in the same way in foreach loops:

```
foreach char in ("123")                // String: Print 1 2 3
    { println(char); }
foreach item in ( List("1","2",3) )    // Print 1 2 3
    { println(item); }
foreach line in (File("f.txt","r"))    // Print every line
    { print(line); }
```

If you look closely at the list example, you'll notice that lists are heterogeneous, that is, they can contain *any* zkl object. In this case, two strings and a number.

The zkl exception system is very similar to that of Java, Python and other languages.

```
try{
    gettingOutOfBedWasABadIdea:=consultHoroscope(today);
    if (gettingOutOfBedWasABadIdea)
        throw(Exception.BadDay("Coffee please"));
}
catch(BadDay){
    println("I heard somebody say: ",__exception.text);
}
```

When this code is run and my horoscope for today isn't so good, the code will print:
    I heard somebody say: Coffee please

---

3   Using the BigNum extension: `fact(BigNum(50))` : `"%,d".fmt(_)` → 30,414,093,201, 713,378,043,612, 608,166,064,768,844,377,641,568,960,512,000,000,000,000

Getting Started

The zkl executable is self contained; it is all you need to get started programming in zkl. Running zkl gives you an interactive shell:

```
> zkl
zkl: 1+2
3
zkl: var x=L(1, "2", 3.4, L(5,"six"), self, fcn(x){ x + 1 })
L(1,"2",3.4,L(5,"six"),Class(__class#0),Fcn(__fcn#1))
zkl: x.apply("type")
L("Int","StringConst","Float","List","Class","Fcn")
zkl: ^C
>
```

To create programs, use your favorite text editor to create a .zkl file and then run it:

```
zkl myprogram.zkl
zkl myprogram
```

Data Things: Numbers, Strings, etc

<u>Numbers</u>

Numbers can be integer or floating point. Which one is determined by the number itself. For example, 1 is an integer and 1.2 is a floating point number. You can do all the number things: add, subtract, etc. It is important to note that the first number in a calculation determines which type of number is the result of a calculation. For example:

```
1 + 2        → 3    // an integer
1.5 + 2      → 3.5  // a float
1 + 2 * 3    → 7    // an integer
1 + 2.5 * 3 → 8     // an integer BUT since multiplication is performed before addition,
// the calculation becomes:
1 + (2.5 * 3) → 1 + 7.5 → 8
```

<u>Strings</u>

A string is a bunch of characters in double quotes. For example: "This is a string". Strings are immutable, that is, they can't change (just like numbers). To change a string, you create a new string from the old one:

```
"New " + "string" → "New String"
```

Lists

A list is an ordered collection of objects. You create them by giving objects to a list and it will hand you back a new list with those objects in it. "List" is the "mother" list (and is usually referred to as "L"). So, to create a list of two objects: `L(1,"two")`. Lists are mutable and can change. To add objects to the end a list, you can use the append method or the plus operator:

```
a:=L(1,"two"); a.append(3.5)      → L(1,"two",3.5)
a + "four"                         → L(1,"two",3.5,"four")
```

You can do many things with lists. For example, to sort it:

```
L(5,12,3.5,7).sort()              → L(3.5,5,7,12)
```

To create a list of hex strings from a list of integers:

```
L(9,10,11).apply("toString",16)  → L("9","a","b")
```

Dictionaries

Dictionaries are like the book: a word (the key) has a definition (the value). Anything can be a key and anything can be value.

```
d:=Dictionary();    // Create a dictionary
d["one"]=2;         // The key is "one" and value is the integer 2
d[3]="four";
d → D( 3:four one:2 )
```

Etc

Other objects include TCP/IP sockets, regular expressions, unit tests, time and date, fibers (continuations and co-routines), threads, a data container/byte stream editor and atomic objects. You can see a list by typing "`Vault.dir()`".

Branching

Conditional branching is the traditional if/else:

```
if (1) println("This is done always");
if ("one"==2) println("Nope")
else           println("Yep");
```

An "if" actually has a value:

```
x:=1;
println( if (x==1) "one" else "not one" );  → "one"
```

Loops

zkl provides three types of looping: while/do loops, foreach loops and "transform the collection" loops.

```
while(condition){ code } // run code while condition is true
do{ code }               // run code while condition
while(condition);        // is true, at least once
```

```
do(n){ code }              // run code n times
```

Foreach loops walk through an object using a Walker (which would be called an iterator in languages such as C++, Java or Python). Most objects support a walker so you can traverse them.

```
foreach n in (object) // run code for each item in object
    { code }
foreach n in (L(1,"two",3)){ println(n); } → "1", "two", "3"
```

Additionally, walkers can be used by themselves:

```
L(1,"two",3).walker().walk() → L(1,"two",3)
w:=L(1,"two",3).walker(); w.peek() → 1
```

Functional languages support various ways of applying a function to a collection of data in one statement. This is a very powerful idea, which zkl supports through these methods: apply/pump, filter and reduce.

```
L(1,2,3).apply('+(5))                  → L(6,7,8) // aka map, mapcar
L(1,2,"three",4).filter("isEven")  → L(2,4)
L(5,3,7,99,8).reduce((0).max)      → 99  // aka fold
fcn enum(x,ref){return(ref.inc(),x)}
L("one","two").apply(enum,Ref(0))  → L( L(0,"one"), L(1,"two") )
```

Most container objects (such as lists, files, strings) support these methods, as do Walkers.

Functions

Code is organized in functions, indicated by the "fcn" keyword. A simple function might be:

```
fcn hello{ println("Hello World"); }
```

hello() runs the function. There is no requirement for functions to be named, so the previous example could be written as a lambda function:

```
fcn{ println("Hello World") }(); // run the lambda function
```

This notation is handy when you want to pass functions to other functions:

```
f(fcn{ println("Hello World") });
```

is the same as f(hello) (the function hello). Functions can return more than one thing,

```
fcn f{ return(1,2,3) }
```

is a function that returns a list of three integers. Then, a,b,c:=f() would set a to 1, b to 2 and c to 3.

Classes

Classes are containers, they hold other objects: classes, functions, and data.

```
class C{
   var c;        // instance variable
   println("This is part of the class constructor");
   fcn init(v){
     println("This function is run when "
             "a new instance is created");
     c=v;                  // set the class variable
   }
   fcn hello{ println("Hello"); }
}
```

Calling the class creates a new instance (copy) of the class:

```
c:=C(1)  →
```

This is part of the class constructor

This function is run when a new instance is created

You can also access the class variables and functions:

```
c.hello() → "Hello"
c.c        → 1
```

The class C is just an "reference" instance; in such classes, all variables are initialized to Void (unless they are set in the constructor).

```
C.hello()  → "Hello"
C.c        → Void
```

Scope

zkl is block (lexically) scoped; if something is created in a block, it wants to stays there. Except functions and classes, which are Class scoped. Closures and partial function application can be used to give functions one way lexical scoping.

The zkl Shell

The shell provides an interactive REPL[4] environment where you can get immediate feedback to your experiments. Often, while writing programs, it is convenient to test a few things in the shell and then paste them into your program. Classes, functions and variables stick around so you can reference them later.

The shell is documented in Objects.startup.

---

4   Read-eval-print loop: http://en.wikipedia.org/wiki/REPL

Shared Libraries

Shared libraries (DLLs) enable objects written in C to be added to the system. Example objects include a zlib (gzip) interface, allowing both streaming and static compression and inflation and a LZO compression object.

```
Zeelib:=Import("ZeeLib");
text:=Zeelib.Compressor(True).write("This is a test").close();
(f:=File("foo.txt.z","wb")).write(text.drain()); f.close();
```

That creates the file "foo.text.z" with the compressed text in it. To check:

```
>gzip -dc foo.txt.z
This is a test
```

Concept to Topic Mapping

Closure, Partial application:
- Function: 'wrap, Partial (Objects.Deferred)
- Objects: .fp (Object).

Command line processing:
- Objects: Utils.Argh

Lambda:
- Keywords: Fcn (anonymous functions)
- Objects: Deferred ('wrap)

Lazy and infinite lists:
- Objects: Walker

Lazy objects:
- Objects: Deferred

Looping, functional:
- Methods: apply, filter, pump, reduce, Utils.zipWith, Utils.Helpers.cycle
- Objects: Fcn (tail recursion),Walker

Looping, imperative
- Keywords: do, foreach, while, continue, break
- Objects: Utils.Generator, VM (yield), Walker

Networking:
- Objects: Network.TCP

Packaging:
- Keywords: pimport
- Objects: Import, Utils.Wad

Parameters (arg lists), manipulating:
- Objects: List (xplode), VM (arglist, nthArg, numArgs, pasteArgs)

Repl (read-evel-print-loop), the command line:
- Objects: startup

Sugar:
- Keywords: ask, print.
- Objects: Deferred ('wrap), Op ('+,'-,'*,'/)

Threads, cooperative (green):
- Objects: Fcn (strand, stranded)

Threads, native:
- Keywords: class (threading)
- Objects: Class (launch, liftoff, splashdown), Fcn (launch, future), Thread.Pipe, Thread.Straw

Unit testing:
- Objects: Test

Use zkl to focus on solutions! Order before midnight and receive a FREE microscope!
-- Zander Kale

The zkl Keywords

Expressions, editorials, expugnations, exclamations,
enfadulations
It's all talk
-- King Crimison

Names

Object names can consist of the characters a-z, A-Z, 0-9 and _ (underscore). A name can't start with a number.

Notes:

- Names are limited to 80 characters (out of convenience for the VM).
- Case matters. "Foo" and "foo" are different names.
- A dot (".") is used to connect names together (foo.bar) to create a "data reference", a compound name that refers to nested object. There is no restriction on the total length of a data reference.
- It is a bad idea to use "_" as a name, some things use that as a placeholder.

Internal Names

The compiler will generally use two leading underscores and a "#" for internal names ("__fcn#1", "__jWalker"); the underscores signify a "system" name and the # is used to avoid any possible conflict with user names (since user source code isn't able to create names with # in them). This also means you can't access them by name either; but then, it is unlikely you will need to.

Keywords

The keywords are:

AKA	const	else	onExit	self	while
Attributes	continue	fcn	onExitBlock	switch	
break	critical	foreach	reg	throw	
catch	_debug_	if	return	try	
class	do	include	returnClass	var	

Reserved Words

Reserved words are words that the compiles deems too important to be replaced by user defined objects. The compiler doesn't restrict these words everywhere, just where it thinks there could be problems. Refer to the section in parenthesis for more information.

and	liftoff (Class)	topdog (Class)
BaseClass (Object)	not	True (Bool)
__constructor (Class)	or	Void (Void)
False (Bool)	resolve (Object)	
init (Class)	splashdown (Class)	
launch (Class, Fcn)	TheVault (TheVault)	

(Bool) = Objects.Bool, (Class) = Objects.Class, (Fcn) = Objects.Fcn, (Object) = Objects.Object, (TheVault) = Objects.TheVault, (Void) = Objects.Void

Syntactic Sugar

The compiler make a few helpful substitutions for commonly used objects.

ask	→ Console.ask
D	→ Dictionary
L	→ List
print	→ Console.print
println	→ Console.println
T	→ ROList
vm	→ VM

These changes are only made if the compiler can't resolve a token. In other words, if you have a function named "print", the compiler will use that, rather than Console.print.

Sugared parameters

Parameters to function and method calls also have some sugar for operators and functions.

`'op`	→	`Op(op)`. Eg `sort('<)` → `sort(Op("<")`
		See Objects.Op
`'wrap`	→	Closure. Eg `r:=5; L(1,2,3).apply('wrap(n){ n+r })` → L(6,7,8), `'wrap` is sugar for a partial function wrapping `r`.
		See Objects.Deferred

__<name>

Syntax: __DATE__, __DEBUG__, __FILE__, __LINE__, __NAME__, __TIME__
See Also: Keywords._debug_, Objects.Compiler, Keywords.AKA

Abstract
These compiler provided constants give you information about what is being compiled.
These constants are only available at compile time.

Discussion
- __DATE__ is when the source code was compiled. The format is "yyyy-mm-dd".
- __DEBUG__ is the value of the debug level sent to the compiler.
- __FILE__ is the name of the source text. It might be the full file name (if a file is being compiled) or something made up (eg "<text>" if text is being compiled).
- __LINE__ is the current line being compiled. The first line is 1.
```
println("foo");                      // "foo"
println("This is line ",__LINE__);   // "2"
```
- __NAME__ is the name of the current top level class (compilation unit). It might be "RootClass#" or something else (the compiler makes this up). It can be changed by AKA.
- __TIME__ is the time when this source was compiled. The format is "hh:mm:ss" in 24 hour local time.

Examples
```
println("The file being compiled is ",__FILE__);
_debug_ { println("This is at source line ",__LINE__); }
```

AKA

Syntax: `AKA(className)`
See Also: Keywords.class

Abstract
Attaches className to top level class instead of the file name.
Also sets the vaultPath property and the __VAULT_PATH compiler const.

Restrictions
- AKA is only valid in the top level scope (root class).

Discussion
When a class is compiled, the default class name is derived from the name of the file that is being compiled or is something like "RootClass#". This is fine for scripts and one offs but might not be a good Vault name. AKA allows you to attach a name of your choosing to the top level class.

Example file contents
- `AKA(Foo);`
- `{AKA(Foo)}`   → error
- `class C {`
      `AKA(C);`   → error, AKA only valid at the top level
  `}`
- `AKA(Foo);`
  `fcn f {}`
  `TheVault.BaseClass.add(self);`   → adds Class Foo to the Vault
- `AKA(Compiler.Parser);` sets the class name to "Parser" and sets the vault path to "Compiler".

ask

Syntax: `ask(`parameters`)`
See Also: Objects.Console

Abstract
Ask isn't really a keyword, it is syntactic sugar for Console.ask.

Discussion
Ask is used so much that the compiler saves on keyboard wear and tear by redirecting it to the Console object. Since it isn't a keyword, it can be "reused" by things like functions, variables or classes.

assert

Syntax
- **_assert_(**boolExpression,message="")

Abstract
Assert something is True or throw AssertionError.
The error text will look something like this:
   "assert(foo.zkl:2): message"

Discussion
A helpful tool to do some error checking.
For example:
assert(1==3) → AssertionError : assert(../Tmp/foo.zkl:2)

assert((z:=f())==5,"I wanted 5, got "+z); →
   AssertionError : assert(../Tmp/foo.zkl:4): I wanted 5, got hoho

Attributes

Syntax: `Attributes(attribute [,attribute ...])`
Attributes: `static`, `script` and `noChildren`
See Also: Objects.Class

Abstract
Attaches attributes to a class.
You can also set these with `class [attr] C {}`.

Discussion
Attributes subtlety affect class behavior. For a discussion, see Class Attributes in the Class chapter.

The attributes are:

- **static**: There will be only one copy of this class. If you inherit from a static class, you will share the parent class with every other instance of the class. This attribute is typically used at the file level to keep a large class from being unnecessarily replicated. This attribute can only be set in a class.
  ```
  Attribute(static);
  fcn f { Attribute(static); }  // error
  { Attribute(static); }        // error, in a block
  class C1 {                            // not static
     class C2 { Attribute(static); }  // static
  }
  ```
  There will only be one copy of the instance variables.
  Static class variables are not thread safe.
- **script**: This attribute can only be set in the root class.
  ```
  Attribute(script);
  class C2 { Attribute(script); }     // error
  ```
  The script attribute is informational, as far as the VM is concerned. The Import class uses it to determine how to run a class when it is loaded.
- **noChildren**: This attribute tells the VM that this class can not be used as a parent class. It is often paired with static classes.
  ```
  class [noChildren] C { }
  class D(C) {}        // error
  ```

The attributes do NOT propagate to contained or child classes.

break

Syntax
- `while(…){ … ` **`break`**`; }`
- `do{ … ` **`break`**`; }while (…)`
- `foreach … { ` **`break`**`; }`
- **`break(`**`[1-9]`**`)`**

See Also: Keywords.continue

Abstract
Leave the closest enclosing loop block. With a parameter, break out of the nth loop
(`break(1)` is the same as `break`).

Discussion
The break keyword allows for early termination of a loop. The result is as if the loop
had terminated normally. Note that you can only exit the nearest enclosing loop
block.

Example
Print "12":
```
n:=0; while (1){ print(n+=1); if (n==2) break; }
```
Again:
```
foreach n in ("1234567890"){ print(n); if (n=="2") break; }
```

class

Syntax: Creation
- `class [name] { [classes] [functions] [constructorCode] }`
- `class(parentClass [,...]){ block }`
- `class [[attributes]][name][(parent(s))]{ block }`

Syntax: Reference
- `className`

Syntax: Instance Creation
- `className()`
- `className(parametersPassedToInit)`

Returns
- Reference: The Class
- Creation: The new class instance, after allocation, running the constructor and the init function (if it exists).

Notes
- "." (dot) is used to refer to objects contained in a class.
- Classes support multiple inheritance.
- Some OO languages refer to parent classes as "super" (above) classes.
- Parent classes need to have been already defined (in this file) or be in the Vault.
- Any class (or, preferably, class instance) can become a thread.
- Class names can be up to 80 characters long and can use the characters "a-zA-Z0-9_", in other words: underscore, digits, upper or lower case letters. A name can not start with a digit.
- Names are case sensitive.
- The possible attributes are noChildren, private and static. These are the same as that can be set with the Attributes keyword.

See Also
- Objects.Class
- Objects.Fcn, Keywords.fcn
- Keywords.returnClass, Keywords.AKA, Keywords.Attributes
- Objects.Object
- Objects.Compiler.compileFile, Objects.Compiler.compileText

Abstract

Define a new class object. A simple example:
```
class C{ var v=14; fcn f{ println("f",v); } }
C.f();          // prints "f14"
c:=C();         // create a new instance of C
c.f();          // prints "f14"
```

A class can contain any of: classes, functions and/or class variables.

All class objects inherit from Objects.Class.

Discussion
The class keyword is used to define a Class. A Class is basically a "active" container that can hold data (variables), functions and classes. It is active because it can create new instances of itself and run contained code.

Instance
All classes are class "instances". The word instance is used to refer to a copy of an existing class. "Class" refers to the original "ancestral" instance/definition.

The [Virtual] Class Object
When you use the class keyword to create a new class, you implicitly inherit from Objects.Class, which is a virtual object that inherits from Object and contains all the methods, properties and operators listed in the Objects.Object and Objects.Class sections. That statement is pretty obtuse; here is some pseudo code to explain it from another angle:

```
class Class(Object){
    <methods, properties and operators>
}
class myClass(parents,Class){ … }
```
Notes:
- Class is the last class in the inheritance list so it matched last, use BaseClass (Object method) if you need to access it.
- Class and Object are not special names, and are used to name concepts. Use them if you like.

Class Variables (Instance Data)
When var is used to declare a class variable, that variable is created "class local", that is, each instance of the class contains one of those variables, separate from all other instances. When a new instance is created, the variables of the creating class are copied to the new class.

One common error is an implicitly declared register overwriting a class var. Consider:

```
class{
    var x;
    fcn f{ x=3; }      // sets class var
}
```

The class variable "x" is overwritten in the function f. If f had actually meant to use x as a local variable, the programmer is going to be surprised. Thus, it is a good idea to explicitly declare variables (with var or reg) and use longer names for class variables.

Functions

Functions contained in a class are "bound" to a specific instance of that class. Because of this, a function can always refer to objects in its containing class, no matter how that function is referenced, spindled or mutilated.

Attributes

A class can have several attributes. Since the root class (aka file) is declared implicitly, the root class attributes are set with the Attributes keyword. See Keywords.Attributes for a description. The "private" attribute means that resolve will not be able to find this class but it is visible throughout the file it is defined in.

Special Functions

A function marked *Reserved* means you can't create this function, the compiler creates it for you. Functions marked *Restricted* mean that the name can only be created as a class function, not as a class or variable.

- **__constructor**: *Reserved*. The Class Constructor (you create this implicitly).
  As a class is compiled, the compiler collects all the source code that isn't in a function and puts into a function named "__constructor", in the order that the code appears. (You can't create this function by name but you can call it with __constructor()). That code is then compiled and added to the class. When a new instance of a class is created (new copy allocated), the constructor is called to "construct" the new class. This is done just before init is called. The constructor is *usually* called without any parameters[5] and almost always returns the new instance (almost because, sometimes, you don't want the class to act like a class; see Keywords.returnClass).

  The constructor is always the first function in a class, even if it is nullFcn. The only times you should need to call the constructor is when the compiler hands you a class (because the compiler doesn't construct classes, it only creates them) or when you tell the loader not call the constructor.
  These code snippets both run the constructor (the first is preferred):
  ```
  klass.__constructor()
  ```

---

5 Since the constructor is a function like any other, it can be called with parameters. But, by default, the constructor is called with no parameters.

```
klass.fcns[0]()
```

- **init(**[*parameters*]**)**: *Restricted*. The init function is optional. If it exists, it is called during instance creation, just after the constructor has been called. Init almost always returns the new instance (almost because, sometimes, you don't want the class to act like a class; see returnClass). In `ClassC(1,2,3)`, the parameters passed to init are 1,2,3.

  In the constructor and init, the compiler always appends `return(self)` to the code so you don't have to remember to return the new instance (otherwise
  ```
  newClass=ClassC(1);
  ```
  might return some random object instead of the new ClassC). For this reason, the compiler wants the code to run straight through and actively discourages you from leaving (eg "return" is illegal). The `returnClass` keyword is the escape hatch.
- **launch(**[*parameters*]**)**: *Restricted*. Run this class in a thread. See Threading (below).
- **liftoff(**[*parameters*]**)**: *Restricted*. Called when this class is launched as a thread. The parameters are the same as those to launch. See Threading (below).
- **runMe(**[*parameters*]**)**: runMe hijacks the create method. See Objects.Class.Run Me Classes.
- **splashdown(**happyDeath,exception**)**: *Restricted*. Optional. Called when a thread is done running. See Threading (below).
- **toString()**: Optional. If you want to do something different for the name of your class. Be careful however. See Objects.Class.toString.
- **__sGet(**i [,n]**)**: Optional. Implements self[i [,n]]. See subscripts (below).
- **__sSet(**x,i [,n]**)**: Optional. Implements self[i [,n]]=x. See subscripts (below).

Definition

At runtime, an instance of each defined class is created, the "**reference**" (or Eve) instance. This reference instance can then be used to create additional instances of itself (which, in turn, can create copies of the reference instance). The reference is a class instance like any other instance.

Creating a New Instance

- Copy method:
  - A copy is created.
  - Copies of fcns, contained classes, parents, …
  - Class variables are copied/duplicated.

Keywords

- Instance creation: `className([parameters for the init function])`
  Any new class instance created this way is the same as if it was created from the reference instance (although the instance data may be different).
- A new copy of the class is created, using `class.copy()`.
  - Default args for the init function are resolved.
  - The constructor is run.
  - The init function is called (if it exists) with parameters (if any).
    Note: since default parameters are resolved prior to the constructor being called, an init function like
    ```
    class C{
        var x="x";
        fcn init(y=self.x){ println(y) }
    }
    ```
    will always have y set to Void. This is unexpected and not at all obvious. But that is the way it is. If you call the init function directly, the code works as expected (that is, y is "x").
  - The new instance is returned.
  - If class has the "static" attribute set, the class is returned unchanged after running init (the constructor isn't run), no new instances are made.
- Construction order (for contained classes):
  Contained classes are constructed where they are defined.
  ```
  class A{              // constructe4 first
      var av=12;        // initialized here
      class B{          // constructed second
          class C{}     // third
              if(r){ class M{} } // maybe constructed

      class D{          // forth but after dfv initialized
          fcn init{}    // fifth (for A())
          fcn f{ var dfv=5; } // dfv initialized before D
      }
      class E{}         // sixth
  }
  ```
  A defined→ A, av, B, C, dfv, D, E (where A is A.__constructor(), etc)
  A()   → A, av, B, C, dfv, D, D.init, E
  A.D()   → dfv, D, D.init. New D, same A.
- To recap:
  ```
  class C{
      var x="x";
      fcn init(y=5){ x=y }
  }
  ```

```
C's constructor has been called and x is "x".
c=C.copy(); // c.x="x", init not called
c=C();      // c.x=5, a copy of C has been made and
            //   c's constructor and init called
c=C(1);     // c.x=1, copy made, constructor & init called
c=C.init(); // c is C, C.x=5, new instance not created,
            //   but constructor and init ARE called
```

Files

A file (or other compilation unit) that is compiled is wrapped into a class. The name of the class is derived from the file name and can be changed via the AKA keyword. In some cases, a file/class is just a container for the classes of interest (the Exception class is an example). In these cases, it often makes more sense, when creating a new instance, to create a class other than the base class. There are several ways to do this:

- Use one class per file, don't use the class keyword and let the compiler wrap the class. For example, if a file contains:
  ```
  AKA(Foo);
  fcn init{ … }
  fcn f{ … }
  ```
  it is the same as if the code was wrapped by
  ```
  class Foo{ fileContents }
  ```
- Use **returnClass** in the init function (or in the constructor if there is no init). ReturnClass allows you to override the normal behavior of the init function (to return the new instance of the class) and return something else. In a file that contains a collection of utility functions and classes, you might return an instance of a "primary" class, or, based on the input to init, select different classes. For example:
  ```
  AKA(Goodies);
  fcn init(x){
      if (x==1) returnClass(G1());
      returnClass(G2());
  }
  class G1{ … }     // Goodie class 1
  class G2{ … }     // Goodie class 2
  ```
  Then, Goodies(1) will return an instance of G1 rather than Goodies.
- Don't have an init function and use returnClass in the constructor. This works well if there are no parameters involved.

Inheritance

Inheritance is ability to inherit functionality from a "parent" class. For example:
```
class One{ var v=1; fcn two{ println(two); }}
class Two(One){        fcn two{ println("v = ",v); }}
```

Class Two inherits the class variable v from class One. Even though class One has a function named "two", class Two creates its own function two, which hides the one in One. It is important to note that classes act like containers and hold copies of the parent classes, so One.two still exists. Note that the inherited One is a different instance from the original[6].

```
Two.two();                          // prints "v = 1"
Two.v=2;      Two.two();            // prints "v = 2"
Two.One.v=3; Two.two();            // prints "v = 3"
Two.One.two()                       // prints "Fcn(two)"
println(One.v);                     // prints "1"
One.two();                          // prints "Fcn(two)"
```

Multiple inheritance, the ability to inherit from more than one parent class, is supported. A left-first, breadth-first search is used to search for "ambiguous" objects (i.e. references that are not absolute).

Not surprisingly, things can get pretty messy if the class hierarchy is deep, wide or twisted. "Designing for inheritance" is helpful here, of which the abridged version is: "Don't depend on stuff very far above you".

```
class Three(One,Two){}
class Four(Two,One) {}

Three.One.v=1; Three.Two.v=2;
println(Three.v);     // prints "1", Three.One is searched first

Four.One.v=1; Four.Two.v=2;
println(Four.v);      // prints "1"!
```

This last result might be surprising. While Two is searched first, v isn't found in that class so the search moves to Twos sibling class, which contains the v we set to 1. But Four.Two.v is actually Four.Two.One.v. This also illustrates that duplicate classes are not merged; Three and Four both contain two copies of One, one explicit and one implicit (in Two). A picture might help:

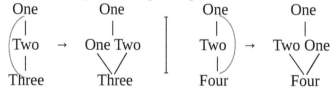

From this, you can deduce that there are two copies of variable "f" in Three: Three.One.f, Three.Two.One.f and similarly for Four.

You can use the Class.linearizeParents property to show the class search order:

```
Three.linearizeParents  →  L(Class(Three),Class(One),Class(Two))
```

---

6   Unless One is static, in which case, all children share the same instance of One.

```
Four.linearizeParents    → L(Class(Four),Class(Two),Class(One))
```

The "diamond" class structure (see <u>Diamond Problem in the Wikipedia</u>)
```
class A{}
class B(A){} class C(A){}
class D(B,C){}
```
is implemented as shown in this
illustration →

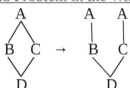

(class A is duplicated[7]). The search order is D,B,C,A (the upper right A is ignored), or more accurately, D, D.B, D.C, D.B.A.

<u>Who's your daddy?</u>
A class can inherit from any class (other than itself) as long as the parent class exists (for example, residing in the Vault) or has already been defined in the source code[8]. But the compiler is a bit myopic when it comes to finding a parent. Thus the following, seemingly perfectly reasonable, things don't work[9]:
```
Null=self.NullClass; class NotSoSpecial(Null){}
class NotSoSpecial(self.NullClass){}
```
If you require this functionality[10], you'll have to create the class manually[11] (see Objects.Class).

You can explicitly reference data in a parent class by using that parents name.
```
class A{ var a; class A2{ var a2; }}
class B(A){ A.a=5; A.A2.a2=6; }
```
If the parent name is a compound name, use the singular name.
```
class B(A.A2){ A2.a2=6; }
```
If you used A.A2.a2, you would be referring to the original Class A, not your parent class, and the wrong a2 would be set.

Anonymous Classes

There is no requirement for a class to be named, it is just a convenience. Nice but not necessary. While this feature is commonly used with functions, it doesn't seem as useful for classes but is used in the same way. Here are two common cases:

---

7   Assuming that A,B or C aren't static classes.
8   The reason is that a class has to exist at compile time in order to inherit from it. Another reason for this restriction - serialized classes. When a class is serialized, parents are not stored with the class, only references. If a parent is dynamic, that reference will be gone when the class is un-serialized.
9   In the case of a variable, the contents are not known at compile time, so the mystery value can't be used as parent. Likewise, "self" doesn't exist until runtime.
10 eg prototype based Class.clone
11 And don't expect to enjoy it.

Keywords

- Passing a "temporary" class as parameter:
  ```
  L(1,2,3).apply(class{ var v; fcn init(x){ v=x; } });
  ```
  This will create a list of three classes, the first has v set to 1, and the last has v set to 3.
- Using a variable instead of a class name:
  ```
  C:=class{ var v=4; fcn f{ println("f" + f); }}
  ```
- Anonymous classes are always private.

Supporting Subscripts

If your class implements subscripts, you'll need to write __sGet and possibly __sSet functions. See Objects.Class.

Threading

Any class can become a thread; all you need is a liftoff function.
Trivial example:
```
class T{
   fcn liftoff{ println("Running in a thread"); }
   fcn splashdown{     // optional
      println(self,"has finished running as a thread");
   }
}
```
`T().launch()` starts an instance of T in a thread and prints:
   Running in a thread
   Class(T) has finished running as a thread

If you pass parameters to launch, those parameters are passed to liftoff when the thread starts.
Splashdown is a optional function, that, if it exists, is called when the thread terminates. Splashdown is passed two parameters, a Bool that is True if the thread ran "normally" and False if something "AB" normal happened. The second parameter is the exception that caused the problem. Or Void if it was a happy death. Splashdown is called in its own thread.

It is worth noting that there is no way to know when the thread starts running. Normally, this is not a problem, but if you need to know, use a Thread.Pipe (to send a message) or set a Atomic.Bool in liftoff and wait for it in the launching function. Just waiting a short amount of time will work until your system is heavily loaded or you move the code to a different system.
```
class Thread{
   var started=Atomic.Bool();
   fcn init{ launch(); }
```

```
    fcn liftoff{
        println("Started");
        started.set();
        Atomic.sleep(5);
        println("Done");
    }
}
t:=Thread();
t.started.wait(); println("Thread is running");
```
→ Started
    Thread is running
    Done

Are You Done Yet?

A somewhat similar problem exists if the main thread exits while other threads are still running – those threads are killed. In the example above, if you are running the code as a script, you won't see "Done"; the main thread will have finished and exited before the thread finished sleeping and printed "Done". You can avoid this by watching the global thread count:

```
    Atomic.waitFor(fcn{ vm.numThreads==0 });
```

If you are coding a subsystem that uses threads and you want to stay in the subsystem until all your threads have finished (which may be before other, unknown to you, threads have finished), you can use a local thread count:

```
var N=Atomic.Int();
class Thread{
    fcn init{ launch(); }
    fcn liftoff{
        println("Started ",vm);
        Atomic.sleep(5);
    }
    fcn splashdown{ println("Done"); N.dec(); }
}
N.inc(); Thread(); N.inc(); Thread();
N.waitFor(0);
```
→ Started VM#1508
    Started VM#1509
    Done
    Done

Note that we don't need to wait for the threads to start. Also, to ensure N is decremented, we do that in splashdown, which is guaranteed to run.

Inheritance and Threads
For the most part, threaded classes "just work". There is one thing to be aware of and that is the search order for the splashdown function. The class that calls launch is the class where searching starts when looking for liftoff and splashdown.
Consider:
```
class P{
    fcn go{ launch() }
    fcn liftoff{}
    fcn splashdown{ println(self) }              // "Class(P)"
}
class C(P){ fcn splashdown{ println(self) }} // "Class(C)"
C.go();        → "Class(P)"
C.launch();  → "Class(C)"
```
You can change this behavior with Class.topdog[12].

Side Effects

A side effect is a calculation that cascades beyond the scope it is running in. A typical example is IO: println("Hello World") is a function call that causes a device somewhere to display characters. Where ever that device is, it is way outside of the scope println is in. Why do you care? You don't, until you try to mix threads and global resources. In this case, two threads writing to the console at the same time will have their characters intermixed, which is annoying but not fatal.

Re-Entrant Functions
In order to be thread safe (something that multiple threads can access at the same time), a function must be re-entrant; that is, it can not contain globally changeable data and it can not access (or return) globally changeable data. The Atomic object provides ways to control access to global data, which mitigates the second point, but, as it is still possible for threads to dead lock, the function would still not be re-entrant[13]. Another place where you have to be very careful about is variables[14], both class and function. Class variables are pretty obviously global data for all functions in the class; every function is bound to the class instance it is defined in, thus accessing a class variable is not re-entrant[15]. Function variables are, surprisingly[16],

---

12 In this case, by changing the function go to `fcn go{ topdog.launch() }`
13 But, you gotta do what you gotta do. Life isn't always simple.
14 As opposed to registers, which are always thread safe.
15 Note that each class instance has a separate copy of the class variables. So there is no conflict if two threads are calling the same function in DIFFERENT class instances. But the function is still not re-entrant.
16 Especially for C programmers. Think of them as "static int".

also class variables, as they [effectively] live in the class instance[17]. Thus, two threads calling the same function, which accesses a function local variable, are accessing the same variable.

Functions have restricted access to data outside of their scope (as discussed above), which can make life difficult for anonymous functions. Consider:

```
fcn f(list,x){ list.filter(fcn(i){ i!=x })}
```

You would expect f(L(1,2,3),2) to return L(1,3). Maybe it would if it would compile, but it doesn't because anonymous functions are also autonomous[18], which basically means they run in their own little sandbox, separate from the scope they were defined in. In this case, that means the filter function can't access f's parameter x. OK, what about this fix:

```
fcn f(list,x){ var y=x; list.filter(fcn(i){ i!=y })}
```

Well, it works. But what isn't obvious is the code is equivalent to:

```
var y; fcn f(list,x){ y=x; list.filter(fcn(i){ i!=y })}
```

Which means f is not re-entrant[19]. What do to (besides curse)? Now you know why many of the [list] methods that take functions (and methods) also take static parameters:

```
fcn f(list,x){ list.filter(fcn(i,x){ i!=x },x) }
```

Now, the filter call is side effect free and f is re-entrant[20].

In general, try to write your code to be re-entrant. If the unexpected happens and your function IS used in a threaded application, re-entrancy errors tend to be randomish and very hard to find. By the same token, library functions should ALWAYS be re-entrant.

---

17 That's just the way it is; they are syntactic surgar.

18 They have to be if they are to live outside of the scope they are defined in; which, of course, they have to be, since they can be stored by whatever they are passed to (they are first class objects). Methods are the same in this regard.

19 It can be argued, quite reasonably, that function variables were a bad idea.

20 Closures are the preferred way to solve this but closures are not [directly] supported. Partial evaluation (.fp) works but static parameters are cheap and easy.

comments: #, //, / */, #define, #if, #ifdef, #text, #tokenize*

There are two types of comments; to end of line and block.
- // All text after the "//" is ignored (to end of line)
- # All text after the "#" is ignored (to end of line)
- #define *name* 0|1
- #if 0|1|name [#else] #endif
- #ifdef *name* [#else] #endif
- #fcn *name* { *body* }
- #text *name text*
- #tokenize *name*
- / * */ All text inside between the starting /* and ending */ is ignored. These can be nested: /* comment /* more comment */ */

See Also: Comments section in the grammar appendix.

// and # comments are stripped out as source code is tokenized; as soon as they are seen[21], they, and the rest of the line are thrown away, never to be seen again.

If you use # for a comment, you should use "# " (sharp blank) so the space will keep the comment from being interpreted as a command. For example,
`#define the following to 4` isn't going to do what you expect. Use
`# define the following to 4.`

The #cmds can only be used when they are preceded by nothing more than space.

Problems
Block comments are stripped out after the source code has been tokenized[22]. This can cause problems for you, the coder. Consider:
```
/* Bad: Comment with a quote (") in it */
/* Bad: Comment with a unquote (0') in it */
```
The tokenizer sees the quote and thinks you are starting a string (it thinks the /* is just another token, not the start of a comment). When it doesn't see a closing quote, it complains about a non-terminated string. The next lines will also cause problems:
```
/* Bad: Comment with a # in it */
/* Bad: Comment with a // in it */
```
because the "#" and "//" are recognized by the tokenizer, which clears the rest of the line and causes the terminating */ to disappear.

---

21 Unless they are quoted or are in a string constant ("//")
22 There are good reasons for this, from a compiler writers view point anyway

#if and /* comments can't overlap. Put the entire comment in the #if block or vice versa.

Usually, the error is pretty clear but it can lead to some really strange errors[23].

Here are some comments that are correct but don't look that way:

```
/* Comment with a "#" in it */
/* Comment with a \# in it */
/* Comment with a \" in it */
/* Comment with a " in it */ " */
```

Nested Comments

Block comments can be nested. This is really nice when you want to "turn off" a chunk of code but not remove it from your program. For example:

```
/* foo isn't being used but the code is cool,
   keep it around for reference.
      /* The foo function does
       * strange and wonderful things
       */
   fcn foo { strangeAndWonderful(); }
*/
```

Shell Scripts

The "#" comments provide the standard Unix shell escape for running scripts:

```
#!/usr/bin/zkl
```

In addition to that, compiled (.zsc) classes can also be treated as scripts by shells. The "--#!" compiler option will add a "#!" line of text to the compiled file ("--#! ." will grab that line from the program text). A shell that is asked to run a .zsc file will look at the first line and see the "#!" comment and invoke zkl on the .zsc file. This also works with Apache CGI scripts.

#define *name* 0|1

Create a symbolic name to be used with #if or #ifdef.

If you need to create the value dynamically, use #fcn and #tokenize. For example, if you want to create #define OnWindows 1 only when compiling on a Windows machine, you can use:

```
#fcn MSWIN {"#define OnWindows "+System.isWindows.toInt()}
#tokenize MSWIN
#if OnWindows
   println("Compiled on a Windows box");
#endif
```

---

23 This is one reason why strings can't span lines; a non-terminated string might not be detected until the end of the file, a long, long way from the actual error. Unfortunately, that is what you get with a non-terminated comment.

or

```
#fcn MSWIN {System.isWindows and "#define OnWindows 1" or ""}
#tokenize MSWIN
#ifdef OnWindows
   ...
```

#fcn *name* { *body* }
Create a function that can be run by #tokenize. The function can take parameters. Body has access to all the objects [previously] created by #define, #fcn and #text (but parameters do not).
If you want debug the fcn, use print; it will be called during #tokenize.

#if 0|1|*name*
#if blocks are basically the same as the equivalent C preprocessor commands. The "#" has to be the first non space character on a line or it is treated as a comment. The only argument is one integer; 0 means don't compile, 1 means compile.
The rest of the line needs to have valid syntax, even though it is currently ignored (future proofing).
Blocks can be nested.
```
#if 1    // compile this code
   println("Compiled");
   #if 0
      println("Not compiled");
   #endif
   /* more compiled code */
#else
   println("Not compiled");
#endif  // done with #if
```
Name is something has been created with #define, #fcn or #text and is evaluated with toBool. If *name* hasn't been defined, an error is thrown. A fcn is always 1, it is not called.

#ifdef *name*
Name is replaced by 1 if it has been created by #define, #fcn or #text and the #ifdef is transformed into #if.

#text *name text*
Create a symbolic name for the rest of the text on the line so it can be tokenized with #tokenize. Leading and trailing white space is removed.

#tokenize *name*, #tokensize *f*, #tokenize *f(a)*
Tokenize some text. If name is a function, run the function and tokenize the result as if it were part of the source code. This is recursive, awkward and error prone.

To remove a previously created item, use `#text` *name* or `#define` *name* `0`.

The #cmds allow you to insert text into the source code before it is parsed. Constants (Keywords.const) are post parse. Keywords._debug_ processing is during parse.

```
#<<<
x:=
#<<<
"#<<< starts a block of lines that are concatenated verbatim
and fed into the parser as one line. #<<< ends the block.
Both #<<< tokens must start the line that is otherwise ignored

Note that is isn't a string, but arbitrary source " + 1 + 23;
#<<<
x.println();
```
Prints:
```
#<<< starts a block of lines that are concatenated verbatim
and fed into the parser as one line. #<<< ends the block.
Both #<<< tokens must start the line that is otherwise ignored

Note that is isn't a string, but arbitrary source 123
```
#<<<#
This marks the start and end of a block of text to be completely ignored. You can use this as a super `#if` `0` or use it to "hide" information for other programs. For example, you can embed shell scripts in a zkl file:

```
File foo.zkl:
#!/bin/sh
#<<<#
echo "A shell script in a zkl program ($0)"
echo "Now run zkl <this file> with Hello World as args"
zkl $0 Hello World!
exit
#<<<#
println("The shell script says ",vm.arglist.concat(" "));
```

Keywords

Now make it executable: `chmod a+x foo.zkl` and run it:

```
$ ./foo.zkl
A shell script in a zkl program (./foo.zkl)
Now run zkl <this file> with Hello World as args
The shell script says Hello World!
$
```

Notes:
- #<<< and #<<<# must start the line.
- #<<< and #<<<# do not nest.
- #<<<# can enclose #<<< but not vice versa; #<<<# inside of a #<<< block is just text (that will be parsed).

Assertions

According to [Wikipedia](#); Assertions can function as a form of documentation: they can describe the state the code expects to find before it runs (its preconditions), and the state the code expects to result in when it is finished running (postconditions); they can also specify invariants of a class.

That can be implemented by talking directly to the tokenizer:

```
fcn assert(fname,lineNum,bools){
    if(False!=vm.arglist[2,*].filter1n('!))
        throw(Exception.BadDay(
                "Assertion failed: %s:%d".fmt(fname,lineNum)));
}
#fcn assert { "assert(__FILE__,__LINE__,
%s);".fmt(vm.arglist.concat(",")) }
```

Then, your code:

```
fcn f(a){
    #tokenize assert("a.isType(1) and a>3","a*3<20");
}
f(4);       // passes
f("hoho"); // fails
```

`#tokenize assert(args)` runs the tokenize time assert function and and tokenizes the result. The args need to be strings because a is not a known quantity at tokenize time, the parser does that (something like `1==1` would not need to be quoted). The above example is turned into:

```
fcn f(a){
    assert("bbb.zkl",23,a.isType(1) and a>3,a*3<20);
}
```

Running the code produces:

Output:

VM#1 caught this unhandled exception:
  BadDay : Assertion failed: bbb.zkl:23

: *(Compose)*

Syntax
- `i:f(_):g(_)` → `g(f(i))` or *X*=i; *X*=f(*X*); *X*=g(*X*)
- `i:f(_,x):g(_,y)` → `g(f(i,x),y)`or *X*=i; *X*=f(*X*,x); *X*=g(*X*,y)
- `i:f().g(_)` → `f().g(i)`
- `i:(x=_)` → x=i
- `i:(_).name` → `(i).name`
- `a:b:c` → `(((a):b):c)` (: has very low precedence)

See Also: Objects.Utils.Helpers.fcomp (function composition)

Abstract

Intermix method and function calls in a left to right ordering.
The expression on the left of the **:** is a parameter to the expression on the right.
The "target" of a compose is _ (underscore) or **(_)**.

Discussion

Compose allows you to treat functions as if they were object methods and maintain an "object, action, action ..." code flow.
Compose only works in expressions (which can be forced by wrapping with ()s).

Examples

- Create a small dictionary from a big dictionary:
  ```
  D("one",1,"two",2).toList() : SD(_)
  ```
- You can use compose to break apart big computations into more bite size pieces without using temporary variables:
  ```
  f:=Compiler.Asm.asm("done\n") :
          self.fcn.build(T("f"),_,Void,False);
  ```
  instead of:
  ```
  code:=Compiler.Asm.asm("done\n");
  f    :=self.fcn.build(T("f"),code,Void,False);
  ```
  or `f    :=self.fcn.build(T("f"),`
  ```
              Compiler.Asm.asm("done\n"),Void,False);
  ```
- `T(1,2,3) : String(_.xplode()) : T(_)` → `L("123")`

Assignment

A composition can be used with assignment: `5 : L(_) : (x:=_)` assigns L(5) to x.
- `f:=name + "zsc" : File.exists(_);`

Keywords

- gz.write("This is a test").close().drain() :
  (f:=File("text.gz","wb")).write(_); f.close();

If
If/then/else (and switch) composes if target is in the control. Further, "_" doesn't propagate into any of the then/else parts (but the entire if can be composed).

```
    f:=name + "zsc" : File.exists(_) :
    (if (_) System.loadFile2(f) : return(_));
```

You should wrap the if in ()[24]:

```
    a<b : (if(_) b-a else a-b) : L(_);
    a b : (if(_) println("less")); ab:=a + b;
    (if(a<b) b-a else a-b) : L(_)
```

```
(a+b) : switch(_){case(3){"Three"} else "Unknown"} :
println("The result is ",_)
```

Functions
Functions can be composed: 5 : fcn(x){x+1}(_) → 6. The function can be anonymous (lambda) or named. If the function starts the composition, you will need to enclose it in ()s: (fcn f(x){x+1}) : listOfFcns.append(_);

---

24 At the start, to force it to be an expression. Because it is expressions that compose. You can also use a ";" but that gets tricky figuring out if the ; is terminating one of the clauses, the entire if or the expression itself.

const

Syntax
- **const** k=*expression*;
- **const** kf=fcn{}
- **const**{ *block* }
- **const** *nameSpace*{ **const** … }

Notes
- const a=b=123 is illegal.
- Only constants of types Bool, Float, Fcn, Int, String and Void can be accessed from code space.
- Constant functions can only be run from code, they are not available to be compiled.
- Parameters to constant functions can be True, False, number (eg 123, 4.56), text (eg "foo"), or Void.
- Constants are visible to the entire class (and all contained classes) they are declared in, independent of where in that class they are declared.

See Also: Keywords.reg, Keywords.var

Abstract
Create a compile time constant.

Discussion
Constants are compile time objects that allow you to perform calculations at compile, rather than run, time. All constants are gathered at parse time, compiled, run and the resulting objects are placed in their enclosing class before that enclosing class is actually compiled[25]. Your code can then access the compiled objects.
Example:

```
const k=123;
println(k);      // prints "123"
println(k + 3);  // prints "126"
```

As the constants are collected at parse time, then compiled, if there is more than one definition of a constant, the last one wins.

---

25 This is a "nested", or phased, compile. The parts of the parse tree marked "constant" are compiled, and run, before the rest of the tree is compiled. This defines a "constant space". Objects created in constant space are then accessible to the rest of the parse tree as it is compiled. Actions performed in constant space can likewise radiate out to the enclosing code.

Keywords

Example:
```
const k=5;
println(k);        // prints "foo"
const k="foo";
```
While this may not be the most pleasant behavior, it is most likely to be a problem when including header files (but that is one reason why it works this way).

Const Name Spaces
Just as classes can be nested, so can constants.
```
const RGB_COLOR{
    const RED=0xf00;
    const BLUE=0x0f0, GREEN=0x00f;
    const CYAN=BLUE + GREEN;   // → 0x0ff
}
const INDEXED_COLOR{ const RED=1, BLUE=2, GREEN=3; }
const BLUE=1;
BLUE                    → 1
RGB_COLOR.BLUE          → 0x0F0
INDEXED_COLOR.BLUE;  → 2
```
This could be further nested as:
```
const COLOR{
    const RGB{
        const RED=0xf00,BLUE=0x0f0,GREEN=0x00f,CYAN=BLUE+GREEN;
    }
    const INDEXED{ const RED=1, BLUE=2, GREEN=3; }
    const BLUE=1;
}
```
Then the example becomes:
```
COLOR.BLUE;             → 1
COLOR.RGB.BLUE;         → 0x0F0
COLOR.INDEXED.BLUE;  → 2
```

Name spaces can be used to wrap header files. For example, if file "bar.h.zkl" contains const X=123;, a poorly named const, you can wrap it with:
```
const FOO{ include(bar.h.zkl) }
```
then FOO.X → 123. The entire contents of bar.h.zkl becomes part of constant space, *even* those parts not declared const. See the next item.

Header/Include files
If you have programmed in C, you are familiar with header (.h) files. You can do the same thing by collecting constants into a file.

Constanst Functions: `const f=fcn {}`

A constant function is a run only object as far as compiled code is concerned. Note that this is actually creating a variable in const space (see next section). If the function name is referenced without parameters, it acts like a proxy variable and the function is run.

Examples:

```
const f=fcn { return(3) }
println(f);        // reference, prints "3"
println(f());      // → "3"

const f2=fcn(x){ return("hoho" + x) }
println(f2);         // error, missing parameter
println(f2(2));      // prints "hoho2"
println(f2(f));      // error, f is invalid parameter to a const fcn
```

Arbitrary code in Constant Space: `const { … }`

Constants can do pretty much anything they like in constant space. They are a class, they have a constructor that is run. Of course, getting carried away here is a good way to hang yourself. Use the `const { block }` to shove arbitrary code into constant space. All const class variables are available in code space; functions, methods, etc are not (if a function is bound to a variable, it is; see previous section).

Examples:

```
caraeconst{
    // "Hello" printed between parse time and compile time
    println("Hello from constant space");
    class C{}
    var k=C.toSring(); // create const k
}
println(k); // prints "Class(C)" at run time
```

- Put an auto-incrementor in const space to create enum like constants.
  ```
  const{ var _n=-1; var [proxy] N=fcn{ _n+=1 } }
  ```
  To use:
  ```
  const X=N;      // → 0
  println(_n);      // → 2 code time is after const time
  const Y=N,Z=N;      // → 1,2
  ```
- To reset the above enumerator, use `const{ _n=-1; }` just before you define the next constants.
- Be aware of the difference between running a function in const space and referencing a const space variable and what happens if mixed.
  ```
  const{ var _n=-1; fcn N{ _n+=1 } }
  const A=N;   // → 0?
  const B=N;   // → 1?
  ```

```
println(B,",",A); //-→ 0,1, oops
```
A and B are bound to the function N at const time but are evaluated at run time (in the print statement).

Debugging

Since constants happen at compile time, not at run time, they can be unpleasant to debug. If your constants are complicated, create them outside of constant space and then convert them to constants. Use print to debug existing constants. Take a look at the parse tree to see what the parser thinks you are doing. You can do this with `zkl --parse file.zkl`. The constants are collected in the "__Constants#" class that is at the top of the parse tree.

Note that `__DEBUG__`, `__FILE__`, etc have NOT been set yet but _debug_ works as expected (ie the debug level has propagated into constant space).

Constant Movement

Constants are moved to the top of the class they are declared in[26] and are compiled before references to them are resolved. This means that a constant declared in a class is visible throughout the class, regardless of where it was declared (if a const is declared in the root class, it is visible to the entire class). This can lead to counter intuitive behavior; consider:

```
x:=K; println(x); const K=1;                → 1
const K=1; x:=K; println(x); const K=2;    → 2
```

Scope

The following show some class scoping:

```
const K=1; class{ const K=2; println(K); }  → 2
const K=1; class{ const K=2; } println(K);  → 1
```

Name Conflicts

If a register or variable name conflicts with a const name, the "closest" declaration wins, which is usually the reg or var as const space is searched last.

```
const k=1; var k=5;    // k = 5
const k=1; var k=k;    // k = Void, k is always seen as a var
```

---

26 Variables also do this, moving to the top of their class or function; registers move to the top of their block.

continue

Syntax
- `while (…){ … `**`continue`**`; … }`
- `do { … `**`continue`**`; … }while (…)`
- `foreach x in (…){ … `**`continue`**`; …}`
- **`continue(`**`[1-9]`**`)`**

See Also: Keywords.break

Abstract
Skip to the next iteration of the enclosing loop. With a parameter, continue the nth loop (continue(1) is the same as continue).

Discussion
The continue keyword jumps to the control part of the nearest enclosing loop.

Example
```
foreach n in ("123"){ if(n=="2") continue; print(n); }
```
Prints "13"

critical

Syntax
- `critical{ block }`
- `critical(lockName){ block }`
- `critical(lockName, acquireName, releaseName){ block }`

  lockName can be any object that has "acquire" and "release" methods, the object of choice being Atomic.Lock. If not a Lock, you need to provide the names of the acquire and release methods (critical prepends *lockName* to the method names).

See Also: Keywords.onExit, Atomic.Lock, Atomic.WriteLock, Keywords.class.Threading

Abstract
Mark a block of code as guarded, usually atomic (executable by only one thread at a time), however, critical can be used for other types of locks or operations.
Useful for controlling access to a global resource, it is a specialized form of onExit.
If control passes out of *block*, (via return, throw, etc), the lock is released.

Discussion
A multi-threaded program may have resources that are shared amongst several threads but can only be accessed by one thread at time. For example, if two threads write to a file at the same time, the result would be garbage – data from one thread's write would be intermixed with the other threads. The critical keyword provides a way to serialize access to that resource by using a lock. When a thread tries to run the block, it attempts to acquire the lock and, if it can, it does and runs the block. While it is running the block, if another threads attempts to run the block, it blocks attempting to acquire the lock and waits until the first thread has exited the block and released the lock. This also illustrates an important point – the critical code should be as short, and fast, as possible to minimize the time other threads might be blocked.

The two forms exist to cover the following cases:
- A resource is protected by more than one critical block and thus needs to share a lock. That lock should be a class variable.
  ```
  class C{
  var [protected] lock=Atomic.Lock(), N;
      fcn a{ critical(lock){ N 1; } }
      fcn b{ critical(lock){ N=2; } }
  }
  ```
  Note that lock and N are read only (to anybody outside of C) so other threads will keep their grubby mitts off of them.

- If there is no resource to protect, or there is only one place the resource needs to be protected:
    - `fcn a{ critical{ file.write("foo"); } }`
    - `critical{ blinkLED(); }`

Non-Locking Uses

Critical can also be used to to wrap a block with a prologue and epilogue. Here is a simple example:

```
class C{
    fcn begin{ println("BEGIN") } fcn end{ println("END") }
}
var c=C();
critical(c,begin,end){ println("My code"); }
```
→ BEGIN
  My code
  END

This provides two benefits: You won't forget to call "end" and you know "end" will be called no matter what. A real world use is with GUI toolkits; a widget is created and then other widgets (such as buttons) are added to the main widget. The code might look something like this:

```
var window=GUI.Window();
window.begin();
    GUI.Button(); GUI.TextEditor();
window.end();
```
(The toolkit adds the new widgets to window until "end" is called).

Which is fine for small amounts of code but when adding lots of widgets (or updating the code at a later date), it is easy to miss the end. A worse problem is if one of the widgets throws an exception; end would not get called and window is now messed up. Contrast the above with:

```
var window=GUI.Window();
critical(window,begin,end){
    GUI.Button(); GUI.TextEditor();
}
```

debug

Syntax
- _debug_ { *block* } [else { *block* }]
- _debug_(*n*) *block*   [else { *block* }]
- _debug_(ON, debugLevel=1) { [*block*] }
- _debug_(OFF) {}

Notes
- If __DEBUG__ is 0 (ie debugging is not turned on in the Compiler), the else clause will always happen.
- ON and OFF can be used to override the compiler settings. Once set, the new setting last for the rest of the compilation unit or until changed with _debug_.

See Also: Keywords.__DEBUG__, Keywords.comments (#if/#else/#endif)

Abstract
Include debugging information or just general verbosity in your code. You can turn this on or off from the command line or within your code.

Discussion
debug provides a way to include or exclude code at compile time. If N and N >= __DEBUG__, debugBlock happens.

Examples:
__DEBUG__ is 0
```
• _debug_ { println("checkpoint"); // This line is NOT compiled
  else { println("hoho"); }        // This line is compiled
```

__DEBUG__ is 1
```
• _debug_ { println("checkpoint"); // This line is compiled
  else { println("hoho"); }        // This line is NOT compiled
• _debug_(2) { println("checkpoint"); // compiled
  else { println("hoho"); }           // NOT compiled
```

__DEBUG__ is 5
```
• _debug_ { println("checkpoint"); // This line is compiled
  else { println("hoho"); }        // This line is NOT compiled
• _debug_(2) { println("checkpoint"); // NOT compiled
  else { println("hoho"); }           // compiled
```

do

Syntax
- **do{** *block* **}while(***control***)**
- **do(***count***){** *block* **}**

See Also: Keywords.foreach, Keywords.while, Keywords.break, Keywords.continue, loop, reduce.

Abstract

A do while condition-is-true loop or a do n-times loop.

Discussion

There are two types of do loop:

1. Repeatedly run the block code while the control evaluates to True. The control is tested after <block> is run, so it is run at least once. Thus
   ```
   do{ println("foo"); }while(False);
   ```
   prints "foo" once.
2. Do a block n times. In this case, count is tested BEFORE the block is run and the block is run until count reaches zero. So
   ```
   do(0){ println("foo"); }
   ```
   doesn't do anything.
   - If count is not positive, no looping.
   - There is no loop index.
   - The count is converted to an integer. Thus, the following are equivalent:
     ```
     do(3)  { println("foo"); }
     do("3"){ println("foo"); }
     do(3.5){ println("foo"); }
     ```

Examples:

```
n:=0;   do{ println(n+=1); }while(n<5);    → 1 2 3 4 5
n:=0;   do(5){ println(n+=1); }            → 1 2 3 4 5
n:=100; do{ println(n); }while (n<5);      → 100
```

fcn

Syntax: Creation
- **fcn** *name*{ *block* }
- **fcn** *name*(*prototype*){ *block* }
- **fcn**{ *block* }   // anonymous (lambda) function
- **fcn**(*prototype*){ *block* }
- **fcn** [[*attribues*]][*name*][(*prototype*)]{ *block* }
- **fcn** ([*type*]*name* …){ *block* }
- **fcn** ([(*fmt*)], …) … or **fcn** ([(*fmt*)]*name*, …) …
- **'wrap**(*prototype*){ *block* }

Syntax: Calling
- *fcnName*()
- *fcnName*(*parameters*)
- Calling object methods has the same syntax.

Returns
- Creation: The function
- Calling: The result of running the function code block, unless interrupted by an exception.

Notes
- `self.fcn` is the running function object.
- `vm.arglist` is the list of parameters to the running function, `vm.numArgs` is length of the arglist.
- The compiler is "style" agnostic.
- Function names can be up to 80 characters long and can use the characters "a-zA-Z0-9_", in other words: underscore, digits, upper or lower case letters. A name can not start with a digit.
- Names are case sensitive.
- The possible attributes are **mixin**=return value, **private** and **public** (the default). A mixin is a object that the compiler assumes the function will return. It is not enforced. For example, `fcn [mixin=1]f{ return(5) }` and `fcn [mixin=Int]f{ return(5) }` are the same.
- The *type* attributes for parameter lists are short hand for mixin (see above). The compiler will verify that an operation on the parameter is valid for a parameter of that type. For example, `fcn f([List]a){ a.bitAnd(0xf) }` will generate an error as bitAnd is not a method of List. The is no enforcement of this outside of the function (eg `f(123)` is legal).
- *Fmt* attributes are used to break apart passed in parameters. A parameter name is optional, but useful if you want to refer to both forms. For example, `fcn f([(a,b,c)])` indicates the first parameter is to be separated into three register values (eg `f(L(1,2,3))` → `a,b,c:=L(1,2,3))`; `fcn([(a,(b,c))])`

specifies a twice nested parameter. As with list assignment, "_" can be used to ignore parts (eg fcn f([(a,_,c)])).

- 'wrap wraps registers and parameters in enclosing blocks for use in a function. One way lexical scoping. See Objects.Deferred.'wrap for more information.

See Also: Objects.Fcn, Objects.Class, Objects.Deferred.'wrap, Keywords.return, Objects.VM.arglist, numArgs, pasteArgs.

Abstract

Create, call or refer to a user defined function.
Functions can be anonymous (lambda functions).
All functions inherit from Objects.Fcn.

Discussion

Functions encapsulate code. The "fcn" keyword is used to create user defined functions, which can then be run (called) or passed to other objects. Functions are "bound" to the class instance they are created in (which may be implicit), thus, a function, in any context, can refer to the class variables in the class instance it is bound to.

All functions implicitly inherit from the Fcn object, which gives them some unique methods and properties.

Special Names

There are several names that are "special" to a Class :
    __constructor, init, liftoff, splashdown
See Keywords.Class for more information.

Function Definition

Almost all zkl programming is creating functions (and classes). Fortunately, it is easy, just wrap code in braces and give it a name:

```
fcn helloWorld{ println("Hello World"); }
```

When run: helloWorld(), the function prints "Hello World".

Some Syntax Details

The compiler pretty much ignores whitespace and doesn't care how your code is arranged, with a few exceptions:

- Function calls: If the compiler sees a word immediately followed by a opening parenthesis, it is assumed to be a function call. Thus println (x) is different from println(x) and will probably cause a syntax error.

Keywords

- Dot (".") is used to create compound references to objects (basically navigate around the object hierarchy). The compiler doesn't care if there is whitespace in front of the dot, dot always is attached to the previous object. Thus `self.fcn` is the same as `self .fcn`. Note that there can not be space after the dot. This can help with code layout for long lines:

```
foo(1,2,3).bar(4,5,6);
```
is the same as
```
foo(1,2,3)
.bar(4,5,6);
```

- Tokens don't need whitespace around them. `1+2` is the same as `1 + 2`, `{print(x)}` is the same as `{ print(x) }`.
- Semicolon (;) is the expression terminator. It informs the compiler that a code construct is done. If the compiler can figure out that the expression is done anyway, the semi is optional, but it good idea not to let the compiler make too many decisions for you.

```
{ print(x); } is the same as { print(x) } and { print(x);;;;;;; }
```
Extras are ignored.

Return Value

All functions return a value, explicitly or implicitly. There is no restrictions on what a function can return or any requirement that the return type has to be consistent. In addition, multivalued return is supported.

The "return" and "returnClass" keywords are used to explicitly end a function and return a value. If return isn't used, the result of the last calculation as the function flows out of the function body is the implicit return value. Thus, the following are equivalent:

```
{ return(1) } and { 1 }
```

A function can return values of different types:
```
fcn f(x){
    if(x==1) return(1);    // return number
    return("2");           // return string
}
```

A multi-valued return is just returning a list. It is up to the caller to know how it wants to handle the list. The following are equivalent:

```
return(T(1,2,3)) and return(1,2,3)
```
See Keywords.return for more information.

Parameters
There is no enforcement of parameter type or the number of, by either the compiler
or the VM. If required parameter doesn't exist, a runtime error occurs. For example:
```
fcn f(x){ return(x + 1); }
f();      // runtime error, not a compile error
```
If there more parameters are passed to the function than are used, or are specified by
the prototype, nobody cares. This can be considered a good thing, as it makes C's
varargs very simple. Another place where this is very helpful is where different
objects share an API but some functions have optional parameters; a program can use
many different objects with no change.
If a parameter is expected to be a certain type, it is up to the function to enforce that,
you can't do it at compile time. Ideally, the parameter will morph into the proper type
(for example, integer to float or string to integer), otherwise a conversion error will
probably be thrown. vm.argsMatch can be helpful in this case.

A function parameter can be many different things: object, function call, if
statements, try/catch statements, function or class definitions.
Here is an example:
```
day=1;
println(
    if (1==(day / 10)) ">10" else "<10",
    " ",
    try  { L("th","st","nd","rd")[day % 10] }
    catch{ "th" });
```
This prints "<10 st". If day is 3, "<10 rd" and if day is 15, ">10 th".

It is common to create functions to pass to other functions. See Anonymous
Functions below.

Attributes
The settable attributes are public (the default) and private. The "private" attribute
means that Class.resolve will not be able to find this class but it is visible throughout
the file it is defined in. The static attribute is set by the VM.

Fmt attribute
Very handy when parameters are composites that would be easier to deal with broken
up. Anything that can be used in list assignment can broken apart. For example, a
dictionaries key/value pairs:
```
fcn f([(k,v)]){ println(k," : ",v) }
Dictionary("one",1,"two",2).pump(Void,f)
    two : 2
    one : 1
```

```
f("foo") → "f:o", f("f") → error
```

Pass By Reference

Function parameters are passed by reference. If a parameter is a mutable type (such as a list), and you modify it, then the calling code will see the change. If the parameter isn't mutable (numbers, strings), you can't change it. This sometimes leads to the following code:

```
fcn f(list){
    tmp:=list.copy();  // make a copy, don't change parameter
    // munge tmp
}
```

Default Parameters

A function prototype can define *defaults* (as in C++ or Java). In addition, the default does not have to be a constant value, it is evaluated at run time and can be almost anything, such as a function call or definition. Any parameter can have a default, or not. The default is run in the context of the class the function is defined in.

Syntax: `fcn … (p1=default,p2=default, …);`

Examples

- `fcn f(x=5){} f(); → f(5)`
- `fcn f(text=ask("Your name is: ")){}`
  `f("Fred");  // sets text to "Fred"`
  `f();        // at runtime, Console.ask is called`
- `fcn f(a=1,b,c=3)){}`
  `f() → f(1), f(6) → f(6), f(6,7) → f(6,7,3)`
- `class C{ var v=123; fcn f(p=v){ p }}`
  `C.f() → 123`
  `cf=C.f; C.v=5; cf() → 5`

Anonymous Functions

The function name is optional. There are places where the name is superfluous, such as passing a function to another function. Such "lambda" functions can be assigned to a variable if you need to keep track of them. That variable then behaves the same as a named function. One place where this is useful is in classes where you want a function to have multiple names, such as a placeholder or when implementing to a API specification.

```
    class C{
        fcn f(x){ … }
        var f2=f;
    }
```

Now, C.f(1) and C.f2(1) are the same (assuming that C's constructor has been run). If we wanted to change bar to another function, that is easy:

```
C.f2=fcn(x){ … }
```
Anonymous functions are used a lot with methods like apply and filter. For example, to find all the strings in a list, you could use:
```
L(1,"two",3.0).filter(fcn(x){ x.isType("") }) → L("two")
```
Anonymous functions are always private.

Nested Functions

Functions can be created inside of other functions but they must be anonymous.
```
fcn f{
    fcn bar{}            // error
    f2:=fcn{}            // OK, put fcn into register "f2"
    f2();                // call the nested function
    someOtherFcn(f2);    // pass the nested function
}
```
This is because nested functions don't really exist (since functions can't contain functions), all functions are promoted to the nearest enclosing class. A named, nested function could cause a name conflicts with another function, and, in practice, there is no difference in usage.

Function Variables
Variables declared in a function are local and persistent to that function (they are instance variables that are invisible outside of that function). They are initialized in the class constructor. They are not thread safe.
See also: Keywords.var, Objects.fcn:Instance Variable
```
class C{
    var cv=123;         // instance variable
    class D{ cv=4 }     // change cv, see fv2
    fcn f{
        var fv1=7;      // good. An invisible instance variable
        var fv2=cv;     // bad, fv2 initialized when?
        fv1+=1;         // f(); f(); → 9
    }
    f.v1;  // won't compile
}
C.f.fv1;  // won't compile
```

"Script" Code
Code that isn't explicitly in a function is collected, by the compiler, into the class constructor. The "RootClass" constructor contains all the code, in a file, that is outside of any function. This is because all functions reside in a class and all code resides in a function. Most of the time, nobody cares, but it is useful to know if you

are rooting around compiled code, using reflection, trying to find something you know is there.

For example, if a file consists of the following:

```
fcn factorial(x){ return(x and x*self.fcn(x - 1) or 1); }
```

and you were to compile the file, how would you run the factorial function? Just running it doesn't do anything. Looking deeper, the file, from the compilers point of view, actually looks like:

```
class RootClass#{
    fcn factorial(x) { return(x and x*self.fcn(x - 1) or 1); }
    fcn __constructor{ return(self); }
}
```

If we want to treat the file as a script, one that runs the factorial program with user input, we could just add a call as part of the script:

```
fcn factorial(x){ return(x and x*self.fcn(x - 1) or 1); }
x:=factorial(ask("Take the factorial of: ").toInt());
println(x);
```

then the constructor becomes:

```
fcn __constructor{
    x:=factorial(ask("Take the factorial of: ").toInt());
    println(x);
    return(self);
}
```

And if we run the "script":

```
>zkl fact.zkl
```

Take the factorial of: 4

24

Knowing this, if we were to compile the file inside a running program:

```
factFile:=Compiler.Compiler.compileFile("fact.zkl");
println(factFile) → Class(fact)
```

(a RootClass takes the name of the file by default)

we can treat it as a script and run the constructor:

```
factFile.__constructor();
```

and it would behave as in the previous example. What if we wanted to run the factorial function itself? Well, since it is a RootClass that contains the function, we can run it:

```
factFile.factorial(4)
```

Script Parameters

Scripts are just constructor functions living a double life. As such, it is sometimes difficult to know if one should treat them as a function or script. They can be both. The most problematic is parameters; constructors don't take parameters but scripts might (command line arguments); without some careful orchestration, a big ugly mess ensues. The first thing your script should do is to use Attributes(script) so that the loader will know that this is a script and there is no confusion about what file is. Then, if the script is run from the command line:

    C:\>zkl myscript arg

the constructor is called with arg. Your script can test this[27]:

    Attributes(script);
    if (vm.numArgs){…}   // I'm being run as a script

If you have loaded the script, you can call it:

    myscript.__constructor(arg);

The difference is, from the command line, arglist will be all strings and won't be all of argv.

Another way of handling parameters is to use init. Since setting the script attribute prevents a script from being copied, init provides a convenient way to run the script:

    Attributes(script);
    fcn init(arg){ doScriptStuff(arg); } // or __constructor(arg)

The compiler doesn't have init call the constructor for static classes (which scripts are) so init becomes a front end for the script/constructor itself. Now, you can run the script:

    myscript(arg);

Binding

The compiler "binds" (that is, statically links) function calls if it can find the function while compiling code. If it can't find the function (it might be in another file for example), it passes off that responsibility to the VM (to find at runtime). This later case is known as late binding. This form is usually transparent to the user (unless an error occurs). You can also explicitly use late binding. Experienced C programmers will be familiar with some of these, the others are also widely used.

- Calling functions stored in list. C programmers will recognize this as a array of pointers to functions:
  ```
  functions:=L(Console.println, fcn(x){ println("fcn 2") });
  functions[0]("foo"); // → "foo"
  functions[1]("foo"); // → "fcn 2"
  ```
- Searching a class for a function by name. There are two ways to do this, the first explicitly looks for a function and is more work than it should be:
  ```
  class C{ fcn f{ println(self.fcn) } }
  names:=C.fcns.apply("name"); // → L("nullFcn","f")
  n    :=names.index("f");       // → 1
  C.fcns[n]();                   // → "Fcn(f)"
  ```
  The next method is easy but will find more than functions. The VM uses this method for late binding:

---

27 Assuming your script takes parameters; if not, just ignore this.

Keywords

```
    C.resolve("f")();                    // → "Fcn(f)"
```
- The resolve method works on any object, so you can use it to find, and call, methods:
```
    (123).resolve("toList")();      // → L(123)
```
Not overly useful as it is the same as (123).toList().

Tail Recursion

Tail recursion[28] is a special case of recursion that converts a recursive function call into a goto. Consider the classic factorial program:
```
1) fcn fact(x){
       if(0==x) return(1);
       return(x*self.fcn(x-1));
   }
```
This program uses the stack to store the intermediate values of x until it can multiply them together to calculate the factorial. We can re-write this to explicitly pass the intermediate values during the recursion:
```
2) fcn fact(x,N=1){
       if(0==x) return(N);
       return(self.fcn(x-1,N * x));
   }
```
This can then be flattened into an iterative function:
```
   fcn fact(x,N=1){
       if(0==x) return(N);
       x-=1; N*=x;
       goto fact;
   }
```
Which is what the compiler does when given (2)[29]. This has great benefits in stack space and time[30] for heavily recursive functions. One of tail recursion optimizations (as opposed to tail calls) is that default parameters are NOT expanded when making the recursive tail call. They are for the initial external call to the function but within the function, it is expected that you know what the parameters should be[31].

Another example: Summing the contents of a list. In a functional language, you might see something like:
```
sum x:xs
   sum []=0
   sum (x:xs)=x+sum(xs)
```
In zkl, we have to make the accumulator explicit, thus this would be:

---

28 See also http://wikipedia.org/wiki/Tail_recursion
29 The compiler isn't smart enough to convert (1) into (2).
30 Function calls are computationally expensive.
31 This is purely an effort to further reduce overhead. A "regular" tail call has parameters expanded.

```
fcn sum(list,s=0){
   if (not list) return(s);
   return(sum(list[1,*], s+list[0])));
}
sum(T(1,2,3)) → 6
sum(T(1,2,3),"") → "123"
```

Tail Calls

A tail call is a goto, with parameters, to another function or method. As such, it doesn't consume stack space because it doesn't ever return to the caller. Consider
```
fcn f1(n){ if(n){ println("f1 : ",n); return(f2(n-1)) }}
fcn f2(n){ if(n){ println("f2 : ",n); return(f1(n-1)) }}
f1(5) → "f1 : 5" "f2 : 4" "f1 : 3" "f2 : 2" "f1 : 1"
```
This is a form of "long chain" recursion, that, because of tail calls, doesn't recurse. The compiler recognizes that return(f2(n-1)) is equivalent to goto f2 and changes the code from a call to a jump. The advantage is that no stack space is used for the recursion (or call). In fact, if n-1 is changed to just n in the example, the code will run forever without using any additional stack space.

It can't happen here
Since a try/catch block has to be able to catch exceptions thrown by the callee, tail call optimization can't be done in the try or catch blocks (the else block is OK). Tail recursion optimization will be done.

In general, tail call optimization just happens and you don't need to know about it. Which is good because there isn't much you can do about it either way, other than write your code so that the compiler can use tail calls.

Functions are not Closures

Unlike closures, functions can *not*, in general, access data outside of their scope. The one exception is that functions have full access to the instance data in their defining class instance[32].

---

32 A function is itself instance data. Usually.

Keywords

Consider:
```
class C{       var v;  reg r;
   fcn f(a){ var v2; reg r2;
      v;                    // OK
      r;                    // error, r is out of scope
      fcn{ r2; a; }         // error, r2 & a are out of scope
      fcn{ v2 }             // OK, v2 is really a class var
   }
   fcn g{ f(); f.v2; } // error, no outside access to fcn vars
}
```
If you need closure functionality, see the Objects.Object.fp methods and Objects.Deferred.'wrap (which provide one way closures).

foreach

Syntax
- `foreach` *i* `in (`Sequence `|` Stream`){` *block* `}`
- `foreach` *i* `in (`Walker`) {` *block* `}`
- `foreach` *i,j,k* `in (`x`){` ... `}`   blow apart x
- `foreach` *i,j,k* `in (`x,y,z`){` ... `}` nested or cascading foreach
- `foreach` *i* `in (){` `} fallthrough{` *block* `}`

Notes
- `{` and `}` are required.
- *i* is the name of the control variable. It is created local to *block* (as a register).
- `__iWalker`: Name of the iterator, its scope is inside *block* (or just outside *block*).
- If there are are multiple control variables, list assignment is used and the first is used for the walker name (eg __iWalker).

See Also: Keywords.while, Keywords.do, Objects.Walker, Objects.Utils.range, filter, pump, reduce.

Abstract
Foreach iterates over each item in a sequence or stream.

Discussion
Foreach is a variation on the classic for or while loop. Objects that support iteration will have a walker function.

Examples
- To process every line of a text file:
  `foreach line in (File("text.txt")) { process(line); }`
- To look at every character in a string:
  `foreach char in ("foo") { println(char); }`
  prints "f", "o" and "o".
- `foreach n in (5)` is short hand for `foreach n in (Utils.range(5))`. `n` ranges between 0 and 4.
- `foreach a,b in (L(L(1,2),L(3,4))) { println(a,b) }` → "12", "34" zip can be handy here.
- `foreach a,b in (3,4){}` expands to `foreach a in (3) { foreach b in (4){}`.

Ranges (See Objects.Utils.range)
Ranges allows foreach to emulate the C for loop:

Keywords

zkl	C equivalent (int i; float f;)
`foreach i in (10)`	for (i = 0; i < 10; i++)
`foreach i in (Utils.range(10))`	for (i = 0; i < 10; i++)
`foreach i in (Utils.range(3,10))`	for (i = 3; i < 10; i++)
`foreach i in (Utils.range(10,0,-1)`	for (i = 10; i > 0; i--)
`foreach f in (Utils.range(0.0,1,0.001)`	for (f = 0.0; f < 1.0; f += 0.001)

```
foreach j in (s) { block } is equivalent to:
    {
        reg __jWalker=s.walker();
        while(_jWalker._next()){
            reg j=__jWalker.value;
            <block>
        }
    }
```

`[a..b]`, `[a .. b]` and `[a..b,step]` are syntactic sugar for ranges that include b. So `foreach I in ([3..10])` is equivalent to C's `for(i=3;i<=10;i++)`

Ranges usually iterate over ints, floats or characters. See Objects.Utils.range for the finer points (especially regarding floats).

fallthrough
A fallthrough block is run if running code "falls off" the end the foreach loop, ie the loop runs to completation, ie a break statement isn't run.
Notes:
- The fallthrough block is in the *same* scope as the foreach block, ie you can access registers created in the foreach block.
- **Break** and **continue** are *outside* the foreach block, ie `break(n)` becomes `break(n+1)`.
- If a fallthrough block is attached to a cascading foreach, it is undefined *which* foreach it gets attached to.

if else

Syntax
- `if(control) true-expression`
- `if(control){ true-block }`
- `if(control) true-clause else false-clause`
- `if(control) true-clause else if(control) true-clause`
- `if(control) true-clause else if(control) true-clause else false-clause`
- `if(c) true-clause else if(c) true-clause else if(c) true-clause` ... `[else ...]`[33]
- *clause* is a expression or block
- Controls include assignment, if, and try in addition to the expected.

Result
- The last calculation, which could be the control, true-clause or false-clause, if control flows off the end of the if (ie not terminated by return, etc).

Abstract
Conditional branching.

Warnings
- `n:=5; if (n+=1>5) n=0;` isn't going to do what you expect. In fact, n isn't even incremented. The control is parsed as `n+=(1>5) == n+=0` (because "+=" has a lower precedence than ">"). You meant `n:=5; if((n+=1) > 5) n=0;`
- Similarly, `if(g(v=f(),2,3))` doesn't compile, as the compiler gets confused, seeing `if(g(v=(f(),2,3)))` which looks like a badly formed multiple assignment. You can rewrite this as `if(g((v=f()),2,3))`.
- This will also surprise you:
  `x:=1; if(0) try{} catch{} else { x=2; }`
  x is 1, NOT 2. This is because try also has a else clause. Wrap this in a block:
  `x:=1; if(0){ try{} catch{} } else x=2;`
  The following are equivalent:
  `if 0){ try{} catch{} else { x=2; }} else x=3;`
  `if(0)  try{} catch{} else { x=2; }  else x=3;`
- Be careful if you use side effects:
  `a:=1; if (a or  a+=1) println(a);` → 1
  `a:=1; if (a and a+=1) println(a);` → 2
- If you use if as part of an expression, you may need, or want, to wrap it in ()s:
  `(if(X) 2 else 3) + 5` or `(if(X) 2 else 3; + 5)`
  `r=(if(X) 2 else 3.0); println(r.type);`

---

33 I need a sanity-clause!

Discussion

Conditions are evaluated on an "as-needed" basis and order is not specified.

Conditional Compilation

Conditional compilation makes it easy to comment out a block of code or switch between multiple blocks of code. The code has to parse but it doesn't have to compile. It can be used in the same way as C's #if 0 ... #elif ... #else ... #endif but is not as powerful or useful since only 0, 1, True, False are evaluated and functions and classes are compiled no matter what (due to the way the compiler rewrites code).

- if (True) *block* is the same as *block*, in other words, *block* is never compiled.
    if (1) ... is the same, as is const doit=1; if (doit) ...
- if (True) *block1* else *block2* is the same as *block1*
- if (False) *block* generates no code; ditto with if(0)
- if (False) *block1* else *block2* is the same as *block2*

Result

The if statement actually has a result that you can use. For example, consider:
    x:=if(0) 1 else "two";
This will always set x to "two". You can use this to duplicate C's "?" conditional operator.

zkl	C
if (expression) true-clause else false-clause	expression ? true-clause : false-clause

The if statement can be part of a another if statement, assignment, a function parameter and other places.

- if can used as a parameter:
    f(if (1) 2 else 3);   // → f(2)
- You can even use if inside an if:
    if (if (0) 1 else 2) f();   // → if (1) f() → f()

A particularly ugly example is found in Date.prettyDay. Here is part of the code:

```
fcn prettyDay(year, month, day){
   return("%s, the %s%s of %s %s".fmt(
      ...,
      if (1==(day/10)) "th"              // 1*
      else                               // *0, *1, *2, *3
         try  { T("th","st","nd","rd")[day%10] }
         catch{"th"}                     // all other days
      , ... );
}
```

Here, the if statement is a function parameter (to fmt) and has a gnarly else clause, all in an attempt to calculate the suffix of a day in a month.

It should be noted that if the one of the clauses leaves the if statement (such as return or break), there will be no result.

include

Syntax
- `include(`*`filename`* `[,` *`filename`* `...])`
- `include("`*`filename`*`" [,` *`filename`* `...])`

Notes
- If the file name includes a "/", quotes are needed because the tokenizer sees "/" as division, not as a path name.
  `include(bar.zkl, "foo/bar.zkl");`
- On Windows, you can use back slashes ("\") in the file name. Quotes are optional in this case. You will need to double the backslashes or use a raw string. The following are equivalent:
  `include(foo\\bar.zkl);`
  `include("C:\\foo\\bar.zkl");`
  `include(0'"C:\foo\bar.zkl");`
  `include("C:/foo/bar.zkl");`
- System.includePath ($zklIncludePath) is searched.
- On Windows, it doesn't matter if you use slash "/" or back slash ("\").
- There is no restrictions on the file name, just that it can be opened.

Throws: SyntaxError

Abstract
Treat the contents of a file as part of the file being compiled. The include keyword is replaced by the contents of the file and parsed.

Discussion
Search order (success stops the search, failure throws a SyntaxError):
1. An attempt is made to open filename.
2. The include path is searched:
   - The include search path is stored in `System.includePath`, which is a list generated from the system environment variable `zklIncludePath` (if it exists, otherwise a default is used).
   - Each element of the list as the file name appended and an attempt is made to open that file.

Include is very useful for sharing constants between programs. For example, if classes in several files use a magic cookie whose value is "MagicCookie", rather than hard code this value in each file, you could put it into a file (named "cookie.h.zkl" for this example): `const MAGIC_COOKIE = "Cookie Monster";` Then, in each of the code files, use

```
    include(cookie.h.zkl);
    println("The magic cookie is ",MAGIC_COOKIE);
```
to print "The magic cookie is Cookie Monster".

[[ ]] (List Comprehension)

Syntax: `[[(parameters); sequence; action]]`
              `[[([parameters]); sequence,filter,…;s,f,…; action]]`
              `[[…;_]]`: Action is the identity function.
              `[&…]]`: → Walker
Returns: List or Walker
See Also: Keywords.Range ([]), Objects.Utils.zipWith, Objects.Walker

Abstract

List comprehension[34] is a way of describing list generation, typically done with nested loops, concisely.
If action is "_", it is converted to `self.fcn.idFcn` (the identity function).

Discussion

For example, to construct the list L(L(0,"a"),L(0,"b"),L(1,"a"),L(1,"b")), you could use

```
r:=L();
foreach n in ([0..1])
    { foreach c in (["a".."b"]){r.append(T(n,c))}}
```

or

    `[[(n,c); [0..1]; ["a".."b"];_]]`[35]

which reads left to right just like the loop version.
The comprehension has the benefit of being able to create an infinite list:

```
r:=[&(n,c); [0..]; ["a".."b"]; T]]
r.walk(8) → L( L(0,"a"),L(0,"b"),L(1,"a"),L(1,"b"),L(2,"a"),L(2,"b"),L(3,"a"),L(3,"b") )
r.walk(2) → L( L(4,"a"),L(4,"b") )
```

(n,c) creates the variables that will be used for each "section" (the areas between semi colons), "n" for the first and "n", "c" for the next two (just as in the loop version). The action is T, which is a shortcut for `T.create(n,c)` → ROList.

What if you want a sequence based on one of the variables? Use a function to create it. And, speaking of functions, there is a short for creating them: **{}** will **prepend fcn(…)** to the braces (the parameters are based on the variables that are in scope for that section).

Another example: Create a sequence of (x,y,2xy) triples where x is 0…100 & $x^2 > 40$ and y is 1…x & y is a multiple of 3 & $y^2 < 100 - x^2$:

---

34 http://en.wikipedia.org/wiki/List_comprehension
35 AKA Cartesian Product

```
[[(x,y); [0..100],{x*x>40}; {[1..x]},{y%3==0},{y*y<100-x*x};
        {return(x,y,2*x*y)} ]]
```
→ L(L(7,3,42),L(7,6,84),L(8,3,48),L(9,3,54))

Or:
```
[[(x,y); [0..100],{x*x>40}; {[3..x,3]},{y*y<100-x*x};
        {return(x,y,2*x*y)} ]]
```
Or, if you just want the 2xys:
```
[[(x,y); [0..100],{x*x>40}; {[1..x]},{y%3==0},{y*y<100-x*x};
        '*(2)]]
```
→ L(42,84,48,54)

Anything that has a walker[36] method can be used as a sequence. Filters and action can be any runnable that handles the parameters (you can use the fp methods to adjust them).

If you use fcn or 'wrap, you need to use the full signature. For example, rewriting the above example:
```
[[(x,y); [0..100],fcn(x){x*x>40};
    fcn(x,y){[1..x]},fcn(x,y){y%3==0},fcn(x,y){y*y<100-x*x};
    fcn(x,y){return(x,y,2*x*y)} ]]
```

If the Walker comprehension doesn't generate any results, TheEnd is thrown:
```
[&(); [1..10],fcn{False}; T]].walk() → TheEnd
```
If you don't like that, use pump instead of walk:
```
[&(); [1..10],{False}; {}]].pump(List) → L()
```
The "do it now" comprehension acts like the pump case.

More Examples
```
xs.apply(f) ≈ [[(x); f]]
    T(1,2,3).apply('+(1)) == [[(); T(1,2,3);'+(1)]]
    → T(2,3,4)
xs.filter(f) ≈ [[(x); xs,f; _]]
    T(1,2,3).filter(fcn(x){x.isEven}) ==
    [[(x); T(1,2,3),{x.isEven}; _]]
    → T(2)
n:=3; [[();T(n),'>(0);_]] → L(3) is a slow way of writing
    n:=3; if(n>0)T(n) else T;
```

---

36 If you supply a Walker, all but the first walker needs to be able to be restarted (eg List but not File or Pipe). If you supply the object, a new walker will be created each time.

onExit

Syntax
- **onExit(**exitObject [,args]**)**
- **{** … **onExitBlock(**exitObject [,args]**)** … **}**

See Also: Keywords.critical, Objects.VM.xxception

Abstract
OnExit funnels exits through an object, usually a block of code. All attempts to leave the fenced code are redirected through the exit code. The exit code is run in a walled garden (or sandbox), from which exceptions can't escape and context in which it was created can't get in (exit functions are not closures). An exit function can access its instance data.

Discussion
OnExit is used to make sure a chunk of code is run no matter what, after another chunk of code has finished running. The best example of this is when you need to make sure clean up happens, such as allocating a resource that needs to be freed before exiting.

Notes
- OnExit queues objects to be run at the end of a function.
- OnExitBlock queues for the end of the block.
- Exit objects are queued, and run, in the order in which they are encountered. If not encountered, it won't be run.
- The exit object is wrapped in a Deferred.once object, thus any parameters are evaluated when onExit is encountered and those are what the code will see when it is run.
  ```
  fcn f(a)
     { onExit(Console.println,a); a=123; println("a=",a); }
  f(5) → "a=123", "5"
  ```
- The exit object can be any object but functions and methods are the most useful.
- There can be more than one exit object per block or function.
- Aside from changes via parameters, and side effects, the originating code is oblivious to the running of the exit code.
- If a thrown exception caused the exit code to be run, vm.xxception has the exception. If an uncatchable exception was thrown (such as OutOfMemory), xxception is True.

- An exit object is run only once although it may be recreated many times and the new instance run (for example, calling a function more than once).

Examples

- Write to a file until something happens, then close it[37]:
```
f:=File("foo.txt","w"); onExit(f.close);
while (True) { x:=something(); f.write(x); }
```
- Don't leave a Lock locked if an error occurs (this is basically critical):
```
lock:=Atomic.Lock(); lock.acquire(); onExit(lock.release);
doSomething();
```
- `foreach n in (5) { onExitBlock(fcn(a) { println(a) },n); }`
  → 0,1,2,3,4
- By adding these two lines to the start of a function, you can add tracing to that function:
```
    println("Entering ",self.fcn.name,vm.arglist);
    onExit(Console.println,"Leaving ",self.fcn.name);
```
You can make this easier to use with:
```
fcn trace(f,args){
    println("Entering ",f.name," ",args);
    Console.println.fp("Leaving ",f.name);
}
#text TRACE onExit(trace(self.fcn,vm.arglist));  [38]
fcn g{
    #tokenize TRACE  // cut&paste this line
    … println("widget made"); …
}
g(1,2,3);
```
→ "Entering g L(1,2,3)", "widget made", "Leaving g"

Warnings

- While the exit code is called by the running thread, that does not imply it is thread safe; another thread may also be running it or it may access data that another thread is also looking at. Take precautions if cross threading is a possibility.
- Tail calls can change the onExit order. Consider:
```
fcn g{ print("G") }
fcn f1 { onExit(Console.print,"F"); r:=g(); return(r); }
fcn f2 { onExit(Console.print,"F"); return(g()); }
fcn f3 { onExit(Console.print,"F"); try {return(g())}catch{} }
f1() → "GF", f2() → "FG", f3() → "GF",
```

---

37 GC will also close the file, but we don't know when.
38 Doing it this way also allows you to turn off TRACE for all fcns (with #if or _debug_)

f1 is pretty clear, f2 isn't so. `return(g())` is turned into a "goto g", which is the exit of f2[39]. f3 can't be turned into a tail call because that would obliterate the try.

Details

Here is a peek under the covers: `OnExit(f,a,b,c)` is transformed into something like `reg __onExitFcn=ROList; __onExitFcn+=Deferred.once(f,a,b,c);` and stashed where the VM can find it. One take away from this is that you need to be careful if f can return a Deferred as it will be evaluated, which may not be what you want.

Acknowledgments

This functionality was inspired by/copied from Google's Go language, keyword defer.

---

39 Indeed, g can not detect that it was even called from f2 as f2s presence on the call stack is obliterated.

pimport (packaging)

Syntax
- `i=`**`pimport(`**`"fileName"`**`)`**`,` `f(`**`pimport(`**`"dir/fileName"`**`))`

Notes:
- When pimporting a code file, do not include the extension. If pimporting a data file (such as a gif), do include the extension.
- The filename is relative to the current directory, no path search is done.

See Also: Objects.Import, Objects.Utils.wad

Abstract
pimport imports a file (just like Import) and caches the result.
"zkl **--package** top_of_tree.zkl" compiles and packages the entire tree.

Discussion
Pimport expands the functionality of import for use in a "packaged" program; a program made up of more than one file (both source and data/resource files). Recursive pimports are handled and pimport also tells the compiler the complete program structure. When *fileA*.zkl is compiled with the **--package** option, all the files pimported by *fileA* are compiled (or loaded if data) and bundled into one runnable .zsc file. This process is recursive: if *fileA* pimports *fileB* and *fileB* pimports *fileC*, both *fileB* and *fileC* will be bundled with *fileA*.

Creating a program "tree" with a bunch of files
When a program passes a certain size, it is easier to deal with it by chunking; dividing functionality into files of code and resources. A program can then exist in any of four states: all source code, all compiled, a mix of source or compiled, or packaged into a ZSC wad. For ease of development, a program needs to be runnable in any of these states and pimport facilitates that.

By way of illustration, consider the Frame-O-Matic program, a collection of fifteen files: eight source files, five images, one text file and a DLL. The root of the tree, frameOmatic.zkl is the "main" file and "wraps" the program into one unit.
Here are the dependencies (most of which are recursive, either directly or indirectly):

frameOmatic.zkl		
frame.zkl	io.zkl	plot.zkl

frame.zkl	io.zkl	plot.zkl
data.zkl io.zkl trig.zkl utils.zkl	data.zkl frame.zkl trig.zkl utils.zkl	data.zkl frame.zkl plotFLTK.zkl trig.zkl

data.zkl	io.zkl	trig.zkl	utils.zkl
frame.zkl io.zkl	frame.zkl data.zkl utils.zkl trig.zkl	data.zkl utils.zkl	data.zkl trig.zkl

plotFLTK.zkl			
frame.zkl io.zkl	applications.gif, help.gif, open.gif, pen.gif, save.gif	help.txt	zklFLTK.dll

As you can see the dependencies are very recursive (eg frame.zkl ↔ data.zkl, frame.zkl → utils.zkl → data.zkl → frame.zkl). When one file imports another file that, in turn, imports the first file, it is an infinite loop and thus very slow. Some languages, such as C, take a "see no evil" and "have the programmer save explicit state" approach (using header files with prototypes and state, and linking after compiling). Another approach is to [indirectly] cache the imported files and let the compiler reference the cache as needed.

The biggest advantage of the latter method is that the program describes itself and all of its code files and resources so no Makefile or external description is needed[40].

Some code. Note that .zkl and .zsc extensions are not included:

- frameOmatic.zkl
  ```
  var [const] Frame=pimport("frame");
  Frame.buildAbike();
  ```
- frame.zkl
  ```
  var[const] FrameData=pimport("data"),Utils=pimport("utils");
  FrameData.getData("wheel");
  Utils.distance(p1,p2);
  ```
- data.zkl
  ```
  var [const] Frame=pimport("frame");
  Frame.find(z);
  ```

---

40 The drawback being no incremental app compiles – making a package is a whole program compile.

- plot.zkl
  ```
  reg [const] PlotFLTK=pimport("plotFLTK");
  plotter=PlotFLTK(Plotter,minX,minY, maxX,maxY);
  ```
- plotFLTK.zkl
  ```
  Attributes(static);
  var FLTK=Import("zklFLTK");    // DLL
  FLTK.get_image("pen",pimport("pen.gif"));
  ```

A twisty maze of references, all alike[41]

Each .zkl files can be compiled into a .zsc file (or not) or the tree toped at frameOmatic.zkl can be compiled and packaged into frameo.zsc (if it were named frameOmatic.zsc, it is ambiguous which should be run, the .zsc or .zkl?). The reason to not compile files is when writing a program, files change a lot and the edit/recompile/re-run cycle is slower than edit/re-run. When the contents of a file become stable, compiling it can be worth the quicker load time.

Here is what happens when frameOmatic is run in each of the four states.

- All source (zkl frameOmatic.zkl in the FOM directory)
  FOM pimports frame (.zkl is appended), which pimports data, which pimports frame again, etc. When FOM imports frame, it caches it. When data.zkl wants to import frame, it checks the cache, finds frame and uses that. When plotFLTK.zkl pimports pen.gif, the gif file is read into a Data.
  Note that zklFLTK (the FLTK DLL) is loaded with Import, not pimport. pimport doesn't handle libraries, it thinks they are just Data. So the DLL is loaded at runtime (and cached by the VM), and not packaged in the wad. FOM is then run as if it were a single file.
- All compiled (zkl frameOmatic.zsc in the FOM directory)
  This is the same as above, except that .zsc is appended (instead of .zkl) and FOM.zsc is run as if it were a single file.
- A mix of source and compiled (zkl frameOmatic.zsc or .zkl in the FOM directory)
  This is the **usual case** when writing an application.
  When a file is pimported, file.zsc is looked for first (on the assumption the compiled file is more desirable), then file.zkl. Then things proceed as above.
- Packaged into a ZSC wad (zkl frameo.zsc from any directory)
  "zkl **--package** frameOmatic.zkl -o frameo"
  The compiler processes pimports as above (which describe the entire program and its resources), compiles (or reads) the pimported files, adds code to build the cache and writes the entire wad to frameo.zsc, which is one file and can be run as such.

---

41 For those who remember the Colossal Cave Adventure.

Keywords

- Once frameo.zsc has been created, it is the complete application and the other files are not needed to run it. Just the VM (zkl) and DLLs.

Notes:
- Notice the Attributes(static) in plotFLTK.zkl. This is because plot does a PlotFLTK() which treats the entire file a class and [attempts] to create an new instance. This is not a "best practice". If the file were not static, a copy would be made and all the pimport information would be reset to Void (in the new class), which breaks things.
- When loading a Data object (such as a image or text file), the packaged application returns a const Data (since the data is in the application itself), otherwise, it is a writable Data. This is an issue if you want to edit the data; in that case make a copy:
  ```
  html:=pimport("frameOmatic.html").copy();
  ```

print, println

Syntax
- `println(args)`
- `print(args)`

Notes
- Print and println aren't actually keywords.

See Also: Objects.Console, Objects.Object.print

Abstract

`Print` and `println` are syntactic sugar for `Console.print` and `Console.println`.

Discussion

Print and println are used so much that the compiler saves on keyboard wear and tear by redirecting these to the Console object. Since they aren't keywords, they can be redefined by things like functions, variables or classes.

If you want to pass print to a function or store it in a list, use the "real" name:
```
L(Console.println);
println(Console.print);
p:=Console.println; p("Hello");
```

[ ] (Range)

Syntax: `[start..]`, `[start..stop]`, `[start..stop|*,step=1]`
Returns: Walker
See Also: Keywords.foreach, Objects.Int.Walker, Objects.Walker

Abstract

Range creates a Walker that provides the functionality of the "traditional" for loop: iterating in discrete steps. Ranges are over Ints, Floats or characters.
`[a..b]`, and `[a .. b]` create ranges that include b. `[a..b,step]` might include b.
`[a..]` is the same as `[a..*]`, which is an infinite range starting at a. To create an infinite stepped range, use *: `[a..*,step]`.

Discussion

A range provides more information than a do() loop; mainly control of the step size and an index variable at the expense of verbosity and overhead. Range is intended to provide similar functionality to C's for loops. A range Walker has all the functionality of a Walker.

zkl	C equivalent (int i; float f;)
`foreach i in ([3..10])`	for (i = 3; i < 10; i++)
`foreach i in ([10..0,-1])`	for (i = 10; 0 < i; i--)
`foreach f in ([0.0 ..1,0.1])`[42]	for (f = 0.0; f < 1.0; f += 0.1)
`foreach i in ([3..*])`	for (i = 3; 1; i++)
`do(10)`	for (i = 10; --i;)

- The `[a..b]`[43] notation indicates a range that includes b. So `foreach i in ([3..10])` is equivalent to C's `for (i=3; i<=10; i++)`
- A range doesn't need to be created with constants, any calculation will do. `a:=2; b:=5; [a+b..a*b]` → `[7..10]`.
- `[1..0].walk()` → TheEnd as that range is empty. `[1..0].pump(List)` → L().

<u>Special Cases</u>
- Character ranges: `["a".."d"]` → "a", "b", "c", "d"
  * isn't special: `[(40).toChar()..*]` → "(",")", "*", thus `["a"..]` == `["a"..*]` == `["a".."*"]` → [] as "a" > "*".
  Only the first character is used. `["efg".."abc",-2]` → "e", "c", "a"
  This is restricted to ASCII characters.

---

42 Usually. See Special Cases.
43 For ints and characters.

- If start is a float, the values are floats.
  - If all start, stop and step don't have fractioal parts, the range is the same as with ints.
  - Otherwise, ½step is added to stop so the terminal value is "close to" stop.

  ```
  [1.3..5]            → 1.3, 2.3, 3.3, 4.3, 5.3
  [0.0..0.29,0.1]     → 0.0, 0.1, 0.2, 0.3
  [1.5 .. 0.1,-0.5]   → 1.5, 1.0, 0.5, 0.0
  ```
- That isn't the case with integers (or characters); if a step takes the range beyond the terminal, the terminal is skipped:

  ```
  [1..6,2]        → 1, 3, 5
  [7..0,-2]       → 7, 5, 3, 1
  ["a".."d",2]  → "a", "c"
  ```

reg

Syntax
- **reg** *name*;
- **reg** *name=expression* | fcn | class;
- **reg** *name=(expression)*;
- **reg** *name=expression*], *name* [= *expression*] ...;
- **reg** [[attributes]] *name*=...
- *name=expression* | fcn | class | *block*; (*name* exists)
- *name:=expression* | fcn | class | *block*; (*name* might exist)
- n1:=n2:= ... := ...
- n1,n2, ... := ...

Notes
- Registers are created with value Void. reg r; is the same as reg r=Void;.
- Registers can be created almost anywhere and are local to "their" block.
- Assignment happens at run time.
- Registers are typeless, they can hold any object.
- Register names can be up to 80 characters long and can use the characters "a-zA-Z0-9_", in other words: underscore, digits, upper or lower case letters. "_" is not a valid name and the name can't start with a digit.
- Names are case sensitive.
- Attributes are **const**, **mixin**, **private**, **protected**, **proxy** and **public**.
  - The default is [private], public and protected are ignored.
  - See Keywords.var for what the attributes do.

See Also: Keywords.var

Abstract

Create a block local variable. The scope of a register is limited to the block it is declared in and blocks contained in that block. Registers can be created implicitly by assignment: r:=5; is the same as reg r=5; if there isn't another object named "r" in this block.

Discussion

Register variables are variables whose life span is that of the block they are in. You can create them with the reg keyword or implicitly with assignment. For example, foo:=Void; creates a block local variable. Reg is preferred when you want to be explicit about the scope of the variable.

Registers are never instance data and are not visible outside of their scope and are only alive at run time.

:=

`r:=5` is roughly equivalent to `reg r=5`. If r doesn't exist in the block, it is created as a register. If r already exits (as a register), `r:=5` is the same as `r=5`. Examples:

- `reg a; a:=b:=5;` creates two registers and assigns 5 to both of them.
- `a,b,c:=T(1,2,3)` creates three registers and assigns 1 to a, 2 to b and 3 to c.
- `if((r:=something())==5){ println(r); }`
- `r:=1;`
  `{ r:=5;`   // this r is 5, a different register from above
  `}`   // r is 1 here, previous r is out of scope

`:=` is restricted to registers. For chained assignment, `:=` can be intermixed with `=`:
`var v; v=r:=5;` assigns 5 to v and creates and assigns 5 to r.
In list assignment, "_" is thrown away. `a,_:=L(1,2)` is the same as `reg a=1`.

Typeless

Registers are typeless and have no restrictions on the objects they can hold. Thus, the following:

```
r:=Void;
r:=123;
r:="foo";
```

is valid and assigns objects of three different types to the same register.

Scope

"reg" is short for register, a type of variable that has a limited life span. In this case, the scope (where and when the variable is accessible) is the block it was created in and all blocks that enclosed by that block. This is compile time, not run time (dynamic), scoping.

It is import to note that a register is always visible in its entire scope, regardless of where it is declared (explicitly or implicitly). This will surprise most programmers. Even in languages such as C++, where you can declare variables pretty much at will, you usually can't access them until after they have been declared.

Note

The "write-onceness" is block local; in some situations, there can be multiple writes. Consider:

```
foreach j in (3){reg [const] r=j;}  → r is 0,1,2
```

Keywords

Examples
- Create two registers, one explicitly and one implicitly:
```
reg r1=1;
r2:=2;
```
- Declare registers after use:
```
    println(x,y); reg x=1; y:=2;      // prints "VoidVoid"
```
Even though the variables were declared after use, they were not set until after the print statement.
- Scoping
```
{
    reg r1=1;
    {
        reg r2=2;
        println(r1);      // prints "1"
    }
    println(r2);    // error, out of scope
}
```

return

Syntax
- **return(**object**)**
- **return(**object,…**)** → **return(**ROList(object,…)**)**
- **return()** → **return(**Void**)**

Notes
- Return is a function so the ()s are required, no spaces between them and return.
- Return is illegal in a constructor or init function.

See Also: Keywords.returnClass, Keywords.fcn

Abstract

Return from a function to the calling function.

Discussion

All functions return a value (implicitly if execution flows off the end of the function). Return explicitly ends the function and returns a single object. If that object is a List, the caller is free to interpret that as a multi-valued return (see below). A function can return any object, it can return different types of objects in the same function (unlike statically typed languages such as C). For example, the following is legal:

```
fcn f{
    if (wrong) return(Void);
    return(True);
}
```

Constructors and init functions are "special" and don't allow you to use return. The reason is, when you are building a new class, the only way you can access the new class is if it returns itself, which it does at the end of init or the constructor. Return would short cut that and, aside from side effects, effectively turning the class instance creation into a no-op. Of course, there are cases where you are only interested in those side effects, which is why returnClass exits.

Multi-valued Return

It can very nice for a function to return more than one value, for example, the result of a calculation and a status to indicate if the calculation is valid or not. If you have used C, you are familiar with errerno, passing in a pointer to status code, and other annoyances. Multi-valued returns allow you more concisely express the results and allow the caller more freedom to deal with those results. For example, in

Keywords

```
fcn calc{… return(result, status)}
r,s=calc();
```

the caller can decide what to do if the status indicates something is amiss. (*Aside*: in many cases, calc may deal with an invalid status cases by throwing an exception but that may not be the best way or place to deal with the problem). One interesting things to note:

- x=calc() will assign an ROList to x, which is ROList(r,s).
- If you only want the result, you could use
  `r=calc()[0];` or `r,_=calc();`
  which assigns the first returned item to r. Note that this is a "special" case because the compiler can't tell, in `r=calc()`, if you want all of the result or just the first item.
- For the general case, assignment works as follows:
  - `x=… return(a,b,c,…)`
    x gets a read only list of the returned items.
  - `x1,x2,…,xn=… return(a,b,c,…,n)`
    x1 gets the first element of the list, x2 gets the second and so forth through xn. If the list contains more than n items, the leftovers are discarded. Thus
    `a,b=… return(1,2,3,4,5);`
    a=1, b=2 and 3,4 and 5 are discarded. If there are less than n items in the list, an error is thrown at run time.
  - If one of the items is "_", it is thrown away. `a,_,c=…`

returnClass

Syntax: `returnClass(`*object*`)`
Notes
- returnClass is only legal in a constructor or init function.
- But not legal in constructors if the class contains init. Put returnClass in init.
- One parameter is required and is usually a class instance (hence the name).
- returnClass is a function, so no space between returnClass and the ()s.

See Also: Keywords.return

Abstract
In the normal course of events, return is illegal in init() or a constructor. ReturnClass is for those abnormal events. ReturnClass is legal where return is illegal and vice versa (subject to the fine print in the Notes section above).

Discussion
Normally, class constructors and class init functions have a single exit point and return self when the code finishes running. This is almost always what you want (otherwise the class you just created would be invisible and get garbage collected, never to be seen) but there is the rare occasions when you want or need to return something other than self.

ReturnClass is named based on the assumption that you'll use it to return a class instance other than self but that isn't required; you can return any object. But, if you do return a non instance, you might want to say to yourself "hmmm, I wonder if there might be a better way to do this".

The usual case is a root class (file) that you would like to impersonate one of its contained classes.
Examples:
- The Exception class is big class that contains lots of exception classes and exception templates. You don't use the big class directly, it has too much baggage, you use a contained class. To throw an generic exception, the "correct" code is `throw(Exception.Exception("Boo"))` but people forget and it's extra work so init helps out by returning a `Exception.Exception` instance for you:
    ```
    fcn init(text) { returnClass(Exception(text)); }
    ```
    Thus, throw (`Exception("Boo")`) is equivalent to
    ```
    throw(Exception.Exception("Boo"))
    ```

Keywords

- The test suites are contained in files that use an instance of Test.UnitTester to test a small piece of functionality and, since there is a lot of functionality to test, there are lots of files. The tests are run in the constructor:

```
tester.testSrc(test-code);
tester.testSrc(another-test);
...
```

A UnitTester instance collects the stats for all the tests run in the constructor, and, when the all tests have finished running, prints the results. This is all well and good if you are just testing one area but, if you are doing a system test, there is too much data. The solution is to have a test collector that runs all the tests, collects the results (contained in UnitTesters) and summarizes. But how does it collect the UnitTesters? The test suites would normally return instances of themselves (since the file is just a constructor), not UnitTesters. You could dig around in the test looking for an instance of a UnitTest or force the test to contain a variable of a certain name that holds the tester but that would be a pain in the butt. ReturnClass to the rescue:

```
tester.stats();      // print test results
returnClass(tester); // return UnitTester instance
```

Now, as each test finishes, it returns the test results (and gets garbage collected since its job is done) so somebody can do an executive summery.

You can also use returnClass to return self if, for some reason, you don't want to flow off the end of the constructor.

self

Syntax
- `self`, `self.*`
- `self.fcn`, `self.fcn()`

Notes
- self must the first word in a data reference.
- self.fcn() is a recursive call.

See Also: Objects.class, Keywords.fcn (tail recursion)

Abstract
Refer to the current class instance.

Discussion
Self is the name of the current class instance, which always exists. It can be used to remove ambiguity from a reference or to clarify code. See class for a full list of things it can refer to.

`self.fcn` is special and refers to the currently running function. It can be used for recursion, and is used by the compiler as hint to check for tail recursion.

Examples
- ```
  class C{
      var c;
      println(self);        // prints "Class(C)"
      fcn init(c){
          var f;
          println(self.fcn); // prints "Fcn(init)"
          self.c=c;    // sets instance var C.c to function arg c
          self.fcn.f=1;      // error, use f instead
                             // to refer to function var
      }
      self.fcn();     // error, infinite recursion if
                      // constructor calls itself
  }
  ```
- ```
  fcn(x){       // factorial
      if(0==x) return(1);        // 0! = 1
      return( x*self.fcn(x - 1) );    // x! = x*(x-1)!
  }
  ```

switch

Syntax
- `switch(`*control*`) { case(`value`){ `*do_this_if_eq_block*` } }`
- `switch (`*control*`){ case(`*value,value*`) ` *block* `else` *default* ` }`
  default is a block or expression, else is the last clause
- `switch(`*control*`){ case(`...`)[fallthrough]` *block* `case(){} }`
- `switch [arglist]{ case(`*object* ...`) ... }`
- Note: `break` does not apply to switch.

Result
- The last calculation, which is usually one of the block results, if control flows off the end (ie not terminated by return, etc).

Abstract
Conditional branching, a more compact syntax than `if/else if`.
Also allows switching on the calling parameters.

Discussion
The switch statement is [somewhat] equivalent to a if/else if/else construct.

```
switch(x){
    case(a)  { fa();  }
    case(c,d){ fcd(); }
    else     { default(); }
}
```
is equivalent to
```
reg X=x;
if(X==a){ fa(); }
else if(X==c or X==d){ fcd(); }
else { default(); }
```
The default case ("else") has to be the last case and will be run if none of the other cases match. Case statements have the same syntax as a function call. The order in which the cases are tested is not specified, all of the cases may or may not be evaluated (so don't use side effects).

fallthrough
When a matched case block finishes running, the switch is done. Unless the case is tagged as "fallthrough", in which case it jumps to the next case block and continues running there. Execution will continue falling until it falls into an untagged block. The default case can be fallen into. For example

```
switch(4){
   case(4)  [fallthrough]{ print(44) }
   case("a")[fallthrough]{ print("A") }
   else {print("**")}
} → "44A**"
```

switch as cond

Lisp's cond: (cond (test)(action) …) can be modeled as switch(True)
{case(test){}… }. This can result in "cleaner" code than a wad of if then elsess.

```
n:=someResult();
switch(True){
   case(n==4)    {}
   case(n.isOdd){}
   else          {}
}
```

Result

Switch has a defined result if the control flows though the entire switch statement.

- If a block is run, the switch result is the block result.
- If there is no match, the result *might* be the control but might not be so use a default case if it matters.

Example

```
r:=switch(4){ case(2){ 22 } case(4){ 44 } }; → 44
```

Oddities

- switch(n){} works and doesn't do anything.
- switch(n){case(){x}} is a no-op and switch(n){case{x}} is an error.
- switch(n){ else { println("Always prints"); }}

Notes

- You can use switch in an expression but you may need to wrap it in ()s or terminate it with a ";":
  ```
  (switch(X){case(Y){1}} +5) or (switch(X){case(Y){1}}) +5
  if (X) switch(Y){ case(Z){1} }; foo();
  ```

[arglist]

Switch [arglist] is a VM.argsMatch wrapper to make it a bit more palatable/useful.
For example:

Keywords

```
fcn f{
    switch [arglist]{
        case(1) [fallthrough] {}
        case(self.NullClass)  { println("number or class") }
        case(List)            { println("list") }
        case(*,*)             { println("match any 2 args"); }
        case()                { println("no args"); }
        else                  { println("anything"); }
    }
}
f(self), f(5), f(6.7)   → "number or class"
f(Void)                 → "anything"
f()                     → "no args"
f("test",4)             → "match any 2 args"
```

The cases are evaluated in order so put the long matches and specific matches first, followed by the more and more general cases.

throw

Syntax: `throw(`*Exception*`)`
Notes
- The exception has to an Exception class, that is, a Class that inherits from Exception.

See Also: Keywords.try/catch, Objects.Exception

Abstract
Throw is used to signal that something out of the ordinary has occurred and it can't be handled here so control is being transferred to somewhere where it can be handled.

Discussion
Throw is a rich mans goto. Modern coding societies consider goto to be poor hygiene so we use throw instead. Throw is a goto with a wealth of constraints attached (golden handcuffs if you will). In exchange, we get cleaner code that is easier to understand and less prone to error. Hopefully, you have already been indoctrinated about the benefits, failing that, you'll have to trust me. Or not, no matter because goto doesn't exist so it can't be abused.

For example `throw(`Exception.BadDay`)` stops the current control flow and searches for the nearest catch block that can deal with a bad day. See try for the gory details.

See Objects.Exception for a list of already created exceptions (like BadDay) that you can use.

Note that some exceptions can't be caught. If you come across a situation so dire that recovery is impossible, you can throw something like Exception.KissOfDeath.

Most exceptions allow you to do minor run time customizations, most often adding a custom message. To reuse the bad example, you could `throw(`Exception.BadDay`("My hair is a mess!"))` and the catching code would be able to determine why this is such a bad day.

What if a suitable exception just doesn't exist? You can create your own:
```
class YouBad(Exception.Exception){
    Exception.init("You bad boy you");
    fcn init(msg=Void){ if(msg) text=msg;  }
}
```

This is the "standard" way to create a new exception, one that acts like those in the Exception class. The new exception name is "YouBad" and the default text is "You bad boy you". Now, you can use the following:

```
throw(YouBad)
throw(YouBad("Thats just crazy")) if you want to change the text.
```

In general, use one the provided exception if it is at all close, people who use your code will more likely expect one of those. Definitely create your own exception if your new class doesn't fit the mold or it help avoid confusing your class with another class.

Wishing for Goto

Sometimes, it just seems it would be easier to just use a goto to get stuff done. Consider:

```
walker=File("test.txt").walker();
foreach line in (walker){
    if (Void!=line.find("GO!")) goto printRestOfFile;
}
throw(Exception.AssertionError("GO not found in file"));
printRestOfFile:
walker.walk(Console.print);
```

All we want to do is read from a file until we find a line with "GO!" in it, then print the rest of the file. If "GO!" isn't found, that is an error. Goto seems to be pretty nice way to skip around the error processing and get on with things. And it is. But, there is no goto, so we have to do something else. The usual way is to use a boolean flag:

```
foundGO=False;
foreach line in (walker){
    if (Void!=line.find("GO!")){ foundGO=True; break; }
}
if (not foundGO)
    throw(Exception.AssertionError("GO not found in file"));
```

which seems like a step backwards in readability. And it really gets bad when you need to nest these. Exceptions give a way of simulating goto and "break to label".

```
try{
    foreach line in (walker){
        if (Void!=line.find("GO!")) throw(Exception.TheEnd);
    }
    throw(Exception.AssertionError("GO not found in file"));
}catch(TheEnd){}
```

Still not as direct as a goto but it is a nice alternative to flags. You can also create your own exceptions and use those.

```
class Label1(Exception.Exception){ fcn init{} }
try{ … throw(Label1); … }catch(Label1){}
```

A more twisted version of this is to use exceptions to simulate C's switch statement. For example, processing user input or method handling.

try/catch

Syntax

- `try { ` *block* ` } catch { ` *block* ` }`
- `try { ` *block* ` } catch(` *exceptionName* ` [,` *exceptionName* ` ...])`
  `{ ` *block* ` }`
- `try { ` *block* ` }`
  `catch(` *exceptionName* `(s)) { ` *block* ` }`
  `[ catch( ... ) { ... } ]`
  `[ catch { ... } ]`
- `try { ` *block* ` } catch[( ... )] { ` *block* ` } fallthrough { ` *block* ` }`
- `try { ` *block* ` } catch[( ... )] { ` *block* ` } fallthrough try`
- `try { ... } catch { println(__exception); }`

Result

- The last calculation, if control flows through to the end of the try/catch (ie not terminated by return, etc).

Notes

- Exception names are the names of Exception classes. For example, `throw(`Exception.BadDay`)` throws an Exception class named "BadDay". To catch that exception, use `catch(`BadDay`)`.
- Names are plain text fixed at compile time; no consts, vars, etc.
- catch and catch() match all catchable exceptions.
- Catch order is important. It is first come, first served, so put "catch" as the last catch block.
- Some exceptions are uncatchable. For example: Exception.KissOfDeath and Exception.OutOfMemory.
- Special exception names: "*", "!*name*", "*name*.", "0" and words starting with "+" or "-".
  - "*" means match any catchable exception; `catch(*)` is longhand for `catch` or `catch()`.
  - "!*name*" means "don't catch this exception". If you want to catch all exceptions but BadDay, use `catch(`!BadDay, *`)`. Exception names are matched from left to right.
  - "*name*." (name dot) means match if the thrown exception is, or is a child of, Exception *name* (ie look up through the parent tree for *name*)[44].
  - "+" and "–" set catch options.
    The options are:
    - +trace: Print a stack trace

---

44 __exception.isChildOf(*name*) = True

- -trace: Don't print a stack trace.

These options remain set for the remaining catches (attached to the current try) or until changed. By themselves, the options don't match anything. For example:

```
try { … }
catch(NoTrace1,+trace,Trace1,-trace,NoTrace2) { … }
catch(+trace,Trace2) { … }
catch { … } // will get stack trace from above
```

The NoTrace* exceptions won't get stack traces, all others will.
If you want to catch everything and get a stack trace, use:

```
catch(+trace,*) { … }
```

Which is equivalent to:

```
catch(+trace) {}  // doesn't match anything
catch { … }       // match everything, trace is on
```

- 0 means match all uncatchable exceptions. Needless to say, don't use this! They are uncatchable for a reason. If you feel compelled to, try to use critical or onExit first. I'm not going to tell you the syntax but it is probably obvious.
- Inside of a catch block, register __exception contains the thrown exception. If your catch block handles an exception and you want to re-throw it, use

  ```
  throw(__exception).
  ```

- throw is legal in a try, catch or fallthrough block.
- A finally clause isn't provided, onExitBlock provides similar functionality.
- Try can also be used in a function parameter and in a control expression (if, loops).
- Or in an expression. You may need to wrap it in ()s or terminate it with a ";":
  ```
  if (X) try{Y}catch{}; a+b;    (try{X}catch{Y}) + 5;
  ```

See Also: Keywords.throw, onExitBlock, critical, Objects.Exception

Abstract
Try to run some code, catch any errors that occur.

Discussion
Like all good modern computer languages, zkl lacks a goto statement (C doesn't count because it is a perfect language). To make up for this grievous loss, zkl uses that other common feature: exceptions. If you've used Java, C++, C# or Python, you know how this works, but the syntax and rules are a bit different:

Keywords

```
fcn consultHoroscope {
    gettingOutOfBedIsABadIdea = throwTheBonesForToday();
    if (gettingOutOfBedIsABadIdea)
        throw(Exception.BadDay("Coffee please"));
}
try { consultHoroscope(); }
catch(BadDay) {
    println("I heard somebody say: ", __exception.text);
}
```

When this code is run and my horoscope for today isn't so good, the code will print: "I heard somebody say: Coffee please"

The rules are, basically: You have to throw something derived from the Exception class and you can catch anything, everything or nothing (well, not quite but you get the idea).

Try doesn't have a "finally" clause like Java or Python, the "onExitBlock" keyword provides that functionality.

fallthrough

The fallthrough clause is useful for minimizing the amount of code under try control. Usually, try is used where you expect it is reasonable for an exception to occur; you write your code against that expectation. If you enclose a big block of code in a try, you might get exceptions that you are not expecting and thus don't handle correctly. In that case, it might be better not to catch the exceptions at all and let them propagate. Fallthrough helps you do this by basically extending the try clause minus exception handling. Using an fallthrough usually boils down to personal preference. **Note**: The fallthrough block has the same scope as the try block, ie you can access registers created in the try block.

In this example, in the no error case, we want to doSomething and doSomeMore but if doSomething has issues, we have to catch them. After catching, we do not want do anything and the fallthrough clause lets us jump around doSomething. You can read this as "try to doSomething and catch these exceptions, else, if there were no exceptions, doSomeMore".

```
try { doSomething(); }
catch(E1) {}
catch(E2) {}
fallthrough { doSomeMore(); }
```

Control Flow

The control flow through a try catch fallthrough is:

- Do the try block.
- If no error is thrown, flow off the end of try block into the fallthrough block, if it exists, otherwise, just flow off the end (unless throw, return, continue or break is called).
- If an error is thrown:
  - Move up the call stack one level (ie if thrown in a try block, don't look for a match there).
  - Continue walking until a catch block is found and check to see the exception name matches one of the catch name(s).
  - If it doesn't, continue walking up the call stack
    If nobody catches the exception, the current VM is halted and the exception flows up to the calling VM[45]. If that VM doesn't catch it, repeat until we pop out of the current thread, which terminates the thread[46] (which may stop the program if the thread is the main thread).
  - If a catch if found:
    - The exception is stashed in __exception (a register in the catch block).
    - The catch block is run and the fallthrough clause is ignored (as are other catches).

Avoiding Yucky Code

Try can be used to avoid value checking. Let's say you are looking at something that contains all kinds of things, but you only care about one case and, unfortunately, that case is a bit nasty to test as it is pretty convoluted. How to avoid checking? Here is a real world example from the compiler: checking to see if a function call is tail recursive. Check out this code:

```
reg s;
try{  // if the the next line to blows a gasket, s remains Void
   s=((arg := self.args[0].objs[0]).isInstanceOf(FcnCall) and
      arg.name=="self.fcn");
}catch{}      // nope, not tail recursion
fallthrough{ // might be ...
   if (s){  // s is not Void or False, we made a valid assumption
      println("Tail call!");
      rewriteCodeToDoTailRecursion();
   }
}
```

The code has to look in two lists, which can be empty or hold all kinds of things we don't care about, for a function call to "self.fcn"[47]. Without using a try, the code

---

45 VMs and methods create VMs on an as needed basis to run code. Eg fibers.
46 And that isn't a happy death, see Keywords.class.splashdown
47 This is checking for "return(self.fcn(...))"

would have to check that each list was not empty[48], then check that each has the right kind of item in the right place, all before it can check for the function call. What a hair ball. Instead, we just assume it is going to work and write the code accordingly. If it doesn't, an exception is thrown, we catch it and go on our merry way. The other important point is that the real work is done in the fallthrough clause. We do that so, if we screw up, we won't catch those exceptions. If rewriteCodeToDoTailRecursion was in the try block, our catch would have to catch specific exceptions, and further, we would have to test to find out what those exceptions might be and we definitely don't want to do that much work.

Exception Hierarchies
The core exception tree is pretty flat, this keeps things simple. However, sometimes a deeper hierarchy can make your code cleaner; you can catch a particular exception or an exception tree. This exception specializes a BadDay:

```
class WorseDay(Exception.BadDay){
    const TEXT = "I'm having a really bad day";
    text = TEXT;        // globally set self.BadDay.Exception.text⁴⁹
    fcn init(msg = TEXT) { BadDay.init(msg); }
}
```
In use:
```
try { doSomething() }
catch(BadDay.)  {}   // catch exceptions based on BadDay
```
If doSomething throws WorseDay or BadDay, it will be caught. You could also catch WorseDay or both:
```
try { doSomething() }
catch(WorseDay) {}   // extra strength aspirin
catch(BadDay)   {}   // warm milk and cookies
catch(BadDay.)  {}   // a bad day I don't know about: Advil
```

And finally
To add a "finally" clause to try, use onExitBlock:
```
fcn f(t){
    try{ onExitBlock(fcn{println(vm.xxception)});
        if(t) throw(Exception.BadDay);
        print("try succeeded: ");
    }catch { println("try failed: "); }
}
```

---

48 With if (args) ... or args[0,1]

49 This is done so throw(WorseDay) will have have "right" text without having to create an instance. In this example, throw(WorseDay()) has the same result but does more work.

```
f(0) → "Try succeeded: Void"
f(1) → "BadDay(I'm having a bad day)"
        "Try failed: "
```

If you want to do the finally *after* catching, use:
```
fcn f(t){
    {   // block wrapper for onExitBlock & try
        onExitBlock(…);  // in same block as try
        try{…}catch{…}
    }
}
```
```
f(0) → "Try succeeded: Void"
```
```
f(1) → "Try failed: Void"
```
Using a block wrapper ties onExitBlock and try into one unit with the exit code running immediately after the try/catch code.

var

Syntax
- **var** *name*
- **var** *name=expression* | fcn | class
- **var** *name=(expression)*
- **var** *name* [= *expression*], *name* [= *expression*] …
- **var** [*attributes*] name [= …]
- **var** [**mixin**] *name*=class | Vault object …
- **var** [**mixin**=class | Vault object] *name* [= …]
- v1=v2= … = … Set exiting variables or registers to the same value
- v1,v2, … = X List assignment
- v1,v2, … = 1,2,3 Mulitple assignment

Notes
- Variables are typeless, they can hold any object.
- Variables are created with value Void.
- Even though creation and assignment can be co-located, the compiler moves variable creation to the start of the class they are declared in while assignment remains at the point of declaration. Except when it doesn't (see function variables).
- For class variables, assignment happens at run time, in the constructor.
- Function variables (variables declared in a function):
    - Are actually class variables[50]. This notation makes it easier to "confine" class variables to a function and hide those variables from other functions.
    - Variables declared in "init" are treated the same as variables created in the constructor (init is considered an extension of the constructor).
    `class{ fcn init{ var v=1; }}` is the same as
    `class{ var v; fcn init{ v=1; }}`
    Assignment happens when init is run.
    - For other functions:
        - Initialization values are restricted to things that are available to the containing class constructor. You can't use parameters and usually can't use other co-located variables.
        - Variable initialization occurs early during class construction, after the parent class constructor(s) are run but before the class constructor is run. This is good and bad. Ideally, initializers should be totally contained (eg `fcn f{ var v=123; }`).

---

50 If you are a C programmer, think of them as in "void fcn(){ static int var; }"

- You can use a contained class constructor to initialize variables you might otherwise not have access to. The following doesn't work because BigNum is initialized after b is initialized:
  ```
  var [const] BI=Import.lib("zklBigNum");
  fcn f{ var b=BI(5); } // b is Void
  ```
  This does work (C is constructed where defined, order is important!):
  ```
  var [const] BI=Import.lib("zklBigNum");
  class C{ fcn f{ var b=BI(5); } }
  ```

  Even better (assuming BigNum isn't needed else where):
  ```
  fcn f{
     var [const]
           BI=Import.lib("zklBigNum");
     var b=BI(5);
  }
  ```
  - You will not be able to access the variables from outside of the function[51].
- When doing an assignment as part of a var declaration, you may need to wrap the expression in ().
- Variable names can be up to 80 characters long and can use the characters "a-zA-Z0-9_", in other words: underscore, digits, upper or lower case letters. "_" is not a valid name and the name can't start with a digit.
- There is a limit of 200 variables per class.
- Names are case sensitive.
- **Attributes** are **const**, **mixin**, **private**, **protected**, **proxy** and **public**.
  - The default attribute is public.
  - **Const**/"write-once" variables are protected variables that can be set only once. You need to set them in the var statement. Actually, "write-once" is more like "write-in-only-one-place", see below.
    Const vars try to become mixins.
  - A **mixin** is a variable that the compiler pretends has the same type as the mixin value. This allows the compiler to do some static checking. It can be set to anything at runtime[52]. Use as a "this is the API" var and set to the real object at runtime. As an example,
    `var [mixin] t=L(1,2,3);`[53]

---

51 Not strictly true – you can poke around the class vars and find the fcn vars
52 It really is just a variable with a compile time chaperone.
53 The compiler doesn't always know the result of a function call, so something like
   `var [mixin] plus1=Op("+",1)` generates a syntax error. Rewrite as

tells the compiler to expect a List or something with List semantics. It then knows that `t.pmp(f)` is an error and
```
t=t.walker(); t.pump(List,f);
```
is OK since both List and Walker contain pump.
See also: Device Drivers in the Illustrated Examples Appendix.

- **Private** variables are not found by resolve but are visible throughout the file they are defined in.
- **Protected** means the variable is read only outside of the class it is defined in or child classes.
- A variable with the **proxy** attribute is an "active/trampoline" variable, referencing it causes an action to happen. For example
```
var [proxy] f=fcn{ println("test"); }  f; → "test"
```

See Also: Keywords.reg (:=), Objects.Class.varNames, Objects.Class.vars

Abstract

Create a class local (instance) variable. The scope of a variable is the class it is created in.

Discussion

Variables are instance data and differ from registers in that they live as long as the class they are in lives. The only way to create an instance variable is with var. Creating a variable implicitly always creates a register.

Typeless

Variables are typeless and have no restrictions on the objects they can hold. Thus, the following
```
var r=Void;
r=123;
r="foo";
```
are valid and assign objects of three different types to the same variable.

Creating

Var creates object local variables in the nearest enclosing class. Vars are noted at parse time and are visible throughout the object, regardless of where they were declared. This will surprise most programmers. Even in languages such as C++, where you can declare variables pretty much at will, you usually can't access them until after they have been declared (ie they are Void, which is not good).

Constructor and init variables are initialized where they are declared.

```
var [mixin=Op] plus1=Op("+",1)
```

Variables in init are moved to the constructor
If a variable is created in the init function, it is promoted to the constructor of the
enclosing class. For example:

```
class C{ fcn init(x){ var [const] v=x; }}
```

is the same as

```
class C{ var [const] v; fcn init(x){ v=x }}
```

if the latter worked.

Scope

- Class (instance) variables
  These variables can be referenced, by name, from anywhere, inside or outside
  of the class, from other classes or files. The var is wholly contained in the
  class and every instance of the class (including the "reference" instance) has
  it own set of vars. If the var exists in the file being compiled, the compiler is
  usually able to resolve the reference, otherwise, it leaves the resolution to
  runtime. The class constructor will initialize vars that have initializers, before
  that, the var's value is Void.
- Function variables
  These are class variables with limited visibility. They are not shared amongst
  other copies of the same function. In other words, if class C contains function
  f and f contains var v:
  ```
  class C{ fcn f{ var v; } }
  ```
  and there are two instances of C, the two variables v are separate.

Constant (Write Once) and protected Variables

If the variable was declared const, the compiler will only allow the variable to be set
when it is declared.

```
var [const] v=5;      // OK
v=6;                  // error
class C{ var [const] v=1; }         // OK
class C{ var [const] v=1; v=2 }  // error
class C{ fcn init{ var [const] v=1; }}  // C().v → 1
```

Write once variables are set when the function they are declared in is run.
Protected variables are similar, except they can be modified in their class or children
classes.
Note: The "read onlyness" has no effect on values that are mutable. For example, if a
read-only variable is a list, that list can be changed:

```
class C{ var [protected] v=L() }
C.v.append(1);    // OK, v hasn't changed, but contents have
C.v[0]=1;      // ditto
```

Note

The "write-onceness" is not strict; variables are set in one of two places:

- The init fcn for vars initialized declared there.
- The constructor for all other initialized vars.

This means direct calls to init or __constructor will reset all vars, including const ones.

```
class C{ fcn init(n){ var [const] v=n; }}
c=C(4);              // c.v=4
c.init(654);         // c.v=654
```

A little more on mixins

Let's say you are using the BigNum DLL and wish to use it as a mixin. This is a problem because it is not part of the system and your program will load it at run time. The work around is to also load it at compile time so the compiler can access it.

```
const IMPORTS                    // compile time
   { var BigNum=Import("zklBigNum"); }
var [mixin=IMPORTS.BigNum]       // run time
   BigNum=Import("zklBigNum");
r:=BigNum.rand(0,10);            // compile time check
```

generates a SyntaxError as rand should be spelled random.

"Template" classes can also be put into const space, where they can be used for syntax checking but won't take up any space in compiled code.

List assignment

In **a, b, c=X**, a, b and c are assigned the first three items of X, where X gets to decide what those three items are. The most obvious examples are:

```
var a,b; reg c;
a,b,c=L(1,2,3)      → a=1, b=2, c=3
a,b,c=L(1,2,3,4,5)            → same as above, the rest of the list is ignored
a,b,c=L(1)                  → error, not enough data
fcn f{ return(1,2,3) } a,b,c=f();   → same as first example
```

However, it get even better:

```
a,b="ABCDE"       → a="A", b="B"
class C{ fcn __sGet(n){ return(n+5) }} a,b=C  → a=5, b=6
```

Any object that supports sub-scripting (a __sGet method or function) also supports multiple assignment. Functions implement multi-value returns in a way that mimics returning a list of the return values.

If the assignment is of the form **a,b,c=x,y,z;** then it is the same as **a=x; b=y; c=z;** Note it takes [at least] a y to to get this form.

If the assignment is of the form **a=b=c=x;** then it is the same as **(a=(b=(c=x)));** Note of caution: if the left hand sides are compound into the same class (eg n.left.right=n.left=x) there is a good chance that you will get the wrong result depending on how and when the left sides are computed.

Single assignment and multiple assignment can be mixed, as long as multiple is to the left of the single:

    a=b,c=L(1,2) → error
    a,b=c=L(1,2) → a=1, b=2, c=L(1,2)
"_" is thrown away: **a,_=L(1,2)** assigns 1 to a.
All the variables/registers must exist.

Note: The order of the assignments is undefined.

Proxy Variables

Proxy variables enable lots of wild and wacky things but can also be used to give classes Property like functionality.

    class C{ var [private] broken=False, closed=False;
             var [proxy] isClosed=fcn{ (closed or broken) }}
Then, C.isClosed → False
A proxy variable is always called when it is referenced, which can yield odd results.

    var [proxy] p=1; p → 0 (as (0)() → 0)
If you want to proxy another variable (or proxy), use Property:

    var v=123; var [proxy] p=Property("v");   p → 123
    fcn f{123} var [proxy] p=f, p2=Property("p"); p2 → 123
Proxies can be very handy when changing, updating or refactoring an existing API.

Off the Wall Examples
- class One{ var v; } println(One.v);   // prints "Void"
  class Three{ println(v); var v=4; } // prints "Void"
  Even though the variable is declared, it is not set until the constructor is run and the constructor does the println before it does the assignment.
- Class var assignment after the constructor is run and after a new instance is created:
  class Two{ var v=1; fcn init{ v=2; } }
  println(Two.v);   // post constructor: prints "1"
  println(Two().v); // new instance: prints "2"

Keywords

- What does this do: `{ reg a=1; var a=2; } println(a);` ? Probably not what you think, and it is probably a surprise it even compiles. But compile it does and prints out Void. Bet you didn't expect that. Not very intuitive; the key is to remember that creation and assignment are separated, the code is transformed into `var a; { reg a; a=1; a=2; } println(a);` and variables default to Void. The block register "a" is set twice and then thrown away. Save yourself some grief and declare your variables and registers before you use them.

while

Syntax
- `while (control){ block }`
- `while(control) { block }`
- `while(control) { block } fallthrough{ block }`

See Also: Keywords.foreach, do, break, continue

Abstract
A while loop.

Discussion
Repeatedly run the block code while the control evaluates to True. The control is tested before *block* is ever run, so if the initial test is False, *block* is never run.

Examples
Two ways to write the same infinite loop:
```
while(True){ … }
while(1)    { … }
```

This doesn't do anything: `while(0) { println("hoho"); }`

Print "123": `n:=0; while((n+=1)<4){ print(n); }`
Note that that the above is very different from:
```
n=0; while(n+=1<4){ print(n); }
```
This second loop is infinite; the control is parsed as `(n+=(1<4)) ≈ n+=1`.

fallthrough
A fallthrough block is run if running code "falls off" the end the loop, ie the loop runs to completion, ie a break statement isn't run.
Note: The fallthrough block is in the *same* scope as the loop block, ie you can access registers created in the while loop. **Break** and **continue** are *outside* the loop block, ie `break(n)` becomes `break(n+1)`.

Keywords

The zkl Objects

Young man, it's objects all the way down!
-- Elderly woman
        who clearly understands OOP

In zkl, objects are pervasive and first class, but it is not a "pure" object oriented language (like, for example, SmallTalk). However, it is close enough that even those things you wouldn't normally think as objects, such as numbers, are. Classes, functions, methods, etc are all objects that can be assigned to variables, passed in function calls, created at run time, etc. If something is an object, it is a first class object.

Attributes of Objects (See Objects.Object)
All objects have a common set of attributes:
- Name
- Type
- Methods
- Properties
- Operators: All objects have the same set of operators. But they might not be implemented.

It if often convenient to store a "pointer" to an object you are going to be using a bunch and use that to save some typing.
For example:

```
tester:=TheVault.Test.UnitTester();
tester.testSrc("return(Void);","SyntaxError");

Date:=Import("Time.Date");
Date.nthDayInYear(2006,1,1);
println(Date.ctime());
```

Objects

Some the the classes just contain utility functions so you don't need to create a class instance to use it, just use the "static" class, as in the Date example above.

Attributes of Classes (See Objects.Class)
Classes are "fat" Objects – in addition to all the Object attributes, they can also contain classes, functions, variables (instance data) and have parents (inheritance).

Programming
Creating a program in zkl is the process of creating new objects by combining existing objects. This process looks pretty much like any other Algol like (or "curly-bracket") language (such as C or Java), if you have done any programming at all, zkl will very likely look familiar. Where it differs is the object system; in zkl, it is typeless and dynamic, similar to that of SmallTalk and Python.

Environment Variables

Environment Variable Name	zkl Property	What and Default Value
zklRoot	N/A	This is used if a path needs to be constructed. It can contain more than one path, each of which is a directory. Windows: C:/ZKL Unix:
zklClassLeafs	N/A	After classPath has been built, this variable is used to augment classPath. classPaths are searched to find a leaf directory in the subtree.
zklClassPath	System .classPath	Where the loader looks for classes (source or compiled). "$zklRoot/.;$zklRoot/Src/Scripts;$zklRoot/Src;$zklRoot/Built"
zklLibPath	System .libPath	Where zkl looks for shared libraries. "$zklRoot/.;$zklRoot/Lib"
zklIncludePath	System .includePath	Where the compiler looks for include files when compiling the "include" keyword. "$zklRoot/.;$zklRoot/Include;$zklRoot/Src;$zklRoot/LibSrc"

Environment Variable Name	zkl Property	What and Default Value
zklIgnoreWad	N/A	If 1, zkl will attempt to load the Core classes from the file system. Used for debugging or when building a new system. 0; classPath is "C:/ZKL/Built", libPath and includePath are not set.

When the VM starts up, it creates these properties (see Objects.System Properties). If the associated environment variable exits, it is used; otherwise, $zklRoot[54] is prepended to the default paths to create the property. In both cases, if the resulting directory doesn't exist, it won't be in the property[55].

Names

Object names (variables, etc) start with a letter and have up to 80 case sensitive upper or lower case letters, digits or underscores (a-zA-Z0-9_). Don't use a lone underscore, some things interpret it as a placeholder.

What thread-safe and not thread-safe mean

A *thread safe* method means two or more threads can call that method on that object and all will have to expected result. If a method is *not thread-safe*, then only one thread [at a time] can call that method on that object. Note that methods are bound to objects and it is the underling object that determines thread safety, not the method per se (two threads calling the same method on two objects is always safe (unless noted).

Notes on the Pump Method

What pump does: It is basically a stream processor, rolling a value through a fixed set of actions into a sink. Values from the pump source are fed to the first action and that result is fed to the next action. Rinse and repeat. The end result is then fed to a sink (which typically aggregates the result into, for example, a list).
The syntax is:
```
object.pump(sink [,action ,action …])
```
The object may have optional parameters before the sink, such as a count:
```
[0..].pump(count,sink [,action ,action …])
```

---

54 The use of "$zklRoot" notation is informational only, no attempt is made to recursively parse/expand $envVar.
55 Note that if directories [dis]appear after startup, the properties don't change to reflect this.

If an object has a pump method, it has the following attributes:
- The **sink** parameter:

Data	A data Data (vs string Data) is the sink. If the word Data is used, a new sink is created (eg `"123".pump(Data)`). To append to an existing Data, use it (eg `"123".pump(Data(0,String))` creates and appends to a string Data, which is returned).
List ROList	If the name of the sink is List, L, ROList, or T (or anything that points to one of those Vault objects), the sink is a [empty] ROList. If the sink is a non-empty ROList, the [new] sink is initialized to that. If the sink is a user created List (empty or not), it will be appended to.
Deferred Fcn Method	Pump doesn't aggregate and returns Void. A good way to aggregate to your object is to use *object*.write as the sink: eg `[1..9].pump(Console.println,factorial)`
Sink	Calls sink.write. The sink isn't closed (unless the Sink requests that).
String	Concatenate the results into a string or append to a string. Use the word "String" for clarity: `T(1,2,3).pump(String)` → "123". A new string is created.
Void	Don't aggregate. The last result is returned.
else	If the sink object has a write method, use that method as the sink. `T("testing",1,"two",3).pump(Console)` prints "testing1two3". This means many other objects can to be used as sinks (such as Files, Pipes or Sockets). When done, pump returns the object (which isn't closed).

If aggregating, the sink is usually returned. Otherwise, the last result (or Void) is returned.

- The pump **action**(s) can be anything.

Action	Result
None	Same as Void. `"123".pump(List)` → L("1","2","3")

ROList	Specifies an action and static parameters. See String for an example. Specify a constant: `(3).pump(List,T(Void,""))` creates a list of three empty strings. If the list is empty, the action is `ROList.create`.

String	Resolve and run: i.string().
	`T("one").pump(Void,"len")` → 3
	`T("1","two").pump(List,"len",'+(1))` → L(2,4)
	`T(10).pump(String,T("toString",16),"toUpper")` → "A". This is the same as
	`T(10).pump(String,fcn(n)`
	`{ n.toString(16).toUpper() })`
	
	If string isn't found, i is ignored.
	To pump a string constant, use `T(Void,"string")`.
	If the string is "", the action is `String.create`.

Void	Use the identify function: fcn(i) → I
Void.Filter	If v_0 is the first value fed to the actions and v_n is the value that reaches Void.Filter, the result is: `fcn(v₀,vₙ){ if(vₙ) v₀ else Void.Skip }` `[0..4].pump(List,'-(1),'>(1),Void.Filter,'+(10))` → L(13,14)
Void.Xplode	If the result the from previous action is a ROList, the list is blown apart into separate parameters for the next action. If Xplode is the last action (or not ROList), it is ignored. This is nice when you want to pump a Dictionary, the (key,value) pairs can be transformed when the next action wants two parameters (eg Dictionary to Dictionary transformations).
Bool Number	The number or bool
else	The action, such as a function or method

- Special **return values** (`return(v…)` is the same as `T(v…)`):

Return Value	Meaning
Void.Again	`return(Void.Again,r)` repeats the call to this function with two parameters: (next,r)

Void.Drop	Used for preambles. When an action returns Void.Drop, the action is marked as a no-op. The instance returned with Drop is written to the sink (the default is the passed in parameter). See the concat and reduce fcns below for usage. Drop is treated as a Skip. If you don't want to write to the sink, make the second parameter Void.Void, as in `return(Void.Drop,Void.Void)`
Void.Read	Read n more items from the source, appending them to the existing parameter(s), and passing the lot as parameters to the next action. N is limited to a smallish number (in the tens). Usually, this is used as an action by itself, eg `pump(sink,T(`**`Void.Read`**`,1),fcn(a,b){})` If n items can not be read, TheEnd is thrown. Unless the third parameter is False (`T(Void.Read,5,`**`False`**`)))`. If the fourth parameter is True (`return(Void.Read,n,x,`**`True`**`)`), the action is retried.
Void.Recurse	`return(`**`Void.Recurse`**`,i [,pump parameters])` calls `i.pump(sink,parameters)`, reusing the sink. As this is recursion, there is a depth limit.
Void.Skip	`return(`**`Void.Skip`**`)` causes this action/result, and all following actions, be ignored. `return(Void.Skip,r)` writes r to the sink and skips the rest of the actions.
Void.Stop	`return(`**`Void.Stop`**`)` stops the pump (equivalent to `break`). `T(Void.Stop,r)` writes r to the sink and stops.
Void.Write	`return(`**`Void.Write`**`,x,y,z)` writes x, y and z to the sink and skips. `return(`**`Void.Write`**`,`**`Void.Write`**`,T(x,y,z))` writes x, y and z to the sink and skips. `T(`**`Void.Write`**`)` writes the parameter list as a list and skips. If one of the xyzs is **`Void.Drop`**, p is written in it's place (where p is the [first] parameter passed to this action).

If you wish to use one of the Void signals by itself, you can do so like this:
`T(1,2,3).`**`pump`**`(List,'+(1),`**`Void.Write`**`,'+(1))` → L(2,3,4)
`T(1,2,3,4).`**`pump`**`(List,`**`Void.Read`**`)` → L(L(1,2),L(3,4))
`T(1,5,3,7,2).reduce(Void.Write,String,(0).max,0)` →"15577"

fcn.pump: This functionality can be written as `(0).pump(*,f)` or
`(0).pump(*,f.fp(x))` where f is something like `fcn f(x)`
`{...; return(`**Void.Stop**`) }`.

Flattening a List (ie `a.flatten`) can be written as
```
T(1,T(2,T(3)),4).pump(List,
      fcn(i){ if(T.isType(i)) return(Void.Recurse,i); i })
```
→ L(1,2,L(3),4)
If you wanted to flatten all the way down[56] this will do:
```
T(1,T(2,T(3,T(T(T(4)))))),5).pump(List,
      fcn(i){ if(T.isType(i)) return(Void.Recurse,i,self.fcn); i })
```
→ L(1,2,3,4,5)

Concatenate to string can be written as
```
fcn concat(src,sepr){
   src.pump(String, Void.Drop,
         T(Void.Write,sepr,Void.Drop));
}
```
Then
```
   concat(T(1,12),".") → "1.12"
   concat(Data(0,String,"x","y","z"),"-") → "x-y-z"
```

A simple reduce can be written as
```
fcn reduce(src,f){
   args:=L();
   src.pump(Void,'wrap(i){ args.append(i); return(Void.Drop,i); },
      'wrap(i){
         args.append(i) : (r:=f(_.xplode())) : args.clear(_);
         r
      });
}
```
Then
```
   reduce(T(1,2,"3"),'+) → 6
   reduce(Data(0,String,"Hello"," ","World"),'+) → "Hello World"
```

Decoding URL strings: If urlText is "http%3A%2F%2Ffoo.com%2Fbar" then
```
urlText.pump(String,
   fcn(c){ if(c=="%")return(Void.Read,2); return(Void.Skip,c) },
   fcn(_,b,c){ (b+c).toInt(16).toChar() })
```
results in "http://foo.com/bar".

Chunking can be done with Read:

---

56 And the list isn't recursive or cyclic.

Objects

```
"12345".pump(List,T(Void.Read,2,False),String)
→ L("123","45")
T(1,2,3,4,5).pump(List,T(Void.Read,2,False))
→ L(L(1,2,3),L(4,5))
```

Decoding a character stream to UTF-8 characters:

```
fcn readUTF8c(chr,s=""){ // transform UTF-8 character stream
    s+=chr;
    try{ s.len(8); return(s) }
    catch{ if(s.len()>6) throw(__exception) } // 6 bytes max/UTF-8
    return(Void.Again,s);   // call me again with s & next chr
}

s:="-->\u20AC123";   // --> e2,82,ac,31,32,33
s.pump(List,readUTF8c) //--> L("-","-",">","€","1","2","3")
File("foo.txt","rb").howza(3).pump(List,readUTF8c,"print");
```

Mixing metaphors:

```
println(" x    1    2    3    4    5\n"
        "    ------------------");
foreach a in ([1..5]){
    print("%2d|".fmt(a)," - "*(a-1));
    [a..5].pump(String,'*(a),"%3d ".fmt).println();
}
```

```
  x   1   2   3   4   5
      ------------------
1|   1   2   3   4   5
2|   -   4   6   8  10
3|   -   -   9  12  15
4|   -   -   -  16  20
5|   -   -   -   -  25
```

Notes on the apply and filter methods

These methods apply an action on a stream to produce a result. The action is the same as in pump and the result is determined by the source object (usually a list). These are special cases of pump.

Apply is pump with a default sink and one action:

`src.apply(f [,static parameters])`

Each i in obj is passed to f (f(i,static parameters)) and collected in a sink (specified by the src object, such as an object of the same type or list).

Filter collects those things that make it though the filter (ie action(i).toBool() is True).

The parameters are the same as for apply, with the addition of a list of actions and a list of lists of actions. This latter case is a conditional and – each filter has to pass and the first that fails causes a skip.
`src.filter(action=Void)`
The syntax for many actions:
`src.filter(T(action, T(action, static parameters) ) )`
If you just want side effects, you can use False as the last action.
See pump ROList action for more information.

Special return values: Only **Void.Stop**, **(Void.Stop,r)** and **Void.Skip** are reconized, all others are treated as **Void.Stop**. Use pump if you want to use other specials.
Filter to different sinks: If you want the filtered results collected into your choice of sink (perfering, for example, a String), use a pump and **Void.Filter**:
> `L(1,"2",3,4.5).filter(Int.isType)` → L(1,3)
> `L(1,"2",3,4.5).pump(String,Int.isType,Void.Filter)` →> "13"

Other Filters:
- **filter1**: This filter stops on the first "true" value and returns it.
- **filter1n**: As above but returns the index (in the source) of the first "true" value.
- **filter22**: The "true" value go in one list and the false value are collected in anther list.
- **FilterNs**: As in filter1n, but returns the indexes of all "true" values.

Notes on the reduce method

Reduce the stream to a single value or calculate a value from the contents of a stream. Another form of a feedback loop.
The syntax is `src.reduce(action [,initialValue [,staticParameters]])`
or `src.reduce(Void.Write,sink,action,…)` // aka scanl
Reduce is equivalent to:
> `p:=initialValue;`
> `foreach i in (src)`
> `   { p=action(p,i,static parameters) }`
> `""`.reduce(f)   → Void
> `""`.reduce(f,i)   → i
> `"x"`.reduce(f)   → "x"
> `"x"`.reduce(f,i) → f(i,"x")

Special return values: Only **Void.Stop**, **(Void.Stop,r)**, **Void.Skip** and **(Void.Skip,r)** are reconized, all others are treated as **Void.Stop**.

Atomic

Objects: Atomic.Bool, Atomic.Int, Atomic.Lock, Atomic.WriteLock
Inherits from: Object
See Also: Keywords.critical, Objects.Class.launch, Objects.Fcn.launch,
Objects.Thread

> *Programs that generate atomic power! Just think, they could heat our homes,*
> *power space ships. The possibilities are endless.*
> -- Zander Kale, not quite grasping the concept

Abstract
The Atomic Object is a container for several threading Objects and constructs that
are useful for course grained concurrent (multi-threaded) programming.

Methods

- **Bool(**initialValue=False**)**: Create an instance of a Atomic Bool object.
  See Atomic.Bool.
- **Int(**initialValue=0**)**: Create an instance of a Atomic Int object.
  See Atomic.Int.
- **Lock()**: Create an instance of a Atomic Lock object.
  See Atomic.Lock.
- **WriteLock()**: Create an instance of a Atomic WriteLock object.
  See Atomic.WriteLock.

- **setAndWait(**Atomic.Bool,timeout/seconds=True [,i...]**)**: Set a bool
  and wait for a write/change event on one or more of the objects. The
  following two lines are equivalent:
  ```
  ab.set(); Atomic.wait(10,c);
  Atomic.setAndWait(ab,10,c);
  ```
  except that the latter is atomic: The waiting starts before the bool is set; thus
  any changes to the objects *after* the bool is set won't be missed.
  This is useful for testing threads and avoiding sleeps:
  ```
  b:=Atomic.Bool(); lock:=Atomic.Lock();
  fcn(b,lock){b.wait(); lock.acquire();}.launch(b,lock);
  Atomic.setAndWait(b,10,lock);
  ```
  This waits for a thread to acquire a lock. If a set/wait combination were used,
  there is a race between the set and when the wait starts that could miss the
  acquire.

`lockAtomic.setAndWait(b,True,b)` works, `Atomic.setAndWait(b,True)` sleeps after setting b as does `Atomic.setAndWait(b)`.
See also: Atomic.wait
Interruptible: Yes
Throws: No
Returns: Void or list of objects have changed.

- **sleep**`(timeout/seconds=True)`: Sleep for a while or until interrupted. Seconds is an integer or real value, resolved to (typically) a millisecond value.

Timeout	Blocks
True or Void	Forever
False or 0	Don't block, either works immediately or fails
n (Int or Float)	Max seconds to wait for success (0 is the same as False)

Returns: True if slept for the duration, False if interrupted (not that you could tell, it was an exception that did the interrupting).
Interruptible: Yes

- **wait(**`timeout/seconds=True`**)**: The same as sleep.
- **wait(**`timeout/seconds,i...`**)**: Wait for a write/change event on one or more of the objects. The objects can include Atomic Ints, Atomic Bools, Pipes, Straws and VMs. If an object doesn't support asynchronous events, it is ignored.
  If a write happens before the wait starts, it will be missed.
  Note: This an asynchronous method that doesn't consume CPU cycles.
  To wait for a thread to die or for a write or close on a Pipe, you could use
      `Atomic.wait(True,threadVM,pipe);`
  See also: Atomic.setAndWait
  Interruptible: Yes
  Throws: No
  Returns: Void or list of objects that have changed.

- **waitFor(**`Fcn|Method|Property,`
  `timeout/seconds=True,throw=False`**)**: Wait for something to happen.
  To wait for five items to show up in a Pipe, you could use:
      `Atomic.waitFor(fcn(len){ len()>=5 }.fp(pipe.len));`
  We need to use >= in case more than five items get in the pipe before we notice.
  Note: This is a polling method and uses CPU cycles and can miss quickly changing events.
  Interruptible: Yes
  Throws: TypeError
          ValueError if timeout can't be converted to a Float

> Timeout if throw is True
> Returns: True if event waiting for happened, False if timed out or interrupted

Properties: None
Operators: None

Discussion
When more than one thread can change a chunk of data at the same time, some mechanism must be provided to "serialize" those changes such that one change is completed before another is attempted or data corruption is guaranteed. Some languages do that for the programmer but zkl only does that for objects that are expected to be used in threads[57] or it is forced to[58]. The programmer is required to know when their program will share data amongst threads and take care to protect it. The constructs in this class are "atomic", that is, they are guaranteed to allow only one thread at time to access them. Attempts to use them while they are in use will cause a wait or access denial. Other constructs facilitate inter-thread communication. And, importantly, since they are low level (or primitive), they provide a basis on which to build higher level constructs.

WaitFor is a very powerful construct that allows one thread to basically sleep while waiting for another thread to do something. The calling thread waits until that something happens, it waits longer than it should or another thread throws an exception at it. Waitfor can wait for more than one something but that requires more work than just listing them. On the other hand, waiting for some things is very simple.

Simple Waits: Events

Let's say e is an Atomic.Bool. To wait for another thread to set it, all you have to do is e.wait(); This will cause the current thread to wait until e is set (which might never happen). Here is an example program:

```
var e=Atomic.Bool();
// start a thread that sleeps for 10 seconds, then sets e
fcn sleeper{ Atomic.sleep(10); e.set(); }.launch();
println("Waiting …");
s:=e.wait();        // wait until the thread sets e
println("done: ",s);
```

---

57 For example Thread.Pipe.
58 The VM requires certain types of objects to be thread safe, List and Dictionary being two.

This program is a complex way to wait for ten seconds[59]. A thread is created that just sleeps for ten seconds and then sets e. The main thread then waits for e to be set and stops. Here is the output when the program is run:

    Waiting …
    <ten seconds>
    done: True

Now, suppose you don't want to wait ten seconds. Five should be plenty, you have better things to do than to wait (which you could be doing, instead of waiting, but that is another story). One small change:

    s:=e.wait(5);

Now, when the program is run:

    Waiting …
    <five seconds>
    done: False

We'll ignore exceptions here, but it is possible (and easy) for another thread to throw an exception at us and interrupt the wait.

Waiting for a Method

The other type of waiting is waiting for something to return True (or evaluates to True). That something can be any object method but, if it is not a Atomic method, be very careful that you won't be calling the method while another thread is changing something. Thus, the above program can be written as:

```
var e=Atomic.Bool();
   // start a thread that sleeps for 10 seconds, then sets e
fcn sleeper{ Atomic.sleep(10); e.set(); }.launch();
println("Waiting …");
s:=Atomic.waitFor(e.isSet); // wait until the thread sets e
println("done: ",s);
```

The only change is in bold; the program works similar to the previous one, the difference is that it polls (ie loops) and thus uses CPU cycles. It can also miss events if they occur in rapid succession.

Waiting for a Function

Waiting for a function to return True allows you to wait for lots of different things. For example, to wait for integer to count up to five:

---

59 Or use a thread future: `s:=sleeper.future().noop();`

Objects

```
var n=Atomic.Int();
    // start a thread that counts forever
fcn{ while (1){ Atomic.sleep(1); n.inc(); }}.launch();
println("Waiting …");
s:=Atomic.waitFor(fcn{n>=5}); // wait for n to reach 5
println("done: ",s);
```

Again, as before:

    Waiting …

    <five seconds>

    done: True

Note: the counting thread never ends, it just keeps counting.

What ensures that this works is that Atomic Ints are atomic. In this case, that means inc() won't allow anybody else access to the value until it has changed and when it retrieves the value, nobody else is modifying it. Thus, while one thread is reading n, the other can be trying to increment it but can't until the first thread has read the value. And vice versa.

Note that we check to see if n is greater than or equal to 5 because it is possible for the counting thread to increment n twice between checks. It is also the thread could start and move past 5 before the wait starts.

A much better way to write this example is to use Atomic.Int.setAndWaitFor:

```
var n=Atomic.Int(), b=Atomic.Bool();
    // start a thread that counts forever
fcn{ b.wait(); while (1){ n.inc(); }}.launch();
println("Waiting …");
s:=n.setAndWaitFor(b,5); // wait for n to reach 5
println("done: ",s);
```

Waiting for Multiple Objects

If you need to wait on multiple objects or functions, you can put then into a list and use the runNFilter method in waitFor.

```
b =Atomic.Bool();
f:=fcn{ return(etCallHome()==ANSWER); }
list:=T(b.isSet,f);
// return when b is True or somebody answers the phone
Atomic.waitFor(list.runNFilter);
```

The above example, while more expressive, is also more wasteful of system resources (and can miss rapidly changing events). This rewrite won't miss events (assuming the events happen after the wait begins) and is efficient.

```
b:=Atomic.Bool();
p =Thread.Pipe();
// return if b is set or the pipe is written to or closed
Atomic.wait(True,b,p);  // or use Atomic.setAndWaitFor()
```

Atomic.Bool

Inherits from: Object

Abstract
Atomic Bools are Bools that change state atomically.
Bools also can also act like events and are used by threads to signal other threads that something has happened.

Create this object with `Atomic.Bool()` or by calling the create method on an existing AtomicBool.

Methods (All methods are atomic and thread safe)
- **clear()**: Set the current *value* to False.
  Returns: Bool (previous *value*)
- **create(**value=False**)**: Create a new AtomicBool instance. Value is used for the initial value.
  Returns: AtomicBool
- **isSet()**: Returns *value*.
  Returns: Bool
- **set()**: Sets the current *value* to True.
- **set(b)**: Sets the current *value* to b.
  Returns: Bool (previous *value*)
- **setIf(***newValue, expectedValue***)**: Sets *value* to *newValue* if *value* is equal to *expectedValue*.
  - If *value* is equal to *expectedValue*, *value* is set to *newValue* and True is returned.
  - If *value* is not equal to *expectedValue*, *value* is unchanged and False is returned.
  Returns: Bool
- **setAndWaitFor(***atomicBool, v=True, timeout=True, throw=False***)**: Sets *atomicBool* to True and waits for self to be set to *v*.
  Timeout is seconds, True (to block), False is the same as 0 (see wait).
  Throws: Error if timeout can't be converted to a Float
          Timeout if throw is True
  Returns: Bool
- **toBool()**: Returns *value*. This is the same as isSet().
  Returns: Bool

Objects

- **toString()**: Returns "AtomicBool(*value*)".
  Returns: String
- **tryToSet()**: Sets *value* to True if False. Equivalent to setIf(True,False).
  If the current *value* is True, returns False.
  If the current *value* is False, set *value* to True and returns True.
  Note: If two or more threads are calling this at the same time (and *value* is False), only one will see True; *value* will be set to True in all cases.
  Returns: True if signaled, False if timed out.
- **wait(**timeout/seconds=True, throw=False**)**: Wait for the self to be signaled (ie become set, which it might already be). If no timeout, wait will block forever waiting to be signaled or until interrupted (by an exception thrown by another thread).
  Timeout is in seconds and can have the following values:

Timeout	Block
True	Forever
False	Don't block, either works immediately or fails
n (Int or Float)	Max seconds to wait for success (0 is the same as False)

  If wait catches an exception, that exception will interrupt wait, and the exception will be processed in the normal way.
  wait(0) is the same as isSet().
  Note: This is an asynchronous wait, one that waits for writes to self.
  Throws: Error if timeout can't be converted to a Float
  　　　　Timeout if throw is True
  Returns: True if signaled, False if timed out.
- **waitFor(***b*=Bool/1/0,timeout/seconds=True, throw=False**)**: Wait for *value* to be set to *b* (which it might already be). If no timeout, wait will block forever waiting to be signaled or interrupted (by an exception thrown from another thread).
  If wait catches an exception, that exception will interrupt the wait, and the exception will be processed in the normal way.
  Note: This is an asynchronous wait, one that waits for writes to self.
  Throws: ValueError if timeout can't be converted to a Float
  　　　　Timeout if throw is True
  Returns: True if signaled, False if timed out.

Properties (All properties are atomic and thread safe)
- **value**: Returns isSet().
  Returns: Bool

Operators: None

Discussion

Events

An event (aka Atomic.Bool) just sits around waiting for somebody to kick it. An example would be waiting for the dinner bell to ring: there are a lot of people waiting for that bell but only one person who can ring it. When it does ring, suddenly there is a lot of action by a lot of people who may have not been doing much until now. The bell is the event, the cook is the thread who calls event.set() and the hungry people are the threads who called event.wait(). A thread that calls event.isSet() is equivalent to somebody who is doing work, and every now and then, calls out to see if dinner is ready yet. You could also think of a beacon that lights up when event.set() is called and turns off when event.clear()is called. During that time, anybody who looks will see the beacon if it is turned on.

Atomic.Int

Inherits from: Object

Abstract
Atomic Ints are integers that change state atomically.
On Windows, these are 32 bit integers.

Create this object with Atomic.Int() or by calling the create method on an existing AtomicInt.

Methods (All methods are atomic and thread safe)
- **create(**value=0**)**: Create a new AtomicInt instance. Value is used for the initial value.
  Returns: AtomicInt
- **dec()**: Atomically decrement *value*.
  Returns: *value-1* (Int)
- **inc()**: Atomically increment *value*.
  Returns: *value+1* (Int)
- **isSet()**:   Returns True if *value* is non-zero.
- **isSet(**n**)**: Returns True if *value* is equal to n.
  Returns: Bool
- **set(**n**)**: Atomically sets the current *value* to n and returns the previous value.
  For example: n:=Atomic.Int(1); x:=n.set(2);

The value of n is 2 and x is 1.
Returns: Previous value (Int)

- **setAndWaitFor(**`Atomic.Bool,n,timeout/seconds=True,throw=False`**)**:
Set a bool and wait for self to be set to n. The following two lines are equivalent:
    ```
    ab.set(); an.WaitFor(n,10);
    Atomic.setAndWait(b,n,10);
    ```
except that the latter is atomic: The waiting starts before the bool is set; thus any writes to self *after* the bool is set won't be missed.
Interruptible: Yes
Throws: Error if timeout can't be converted to a Float
       Timeout if throw is True
Returns: Bool

- **setIf(**`newValue,expectedValue`**)**: Sets *value* to *newValue* if *value* is equal to *expectedValue*.
    - If *value* is equal to *expectedValue*, *value* is set to *newValue* and True is returned.
    - If *value* is not equal to *expectedValue*, *value* is unchanged and False is returned.

    Returns: Bool

- **toBool()**: Returns True if *value* is non-zero. This is the same as `isSet()`.
Returns: Bool

- **toInt()**: Returns the current *value*.
Returns: Int

- **toString()**: Returns "AtomicInt(*value*)".
Returns: String

- **waitFor(**`n,timeout/seconds=True,throw=False`**)**: Wait for *value* to be set to *n* (which it might already be). If no timeout, wait will block forever waiting to be signaled or until interrupted (by an exception thrown from another thread).
Timeout is in seconds and can have the following values:

Timeout	Block
True	Forever
False	Don't block, either works immediately or fails
n (Int or Float)	Max seconds to wait for success (0 is the same as False)

If waitFor catches an exception, that exception will interrupt the wait, and the exception will be processed in the normal way.

One common use for this method is waiting for threads to exit:

```
var N=Atomic.Int();
do(10){ N.inc(); thread.launch(); }
fcn thread{ N.dec(); }    // decrement N and exit
N.waitFor(0);  // wait for threads to start and finish
```

Note: This is an asynchronous wait, one that waits for writes to self. If you start waiting after self has passed the target value, you will not catch it. If self reaches and stays at the target value (as in the example), or is set to the target after the wait starts, you will never miss it.

See also: setAndWaitFor

Throws: Error if timeout can't be converted to a Float

   Timeout if throw is True

Returns: True if signaled, False if timed out.

Properties (All properties are atomic and thread safe)
- **value**: Returns *value*.
  Returns: Int

Operators (All operators are atomic and thread safe)
Note that if two Atomic Ints are compared, the comparison is not atomic, it is equivalent to (a1.value op a2.value). Thus in n:=Atomic.int(5), (n==n) can be False if other threads are modifying n[60]
- **==, != :**   The operand has to be an Int, Float or AtomicInt.
- **<, <=, >, >= :** The operand is as above or something that supports toInt.

Discussion
An atomic integers is an integer that can shared amongst many threads, and those threads can all be trying to change it at the same time. This puts constraints on what an int can do because any operation has to be atomic, that is, any one action has to complete before another one can start. These integers are targeted at a narrow class of threaded programs (as should be obvious by noting the lack of many common integer operators).

Atomic.Lock

Inherits from: Object
See Also: Keywords.critical

---

60 var N=Atomic.Int(5); fcn{while(1){N.inc();N.dec();;}}.launch()
  while(1){if (N!=N) println("Bingo ")}

Objects

Abstract
Also known as a mutex.

Create this object with `Atomic.Lock()` or by calling the create method on an existing Lock.

Methods (All methods are atomic and thread safe)
- **acquire(**`timeout/seconds=True`**)**: Grab ownership of the lock, if it is available. With no timeout, acquire will block until it gets the lock, possibly forever, or until interrupted (by an exception thrown from another thread). Timeout is in seconds and can have the following values:

Timeout	Block
True	Forever
False	Don't block, either works immediately or fails
n (Int or Float)	Max seconds to wait for success (0 is the same as False)

  Returns: True if lock acquired, False if timed out.
- **create()**: Create a new Lock instance. The lock is created unlocked. Returns: Lock
- **release()**: Unconditionally release the lock. Any thread waiting for the lock can then acquire it, and it is unknown which thread that will be (if there is more than one thread waiting). Any thread can release the lock. Returns: self

Properties (All properties are atomic and thread safe)
- **isLocked**: The current value of the object: True if locked, False if not.
- **value**: Same as `isLocked`.

Operators: None

Warning: If a thread acquires a lock and then attempts to acquire it again, it will dead lock (or until acquire times out). You might run into this inadvertently via recursion.

Discussion
A Lock is an object that has two states: locked or unlocked and the transition between those states is atomic, that is, effectively instantaneous. A lock is only useful in threaded applications; in a single threaded application, its functionality is identical to that of a Bool. Unlike locks in other languages and operating systems, nobody "owns" a lock, that is, you can't restrict access to a lock other than by hiding it; if another thread can find it, it can acquire or, more critically, release it.

Atomic.WriteLock

Inherits from: Object

Abstract
A WriteLock is used to control access to a "read mostly" resource – one that has many readers but not many writers. Only one writer at a time may access the resource at a time but an unlimited number of readers can read from the resource at the same time.

Create this object with `Atomic.WriteLock()` or by calling the create method on an existing WriteLock.

Methods (All methods are atomic and thread safe)
- **create()**: Create a new WriteLock instance. The lock is created unlocked. Returns: WriteLock
- **acquireForReading(**timeout/seconds=True**)**: Called when a reader wants access to the protected resource.
  Cases:
    - Access is granted if there are no writers; the number of readers is irrelevant.
    - If the lock is held by a writer, access is blocked until the writer releases the lock.
    - If the lock is held by a writer, and it is being contested by another writer and a reader, it is unknown which will acquire the lock when it is released.
    - If the lock is held by a reader and a writer is waiting to acquire the lock, the writer will get the lock before any more readers can.
  Without a timeout, acquire will block, possibly forever, until it gets the lock or until interrupted (by an exception thrown from another thread).
  Timeout is in seconds and can have the following values:

Timeout	Block
True	Forever
False	Don't block, either works immediately or fails
n (Int or Float)	Max seconds to wait for success (0 is the same as False)

  Returns: True if lock acquired, False if timed out.
- **acquireForWriting(**timeout/seconds=True**)**: Called when a writer wants access to the protected resource (so it can change it).

Objects

Cases:
- Access is granted if there are no readers and no writers. Otherwise, access is blocked until nobody is accessing the resource.
- While a writer is waiting to acquire a WriteLock, readers are blocked and acquireForWriting will succeed before acquireForReading.
- If a writer holds the lock and both readers and writers are waiting to acquire the lock, it is unknown if a reader or write will get the lock after this writer releases it.

Without a timeout, acquire will block forever waiting for the lock or until interrupted (by an exception thrown from another thread).
Returns: True if lock acquired, False if timed out.
- **isSet()**: Returns True if a writer has the lock, otherwise False, irregardless of the number of readers. If True, the number of readers is zero (since there can be no readers while writing).
Note: Even if True, it doesn't mean the writer can actually write, the writer may be waiting for the number of readers to drop to zero (and is still stuck in acquireForWriting).
Returns: Bool
- **readerRelease()**: Decrement the number of readers accessing the resource. When the number of readers is zero, a writer may acquire the lock. If more than one writer wants the lock, the writer that asked first gets the lock.
Any thread can release the lock.
The reader count will not drop below zero.
Returns: self
- **writerRelease()**: Called when the current writer has finished changing the resource. The lock can now be acquired by one or more readers or a writer. If more than one writer wants the lock, which one gets it is undefined. If both readers and writers want the lock, all you know is somebody will get it but not who.
Any thread can release the lock.
Returns: self

Properties (All properties are atomic and thread safe)
- **value**: Returns isSet().
- **readers**: Returns the number of readers.

Operators: None

Notes
- Readers can't starve writers but writers can starve readers.

- If you want to use critical with a write lock, you'll need to tell it which methods to use:

```
var wlock=Atomic.WriteLock();
critical(wlock,acquireForReading,readerRelease){
    doStuff();
}
```

  If doStuff causes an exception, throws an exception, returns, whatever, the lock will still be released.

Warnings:
- If a thread acquires a write lock and then attempts to acquire it again, it will dead lock (or until acquire times out or is interrupted).
- The lock makes no attempt to keep track of who is a reader, writer or the order in which they acquire and release the lock. It is up the application(s) readers and writers to acquire and release the lock in order (ie acquire the lock, access the resource, release the lock). So, don't write sloppy code, minimize the amount of code in a lock and protect against exceptions (especially if you don't expect them; use critical).

Discussion

WriteLocks are used to control access to resources. This is only a concern in multi-threaded applications, in a single threaded application, there will never be more than one thread accessing a resource and, thus, no contention. WriteLocks are useful when the resource is a "read mostly" resource; one that is read a lot more than it is changed. One example would be a phone book: Lots of people look up phone numbers, sometimes at the same time, but the book is rarely changed. However, when it is changing, the last thing the writer needs is someone looking over their shoulder and trying to read a number while it is changing. A WriteLock allows, at most, one writer at a time access to a resource and when there are no writers, an unlimited number of readers can access the resource.

Objects

Example: `lock=Atomic.WriteLock();`

<table>
<tr><td colspan="2" align="center">Thread One (writer)</td></tr>
<tr><td colspan="2">

```
lock.acquireForWriting();
  resource.change();
lock.writerRelease();
```

When this thread has the lock, Two and Three are blocked.

If Two or Three (or both) are reading, One blocks until neither Two nor Three are reading. While One is blocked, neither Two nor Three can start reading.
</td></tr>
<tr><td align="center">Thread Two (reader)</td><td align="center">Thread Three (reader)</td></tr>
<tr valign="top"><td>

```
lock.acquireForReading();
  x=resource.read(4);
lock.readerRelease();
```

If One is writing, Two is blocked.

If Three is reading, Two can also read.

If Two is reading and Three isn't, AND One wants to write, Three can't start reading.
</td><td>

```
lock.acquireForReading();
  x=resource.readLog();
lock.readerRelease();
```

If this thread is reading, One can't write but Two can also read.

If Three is blocked because Two is reading and One is also blocked, when Two releases the lock, One will get it and Three remains blocked until One is finished.
</td></tr>
</table>

Resource

Bool

Syntax: True, False
Full name: [TheVault.]Bool
Inherits from: Object

Abstract

The Bool object is the Boolean object and there are two of them: True and False. They are usually used to indicate the success or failure of something.

Examples:
- `x=True;`
- `x=(1==2); // same as x=False;`
- `return(True);`
- `(1).toBool(); self.toBool(); (Void).toBool()`

Methods

- **create()**:   Returns self. Eg `True(False)` → True. This is useful if you need a callable that always returns True or False.
- **toBool()**:   Returns self.
- **toString()**: Returns "True" or "False".
- **toInt()**:   If True, returns 1, otherwise returns 0.
- **toFloat()**: If True, returns 1.0, otherwise returns 0.0.

Properties: None

Operators

- **eq (==)** : True if both operands are Bools and have the same value.
- **ne (!=)** : True if either operand is not a Bool or the values differ.
- **negate (not)** : Inverts value, ie True becomes False and vice versa.
- **+, -, *** : Behaves like Int, True = 1 and False = 0.
  `(True + 2)` → True but `(2 + True)` → 3

Discussion

True and False

True and False are reserved words that return their respective Bool values.

Class

Inherits from: Object
See also: Keywords.class

Abstract
The Class object is the base class for all classes (that is, all classes inherit from Class). Classes are typically defined by programs using the "class" keyword, they can also be created "on the fly" (the compiler and the VM do this).

Methods
- **BaseClass(***name***)**:
  Look for name in self, ignoring everything but methods and properties.
  Note: The BaseClass methods resolve, toBool and toString are different from Class methods listed here; they have minimal Object level functionality.
  See Also: Objects.Object.BaseClass.
  Throws: NotFoundError
  Returns: Object
- **copy(**copyVars=False**)**: Returns a new class instance based on self. Topdog is the new class, all vars are set to Void and container is self.container.
  If copyVars is True, the [new] vars are *references* to the original ones.
  Notes:
  - NullClass.copy() always returns NullClass, no copy is made.
  - If a class is static, no copy is made, the class is returned.
  - The constructor is not run.
  Returns: Class
- **create(**[*parameters*]**)**: This is the same as self(*parameters*).
  The algorithm to create the new instance of self is:
  - newInstance = self.copy() (equals self if self is static)
  - init = newInstance.fcns[self.theInitFcnIs] (init or __constructor)
  - init(vm.pasteArgs()) (use parameters. Or not)
    If self isn't static, init calls the constructor (first), otherwise, it doesn't.
  - or: self.copy().fcns[self.theInitFcnIs](vm.pasteArgs())
  Returns: New instance of self (Class) (unless init does a returnClass())
- **defer(**[*parameters*]**)**: Returns Deferred(self,*parameters*). For example, Date:=Import.defer("Time.Date") postpones importation until Date is used (Date.prettyDay() will import and call prettyDay).
  Returns: Deferred

- **isChildOf(** *class* **)**: Returns True if self is *class*, is an instance of *class* or has inherited from *class*. Thus, self is a child of itself.
     `self.isChildOf(1) →` False
  Returns: Bool
- **isInstanceOf(** *class* [*,class* ...] **)**: True if self is an instance of *class*. Self is an instance of itself.
  If Ci is an instance of class C or an instance of C (C()) then
     - `A.isInstanceOf(C)` is True iff: A == Ci or A == Ci()
       Note that Ci can be any class instance that was created from C or any instance of C.
     - Given B(A) (class B inherits from class A), then:
       `A.isInstanceOf(A) →` True
       `A.isInstanceOf(B) →` False
       `B.isInstanceOf(A) →` False
  isInstanceOf differs from Object.isType only for classes and functions.
  `self.isInstanceOf(1) →` False
  If there more than one parameter, True is returned if self is an instance of any of them.
  Returns: Bool
- **launch(** *parameters* **)**: Create a thread and, when the thread starts, that thread calls **liftoff(** *parameters passed to lauch* **)**. Liftoff is a [required] user defined function that is called when the thread starts running. Note: There is no way [for the caller of launch] to know when the thread starts running. Normally, this is not a problem, but if you need to know, use a Thread.Pipe (to send a message) or set a Atomic.Bool in liftoff and wait for it in the launching function. Or you could set (in liftoff) a class variable to vm (which is the running thread) and watch that. Just waiting a short amount of time will work until your system is heavily loaded or you move the code to a different system.
  The **splashdown** [is a optional] function is called when a threads ends. Its parameters are (False, exception) or (True, Void) where exception is the exception that killed the thread.
  Note: A new instance of the class is NOT created.
  Template:
  ```
  class C{ fcn liftoff(x){ println(x) }
     fcn splashdown(b,e){}
  }
  C().launch(5);   //-→ print 5
  ```
  See also: Keywords.class for more on threads, Objects.Fcn.launch.
  Throws: TypeError
  Returns: self

- **nthClass(n)**: A Class can contain other classes. This method implements `self.classes[n]`. Note that if you are creating (compiling) a class, the class you KNOW is supposed to be there may not have been created yet.
  Throws: IndexError
  Returns: Class
- **Property(name)**: Search self for a variable or property and return a Property instance for it. The class variables are searched first (parents are NOT searched), then the properties are searched. For example:
  ```
  class C{ var v=123; }
  p:=C.Property("v");
  p();  → 123
  ```
  See Also: Objects.Object.Property
  Throws: NotFoundError
  Returns: Property
- **resolve(*name*)**: Search self for an object named *name* looking at:
  - Class (instance) variables
  - Functions: The following are ignored: The constructor (whatever its name is), functions whose names contain "#"[61] and nullFcns. If you name your constructor "__constructor", you won't notice because the __constructor property will provide the match.
  - Classes: The following are ignored: classes whose names contain "#"[62] and NullClass.
  - Parents

  The above four are searched up through the parent classes, breadth first. If no match, then look in self for:
  - Methods
  - Properties

  Resolve is called by the VM (at runtime) when there is an unknown name being referenced in self. This happens when the compiler couldn't find the name during compilation (common in typeless systems when referencing through variables and functions). If still not found, the function **__notFound**(*name*) is called (if it exists). If that function returns Void.Void, resolve carries on to the parents. Note that __notFound is only used for this instance of the resolve method.

---

61 Anonymous functions (fcn{ }) are given names such as __`fcn#1_line#`, the compiler also creates anonymous functions.
62 These are typically anonymous classes; for example __`class#1_line#`

`BaseClass.resolve` is a different resolve method. It ignores everything above the class object; it will only examine methods and properties while ignoring variables, functions, parents, etc.

For more information, see Data Reference Resolution in Appendix A (Grammar).
Throws: NotFoundError, TypeError, IndexError
Returns: Object

- **resolve(**_name_,`False|Void`**)**: Parent classes are searched.
    - False: Same as `resolve(`_name_`)`.
    - Void. Same as `BaseClass.resolve(`_name_`)`.

Throws: NotFoundError
Returns: Object

- **resolve(**_name_,`N|*`,`searchParents=True`**)**: This variant checks for the existence of a variable, function, class, parent, method or property named _name_. It can also be used to directly access the Class object.
    - N == 1: Check to see if _name_ is a method. Result is MethodType (Int).
    - N == 2: Check to see if _name_ is a property. Result is PropertyType (Int).
    - N == 4: Check for variable, function, class or parent. Result is True if found.
    - N == 8: Check for variable (as above).
    - N == 0x10: Check for parent (as above).
    - N == 0x20: Check for function (as above).
    - N == 0x40: Check for class (as above).
    - *: All of the above. You can also bit-or (ie just add up) any of these; to check for a function or variable: N = 0x20 + 8 = 0x28 (40).
    - If searchParents is False/0 the search is confined to self and the parent classes are ignored. If True/1, all parents are checked.
    - MethodType and PropertyType are defined in vm.h.zkl (they are nonzero). Constants for N can be found in zkl.h.zkl.

Notes:
    - The match order is undefined, if resolving more than one type and there are multiple matches, you will get one of them. Except methods and properties are searched last.

See Also: whatIsThis, Objects.Object.resolve, zkl.h.zkl for symbolic names.
Returns: Bool, non-zero Int

- **resolve(**_name_,`N`,`Void`**)**: This variant returns the index of a variable, function, class, or parent Parents are not searched.

- N == 8:   Check for variable.
- N == 0x10: Check for parent.
- N == 0x20: Check for function.
- N == 0x40: Check for class.
- If N is *not* one, and exactly one, of these values, Void is returned.

For example, class C { var b,a; }; C.resolve("a",8,Void) → 0 and C.resolve("b",8,Void) → 1 (variables are sorted).

See Also: whatIsThis, Objects.Object.resolve, zkl.h.zkl for symbolic names.

Throws: ValueError.

Returns: Int or Void (*name* not found).

- **setVar(**name[,object]**)**: Set variable *name* to object. If name doesn't exist, NotFoundError is thrown. Parents are searched. If object is omitted, the current value of the variable is returned.
- **setVar(**n[,object]**)**: Set the nth variable to object. Parents are NOT searched. If n is out of range, IndexError is thrown.

  Throws: IndexError, NotFoundError, AssertionError (var is read only)

  Returns: Current value of variable
- **__sGet(**i**)**: Calls function "__sGet" if it exists, otherwise calls Object.__sGet.

  self[i] gets translated into self.__sGet(i).

  More generally, self[*parameters*] is translated into __sGet(*parameters*).

  Throws: NotImplementedError if self doesn't implement __sGet.

  Returns: This should return self[i], whatever that is
- **__sSet(**v,i,len**)**: Calls function "__sSet" if it exists, otherwise calls Object.__sSet.

  self[i]　=x is translated into self.__sSet(x,i).

  self[i,n]=x is translated into self.__sSet(x,i,n).

  More generally: self[*parameters*]=x is translated into __sSet(x,*parameters*).

  Throws: NotImplementedError if self doesn't implement __sSet.

  Returns: This should return v. This lets x=self[0]=123 work as expected.
- **toBool()**: This method can be shadowed by the toBool function.

  Throws: ValueError if function toBool doesn't return a Bool. Note that this check doesn't happen if you call toBool directly (ClassC.toBool()) but is when used in a expression: True==ClassC

  You can bypass this with: self.BaseClass.toBool() (which returns True).

  Returns: Bool. If not a function, True.
- **toString()**: By default, returns "Class(*name*)".

  The toString method can be overwritten by a class function named toString.

Warning: Be careful of when overwriting toString. For example, calling `println(self)` inside of toString is infinite recursion (you probably mean `println(self.name)`).

You can bypass this with: `self.BaseClass.toString()`.

Throws: TypeError (if function toString doesn't return a String). Note that this check doesn't happen if you call toString directly, only when toString is called by the VM.

Returns: String

- **whatIsThis(**_name_, searchParents=True, _fullDisclosure_=False**)**:
  Search self for something named _name_ and return information about it. Somewhat like resolve.
  Returns: List(type,container,index,object) or List(Void,Void,Void,Void)
    - Type is ClassType (2), FcnType (3), ParentType (112) or ClassVarType (103).
    - Container is the class that contains the found object.
    - Index is the slot the object is in. For example, if f is a function in class C with index 3, then C.fcns[3] is f.
    - **Note**: If _fullDisclosure_ is False, vars are Void and functions usually have the wrong container (they are otherwise correct however). If True, index is Void.
  See also: vm.h.zkl

- **unasm(**outputStream=Console**)**:
  Unassemble the class – dump the machine code. This is the equivalent to `return(Compiler.Asm.disClass(self,outputStream))`
  You can send the output to a
      File: `self.unasm(File("foo.txt","w"))`
      Data: `self.unasm(d=Data()); // d.text → the output`
      List: `list:=self.unasm(L())`
  Returns: Result of calling Asm.disClass (outputStream)

Methods for class creation (used by compilers and loaders)
- **embryo(**names, numFcns, numClasses, listOfParents [,varBits] [,attributes]**)**:
  Create an "embryonic" class. It is an empty class that is ready to be populated with variables, classes and functions.

Parameter	Value
names	A list containing, in order: the name of the class (*className*), the vault path (*vaultPath*) and the names of all the class (instance) variables (*varNames*). The number of variables in the class is determined from the size of this list.
names *className*	Name of the class. Eg "ClassC". There are no checks on name, you can create an otherwise illegal name. The compiler uses this fact to create names like "RootClass#".
names *vaultPath*	Where in the Vault this class would like to go, if it were to go there. The usual case is to set this to "", unless this class is destined for bigger and better things[63]. Import and TheVault.add will look at this value if told to put the class into the Vault. Can be overridden but not overwritten.
names *varNames*	A list of the names of the instance variables, sorted (use List.sort). When resolve is looking for a variable value, it uses this list. All variables are initialized to Void.
numFcns	The number of functions that this class will contain. This number is constant and can't be changed later. Function 0 is always the constructor, if there are one or more functions. Functions are initialized to nullFcn (which is a fine constructor). See addFcn.
numClasses	The number of classes that this class will contain. This number is constant and can't be changed later. Classes are initialized to NullClass. See addClass.
listOfParents	The parents that this class has (inherits from). Use List (L) or ROList (T) if no parents.
varBits	See the varBits property. Trailing empty strings ("") don't need to be in the list. For example, if the bits are "0010" and "", you can use L("0010","") or L("0010"). If you need a placeholder, use ROList (T). Bits default to 0.
attributes	A string of space separated class attributes. See the attributes property.

---

63 The compiler uses the value of AKA to set this.

Note on parents: Parents must be added in inheritance (search) order. The topdog of the parent is set to self (if *P* isn't static). Note that if self becomes a parent, all of self's parents topdogs are effectively changed to the new topdog. To illustrate:

```
class A{} class B(A){}      // B.A.topdog is B
class C(B){}                // C.B.A.topdog is now C, not B
```

It is an error to add a class that has the noChildren attribute set.

P must have all of its contained classes and parents added but does not need to be cooked.

P can't already be a parent.

Self can't be a copy of a class.

Warning: It is entirely too easy to create a malformed class. The VM will check as you build the class but can't verify many things. Embryos are for the "advanced" student.

Throws: AssertionError, TypeError, ValueError

Returns: Class

- **addClass(*C*)**: Not thread safe. Append a contained class to the classes in self. *C*.container is set to self (if *C* isn't static). Contained classes are those that are created inside another class:

  ```
  class C{ class Contained_in_C{} }
  ```

  Order is important, be sure you have it synchronized with the functions (as they can reference a class by position rather than name).

  Self can't be a copy of a class.

  C must have all its classes and parents added.

  C can't be a member of another class, it must be an embryo or a static class.

  C should *not* be NullClass (as it will be ignored).

  Throws: AssertionError

  Returns: *C* (Class)

- **addFcn(function)**: Not thread safe. Add a function to an embryo, placing it after the previously added function (the first added function gets slot zero). The constructor must be the first function added. Add the rest of the functions in the order as determined by your code. Once a function has been added, it can't be changed. Functions are bound to their class instance when they are added to the class.

  Notes:

  - There is no requirement that the first function be named "__constructor". It is a convention; the name of self.fcns[0]. On the other hand, this convention is codified by the "__constructor" property. Thus, you can name your constructors "cranberrySauce" and code that calls YourClass.__constructor() will still work.

- If your constructor doesn't do anything (and you need a placeholder), use `self.fcn.nullFcn`.
- If you have an "init" function, it does need to be named "init". When addFcn sees a function with this name, it sets the theInitFcnIs property.

Throws: AssertionError

Returns: function (Fcn)

- **addFcn(**`function,n`**)**: Not thread safe. Set the nth function in a class to function. Use this if you are not going to be adding functions serially (for example, if you are going to add the constructor last).

Warning: Do *not* mix these two methods.

Note: You can only add one function once per "slot". Once a function is in place, it can't be overwritten.

Throws: AssertionError, IndexError

Returns: function (Fcn)

- **cook()**: Not thread safe. Cook self and all the classes and parent classes it contains. This converts an embryo to a "mature" class. This needs to be the last thing you do to an embryo before you begin to use it as a class. A cooked class can not be changed.

Returns: Cooked class, which may be different from self.

Properties

- **attributes**: Returns a space separated list attributes, which is some combination of "", "private", "public", "static", "script" , "noChildren". See the section on Class Attributes (below).

Returns: String (the currently set attributes)

- **__constructor**: Return the class constructor, if one exists. If there is no constructor, Void is returned. Thus, the following always works:
      `class.__constructor();`

Returns: Fcn or Void

- **classes**: Returns a list of the contained classes, in creation order.

Returns: List or ROList (if no classes)

- **container**: Returns the class that contains this class. If this is a root class, Void is returned.

Returns: Void or Class

- **fcns**: Returns a list of the functions in this class, in creation order. The list starts with the constructor. "Data" classes[64], such as NullClass don't have any functions.

Returns: List

---

64 A data class is a class that contains only data, no runnables.

- **fullName**: Returns one of two strings:
  - If the class or an instance of the class, or the class is contained in a class that is in the Vault, returns a "vault" path, where the class can be found in the Vault. For example:
    ```
    c:=Compiler.Asm;
    c.name        → "Asm"
    c.fullName    → "TheVault.Compiler.Asm"
    c().fullName → "TheVault.Compiler.Asm"
    ```
  - Otherwise, the class names up to the root class are concatenated to form the full name. For example:
    ```
    AKA(Top); class A{ class B{ println(fullName) }}
      → "Top.A.B"
    ```

FullName isn't the most useful of properties and may do more than you want. If you only want the second behavior, you can use this function:
```
fcn classFullName(klass){
   container:=klass.BaseClass.container;
   name      :=klass.BaseClass.name;
   if (not container) return(name);
   return(classFullName(container) + "." + name);
}
classFullName(Compiler.Asm) → "Asm"
classFullName(TheVault.Compiler.Asm.Code) → "Asm.Code"
```
Returns: String

- **isClassified**: Returns True if self (usually an embryo) has all classes added, including parent classes. An incomplete class can not be copied, used as a parent or added to a class. Note that this doesn't tell you anything about the functions.
  Returns: Bool
- **isCooked**: Returns True if self has been cooked.
  Returns: Bool
- **isEve**: Returns True if self is a Eve or reference class. Eve classes are the very first instance of a given class, from which all other instances of that class are copies of.
  Returns: Bool
- **isPrivate**: Returns True if the private attribute is set.
  See the Class Attributes section (below).
  Returns: Bool
- **isScript**: Returns True if the script attribute is set.
  See the Class Attributes section (below).
  Returns: Bool
- **isStatic**: Returns True if the static attribute is set.

See the discussion (below) on Static Classes.
Returns: Bool
- **linearizeParents**: Returns a list of parent classes in search order. Also known as method resolution order. The class hierarchy is flattened into a left-first breadth-first path with duplicates removed. See Keywords.class.inheritance for an explanation.
Returns: List of classes. Self is always the first item.
- **name**: Returns the name that the class was created with. For example,
`Compiler.Asm.name` → "Asm"
Returns: String
- **NullClass**: Returns a Class with no variables, functions, classes or parents.
- **parents**: Returns a list of the classes this class inherits from, in creation order.
Returns: List or ROList (if no parents)
- **rootClass**: Returns the class at the top of the class tree, that is, the class that has no container and contains self.
Examples:
    - `Compiler.Asm.rootClass` → Class(Asm)
    - If a file consists of the following line:
        `class C{ var v; class C2{var v;} }`
      then ("RootClass#" is the default name of the top level class):
        `C.rootClass`   → Class(RootClass#)
        `C.C2.rootClass` → Class(RootClass#)
      This might seem surprising until you remember that a file is itself a Class that contains all the Classes in it.
    - Since `class C{ class C2{} }` is static (contains no mutable data), `C.rootClass` → Class(C) and `C.C2.rootClass` → Class(C2).
Returns: Class
- **theInitFcnIs**: Returns the index of "init" in self.fcns.
When a class instance is created, the function marked as the init function is called (by the VM). If it is not the constructor, init will call the constructor. Embryos set the init function to zero. It is reset by addFcn.
Returns: Int
- **topdog**: Returns the class at the top of the class hierarchy, that is, a class that inherits from self, which might be self. The "youngest" child class. Topdog is a child of self. Or grandchild, or great grandchild, etc.
If self has a static class between it and the youngest child, topdog stops at the static class.
Examples:
    - `class A{var v;}.topdog`   → Class(A)

- `class A{var v;} class B(A){} B.A.topdog` → Class(B)
- `class A{var v;} class B(A){var v;} class C(B){}`
  `C.B.A.topdog, C.A.topdog` → Class(C)
- `class A{var v;} class B{var v;} class C(A,B){}`
  `C.A.topdog, C.B.topdog` → Class(C)

Returns: Class

- **varBits**: Returns bits strings for the read only and proxy vars. The ordering is the same as the varNames list. If a var is read only or a proxy, the corresponding "bit" is "1", otherwise it is "0". If there are no ones, the value is "".

  Use this value when creating an embryo or serializing a class.
  Returns: ROList(String(roBits), String(proxyBits))

- **varNames**: Returns a list of the names of all the variables, in creation order (sorted).
  Returns: List of Strings

- **vars**: Returns a list of the class variables and their values, in creation order (sorted).
  For example: `L( L("v1",1), L("v2","hoho") )`
  Returns: List of lists: L(L(name,value), …)

Operators

- **+**: This operator can be shadowed by the function **__opAdd**, it will receive one parameter.
  Throws: NotImplementedError
  Result: Object

- **-**: This operator can be shadowed by the function **__opSub**, it will receive one parameter.
  Throws: NotImplementedError
  Result: Object

- *****: This operator can be shadowed by the function **__opMul**, it will receive one parameter.
  Throws: NotImplementedError
  Result: Object

- **/**: This operator can be shadowed by the function **__opDiv**, it will receive one parameter.
  Throws: NotImplementedError
  Result: Object

- **%** : This operator can be shadowed by the function **__opMod**, it will receive one parameter.
  Throws: NotImplementedError

Result: Object

- ==: Returns True if the two classes are the same. The same, `self.id==X.id`; not instance related, etc.
  This operator can be shadowed by the function **__opEQ**, it will receive one parameter. For example, you may prefer equality to be `self.isInstanceOf(X)`.
  Result: Bool
- !=: `not self.eq(X)`
  This operator can be shadowed by the function **__opNEQ**, it will receive one parameter.
  Result: Bool
- <: This operator can be shadowed by the function **__opLT**, it will receive one parameter.
  Result: Object (but should be Bool)
- <=: This operator can be shadowed by the function **__opLTE**, it will receive one parameter.
  Result: Object (but should be Bool)
- >: This operator can be shadowed by the function **__opGT**, it will receive one parameter.
  Result: Object (but should be Bool)
- >=: This operator can be shadowed by the function **__opGTE**, it will receive one parameter.
  Result: Object (but should be Bool)

- -: Unary minus
  This operator can be shadowed by the function **__opNegate**, it will receive no parameters.
  Result: Object

Discussion
Classes are containers, they can hold variables, functions and other classes. They implement the class keyword. The distinction between class and class instance is artificial; all classes are, in fact, class instances. It does, however, provide useful terminology; a "class" is the original, class instances are progeny of a class.

Use BaseClass

If you want to access the methods or properties of an unknown class, use
`klass.BaseClass.name`. The reason for this is that classes can overload
method/property names[65]. Consider:

```
class C{ var setVar=5; }
f(C);
fcn f(klass){
   klass.setVar(0,7);               // does nothing
   klass.BaseClass.setVar(0,7); // changes "setVar" in C to 7
}
```

One drawback to BaseClass is if you want to set a variable. Using class C (above),
`C.BaseClass.setVar=7` generates a syntax error[66]. To work around this, use setVar:
`C.BaseClass.setVar("setVar",7)`.

Class Attributes

The attributes are set with Keywords.Attributes or when creating an embryo. Setting
an attribute doesn't propagate the attribute to children although it may affect the
children.

<u>script</u>
This is just a informational flag. Class ignores it but other objects might care. This
attribute can only be set on the root class.
See Objects.Import for how this this is used.

<u>static</u>
This is used to inform the VM that this class doesn't want to be copied or new
instances created.
Note: If there is an "init" function, the constructor is only run once, at creation time
(for the reference instance).

```
   class [static] C{} C();        → constructor runs for both instances
   class [static] C2{ fcn init{} } → constructor is run
   C2();                          → init runs but constructor doesn't
```

You can inherit from static classes but a static class can't inherit.
Any class can be static.
A static class doesn't have a container.
See the discussion (below) on Static Classes.

---

65 It is perfectly reasonable for a class creator to reuse names.
66 Because the compiler rewrites it to `C.BaseClass("setVar")=7`

Objects

<u>noChildren</u>
You can not inherit from one of these classes; it can not be the parent of any other class. This is useful for classes that are containers for other classes. For example, the Walker class contains a Walker class and a range function, the Exception class contains a zillion exception classes. You don't want to inherit from one of these, the noChildren attribute allows you to enforce this at compile time.
Any class can be noChildren.

Parent Classes and Top Dogs

When a function is called in a parent class, that function runs in the "parent" space, not in self space. It is as if the parent class was compiled separate from self and the function call is made to an instance of the parent. This is all well and good but a problem arises when the parent wants to access something in the child. This is backwards from the "normal" way of doing things, where the child wants to access something in the parent. The basic problem is that at compile time, the parent class doesn't know about the child class yet (although the programmer should). The topdog property provides a way around this. To illustrate:

```
class A{fcn f{ println(x); var v;}} // doesn't compile, x unknown
class A{fcn f{ println(topdog.x); var v;}}67 // this compiles
class B(A){ var x=123; }
```

Now, when we call the function B.f (which is in parent A), f will have access to B.x:

```
B().f() → 123   // create an instance of B and call B.A.f
```

Topdog returns the the top of a class hierarchy and from there late binding will work its way down the classes (or up through the parents, depending on how you look at it) until it finds a match.

```
class C(B){} C().f() → 123
```

Here, A.f starts looking in C, doesn't find x, moves to B and succeeds.

```
class D(A){ var x="foo"; }
class E1(B,D){}
E1().f() → 123
class E2(D,B){}        // same as E1 but parents are switched
E2().f() → "foo"
```

Here we see the difference parent search order makes.

Topdog does have a limitation and that is it can't access the middle of a class tree, you'll have to do that explicitly. This doesn't seem to be much of a drawback, such a capability would be prone to inducing confusion and head aches. But if you have to, you can do something like:

```
class A{fcn f{println(topdog.B.x);var v;}} // minor change to A
E2().f() → 123   // NOT "foo"
```

---

67 The `var v;` is necessary, otherwise A is static (and `A.topdog` is A) and f() will fail.

Here, A.f started its search at E2, found parent B and then found x, bypassing D explicitly. And, of course, it will fail miserably if the topdog doesn't contain a "B".

The take away here is (although not explicitly shown) is that topdog is "safest" when the parent class that uses it also has a copy of what it is looking for as a fall back should the child classes (if there are indeed any) lack the required resource. This is demonstrated in the virtual class example below.

As you can imagine, there are zillions of permeations awaiting your creativity.

There are a couple of places where topdog is very useful: inheritance testing and calling a child function.

Virtual Classes

"Virtual" classes are basically templates to build classes from. The template will probably contain functions that are meant to be replaced by an inheriting class. But, when running the template code, that code doesn't know about the new implementations. Check out the following code:

```
class Template{
    fcn one{ two(); }
    fcn two{ throw(
        Exception.FcnNotImplementedError(self.fcn)); }
}
class C(Template){fcn two{ println("two"); }}
c:=C();
c.one();      // throws FcnNotImplementedError
```

The fact that c.one throws an exception is clearly not what we want. How to fix? Have the Template look to the derived class for two:

```
    fcn one{ self.topdog.two(); }
```

When this runs, it looks to the top of the class hierarchy and finds the implementation of two in class C. If C doesn't implement two, then resolve will search the parents until it finds Template and one will throw the expected exception.

Testing Inheritance

If you have a "super" class, one that is basically a container for a bunch of other classes, you probably don't want anybody to inherit the mothership just to get one of the contained classes, they should inherit from the child class directly. The following code shows how:

```
class C{
    class C2{}
    if (not self.topdog.isInstanceOf(self))
      throw(Exception.NameError(
```

```
        "%s can't be a parent (of %s)"
        .fmt(self,self.topdog.name)));
}
class B(C){}        // error
class B2(C.C2){}   // OK
```

At runtime, the `B(C)` line throws:

    NameError: Class(C) can't be a parent (of B)

In this case, `Attributes(noChildren)` is a much better solution as it is a compile time check instead of a runtime check.

Static Classes

A static class is one that doesn't make copies of itself (or create new instances), has no container or parents; it is static, unchanging. It can not access anything in the class it is contained in. Usually, this isn't what you want, but it makes sense in the following situation: one or more classes that are part of a class hierarchy are "global" to the entire hierarchy, essentially global "variables" for the hierarchy (class patriarchs/matriarchs if you will). These might be classes that only contain "utility" functions:

```
class File(Stream){
    class [static] FileUtilities{
        fcn isDir(fileName){ … }
        fcn del(fileName)  { … }
    }
    fcn open(fileName,mode){ … }
    fcn close            { … }
}
File.FileUtilies.isDir("foo");
f:=File.open("bar","r");
f.FileUtilities.del("foobar");
```

Clearly, we don't want instance f to contain a new copy of FileUtilities. Declaring File static keeps that from happening.

A cleaner way to do the same thing would be:

```
Class [static] FileUtilities{
    fcn isDir(fileName){ … }
    fcn del(fileName)  { … }
}
class File(Stream,FileUtilites){
    fcn open(fileName,mode){ … }
    fcn close            { … }
}
File.isDir("foo"); FileUtilities.isDir("foo");
f:=File.open("bar","r");
f.del("foobar");
```

The "static-ness" of a class applies to its variables, contained classes and functions.

This also means that the class variables are not unique. Consider
```
class [static] C{ var v; }
C.v                           → Void
c:=C();(C.id==c.id)  → True
c.v=123; C.v            → 123
```
Since variable v is static, both C and c contain the same variable so changing it in either class changes it for both.

The Exception and Import classes use this in conjunction with a "redirecting" init in the root class:
```
    Attributes(static);    // Don't make copies of this class
    fcn init{ returnClass(someOtherFcnInThisClass()); }
```

Auto Static

A class may decide to make itself static if the following are true:
- There are no variables or parents.
- Any containing classes have no variables.

This rarely happens (or rather often in test cases).

Late Binding

Like most dynamic languages, zkl makes extensive use of "late binding". A data reference is "late bound" when that reference is resolved at run time. A data reference is "statically bound" when, at compile time, the data can be referenced directly. As with most things, there are trade offs. Static binding is much more efficient and the compiler can check validity, late binding is much more flexible. The compiler waffles; it statically binds when it can and delays binding when it can't.

Binding Rules
- Variables force late binding. That is, accessing data that is contained in a variable requires a run time examination to determine what is actually in that variable.
- Function calls *usually* force late binding, if the compiler can't ascertain what the function returns.
- Class creation is *usually* statically bound. If the constructor or init use returnClass, the compile may switch to late binding.
- There are no rules. The compiler is free to bind more aggressively.

Objects

Usually, you only care about when data is bound is when:
- Your program fails at run time and you think the compiler should have found the error (expect to experience this a lot if you are used to a statically typed language such as C or Java).
- You are worried about efficiency.
- You want to make use of late binding.

Delegation

One way to do delegation is to inherit from a static class that uses variables to hold the "delegation" information. By making the delegator class static, changing the delegator will cause every inheriting class to change its behavior. An example is a global logging resource:

```
class [static] Logger{  // Only one logging resource
    var [mixin=File] dst; // File like semantics, eg Data, Pipe
    dst=File.DevNull;    // initially, the logger does nothing
    fcn log(msg){dst.writeln(vm.pasteArgs())}
}
```

Then, any class that needs to log can inherit from Logger and call log() when it needs to log an event:

```
class A(Logger){ log("A has been created"); }
class B(Logger){ fcn f{ log("Hello from B"); } }
```

What happens when a new instance of A is created (A())? Not much, the log message is ignored. Ditto when B.f() or B().f() is called.

```
var b=B(); b.f();    // nothing is logged
```

Now, let's turn on logging (magic happens here):

```
Logger.log=Console;   // or A.Logger.log=
```

Now, if we create a new A, something happens:

```
A() → "A has been created"
```

And calling function f in b causes a log message, even though b has not changed:

```
b.f() → "Hello from B"    // b has NOT changed
```

Why is changing Logger.log termed magic? It's not, it is just looking at inheritance from a runtime perspective. Here, there is only one Logger class and every child shares it. When Logger changes, all children "automagically" inherit new logging behavior. By simply changing the log function, a central logging controller[68] can control the behavior for all classes that log (or functions that call Logger.log)[69].

Of course, you don't need to inherit from Logger to get this behavior,

```
class B{ fcn f{ Logger.log("Hello from B"); }
```

does the same thing; you can slice and dice this methodology many ways.

---

68 For example, the system event logger.
69 Thread safety would make this example a bit more complex.

Dynamic Class Creation

To illustrate various points about class creation, let's create a simple class two different ways:

```
1. class Test{
       var x=111;                        // constructor code
       println("Hello World!");      // constructor code
       fcn one{ println("x = ",x); }
   }
```

Create a new instance and call the "one" function:

```
   Test();          → "Hello World!"
   Test.one();    → "x = 111"
```

Now, let's create the same class at runtime:

```
2. text:="class Test{"
   "    var x=222;"
   "    println(\"Hello World!\");"
   "    fcn one{ println(\"x = \",x); }"
   "}";
```

Compile the class, construct it and call one:

```
   x:=Compiler.Compiler.compileText(text);
   x=x();          → Creates a new instance and prints "Hello World!"
   x.Test.one();  → "x = 222"
```

Notice a subtle, but important, difference: Here we created a new instance of Test before calling one. We didn't do that before. Why? Because, if we didn't, x would be Void, not 222. Why? Because all variables are initialized to Void. So why did the first case work? Well, when a file is compiled, all the classes in the file are "wrapped" in a class (the RootClass), and, when that file is loaded, the root class constructor calls the constructors in all the classes it contains. When we call the compiler directly, it just compiles the code and creates the Class, it doesn't construct it, so we need to, directly or indirectly (by creating a new instance). The following would also works:

```
   x:=Compiler.Compiler.compileText(text);
   x.__constructor();   → "Hello World!"
   x.Test.one();            → "x = 222"
```

Also notice that we have to call x.Test.one() and not x.one(). Again, this is because the compiler wraps all source code into a class (RootClass#). And again, we are free to discard that wrapper:

```
   x:=Compiler.Compiler.compileText(text);
   println(x);              → Class(RootClass#)
   println(x.classes);   → L(Class(Test))
   x=x.Test;
   x.__constructor();   → "Hello World!"
   x.one();                  → "x = 222"
```

The Null Class

NullClass is a "convenience" class; it exists as helper class for times when you need a placeholder or some such. It is a static class that contains nothing, not even a constructor; thus you can't run it or create instances (`NullClass()` is an error and all copies are just NullClass).

The Compiler Suite
Full name: [TheVault.]Compiler.*

> *Multi-Pass!*
> -- Leeloominaï (Leeloo), describing the compiler

Abstract

The Compiler suite tokenizes, parses, compiles and assembles source code into Objects.

The suite consists of the Assembler, Compiler, Parser and Tokenizer.

There are two files of constants used by the compiler suite: opcode.h.zkl and vm.h.zkl. They are located in the include directory and can be used with:
```
include(opcode.h.zkl);
include(vm.h.zkl);
```

Compiler.Asm

Full name: [TheVault.]Compiler.Asm
Inherits from: Class
Notes: This is a static class.
See also: Objects.Class, Objects.Fcn

Abstract

The assembler converts VM asm source code into VM machine code. It also provides several utility functions: a disassembler, file/class reader, and class to file writer.

Assembler Classes
- **Code**: This class holds VM machine code. It consists of two Data objects: code, which holds the code and strings, which hold text constants.
- **Label**: This class generates unique strings based on the text "label#" or a passed in tag. It is thread safe; many threads can use the same Label and not worry about name conflicts (as they might have to if they used multiple instances).
- **StringTable**: This class manages a Data object as a symbol table; a "packed" list of strigs.

Assembler Functions

- **asm(**text**)**: Convert text to `Asm.Code`. Text contains lines; strings separated by newlines ("\n").
- **asm(**Data**)**: Data has to be in Strings mode.
- **asm(**File**)**: Assemble the contents of a text file.
- **asm(**List**)**: Convert lines of text to `Asm.Code`.
- **asm(**Pipe**)**: Asm expects separate lines.

    A line can have white space in it and blanks lines are ignored.

    Examples:
    ```
    Compiler.Asm("self\ndone");
    Compiler.Asm(L("self","done"));
    Compiler.Asm(Data(0,String,"self\ndone"));
    Compiler.Asm(Data(0,String,"self","done"));
    Compiler.Asm(File("foo.asm","r"));
    ```
    Note: The requirement that a Data be in strings mode is so the assembler can read a line at a time. You can create it in anyway you wish and set the mode before passing it to asm. Strings mode just makes things easier for everybody. Thread safe.

    See Objects.Fcn for an example.

    Throws: AsmError

    Returns: Asm.Code

- **init(**sourceCode**)**: Since this is a static class, init is just a front end to Compiler.Asm.asm.

    Returns: asm(sourceCode)

Loader

Reader/Writer Functions

- **readRootClass(**fileName, addToVault=False, runConstructor=True**)**

    You probably don't need this, the same functionality is in **System.LoadFile**. This code is the reference implementation.

- **writeRootClass(**klass,fileName,bang=""**)**

    This method writes a RootClass (a class that isn't contained in any other class, a typical case is a code file) or static class to a Stream, typically a file but `Data` and `ZeeLib.Compressors` also work. Note that this is a binary stream.

    If bang parameter is present, it is used to write a [Unix] "#!" at the start of the output ("#!*text*\n"). This is useful is you want to use compiled scripts (for example CGI scripts). The loader skips this text if it sees it.

Examples:
- `Compiler.Asm.writeRootClass(klass,"foo.zsc");`
- `writeRootClass(CGIClass,"cgi.zsc","#!/usr/bin/zkl");`
  This writes "#!/usr/bin/zkl\n"at the start of cgi.zsc. When the Apache web server accesses this CGI file, it will hand the file to /usr/bin/zkl to deal with, which is what you want (because Apache doesn't know diddly about zkl). Note that this also works for the Windows version of Apache: "#!C:/Bin/zkl".

See also: Objects.Data:Stream Example

Disassembler Functions

- **disClass(**klass,outputStream=Console**)**
  Disassemble a class (to VM machine code source) and send the text output to a Stream. This implements **Class.unasm**. The result isn't in a form that can be fed back to asm, but it is close; there is a bunch of additional information to the raw code.
  The outputStream can be File, List, a Class or any object that implements "writeln" and "flush" (although "close" might be added in the future). If you want to process the output, you can store it in a List and post process it, or use a filter class and process on the fly:
  ```
  class Filter {
      fcn flush {}
      fcn writeln(line=""){ // writeln() is called
          // do something with line, like save it
      }
  }
  self.unasm(Filter);
  ```
- **disCode(**Asm.Code, outputStream=Console**)**: Disassemble a Code class.
  For example:
  ```
  Compiler.Asm.disCode(Compiler.Asm("self\ndone")) →
  0:171 self
  1:  0 done
  ```
- **disFcn(**function, outputStream=Console**)**
  Disassemble a function. This implements Fcn.unasm.

Discussion
Currently, a VM code reference doesn't exist so the assembler is likely to be a big black box.

The disassembler functions write to a Stream, which defaults to the Console, but other streams works as well, for example:

Objects

Pipes:
```
   p = Thread.Pipe();
      // the next two are equivalent
   self.unasm(p); Compiler.Asm.disClass(self,p);
```
Files: `self.unasm(File("unasm.txt","w"));`
Data: `d=Data(); self.unasm(d); d.text`

Compiler.Compiler

Full name: [TheVault.]Compiler.Compiler
Inherits from: Class
Notes: This is a static class.
See also: Objects.Class, Objects.Fcn

Abstract
Convert source code into a Class.
The compiler is thread safe and you don't need to create an instance. Just use the static class.

Compiler Functions
- **compileFile(**fileName,debugLevel=0**)**: The file name is the name of a file that contains zkl source code. The ".zkl" extension is optional (actually, if you include an extension, the compiler doesn't care what it is, as long as the file contains text). On Windows, you can use forward slash ("/") instead of backslash (if you do use backslash remember to double them up because backslash is the quote character).
  Throws: SyntaxError, CompilerError, others
  Returns: Class
- **compileText(**text,debugLevel=0**)**: Compile a string, list of strings or some object that will stream lines of text (such as Data or File).
  Throws: SyntaxError, CompilerError, others
  Returns: Class
- **init(**fileName,debugLevel=0**)**: This returns compileFile(fileName,debugLevel). This is a convenience function so you can type `Compiler.Compiler("foo")` instead of `Compiler.Compiler.compileFile("foo")`.

Discussion
The compiler converts source code to a Class.
The compiler can be used from the command line:

```
> zkl -c Src/Compiler/Compiler.zkl
```
In a program:
```
compileFile = Compiler.Compiler.compileFile;
klass = compileFile("Src/Compiler/Compiler");
```
In the zkl shell:
```
Compiler.Compiler("Src/startup")
```

Compiler.Parser

Full name: [TheVault.]Compiler.Parser
Inherits from: Class
Notes: This is a static class

Abstract
The parser converts a token stream into a parse tree that can be consumed by the compiler.
The parser is thread safe and you don't need to create an instance. Just use the static class.

Parser Functions
- **parseFile(**fileName,debugLevel=0,wait=True**)**
  Throws: SyntaxError, ParserError, others
  Returns: Parser.RootClass
- **parseText(**text,debugLevel=0,wait=True**)**

RootClass Functions
- **dump(**indent=""**)**: Print the parse tree

Warning
- This document is almost guaranteed to be out of sync with reality. Treat as informative rather than authoritative.

Discussion
If file "fact.zkl" contains:
```
fcn fact(x){    // the recursive part.  input: x   output: x!
   if (0 == x) return(1);       // 0! = 1
   return( x * fact(x - 1) );   // x! = x * (x-1)!
}
```

Objects

```
then
klass:=Compiler.Parser.parseFile("fact.zkl");
// klass=Class(RootClass)
klass.dump()
   →
class fact    Input source: "fact.zkl"
   class __Constants#()
   { Block(Class)
      vars(Class): L("__DEBUG__", "__VAULT_PATH",
                     "__NAME__", "__FILE__")
      <DR*>__DEBUG__
         <==0
      <DR*>__VAULT_PATH
         <==""
      <DR*>__NAME__
         <=="fact"
      <DR*>__FILE__
         <=="fact.zkl"
   }
{ Block(Class)
   fcns = L("fact")
   vars(Block) = L("x")
   fcn fact(x)
      Default args:
      Void
   { Block(Fcn)
      if
         Exp(
            (
            0
            ==
            <DR>x
            )
         )
         return(
            1
         )
      return(
         Exp(
            <DR>x
            *
            <DR>fact(
            <DR>    Exp(
            <DR>        <DR>x
            <DR>        -
            <DR>        1
            <DR>    )
```

```
            <DR>)
        )
    )
}
<DR*>x
    <==<DR>ask(
    <==<DR>    "Take factorial of: "
    <==<DR>)
<DR>println(
<DR>    <DR>x
<DR>    "! = "
<DR>    <DR>fact(
<DR>    <DR>    (<DataRef>
<DR>    <DR>        x
<DR>    <DR>        toInt()
<DR>    <DR>    )
<DR>    <DR>)
<DR>)
}
```

Compiler.Tokenizer

Full name: [TheVault.]Compiler.Tokenizer
Inherits from: Class
Notes: This is a static class

Abstract
The tokenizer converts a file or other text Stream into a token Stream.
The tokenizer is thread safe and you don't need to create an instance. Just use the static class. The two functions create their own instances.

Warning
- This document is almost guaranteed to be out of sync with reality. Treat as informative rather than authoritative.

Classes
- **SourceCode**: The source code that was compiled.
  Vars: **text**, a string of the entire source.
  Functions:
    - **SourceCode[n]**, where n is one based.
      Returns the nth line from the source.
    - **formatLine(n)**, where n is one based.

Objects

> Returns something like: "foo.zkl:Line 23:x = 5"

Tokenizer Functions
- **tokenizeFile(**fileName, wait=True**)**
- **tokenizeText(**text, wait=True**)**

  Tokenize a file or a bunch of lines of text. Text can be Data, File, List, String, Pipe or any object that supports walker and contains lines of text (Strings). The basic difference between these two is tokenizeFile will open a file if fileName is a String. Otherwise, fileName or text can be a Stream object.

  Throws: SyntaxError, TokenizerError, PipeError,

  Returns: L(List, SourceCode)   if wait

  Returns: L(Thread.Pipe, SourceCode)   if not wait

Discussion
The Tokenizer reads text and converts it into a stream of tokens that are typically fed into the Parser. It strips out comments ("#", "//" and "/* */") and does some text transmogrifications as the mood strikes it. The Tokenizer is threaded.

If wait is True, you won't get a result until the source has been completely tokenized, then a list of tokens is returned. Otherwise, you'll get a Pipe immediately, which will be filled as tokens become available. The pipe will close once the source has been tokenized. It will break if there is an error.

The output stream contains both strings and integers. The strings are the tokens and the integers are the line numbers. A line number proceeds the tokens for that line.

It is required that the source stream be line based, that is, it contains lines in the form of a String terminated with a newline ("\n"). As the tokenizer is free form, the line concept is pretty liberal, the newline requirement is so the embedded line numbers will track the source.

Example
If file "fact.zkl" contains:

```
//-*-c-*-
/*
 * Factorial the recursive way
 */
fcn fact(x)     // the recursive part.  input: x  output: x!
{
    if (0 == x) return(1);        // 0! = 1
    return( x * fact(x - 1) );    // x! = x * (x-1)!
}
```

then
```
    tokens,sourceCode := Compiler.Tokenizer.tokenizeFile("fact.zkl");
```
results in the Tokenizer collecting all the tokens into a List and returning them.
tokens = L("{",5,"fcn","fact(","x",")",6,"{",7,"if","(","0","==","x",")",
    "return(","1",")",";",8,"return(","x","*","fact(","x","-","1",")",")",";",9,"}","}")

```
sourceCode[1]          → "//-*-c-*-"
sourceCode.formatLine(3) → "fact.zkl:Line 3: * Factorial the recursive way"
sourceCode.text          → the source text as one big string
```

Console

Full name: [TheVault.]Console
Inherits from: Object

Abstract
The Console object interacts with the text console. It is the basic user I/O interface.

Methods
- **ask(**prompt**)**: Concatenate the prompt, write it to the console and wait for input from File.stdin. Newline (ie the Enter key) signals the input is ready. For example:
  ```
  ask("The answer is: ");
  pw := ask("Hello ",name,", the password is: ");
  ```
  Returns: The input text, with the attached newline.
- **ask(**n [,prompt]**)**: If *n* is an integer *and* vm.nthArg(n) doesn't throw, return vm.nthArg(n).toString(). Otherwise, return ask(prompt).
  This is usful in scripts where parameters may or may not have been passed in on the command line.
  Returns: String
- **close()**: This method does nothing. It is here so Console acts like a Stream.
  Returns: self
- **flush()**:This method does nothing. It is here so Console acts like a Stream.
  Returns: self
- **print(**object(s)**)**: Converts parameters into Strings and write the results to File.stdout. It is the same as the write method.
  Returns: The text printed.
- **println(**object(s)**)**: Convert the parameters into a Strings and write the results to File.stdout, appending a newline. It is the same as the writeln method.
  Returns: The text printed.
- **write**: This method is another name for print.
- **writeln**: This method is another name for println.
- **toBool()**: Returns True.

Properties: None
Operators: None

Data

Full name: [TheVault.]Data
Inherits from: Stream, Object

Abstract
The Data object holds an arbitrary byte stream or sequence of bytes – a bag-O-bytes.
It grows and shrinks as needed.
It is, in effect, a byte editor and a byte stream.
It is NOT thread safe. However, if the content is static and only one thread moves the cursor, it can be used in a thread safe manner.

Terms
- *"bytes"* refers to the contents of a Data object.
- *"offset"*: See **Rules for *Offset*** (below)
- *"numBytes"*: See **Rules for *numBytes*** (below)
- *"cursor"*: Data's internal notion of offset. Used by the Stream methods.

Methods
- **append(**x, …**)**: Appends data to *bytes*.

Object	Action	
Data	Appends the bytes of x to *bytes*.	
Int	Appends the LSB (ie x[0] or x.bitAnd(0xFF)) to *bytes*. For example: append(0x1234) appends 0x34	
List	Recursively appends the contents of the list to *bytes*. Warning: If list is circular, this is infinite recursion.	
String	Mode	Action
	Int	Appends the characters of string, not including the trailing \0
	String	Appends the characters, including the \0

  The *cursor* doesn't change.
  Throws: TypeError
  Returns: self
- **bytes**: Returns bytes from *bytes* as (unsigned) integers.
- **bytes()**: Returns the entire data set.
- **bytes(***offset***)**: Returns one byte at offset as an Int
- **bytes(***offset*,*numBytes***)**: Returns numBytes in a list of Ints
- **bytes(***offset*,***)**: Returns all bytes at, and after, offset.
  Each Int is one unsigned byte of *bytes*.

If there are not bytes (eg data is empty or numBytes is zero), Void is returned.

Bytes is basically an alternative to subscripting ([]), providing the same semantics, but returning the data as numbers.

For example, if *bytes* is 0,1,2,3 (d:=Data(); d.append(0,1,2,3)):
```
Bytes(0)      → 0
bytes(0,2)       → L(0,1)
bytes(0,*)≈ bytes() → L(0,1,2,3)
```
The mode is ignored and the *cursor* doesn't move.
Returns: List, Int, Void
- **charAt(***offset,length=1***)**: Same as get but always returns a String.
  Throws: IndexError
  Returns: String
- **clear(**[stuff]**)**: Clear self, ie reset it to a just created state, optionally appending stuff. Mode doesn't change.
  Returns: self
- **close()**: Does nothing. For Stream compatibility.
  Returns: self
- **copy()**: Creates a copy of self. The contents and cursors are the same.
  Throws:
  Returns: Data
- **create()**:
- **create(**Void,*bytes***)**:
- **create(***initialSize=0*, mode=Int|String [,*someData* ...]**)**:
  Create a new Data instance. If *initialSize* is zero, a default size is used. Otherwise, space for *initialSize* bytes is allocated.
  A "silent" "\0" (string terminator) is always implicit at the end of the buffer, no matter what the mode is. This terminator isn't counted.
  If *someData* is present, it is appended to the new Data.
  Throws: ValueError (size too big)
  Returns: Data
- **del(***offset***)**: Delete one byte at *bytes*[offset]
- **del(***offset,numBytes***)**: Delete numBytes bytes starting at offset.
- **del(***offset,*****)**: Delete all bytes from offset on.
  Delete some bytes from *bytes*, starting at, and including, the bytes at offset. The *cursor* is ignored.
  Throws:
  Returns: self
- **fill(**byte**)**: Stuff as many bytes into self as it will hold (without growing).

fill(byte,sz**)**: Fill self with with sz bytes, length is set to sz.
Returns: self
- **filter(**[f [,static parameters]]**)**:
Push content through a filter and return a Data of those that pass (**f(**d**)** is
True).
The cursor usually moves and howza determines how content is read.
Returns: Data with the same mode as self.
- **find(**string|Data,*offset=0,length=**)**: Searches *bytes* for string.
- **find(**string|Data**)**: This is the same as findString except that partial
matches work:
```
d:=Data(); d.append("one","two");  → "onetwo\0"
d.find("et") → 2;   // findString would fail.
```
You can also search for binary data using a Data:
```
Data(0,Int, 1,2,3).find(Data(Void,2)) → 1
```
The *cursor* is ignored and doesn't move.
Returns: Int (index of start of string), Void
- **findString(**string,*offset=0,length=**)**: Searches *bytes* for string,
including the \0. Returns the offset where string starts, else Void. The entire
search string has to fit in length characters.
The cursor is ignored and doesn't move.
Note that mode has an effect. For example:
```
d:=Data(); d.append("one","two");  → "onetwo\0"
```
d.findString("one") will return Void, d.findString("two") returns 3
but
```
d:=Data(0,String); d.append("one","two");  → "one\0two\0"
```
now d.findString("one") returns 0 and d.findString("two") returns 4.
findString("onetwo") only succeeds in the first case.
A match has to be a "complete" match; all of string has to match. In the
examples above, findString("o") won't match the "o" in "one" but will
match the "o" in "two" (→ 5).
If string is "", findString returns the end of the current string. You can use
that to sequentially find the start of every string[70]:
```
d:=Data(0,String,"one","","two"); offset:=n:=0;
while(offset < d.len()) {
    n+=1;
    println("String %d starts at %s".fmt(n,offset));
    offset=1 + d.findString("",offset);
}
```
→ String 1 starts at 0
    String 2 starts at 4

---

70 Or, write less code and do it with readString and cursor. Or with walker(2).

> String 3 starts at 5

Since there in an implicit "" at the end of a Data, findString will not go out of bounds.

Throws:

Returns: Int (index of start of string), Void

- **flush()**: Does nothing

  Returns: self
- **get(**_offset_,numBytes**)**: Same as __sGet.

  Throws: IndexError

  Returns: Data | String | Int (depending on mode and numBytes)
- **howza()**: Return the current value.

  Returns: Int
- **howza(**int**)**: Howza determines the default way data streams out of Data (by filter, pump, reduce and walker). The initial value is 1 (lines).

  See walker for values.

  See also: mode

  Returns: self
- **howza(**int,True**)**: Same as howza(int) but the change is temporary, it is reset after the next filter, pump, reduce or howza.

  Returns: self
- **index(**x**)**: The same as **find**, but throws IndexError if x isn't found.

  Throws: IndexError, TypeError

  Returns: Int
- **inlineCursor(**[False]**)**: Returns the current text cursor position.
- **inlineCursor(**True**)**: Return text cursor with tab stops counted.
- **inlineCursor(**0|1**)**: Move the cursor to the beginning of the line. Returns self.
- **inlineCursor(*******)**: Move the cursor to the end of the line. Returns self.
- **inlineCursor(**offset,expandTabs=False**)**: Move the cursor to the requested position in the line. Returns self.

  The text cursor is the cursor offset from the beginning of the line. It is one based; the first character in a line is at offset 1. This method moves the cursor back and forth in the current line and will not leave the current line. If tab expansion is requested, tab positions are every eight characters (offset 9, 17, etc). A tab ("\t") is counted as if spaces were used to move the cursor to the next tab stop.

```
var d=Data(0,String,"one\ttwo","1\t2\t\t3");
(0).pump(d.len(),List,
    d.seek, d.inlineCursor.fp(True,False));
→ L(1,2,3,4,9,10,11,12, 1,2,9,10,17,25,26)
```

Throws: Tries not to.

Returns:

- Int; the current cursor position relative to the start of the line. Tab counting is done as requested.
- Self

- **insert(*offset*, item, …)**: Insert items *before* the byte at offset. *Bytes* grow to fit.
- **insert(0, …)**: Insert at the beginning of *bytes*.
- **insert(len(), …), insert(*, …)**: Append to *bytes*.
- **insert(-1, …)**: Insert before the last byte.
    ```
    d:=Data(); d.append("13");   → "13"
    d.insert(1,"two");           → "1two3"
    ```
  The *cursor* is ignored and doesn't move. Use write if you want cursor semantics.

  Throws:

  Returns: self
- **len()**
- **len(0, fromCursor=False)**: Returns the number of bytes in self.

  Returns: Int
- **len(1, fromCursor=False)**: Returns the number of lines, optionally starting at the cursor.
- **len(2, fromCursor=False)**: Returns the number of strings.
- **len(True, *numBytes*)**: Sets the size of self to *numBytes*.

  Throws:

  Returns: *numBytes*
- **mode()**: Returns the current mode.
- **mode(mode)**: Sets the mode. Mode is word Int or String.

  The mode determines how data enters Data.

Mode	Action
Int	*Bytes* is treated as a byte stream. This is the default mode.
String	*Bytes* is treated as consecutive \0 terminated strings.

  See the discussion below.

  Throws: ValueError (can't make the change)

  See also: howza

  Returns: self
- **open(initialSize=0, mode=DATA)**: A synonym for **create**.

  Throws:

  Returns: Data
- **pop(*offset*)**: Remove a byte and return it (as an Int).
- **pop(*offset, length*)**: Remove some bytes and return them (as a Data).

This method behaves the same as:
```
result=bytes[offset,length]; bytes.del(offset,length);
```
Examples:
```
Data(0,Int,1,2,3).pop(1);    → 1
d:=Data(0,Int,1,2,3); d.pop(1,2);  → Data(2,3) & d is Data(1)
```
Throws: IndexError
Returns: Int or Data

- **pump(**sink[,action ...]**)**: Another type of loop, similar to apply but with multiple actions. The calls are r=a$_1$(readln()); r=a$_2$(r); r=a$_3$(r) ... or r=a$_1$(readString()); r=a$_2$(r); r=a$_3$(r) ...
The read used depends howza.
The cursor usually moves.
See also: Notes on the pump method at the start of this chapter, howza, walker.
Returns: sink

- **read(**numBytes**)**: Read *numBytes* at the *cursor* and return a Data. The *cursor* moves. Similar to **bytes**. This is a binary read (that is, there are no data translations).
If *num* is greater than the number of bytes available, all the remaining data is returned.

- **read()**, **read(*)**: Reads all of the available data (post *cursor*).
If a Data isn't much use as a result, explode it with **bytes**, **text** or **toBigEndian**.
See also: **seek**, sGet ([])
Throws: TheEnd
Returns: Data

- **read(**numBytes|*,data**)**: Read into a user created Data
Read bytes from a file into a Data.
d:=Data(N); f.read(M,d); reads min(data.space,M) bytes into d (overwriting). Note that N is just a hint to Data.create so space may actually be different.
Returns: Data

- **readln(**n=1**)**: Read line(s), starting at the *cursor*. The *cursor* is updated.
- **readln()**: Read one line and return it (string).
- **readln(**n > 1**)**: Read lines into a list of strings.
- **readln(**n <= 0**)**: Returns "".
A line is terminated by a newline, \0 or both. Newlines are retained.
The mode is ignored.
Throws: TheEnd
Returns: String or List of Strings.

- **readNthLine(***nthLine* [,*offset*=0]**)**: Read the nth line. readNthLine(0) reads the first line. *NthLine* and *offset* don't have any special semantics (such as * or -1). If an attempt is made to read off the end of data, "" is returned.
- **readNthLine(n)** → String
- **readNthLine(n,***offset***)** → List(String,offset to start of next line) Reads the nth line (start counting lines from byte *offset*).

      d:=Data(0,String,"one","two","three"); d.readNthLine(0,5);
      → L("wo",8) as the bytes are "one\0two\0three\0"

  The cursor is ignored and doesn't move.

  Returns: String ("" if out of range) or List(String,Int)
- **readString()**: Reads from the cursor until the end of the string/buffer is found. The *cursor* is updated. This is the same as readln(), except newline is ignored.

  Throws: TheEnd

  Returns: String
- **readString(**offset**)**: Reads from offset until the end of the string/buffer is found. The *cursor* is ignored.

  Throws: TheEnd

  Returns: String
- **reduce(**f,*initialValue*=self.read() [,parameters]**)**: A feedback loop which starts at the beginning of Data and runs f until the end of Data is reached. The calls are:

      p:=initialValue;
      p=f(p,self.read(),parameters);
      p=f(p,self.read(),parameters);
      ...

  The read used depends on howza.

  To stop the loop, return(Void.Stop) or return(Void.Stop,result).

  The cursor [usually] moves.

  See also: howza, walker.

  Returns: p
- **replace(**text, replaceWith**)**: Replace text. Text and the replacement text can be String or Data (eg binary)

      Data(Void,"onetwo").replace("one",Data(Void,0x31))
      → "1two"

  The *cursor* is ignored and doesn't move.

  Returns: Self
- **seek()**: Returns the current cursor position. The cursor is a zero based offset.
- **seek(***offset***)**: Sets the *cursor* to offset.
- **seek(***offset***,n)**: Sets the *cursor* to offset and moves it n lines.

- **seek(**Void,n**)**: Starting at the *cursor*, move it n lines (zero to move to the start of the current line).
  If you want to set the cursor past the end so that a write will append: d.seek(*).
  To set the cursor to the last byte: d.seek(-1).
  Seek throws an IndexError if offset is out of bounds.
  On line movements, TheEnd is thrown if the cursor tries to move too far (and the cursor is left at the edge). Otherwise, the cursor is set to the beginning of a line.
  If n is negative, the cursor is moved to the start of a previous line. Example:
  ```
  d:=Data(0,String,"one","","two"); d.seek(*);
  foreach cursor in (Utils.wap('wrap(){ d.seek(Void,-1) }))
    { println("String starts at ",cursor); }
  ```
  → String starts at 5
    String starts at 4
    String starts at 0
  Since the data text is "one\0\0two\0". Exercise: What happens if d.seek(*) is changed to d.seek(-1)?[71]

  A line is defined as text that ends with a newline ("\n"), a null ("\x00") or newline/null ("\n\x00") but not null/newline (the cursor is left at the newline).

  See also: **inlineCursor** method, **cursor** property.
  Throws: IndexError, TheEnd
  Returns: Int (the current *cursor* position)
- **set(***offset*,bytes**)**: Overwrite the byte(s) at offset with *bytes*. Self does not grow. Use del/insert or [] to change lots of bytes.
  Returns: self
- **__sGet(***offset* [,*numBytes* | *]**)**: Implements subscripts ([]).
- **__sGet(***offset***)**: Implements *bytes*[offset]
- **__sGet(***offset*,numBytes**)**: Implements *bytes*[offset,len]
- **__sGet(***offset*,***)**: Implements *bytes*[offset,*]. "*" is short hand for *bytes*.len().

Mode	self[offset]	self[offset,len]
Int	One byte @ *offset*	Data(len)
String	One character @ offset	Len character string

See **Subscripts** and **Rules** (below).
The *cursor* is ignored, doesn't move.

---

71 "String starts at 4","String starts at 0". The last character is \0 (end of line) so seek(*) is past the last line and seek(-1) is in the last line.

Throws: IndexError

Returns: Data | String | Int

- **shuffle()**: Shuffle the contents using Knuth's Algorithm P.

  Returns: Self

- **_sSet(**v,*offset*[,*numBytes* | *]**)**: Implements subscript assignment (d[x]=y).

- **__sSet(**v,*offset***)**: Implements *bytes*[offset] = v

- **__sSet(**v,*offset*,*numBytes***)**: Implements *bytes*[offset,len] = v

- **__sSet(**v,*offset*,*****)**: Implements *bytes*[offset,*] = v. "*" is short hand for *bytes*.len().

  NumBytes bytes at *offset* are deleted and *v* is inserted at *offset*:

      d.del(offset,numBytes); d.insert(offset,v);

  If the mode is Strings and *v* is a string, the "\0" is also inserted:

      d:=Data(0,String,"test"); d[1]="3"; d.text → "t3"

      d contains "t3\0st"

  The *cursor* is ignored and doesn't move.

  See **Subscripts** and **Rules** (below).

  Throws: IndexError

  Returns: v

- **toBool()**: Returns True if *bytes* contains any data.

  Returns: Bool

- **toBigEndian(**offset=0,len=<*numBytes* max 8>,unsigned=True**)**: Treats *bytes* as the bytes of big-endian number and converts len of them to an Int in big endian format. A big-endian number is one where the MSB (most significant byte) is at the lowest address (ie left most), that is, ordered like you write them. The MSB of 0x1234 is 0x12.

  For example, if *bytes* is 0x12, 0x34, 0x56, 0x78, 0x90

      d:=Data(); d.append(0x12,0x34,0x56,0x78,0x90);

      d.toBigEndian() → 0x1234567890 (decimal 78187493520)

  If *unsigned* is True, *bytes* are treated as unsigned number (although an Int is signed so an 8 byte number with the high bit set will always be negative). If *unsigned* is False, the sign bit is extended (twos complement).

      Data(0,Int,(-4321).toBigEndian(2)).toBigEndian(0,2,False)

      → -4321

  Note: if Data contains a single byte, endianness is both big and little; that is, it is the same *bytes* (unless, of course, you want endianness at the bit level).

  The *cursor* is ignored and doesn't move.

  See also: Objects.Int.toBigEndian

  Returns: Int

- **toData()**: Returns self

- **toList(***offset*=0**)**:

Mode	Returns
Int	L(self) ie a list with a Data in it. *Offset* is ignored.
String	A list of the strings in self. Strings are strings of characters that end with a 0. For example, if self contains "one\0two\0" then toList() returns L("one", "two"). Starts at the *offset*: toList(2) → L("e","two")

  The *cursor* is ignored and doesn't move.
  Throws:
  Returns: List

- **toLittleEndian(**offset=0,len=<*numBytes* max 8>,unsigned=True**)**:
  Same as toBigEndian but the conversion is to a little endian number.

  ```
  d:=Data().append(0x12,0x34,0x56,0x78,0x90);
  d.toLittleEndian() → 0x9078563412 (decimal 620494205970)
  ```

  The *cursor* is ignored and doesn't move.
  See also: Objects.Int.toLittleEndian
  Returns: Int

- **toString()**: Returns "Data(*len*)", where *len* is the number of bytes in self.
  Throws:
  Returns: String

- **walker(**n=howza()**)**: Create a walker, mode is ignored. 1 is the default.

n	walker.next() returns
0	Int (one byte of *bytes*). The *cursor* is ignored and doesn't move.
1	String, one line at a time using readln. The *cursor* moves.
2	String, one string at a time using readString. The *cursor* moves.
3	String, one character at a time using __sGet. The *cursor* is ignored and doesn't move.
11	The same as 1 plus white space stripped from right side
12	The same as 2 plus white space stripped from right side

  Examples:
  - ```
    d:=Data(0,String,"foo","bar");
    d.walker(0).walk() → L(102,111,111,0,98,97,114,0)
    d.walker(2).walk() → L("foo", "bar")
    d.walker(3).walk() → L("f","o","o","","b","a","r","")
    ```
  - ```
    d:=Data(0,String,"foo\nbar");
    d.walker().walk()   → L("foo\n","bar")
    d.walker(2).walk()  → L("foo\nbar")
    d.walker(11).walk() → L("foo","bar")
    ```

  The walker always starts at the beginning of self. Which can be annoying. If you are reading header data using readln and now want process the rest of the

Data in some kind of loop, what to do? Probably "best" way is to tweak a walker:

```
stuff=d.readln(); process(stuff);
stuff=d.readln(); fiddle(stuff);
walker:=Utils.wap(d.readln.fpM(""));  // → Walker w/no args to readln
walker.pump or foreach line in (walker)
```

Throws:

Returns: Walker

- **write(x)**: Inserts data at the *cursor*, the *cursor* is incremented.
  The mode applies (see insert).
  This is the same as d.insert(d.cursor,x);
  X can be Data, Int, List (recursive is OK, circular is not) or String.
  Throws: TypeError
  Returns: self
- **writeln(x)**: Same thing as write(data).write("\n");
  Throws: TypeError
  Returns: self

Properties

- **cursor**: Returns the current *cursor* position.
  Returns: Int
- **text**: Convert *bytes* to a String and return it. *Bytes* are unchanged.
  Returns: String(*bytes*)

Operators

- **add (+)**: data + x is the same as data.append(x).
  Returns: self
- **eq (==)**: Compare two Data objects. If they are of equal length and the contents are the same, returns True.
  Returns: Bool
- **neq (!=)**: Not eq.
  Returns: Bool

Methods that honor the cursor

copy, inlineCursor, read, readln, readString, seek, toList, walker, write, writeln

Discussion

The Data object holds an arbitrary bunch of bytes. A Data has no idea what the bytes are or what they do and doesn't care. It is up to the application to impose its will on the bytes and create order out of chaos. This is both a benefit and deficit; for while they are very general, they can be painful to work with. In fact, they were so painful that a common case was institutionalized: strings. So, in string mode, Data will pretend that the bytes are in fact streams of null terminated text. But, whether or not this reflects reality is up to the application.

STRINGS and Lines

In STRINGS mode, the bytes are assumed to represent back to back null terminated strings. A null terminated string is the string type C programmers are used to, which is eight bit characters terminated by a zero byte (or end of Data). The readln method makes a further distinction, defining a line as a stream of bytes terminated by a new line ("\n") or zero (or both). So, for example, the following data has two strings and two lines (or four lines, depending who is looking at the data):

"one\0two\nthree\n\0four"

Rules for *Offset*

- The first byte is zero: [0].
- The last byte is [-1].
- If *offset* is < 0, it is added to the length. It is an error if the result is out of bounds.

Rules for *NumBytes*

- The default for len is 1.
- "*" is short hand for length of *bytes*. [0,*] is all the bytes.
- If *numBytes* is < 0, it is added to the length. It is an error if the result is out of bounds.
- If *offset* + *numBytes* is greater than the number of available bytes, *numBytes* is truncated to what is available.

Subscripts

There are several ways to pluck out snippets of data from Data. Subscripts provide a convenient method for random access to Data. For example, if d is a Data(8) that contains "one\0two\0" then

```
d[0]    → "o" or Data(1), depending on mode
d[2]    → "e" or Data(1), depending on mode
d[0,3]  → "one" or Data(3), depending on mode
d[0,6]  → "one" or Data(6), depending on mode
```

Things to note from these examples:

- If the mode is DATA, Data is always returned. A lot (most?) of the time, this isn't what you want. **bytes** provides an alternate form that is more likely to fit the bill. It has the same form without the convenience of the bracket syntax:

```
d.bytes(0)    → 111
d.bytes(0,6) → L(111,110,101,0,116,119)
```

- In STRINGS mode, a String is always returned BUT if there is a \0 somewhere in the chunk, it effectively ends the string, which means you might not get all the data you asked for.

Assignment examples (each example assumes d starts as "one\0two\0" (Data(8)):

- `d.mode(String); d[0]="O"` → Data(9)

  Huh, how come the Data grows? Because, in STRINGS mode, the \0 is always appended. Thus, d becomes "O\0ne\0two\0". Probably not what you were expecting. The next example shows what you probably want:

- `d.mode(Int); d[0]="O"` → Data(8)

  `d.text="One"` and d contains "One\otwo\0"

- `d.mode(String); d[0,3]="A test"` → Data(12)

  Ahh, this is more like it. d.text → "A test". This is why a \0 is always appended in STRINGS mode. But all is not good; d contains "A test\0\0two\0". Argh! The "proper" code here is:

  `d.mode(String); d[0,4]="A test"`

- `d.mode(Int); d[0,3]="A test"` → Data(9)

  Yes! d is "A Test\0two\0"

Take aways:

- STRINGS mode can be a pain. If you don't know exactly what is there, you probably won't get what you want.
- DATA mode is more predictable

Stream and Sequence: Twice the fun at one low price

Data is a dual personality object; it is both Sequence and Stream. While the modes can be intermixed, it is probably a bad idea so be careful.

As a sequence, Data acts like a String or List, a random access object, which is its main target. But it can also act like a Stream, like a File: data flows into the front and out the back. The Stream methods are:

   read, readln, write, writeln, seek, cursor

All the action occurs at the "*cursor*", a pointer into the data that indicates where the method should start looking at data. Since the data is in memory, moving the *cursor* around is cheap and fast, which can be a big advantage over disk files. If your Stream will be undergoing a lot of changes, it might make sense to work on it in memory before it hits the disk (assuming enough memory exists).

Objects

Sequence Example: String Tables

One thing that compilers need are symbol tables, usually two kinds: one to hold the symbols while compiling code and another to store symbols and strings used by the compiled code. The first case usually uses fast access tables like Dictionaries while the second case is more concerned with space savings because the code will be retrieving strings from fixed locations and doesn't have to worry about look ups. The Data object is a good fit for this second case. The idea is for a Data to hold a "packed" list of strings and to keep a list of offsets to those strings. The following class shows the implementation:

```
class StringTable{
    var strings;            // Data
    fcn init{ strings=Data(500,String); }
    fcn add(text){
        if (Void!=(offset:=strings.findString(text)))
            return(offset);
        // string not in table
        offset=strings.len(); strings.append(text);
        return(offset);
    }
    fcn theStrings{ return(strings.toList()); }
}
```

When a new instance of StringTable is created, a Data is created to hold the strings. The real action occurs in add – if the text is already in the table, we reuse it (thus the "packed" label). findString will only find an exact match so we don't have to worry about symbols "foo" and "foobar" overlapping. If text isn't in the table, it is added and its location is returned. It is up the code that uses the StringTable to remember the offsets. In the case of the compiler, the offset is compiled into the code that will retrieve the symbol. Let's look at an example:

```
s:=Compiler.Asm.StringTable();
s.add("one");      → 0    // 4 bytes: "one" and \0
s.add("two");      → 4
s.add("three")     → 8
s.add("two");      → 4    // repeat, use entry already in table
s.theStrings();    → L("one","two","three")
```

Now, if we were a compiler generating code for println("two"), the code might look like:

```
[Symbols] "one\0two\0three\0"
getString(4)    // offset of "two"
call println
```

Stream Example: Code Containers

Since both Data and File both inherit from Stream, they, in many cases, can be used interchangeably. One example of where this is the case is the routines that read and write compiled classes (Compiler.Asm.readRootClass and writeRootClass). WriteRootClass "flattens" a class to bytes and (usually) writes it to a file. readRootClass converts a bunch of bytes into a class. For example, to write the Asm class to "foo.zsc":

```
Compiler.Asm.writeRootClass(Compiler.Asm,"foo.zsc")
```
And to read it:
```
Compiler.Asm.readRootClass("foo.zsc")
```
But you can just as easily write to, or read from, Data:
```
d:=Data();
Compiler.Asm.writeRootClass(Compiler.Asm,d);   → Data(16615)
Compiler.Asm.readRootClass(d);                  → Class(Asm)
```
There was only one change made to accommodate both Files and Data, and that was to open the requested file or to prep Data:
```
fcn writeRootClass(klass,fileName){
    if (fileName.isType("")) f:=File(fileName,"wb"); // ←
    else                    { f:=fileName; }         // ←
    rw:=ReaderWriter(f);
    rw.writeClass(klass,klass);
    f.close();
}
fcn readRootClass(fileName, runConstructor=True){
    if (fileName.isType("")) f:=File(fileName,"rb");    // ←
    else                    { f:=fileName; f.seek(0); } // ←
    ...
    rw:=ReaderWriter(f);
    klass:=rw.readClass();
    f.close();

    if (runConstructor) klass.__constructor();

    return(klass);
}
```
Only four lines of code are needed to handle both Data and Files. Or, to put it a better way, File is treated as a special case of Stream for ease of use in the most common case.

Once we have the class in Data, we can play with it. For example, how compressible is it?

```
d:=Data();
Compiler.Asm.writeRootClass(Compiler.Asm,d);  → Data(16630)
z:=Import("zeelib").Compressor(); z.write(d); z.close();
z.len();                                        → 7785
```
Very compressible – the Asm code compresses to about half its original size.

Hmm, while we are here, we notice that ZeeLib also is a Stream. Let's see what happens if we write to it:

```
z:=Import("zeelib").Compressor();
Compiler.Asm.writeRootClass(Compiler.Asm,z); z.close();
z.len();  → 7785
```
Wow! That is pretty cool. But, as someone famous once said: "Trust but verify". So let's blow that baby back up and see what happens.

```
i:=Import("zeelib").Inflator(); i.write(z.drain()); i.close();
d2:=i.drain();
d           → Data(16615)
d2          → Data(16615)
d==d2  → True
```
So, indeed, the uncompressed bits are identical in both cases: if writeRootClass writes directly to a Compressor or we compress a flattened class.

This example illustrates the advantages of a common Stream interface: the interchangeability of Stream objects.

Deferred

Inherits from: Object
See Also: Objects.Object.fp

Abstract
Deferred is an Object that is a deferred, or delayed, computation. It encapsulates the computation (complete with parameters) until it needs to be evaluated.
When it is referenced, the computation is evaluated. A Deferred can be treated like any other object.

`Deferred.noop()` will force evaluation.

Deferreds are not thread safe. After a Deferred has been evaluated, it is thread safe (although the underling object might not be).

A Deferred can also be a **Partial** (as in Partial [Function] Application). These objects fix one or more parameters to the underling deferred object. Essentially a call in progress, waiting to be completed.

Methods
What a method does depends on whether or not the Deferred has been "created" or not. An "embryonic" Deferred will create new Deferred objects, a created object will evaluate. An embryonic Deferred will act like an ordinary object, not a Deferred. If created, these methods (excepting BaseClass) will force evaluation and reference the result.

- **BaseClass(***name***)**: Reference the underlying Deferred object.
  `d:=Deferred(String,"text"); d.toString()` → "text"
  `d.BaseClass.toString()` → "Deferred"
  Throws: NotFoundError, NotImplementedError
  Returns: Deferred.*name*
- **create(***object[, runTimeParameters]***)**: Create a new Deferred object. Typical objects are fcns and classes (eg Import). The second call to create will evaluate and call. Subsequent calls will just call the result of the evaluation.
  `fcn f(a){a+5} d:=Deferred(f,1);` → Deferred
  `d()+4 ≈ d+4→ f(1) + 4 → 10`
  From this point on, d will always be 6 and d+4 → 6+4 (f is no longer called). Note that d()+4 is now 4 because d() is still a call: 6() → 6.create() → 0.

The new object will not be able to create new Deferred objects[72].
Throws: TypeError
Returns: Deferred

- **create(**[nargs]**)**: Evaluate and call:
  `result=f(runTimeParameters)(nargs)`
  Not overly useful as the result usually isn't a Deferred. For a Deferred.once, the result is always the value of the first evaluation. This is for a deferred constant [expression].
    - `Deferred(5,6)(7)` → `Deferred(5.create(6))(7)` → `Deferred(6).create(7)` → 7
    - `Deferred.once(5,6)(7)` → 6

  Throws: Possibly
  Returns: Something
- **once(**f, [runTimeParameters]**)**: Same as [the first] create: create a new Deferred object. The only difference is in subsequent calls to create: there is no call to the underlying result, that result is just returned.
  `df:=Deferred.once(fcn f(x){x/2},10)`
  `df()` → `f(10)` → 10/2 → 5, `df()` → 5, `df(6)` → 5,
  `df+3` ≈ `df()+3` → 8

  Throws: TypeError
  Returns: Deferred
- **toBool()**: Returns True if evaluated.
  `d:=Deferred(String,"text"); d.BaseClass.toBool()` → False and d remains unevaluated. `d.toBool()` → `String("text")` → `"text".toBool()` → True
  This is useful for things like
  `if(deferred.BaseClass.toBool()) println("Evaluated");` since it doesn't force evaluation. You can check if the Deferred was "triggered" without triggering it yourself.
  Returns: Bool
- **toString()**: Returns "Deferred". This doesn't always force evaluation. If called indirectly (eg `println(d)`), it is not evaluated.
  Returns: "Deferred"

Properties

All properties force evaluation and then return `result.property` unless you use BaseClass.

- **f**: Returns the object used in create or Void if has been evaluated (and isn't a Partial).

---

72 Unless you use BaseClass

Returns: Object or Void
- **isCooked**: Has self been evaluated or is self a Partial?
  Returns: Bool
- **isPartial**: Is self a Partial?
  Returns: Bool
- **value**: Returns `self.f` if a Partial, otherwise, evaluates and returns the result.
  Returns: Object

Operators
All operators force evaluation and then perform the operation on the result.

Discussion
There is typically one "embryonic" Deferred object (TheVault.Deferred), which is used to create all other Deferred objects.

As a parameter
Passing a Deferred as a parameter does not force evaluation (obviously, as that would be eager evaluation). As an example, to test if d is a Deferred, use `Deferred.isType(d)`, not `d.isType(Deferred)`.

Evaluation
A Deferred is evaluated only once. After that, any reference is resolved against the result of that evaluation. Any parameters that are required for evaluation must be part of the Deferred. For example, in `f=Deferred(fcn(n){n+1})`, both `f.noop()` and `f(4)` will fail for lack of a parameter. But in `f=Deferred(fcn(n){n+1},4)`; `f.noop()` evaluates to 5 and `f(4)` evaluates to 4: 5(4) → (5).create(4) → 4.

Typically, evaluation of a Deferred is a two step process: A reference is made to the expected result, which forces evaluation, then the reference is resolved. Using `Date=Deferred(Import,"Time.Date")`[73] as an example,
- The creation of the Deferred is split into two parts to keep eager evaluation from immediately performing the import.

`Date.prettyDay()`
- The reference to prettyDay forces evaluation, which causes `Import("Time.Date")` to be run, which returns the Time.Date class. From this point forward, any reference to Date will be to the Time.Date class.

---

73 Which could also be expressed as `Import.defer("Time.Date")` or
   `(Import : Deferred(_,"Time.Date"))`

- `Time.Date.prettyDay()` is run, which returns "Monday, the 13th of September 2010"
- Mixins are convenient in this case as they tell the compiler how to do additional compile time checking[74]:
  ```
  var [mixin=Time.Date] Date=Deferred(Import,"Time.Date");
  Date.pettyDay() → syntax error
  ```

If you don't know if an object is a Deferred or not, a safe way to force evaluation is to use `d.noop()`, since it normally doesn't do anything but as it is a reference, it does force evaluation.

Nested
A Deferred can reside in a Deferred. Evaluation happens "all the way down".
```
Deferred(Deferred(fcn{4})).noop() → Deferred(fcn{4}()) →
Deferred(4) → 4
```

Dead Lock and Recursion
A Deferred can reference another Deferred and if that reference is circular, evaluation might dead lock, so it isn't allowed. Likewise, recursive Deferreds are not allowed. This is detected at run time:
- ```
  var a=Deferred(fcn{b}), b=Deferred(a);
  b.noop();  →  AssertionError
  ```
- `var a=Deferred(fcn{a}); a.noop()      → AssertionError`
- `fcn f{ Deferred(f) } Deferred(f).noop()  → AssertionError`

A limited amount of recursion is allowed (but how much is undefined).

Deferred Function Variable Initialization
Initialization of function variables can be annoying because they are initialized before other variables in the containing class. For example, if you wished to initialize a function variable to a BigNum, the following doesn't work:
```
var BigNum=Import("zklBigNum");
fcn f{ var b=BigNum(5); }
```
Since b is initialized before BigNum is imported[75], b is set to Void. One work around is to defer setting b until it used:
```
fcn f{ var b=Deferred(fcn{BigNum(5)}); }
```
The seemingly extraneous fcn is necessary to prevent eager evaluation of the BigNum variable[76].

---

74 This adds no run time overhead but only works if Time.Date is available at compile time
75 See Keywords.var for why and how.
76 Another way to do this is to use `fcn f{ var b=Import("zklBigNum")(5)}` or use an initialization class (see Keywords.var)
```

Example: Delayed Thread Launch

Sometimes, you want to maybe create a thread. One example is to create the thread if a Pipe is written to.

```
class DeferredThread{
    fcn init{
        var [const] pipe=Thread.Pipe();
        returnClass( Deferred(fcn{self.launch(); pipe}) );
    }
    fcn liftoff{
        println("Thread launched!");
        pipe.close();
    }
}
reg pipe=DeferredThread();
...
if (something()) pipe.write(x);   // create thread
if (pipe.BaseClass.toBool())      // thread was created
    doSomethingWithPipe(pipe);
else pipe=Void;                   // thread not created
```

Note that if pipe is referenced, the thread will be created so be careful not to create it accidentally.

Closures, Partial Application

The Object methods fp* create closures[77] of a runnable over a set of parameters (ie the parameters are bound with/to the runnable). When the closure is called, the parameters in the closure call are appended to the bound parameters. For example:

```
    fcn f(x,y){...} fc:=f.fp(1); fc(2)  →  f(1,2)
```

These closures can be "stacked":

```
    fc1:=fcn f(x,y,z){...}.fp(1);
    fc2:=fc1.fp(2); fc3:=f2.fp(3);
    fc3()  →  fc2(3)  →  fc1(2,3)  →  f(1,2,3)
```

Partial.resolve works by looking at the underlying object, which is usually what you want. The .fp* methods resolve to Object.fp* because that is also what you want (this makes stacking work). However, this can be a problem and if it is, you'll need to be creative (BaseClass doesn't help you here). Note that resolve "tunnels under" the closed over parameters to the underlying object, thus something like fcn(n,a) {println(vm.arglist)}.fp(3).reduce(0,1) won't see the 3.

See Objects.Object.fp.

---

77 Probably more properly called Partial Application: http://en.wikipedia.org/wiki/Partial_application

Syntactic Sugar ('wrap)
Syntax: `'wrap(){…}`, `'wrap(x,y,z){…}`, `'wrap{}`
'wrap is used to create function closures over registers and parameters in the
enclosing scope. It can only be used as a parameter, or in assignment.
Functions can not access the registers and parameters in their enclosing
environments (they do not have lexical scope). Usually, this is easy to work around
by using static parameters or .fp. However, it can be annoying to type the same name
three times:

```
register:=5;
L(1,2,3).apply(fcn(n,register){ n+register },register);
```

Using 'wrap, the compiler will do this work for you:

```
register:=5; L(1,2,3).apply('wrap(n){ n+register });
```

These closures are not "leaky"; changing the closed over value does not change the
original (you can change the contents of containers). Variables are not closed as they
are always accessible [inside a function]. Default parameters are ignored.

Notes

- If you use recursion inside of a wrap, use `vm.pasteArgs` to pass the
  "invisible" closure data.
- Don't use the .fp methods with 'wrap; you won't know where second set of
  closed data is.
- Default parameters don't play well with 'wrap.

Dictionary

Full name: [TheVault.]Dictionary
Inherits from: Object
See Also: Objects.Small Dictionary

Abstract
A dictionary is an array that is indexed by keys that are not numbers (although numbers can be used). For example, if d is a dictionary, d["1"] and d[2] specify two locations in d.

Virtually any object can be a dictionary key. Integer and Float keys are converted to Strings and that is used as the key. So d["1"] and d[1] refer to the same location but d[1.0] is a different location. If the key doesn't convert to a string, its id is used as the key.

Dictionaries are also known as hash tables.

Dictionaries are thread safe.

Methods
- **add(** [*key value pairs* | *List of key/value pairs*] **)**: Does a self[key] = value for each of the parameter pairs.
  For example, d.add("1",2,"3",4) does the same thing as d["1"]=2; d["3"]=4;
  Throws: ValueError (odd number of parameters)
  Returns: self
- **appendV(** *key, value* **)**: Append *value* to the list associated with *key*. If *key* doesn't exist, it is created with value List(*value*). If *key*:value exists and value isn't a List, nothing happens.
  Returns: self
- **appendKV(** List(*key, value*) **)**: Same as **appendV(** kv.xplode() **)**.
  Returns: self
- **copy()**: Make a copy of the dictionary and return it. All entries are duplicated.
  Returns: Dictionary
- **create(** [*key value pairs* | *List of key/value pairs*] **)**: Creates a new Dictionary and optionally adds data to it.

Dictionary(1,2, "three","four") creates a Dictionary with keys "1" and "three" and values 2 and "four".

- To blow apart an HTTP query string into a dictionary[78]:
```
query:="GET /?value=50&action=Do+it HTTP/1.1";
query=query[query.index("?")+1,*]
        .split()[0].replace("+"," ");
```
  → "value=50&action=Do it"
```
query=query.split("&").apply("split","=");
```
  → L(L("value","50"),L("action","Do it"))
```
query=Dictionary(query);  → D(action:"Do it",value:"50")
```
- `Dictionary(L(L("key","value"),L(1,2)))` → D(key:value,1:2)

See also: add, extend

Throws: ValueError

Returns: The new Dictionary

- **del(**key**)**: The same as pop except it returns self.
Throws: AssertionError (dictionary is read only)
Returns: self
- **extend(***Dictionary | List of key/value pairs***)**: Add all the parameter entries to self. The added entries are not copied.
Returns: self
- **filter(**[f [,static parameters]]**)**:
Push key/value pairs through a filter and return a list of those items that pass (f(kv).toBool() is True).
Returns: ROList
- **filter1(**[f [,static parameters]]**)**:
Push key/value pairs through a filter and return the fist item that passes (f(kv).toBool() is True).
Returns: False | object
- **find(**key,defaultValue=Void**)**: Looks for self[key]
Returns: If key exists in self, self[key] is returned, else defaultValue is returned.
- **get(**key**)**: Synonym for __sGet
Throws: NotFoundError if Dictionary doesn't contain key.
Returns: The value stored at self[key].
- **holds(**key**)**:
Returns: True if self[key] exists, else False.
- **howza(**[mode]**)**: Set the format that walker, pump, etc will receive.

---

78 Well, sort of. Fields can have multiple values, be separated by ";" or "&" and be encoded.

mode	Consumer will receive:
0	Key,value pairs
8	Keys
9	Values

Returns: mode (Int) or self
- **incV(***key***)**: Increment the value associated with *key*. If *key* doesn't exist, it is created with value 1. If *key*:value exists and value isn't a Int, nothing happens. Returns: self
- **len()**: The number of keys in the Dictionary. Returns: Int
- **makeReadOnly()**: Freeze self. No further modifications are possible. Returns: self
- **pop(**key,defaultValue=Void**)**: Find and remove a key from the dictionary. If key isn't found, defaultValue is returned. Throws: AssertionError (dictionary is read only) Returns: deleted value
- **pump(**sink[,action ...]**)**: Another type of loop, similar to apply but with multiple actions. The first action is passed List(key,value) as the parameter. To "reverse" d (ie switch keys and values), this works (returning a new dictionary):
  ```
  d.pump(Dictionary(),"reverse")
  ```
  See also: Notes on the pump method at the start of this chapter. Returns: The last calculated value or a list of those values.
- **reduce(**f,*initialValue* [,parameters]**)**: A feedback loop which feeds key/value pairs to f. To stop the loop, return(Void.Stop) or return(Void.Stop,result). Returns: p
- **__sGet(**key**)**: Implements self[key]. Throws: NotFoundError if Dictionary doesn't contain key. Returns: The value stored at self[key].
- **__sSet(**key,value**)**: Implements self[key] = value Throws: Returns: value
- **toBool()**: Returns True if the dictionary contains any items. Returns: Bool
- **toDictionary()**: Returns: self
- **toList()**: Converts the Dictionary to a list of (key,value) pairs. Dictionary("key","value", 1,2).toList() → L(L("key","value"),L("1",2)) Returns: List of Lists

- **toString(***numItems***=N)**: Returns a String that contains the contents of the Dictionary. For example: `Dictionary(1,2,3,4).toString()` returns "D(1:2,3:4)". *NumItems* controls the number of items "stringized". The default is implementation defined, * is all items.
Returns: String
- **walker(n=0)**: Create a Walker that walks the key,value pairs.

n	walker.next() returns
0	Key,value pairs
8	Keys
9	Values

For example:
```
d:=Dictionary(1,2,  3,4);
foreach k,v in (d)
    { println(k,":",v) }  → "1:2" "3:4"
```
Note: Only read only Dictionaries support walkers.
Returns: Walker
- **write([***key value pairs* | *List of key/value pairs***])**: The same as add.
Throws: ValueError (odd number of parameters)
Returns: self

Properties
- **keys**: Returns a List of the Dictionary keys. The list is unordered. To get an ordered list, use `d.keys().sort()`;
Returns: List
- **values**: Returns a List of the Dictionary values. The list is unordered.
Returns: List

Operators: None

Acknowledgments
Dictionaries are based on dynamic hash tables as implemented by Esmond Pitt.

Exception

Full name:　　[TheVault.]Exception
Inherits from: Class
See also:　　　Keywords.throw, Keywords.try/catch

Abstract
The Exception class contains the Exception base classes as well as a core set of reference exception classes that are commonly encountered during programming.

All exceptions have to inherit from `Exception.Exception` or a child thereof.

You can throw any of the contained classes listed here, either the reference class or a new instance.

When creating your own exception classes, don't inherit from Exception, inherit from one of the contained classes, such as Exception.Exception, Exception.SyntaxError or Exception.KissOfDeath.

Use
To throw a reference class: `throw(Exception.IndexError)`
To throw a "customized" exception:
　　`throw(Exception.IndexError("Foo doesn't have 5 entries"))`
Read further for information on creating your own exceptions.

Contained classes
　　Base Classes
　● **`Exception()`**: Inherits from Class
　　Catchable: Yes
　　Class Variables
　　　● **`payload`**: User data.
　　　● **`text`**:　　Text describing this exception.
　　Functions
　　　● **`init(`**`text="An Exception"`**`)`**: Create a new Exception and sets text.
　　　● **`toString()`**: Returns descriptive text. For example:
　　　　`Exception.toString()` → "Exception(An Exception)"
　　　　`Exception.TypeError.toString()` → "TypeError(Invalid type)"
　　Discussion: The "generic" exception. Go ahead and throw an instance of this if nothing else fits and you don't want to create your own exception class.

Objects

- **KissOfDeath**(`exception`): Inherits from Exception.Exception
  The base class for uncatchable exceptions.
  Catchable: No
  Class Variables
    - **theException**: The exception that caused this exception to be thrown. Void for the reference class.
    - **Exception.text**: "Now is a good time to die"
  Functions
    - **init**(`exception`): Create a new KissOfDeath and set theException to the Exception that initiated this regrettable chain of events, or Void.
  Discussion: You can throw this exception but you can't catch it.

Uncatchable Exceptions
- **OSError**(`msg=Void`):   Inherits from Exception.KissOfDeath
- **OutOfMemory**(`msg=Void`): Inherits from Exception.KissOfDeath
- **VMError**(`msg=Void`):   Inherits from Exception.KissOfDeath

Catchable Exceptions
- **AsmError**(`msg=Void`): Inherits from Exception.Exception
  Indicates an assembler error, usually internal.
- **AssertionError**(`msg=Void`): Inherits from Exception.Exception
  An assertion of some type has failed.
- **BadDay**(`msg=Void`): Inherits from Exception.Exception
  A generic exception.
- **CompilerError**(`msg=Void`): Inherits from Exception.Exception
  Indicates a compiler error, usually internal.
- **FcnNotImplementedError**(`func`): Inherits from Exception.Exception
  This exception is useful when creating a virtual class or class with virtual functions. You can just cut and paste the function templates.
  Functions:
    - **init**(`f`): The function f is used to create a message that means something. For example:
    ```
    class C {
       fcn f {
          throw(Exception.FcnNotImplementedError(self.fcn));
       }
    }
    ```
    C.f() thows an Exception with the text set to
    "Class(C) (or parent): Fcn(f) not implemented"
- **Generic**(`msg=Void`): Inherits from Exception.Exception

The most generic of generic exceptions.

- **HeyYou**(`msg=Void`): Inherits from Exception.Exception
Used to kick another thread.
See Also: Objects.vm.kick
- **IndexError**(`msg=Void`): Inherits from Exception.Exception
The index or subscript is out of range.
- **IOError**(`msg=Void`): Inherits from Exception.Exception
There has been an IO error, usually at the OS level.
- **LoaderError**(`msg=Void`): Inherits from Exception.Exception
The loader has problems. For example, if System.loadFile("foo") can't find "foo".
- **MathError**(`msg=Void`): Inherits from Exception.Excpetion
Things like divide by zero.
- **MissingArg**(`msg=Void`): Inherits from Exception.Excpetion
A requested parameter isn't there.
- **Msg**(`payload`): Inherits from Exception.Excpetion
Pass a message via an exception. For example, bailing of out a [nested] method and preserving a result.
- **NameError**(`msg=Void`): Inherits from Exception.Exception
 Something is wrong with that name.
- **NotFoundError**(`msg=Void`): Inherits from Exception.Exception
Something, usually an object, was not found and it needed to be.
- **NotImplementedError**(`msg=Void`): Inherits from Exception.Exception
Homey don't do that.
- **PipeError**(`msg=Void`): Inherits from Exception.Exception
Thread.Pipe has issues.
- **StreamError**(`exception`): Inherits from Exception
Used to indicate an error in a Stream class.
  Class variables:
  - **throwed**: This holds the exception that reflects the underlying error or Void.
- **SyntaxError**(`errorMsg`, `badText`, `N=0`): Inherits from Exception.Exception
Used big time by the compiler suite (Compiler, Parser, Asm, Tokenizer). Error message is the a description of the syntax error, badText is the source code that caused the syntax error and N is the line number the bad text can be found at.
  Class Variables:
  - **lineNumber**: N
  - **textWithError**: badText

Examples:
- `throw(Exception.SyntaxError("Can't change foo",line));`
- `errormsg := "Can't change %s".fmt(name);`
  `text := "%d: %s".fmt(lineNumber,line);`
  `throw(Exception.SyntaxError(errormsg,text,lineNumber));`
- `foo.bar` might cause the compiler to throw
  `SyntaxError("Can't find \"foo\" (in foo.bar)").`

- **TheEnd(**`text`**)**: Inherits from Exception.Exception
  Indicates the end of something has been reached, such as a sequence or stream. Thrown by methods like read().
- **Timeout(**`msg=Void`**)**: Inherits from Exception.Exception
  The requested operation couldn't be complete in the allotted amount of time.
- **TypeError(**`msg=Void`**)**: Inherits from Exception.Exception
  The supplied parameter is the wrong type. For example, if an object can't be converted to the type needed to complete a calculation.
- **ValueError(**`msg=Void`**)**: Inherits from Exception.Exception
  Type is OK, but the value isn't. For example, if the allowed range is 0 to 5, a value of 10 might generate this exception.

Functions
- **init(**`text`**)**:
  Since creating an instance of Exception doesn't make a lot of sense and the instance would be huge, init just returns an instance of Exception.Exception assuming that is what you meant anyway.
  Example: `throw(Exception("Boom"))` is the same as
  `throw(Exception.Exception("Boom"))` and saves some typing.
  Returns: Exception.Exception(text)

Warning
- If you throw a reference class, don't set the class variables, you'll just screw it for up for everybody else.
- Inheriting from Exception is disallowed, inherit from Exception.Exception instead. The reason is Exception is a big class and contains all the reference classes and that can't be what you want.
  ```
  class MyError(Exception)            // throws SyntaxError
  class MyError(Exception.Exception)  // OK
  ```

Discussion
Creating your own exception class is easy. Here is the usual case:

```
class MyException(Exception.Exception){
   const TEXT = "My error message";
   text = TEXT;
   fcn init(msg=TEXT) { Exception.init(msg); }
   // whatever else you would like
}
```
We create our exception this way so the reference exception has the message we want it to have:
```
try{ throw(MyException)}
catch(MyException){ println(__exception) }
```
   → MyException(My error message)

This is quick, easy and faster than creating a new instance. Of course, `throw(MyException("Phooey"))` works just as well. Since constants are confined to the class they are created in, TEXT won't "contaminate" any other code.

Saying that the uncatchable exceptions are uncatchable is not strictly true. You can catch them, but, obviously, you shouldn't. The reason that they are catchable is so that things that HAVE to clean up after themselves can and for test classes.

Runtime Exception Verification

The VM verifies, at runtime, that the thrown exception is valid; that is, the thrown exception must

- Be a child of the Exception class. If the copy the of Exception class in the Vault is replaced, even with a copy of itself, you will no longer be able to throw a new exception.
- Text must be a string.

Payloads

Exceptions can be used for more than just signaling error conditions. They can also be used to break across nested loops (see throw) or carry a payload to the catcher. Consider this contrived example:
```
try{ L(1,2,3,"stop",4,5).apply2(f) }
catch(Msg)
   { println("The payload is: ",__exception.payload); }
fcn f(x){
   if (x == "stop"){
      e:=Exception.Msg("The magic eight ball says \"Hi!\"");
      throw(e);
   }
   println("f(%s)".fmt(x));
}
```
   → f(1)
     f(2)

f(3)
The payload is: The magic eight ball says "Hi!"

The crux of the problem is: How do we communicate out-of-band information from within apply/filter/walk/etc methods? Or any other deeply nested code? The apply method just goes, assuming that the entire dataset needs attention. If your problem doesn't fit within these strict parameters, things can get ugly fast. Exceptions with payloads adds flexibility to these methods without adding complexity to the methods themselves.

Fcn

Inherits from: Object
See also: Keywords.fcn,
                 Objects.VM.[arglist, argsMatch, nthArg, numArgs, pasteArgs]

Abstract
Functions are the containers that hold the program code you write to do something.

Fcn is the base class for all functions.

Functions are bound to a Class instance and will always refer to that instance when it needs to reference class variables, other functions, parents, etc.

Methods
- `copy()`
  Returns: self
- `defer([parameters])`: Returns `Deferred(self,parameters)`.
  Returns: Deferred
- `future(parameters)`: Create a new thread running self and return a result.
  Using the result blocks until the thread has finished running.
  `r:=fcn{123}.future(); println(r+1);` prints "124" when the thread is done. This is useful when you want to do multiple things concurrently but don't want to manage them.
  ```
  rocket:=Rocket().build.future();
  prepLaunchPad(); // build rocket & launch pad concurrently
  rocket.fire();   // launch when both are ready
  ```
  If things are more complicated and you have to get approval before launching:
  ```
  launchSite:=T(Rocket().build.future(),
                prepLaunchPad.future());
  launchSite.apply2("noop");   // wait for futures to arrive
  passInspection(launchSite); // get both inspected
  launchSite[0].fire();       // launch when approved
  ```
  This is a form of a data flow variable.
  Futures can be lazy: `r:=Deferred(f.future)` (or `f.future.defer()`) doesn't create the thread until r is used.
  `.noop()` can be used to "join" a future (ie wait for it to arrive).
  Here is a poorly written parallel quick sort[79]:

---

79 Very inefficient and uses way too many threads. The performance is truly abysmal.

```
        fcn pqsort(list){      // parallel quick sort
           if (not list) return(list);
           pivot:=list[0]; rest:=list[1,*];
           left,right:=rest.filter22('<),pivot);
           T.extend( self.fcn.future(left).noop(),
              pivot, self.fcn.future(right).noop());
        }
```

See also: launch, strand

Throws: If the thread does.

Returns: future (a Deferred)

- **isInstanceOf(f [,f …])**: Returns True if f is the same function as self. "Same" is loosely defined; two functions that have different class instances (and different ids) are considered equal.
Returns: Bool

- **launch(parameters)**: Creates a new thread running self.
`fcn(s){ println(s) }.launch("Hello world")` prints "Hello world" from a new thread and exits. A handy use of launch is to load and run something in the "background": `fcn{ Import("something") }.launch()`
Example: Spin a star like "I'm doing something" thing:

```
    fcn spin{  // a thread that displays the spinner
       try{
          foreach n,rod in ((1).MAX, "\\|/-"){
             print("  ",rod,"\r");
             Atomic.sleep(0.25);
          }
       }catch{} // don't complain about the
                // exception that stops thread
    }
    // main body of code
    spinner:=spin.launch(); // start spinner thread,
                            // returns reference to thread
    Atomic.sleep(10);     // do stuff
    // stop thread by throwing exception at it
    vm.kick(spinner.value);
```

See also: Objects.Class.launch, future

Returns: Ref(Void) and after thread starts Ref(VM), which is the thread.

- **strand(**parameters**)**: Create a cooperative thread running self and return a future. Strands[80] are light weight "green" threads. They are pre-emptive unless they call a blocking method, in which case they can block *all* strands. It is usually a bad idea for a Strand to create strand futures (as using the future can deadlock).
  A Strand can give up its time slice by calling yield (which doesn't set the future).
  See also: future, launch
  Throws: Yes
  Returns: future (a Deferred)
- **stranded(**key, parameters**)**: Create, or add to, a group of Strands, ie worker strands, strands that communicate via pipes or strands you track with other methods.
  Use like so:
  ```
  key=self.fcn.stranded(Void); // function does NOT run
  f.stranded(key,x,y,z);  // create one or more Strands
  ...
  key[0].waitFor(0);  // wait for Strands to finish or
  // Atomic.waitFor(fcn(key){ key[0]==0 or key[1] }.fp(key));
  ```
  - If any of the strands throws, the exception is stashed in *key*[1]. All strands [in the group] will stop running if this occurs.
  - You can stop all the strands in the group by setting the exception: *key*[1]=True.
  - The key count is the number of Strands *currently* running; if another process is adding strands (such a Strand), the count may go to zero before the group is actually done[81]. The count is only good when you know that all strands have been added to the group.
  Returns: Key (List(Atomic.Int, Exception | Void))
- **toBool()**:
  Returns: True
- **toString()**: Returns "Fcn(*name*)"
  Returns: String
- **unasm(**outputStream=Console**)**: Disassemble self and write the results to outputStream.
  Examples:
  ```
  Utils.range.unasm()        → Console
  self.fcn.unasm(L())        → List
  f.unasm(File("f.txt","w")) → File
  ```
  Returns: outputSream

---

80 Strands are built with fibers and use one or more threads to run them.
81 For example, a parallel quick sort.

Methods for Function Creation (used by compilers and loaders):
- **build**(`names`, `Asm.Code`, `defaultArgs=Void`, `private=False`):
  Create a function that can be added to a class embryo.

Parameter	Value
names	A list containing the function name followed by the names of each parameter (in order). For example, the names for fcn f(a,b,c) is L("f","a","b","c"). The number of parameters is calculated from this list.
Asm.Code	The machine code for this function. This is a class (Objects.Compiler.Asm.Code).
defaultArgs	If Void, no defaults. Otherwise, it is a list of Void or Asm.Code objects. Again, Void if that parameter doesn't have a default. The list has to be the same length as the number of parameters.
private	True if the function should be marked private. Private means that, when this function is added to a class, class.resolve won't find it. Among other things, it won't be found with late binding.

  The container property is set to NullClass.
  A function is not runnable until it has been added to a class (which sets the container property). Unless it is a static function.
  See also: Objects.Class.addFcn, Objects.Class.embryo.
  Throws: TypeError, ValueError
  Returns: Fcn

Properties
- **attributes**: Returns a space separated list of attributes. Attribute names are "static" and "private".
  Returns: String
- **code**: Returns the machine code for this function.
  Returns: Asm.Code Class
- **container**: The class that this function is bound to.
  Returns: Class
- **defaultArgs**: Returns the machine code for the parameters. If there is no default for a parameter, Void is returned.
  Returns: List of Void or Asm.code
- **fullName**: Returns "*instanceName.name*". For example, `self.fcn.fullName` might return "RootClass#.__constructor".
  Returns: String

- **idFcn**: Returns `fcn idFcn(x){ return(x) }`
  Note: The idFcn is runnable.
  Returns: Fcn(idFcn)
- **isPrivate**: Returns True is self was created private.
  Returns: Bool
- **isRunnable**: Returns True is self can run. Functions that have not been added
  to a class may not be runnable, static functions always are.
  Returns: Bool
- **isStatic**: Returns True is self was created static. Static functions do NOT
  reference any instance data (but can have side effects). A static function is
  always runnable. The assembler makes the call about static-ness.
  Class static-ness has no effect on function static-ness.
  Returns: Bool
- **name**: Returns "Fcn(*name*)"
  Returns: String
- **nullFcn**: Returns a function that does just about nothing except return its
  class instance, which is usually the NullClass. It can be used as a class
  constructor. This one is bound to the NullClass but will change when
  Class.addFcn makes a copy and adds it.
  Warning: The nullFcn is not runnable until it has been added to a class.
  Returns: Fcn(nullFcn)
- **prototype**: Returns a list of the names of the parameters.
  Returns: Read-only list of Strings.

Operators: None

Discussion

Instance Variables
If you use "var" in a function, you are probably going to be surprised – these
variables last the lifetime of the function, which is the life time of the class the
function is in[82]. This is very unlike a function variable (automatics) in a language
such as C, where the life time is as long as the function is running (use reg if you
want that behavior). You can think of vars as "static" (or state) vars, they don't revert
to their old values as the a recursive function unwinds.
When you initialize a function variable as part of "var", that initialization is moved
to the class constructor, thus the variable is reset to it's initial value each time a new
class instance is created.

---

82 And in fact, fcn variables are just syntactic sugar for anonymous class variables.

Objects

```
    fcn f{ var v=5; v+=1 } do(3){ print(f()," ") } → 6 7 8
```
You can not access function variables or registers from outside a function (the init
function is special, see Keywords.var).
"reg" variables act like C automatics.

Thread Safety

Functions are thread safe (re-entrant) by design. However, that goes out the window
when a function refers to a global resource (that is, a resource outside the function,
such as a instance variable in the enclosing class OR a function instance
variable).This can be most inconvenient. Consider:

```
    class C{ var cv;
        fcn f(x)
            { x==cv }  // not thread safe, cv is a global resource
    }
```

The next case is not so clear:

```
    fcn f(list,nm){ var x; x=nm;
        duplicates:=list.filter(fcn(y){ x==y });
    }
```
First, transform this as the compiler does (functions don't actually contain functions
or variables):

```
    var x;
    fcn f(list,nm){ x=nm; duplicates:=list.filter(g); }
    fcn g(y){ x==y }
```
We see that the filter function (g) actually refers to a class variable, which is
essentially global. If multiple threads were to call f at the same time, g would get
confused (because f.x is changing out from under it). This also shows why
anonymous functions can't refer to parameters in their parent functions: they aren't
actually part of their parent functions; they are in a different scope.
If you have to use a var, the solution is to use locks:

```
    fcn f(list,nm){
        critical{
            var x; x=nm;
            duplicates:=list.filter(fcn(y){ x==y });
            return(duplicates);
        }
    }
```
However, an much better solution is to rethink the problem and get rid of variables:

```
    fcn f(list,nm){
        duplicates:=list.filter(fcn(y,x){ x==y },nm);
    }
```
Which can be shortened to:

```
    fcn f(list,nm){ list.filter('==,nm); }
```

Remember that registers are always thread safe.

Function Creation

We'll create two simple functions to give you an idea of what the compiler does to create a function. This isn't something you'll want to do very often or at all. If you want to create functions "on the fly", it is usually much easier to use the compiler to compile up a snippet of source code (`Compiler.Compiler.compileText(src)`).

Warnings
- The VM *really* wants functions to reside in a class. To have been *added* to its containing class, not just having its container set. Building a function and having it sit around is fine, but running the function is not and the VM may refuse to run a function that hasn't been added to a class.
- Except if the function is static. Static functions don't need to be in a class and are always runnable.
- If the function code refers to class data (eg variables), it had better be correct and in sync with the class embryo. Otherwise, data corruption and VM crashes will result.

Function Creation: First example: `fcn f{ println("Hello World!"); }`
Since this is a function that is completely self contained, it is a static function[83] and doesn't need to be stored in a Class, which makes things simpler.
Step one, we need the parts that are used to build the function. The hard part, by far, is the code. So let's cheat and use existing code:
```
fcn f{ println("Hello World!") }
code:=f.code;  → Class(__Code#)
```
Now we can create the function:
```
e:=self.fcn.build(    // any function can build a function
    T("f"),           // named "f", no parameters
    code);            // code, no defaults, not private
  → Fcn(f)
```
We are actually done! Since this simple function has no parameters and no variables, we don't have anything to add. Let's test:
```
e() → "Hello World!"
```
Nice!

Function Creation: Second example: `fcn f(n){ return(n + 123); }`
This time, we use machine code but we'll still let the compiler generate code and we'll copy it.

---

83 Use the isStatic property to verify this: `f.isStatic` → True

Objects

```
fcn f(n){ return(n + 123); }.unasm() →
    Fcn: f  [static] (class: Cmd)
    Prototype: L("n")
    Code for default arg 0:
        No default
    Code (code: 7 bytes, strings: 0 bytes)
        0:210 arg0
        1:100 push
        2:203 IntB(123)
        4:102 setX/pop
        5: 70 add
        6:  0 done
```

First, let's create the function code. Each line of code is separated by a newline (or we could use a list)[84]:

```
src:="argN(0)\n"    // parameter 0==n
     "push\n"       // push n onto the stack
     "Int(123)\n"   // create integer
     "setX/pop\n"   // put 123 into the X register
                    // and pop n to the R register
     "add\n"        // R=R + X==n + X
     "done\n";      // all done, return R
```

Assemble the code:

```
code:=Compiler.Asm.asm(src);    → Class(__Code#)[85]
```

Now, create the function:

```
f:=self.fcn.build(L("f","x"),code);    // fcn f(x)
```

Does it work? `f(5)` → 128
Yes!

Function Creation: Third Example: A Class

To beat this horse some more, and to give one more example than promised, let's look at an example where the instance is really important:

```
class C{
    var N=5;
    fcn f(n){ return(N + n); }
}
```

In this case, the function has to access N, a variable in its class instance. And, since f references instance data, it can't be static.

---

84 Our code is slightly different because the assembler optimizes to produce smaller code; our manual code is more general and a little less prone to errors. We could use the original code verbatim however.

85 If you want to disassemble a Asm.Code class, use `code.unasm()` or
`Compiler.Asm.disCode(f.code)`

I'll skip over the "how" of where the code comes from, but, as a hint, classes also support the "unasm" method.

First, create a Class embryo with two functions ("__constructor" and "f") and one variable: `classC:=self.embryo(L("C","","N"),2,0,0);`

The function code for __constructor:

```
constructorSrc :=
    "Int(5)\n"        // int 5
    "setVar(0)\n"     // set instance variable 0
    "self\n"          // return self
    "done\n";
```

Create the constructor:

```
cf:=self.fcn.build(L("__constructor"),
        Compiler.Asm.asm(constructorSrc));
```

and add it to the class: `classC.addFcn(cf,0);`

Now, repeat for function f:

```
fSrc:="argN(0)\n"    // R=first parameter (n)
        "setX\n"         // X=n
        "getVar(0)\n"  // R=first instance variable (N)
        "add\n"          // R=R + X==N + n
        "done\n";        // return R
ff:=self.fcn.build(L("f","n"),Compiler.Asm.asm(fSrc));
classC.addFcn(ff,1);
```

Now, finish up, run the constructor and test:

```
classC=classC.cook();
classC.__constructor(); classC.f(10) → 15
```

Or: `classC().f(15) → 20`

File

Full name: [TheVault.]File
Inherits from: Stream, Object

Abstract
The File object knows about files stored on mass storage devices.

Methods
- `ask()`: Same as readln.
- `close()`: Flush the file and close it. When writing to a file, the contents might not make it to the media until the file is flushed or closed.
  Once a File object has been closed, you can not read from it, write to it or reopen it. You can, of course, recreate a new File pointing at the same file. When a File is garbage collected, close is called[86].
  Throws:
  Returns: self
- `create(filename, mode="r")`: See **open**.
  Throws: IOError, NameError
  Returns: File
- `flush()`: Send all in-memory data to media.
  Throws:
  Returns: self
- `howza()`: Return the current value.
  Returns: Int
- `howza([int])`: Howza determines the default way data streams out of File (by filter, pump, reduce and walker). The initial value is 1 (lines).
  See walker for values.
  Returns: self or Int
- `info()`: Returns information about the file opened by **open**.
- `info(fileName)`: Returns information about a file.
  Returns the file size (same as len()), file last status change time and the last modification time. The times can be converted to time and date with `Time.Clock.tickToTock` and back with `Time.Clock.mktime`.
  Throws: NameError, IOError

---

86 Which means you don't (usually) need to explicitly call close(). But that can be considered bad practice. Especially if you re-open the file later as then you could be "competing" with the garbage collector (over a global resource); GC might flush a file buffer on top of you.

Returns: List(file size, creation time, last modification time, True if a directory)

- **len()**: Returns the number of bytes in the file opened by **open**.
- **len(**fileName**)**: Returns the number of bytes in file.

Note that if you read the file, you might get a different number of bytes. This is because text files may have their line terminators changed (Windows mostly).

Throws: NameError, IOError

Returns: Int

- **open(**filename, mode="r"**)**: Open a file.

Mode is whatever C's fopen supports:

Mode	Action
"r"	Open a text file for reading. Might do "text file" end of line conversions.
"rb"	Open a file in binary mode.
"w"	Create text file for writing. If file exists, it is cleared.
"wb"	Create file in binary mode.
"a", "ab"	Open or create [text] file for appending.
"r+", "r+b"	Open [text] file for update: reading and writing
"w+", "w+b"	Create binary file for update.
"a+", "a+b"	Open or create a file for appending and updating

Both forward ("Dir/foo.txt" and back slashes ("Dir\\foo.txt") work on Windows but remember to quote back slashes in constants or use raw strings (0'|Dir\foo.txt|).

Throws: IOError, NameError

Returns: File

- **print(**string, …**)**: Same as **writeln** without the newline
- **printpn(**string, …**)**: Same as **writeln**.
- **read(), read(***)**: Read the entire file (starting from last read)
- **read(**numBytes**)**:   Read up to numBytes from file.
- **read(**numBytes|*,data**)**: Read into a user created Data

Read bytes from a file into a Data.

d:=Data(N); f.read(M,d); reads min(f.size,N,M) bytes into d (overwriting). Note that N is just a hint to Data.create so it may actually be different.

Returns: Data

- **read(**numBytes|*,data,throw=True**)**: Same as above, except TheEnd isn't thrown if throw is False.

This is for loops like:

```
out,f,buf := Sink(String), File("forth.blk","rb"), Data(1024);
while(blk:=f.read(1024,buf,False)){
  blk.walker(3).chunk(64,String).pump(out,"strip",'+("\n"));
}
// blk is empty here. Without throw==False,
// TheEnd would have been thrown
```
Returns: Data

- **read1()**: Read one byte.
Throws: TheEnd, IOError
Returns: Int
- **readln()**: Read one line and return it as a string.
- **readln(*)**: Read the entire file into a list.
- **readln(*numLines*)**: Read up to *numLines* and return them in a list.
    - If *numLines* is <= 0, returns L().
    - If *numLines* can't be read (because there aren't that many lines left in the file), as many as can be read are returned.

Comments
    - If no lines can be read (because we are at the end of the file), TheEnd is thrown.
    - If a line ends with a newline, it stays with the line. The last line in a file is the one that might not end with a newline.

Throws: TheEnd, ValueError
Returns: List, String

- **toBool()**: Returns True if self is connected to an open file.
Returns: Bool
- **toString()**: Returns "File(*fileName*)"
Throws:
Returns: String
- **walker()**: Returns a Stream Walker using readln. This allows you to iterate over a file line by line. The following prints each line in a file, one line at a time:
```
foreach line in (File("foo.txt")){ println(line); }
```
- **walker(n=1)**:

n	walker.next() returns
0	Int (one byte)
1	String, one line at a time using readln
2	Same as 1
3	String, one character at a time.
11	Same as 1 plus white space stripped from right side
12	Same as 11

Returns: Walker
- **write(**data, …**)**: Write data to a file (assuming it has been opened for writing). The total number of bytes written is returned. The following data types are supported:

Object	Action
Data	Write all bytes in data
Int	Write the integer as a byte stream. Endianess is undefined and may change from computer to computer.
List	Recursively writes the list contents. If the list is circular, the recursion is infinite.
String	Write the string bytes, excluding the trailing \0

Throws: TypeError
Returns: Int
- **writeln(**string, …**)**: Write one or more strings to the file. A newline (or carriage return and newline) is appended after the last string is written. If a parameter isn't a string, it is converted to one, if possible.
The following shows a difference between write and writeln:
```
f:=File("foo.txt","w");
d:=L("one","two");
f.writeln(d); f.write(d);
f.close();
```
Contents of foo.txt:
```
L("one","two")
onetwo
```
Returns: self

Utility Methods

- **delete(**fileName**)**: Delete the file named *filename*.
Throws: IOError
Returns: Bool
- **exists(**fileName**)**: Checks to see if fileName is the name of a "regular" file.
Returns: Bool
- **filter(**[f [,static parameters]]**)**:
Stream the file through a filter and return a list of those things that pass (f(line).toBool() is True).
howza determines how the file contents are streamed.
Returns: ROList
- **glob(**wildCardPattern,flags=0**)**: Match file names.
- **glob(**Data,flags=0**)**: See next entry.

The pattern is the same as used by UNIX shells:

Pattern	Matches
\x	Turns off the special meaning of x and matches it directly; this is used mostly before a question mark or asterisk, and has no special meaning inside square brackets.
?	Matches any single character.
*	Matches any sequence of zero or more characters.
[x...y] [x-y] [x-y-] [-...] []] []x...y] []-] []x-]	Matches any single character specified by the set x...y, where any character other than dash or close bracket may appear in the set. Exceptions: "]" can be the first character in the set and "-" can be the last, if you use both. Otherwise, either can be first. "[" is not special inside the set, so "[[]]" and "[a-z[]" will match "[" A **dash** may be used to indicate a range of characters. That is, [0-5abc] is shorthand for [012345abc]. More than one range may appear inside a character set; [0-9a-zA-Z._] matches almost all of the legal characters for a host name. [-], [x...y-] and [-a-z] all match "-". [[-]], []-a-z] are undefined. [\] matches "\".
[^x...y] [^]]	This matches any character not in the set x...y, which is interpreted as described above. ^ is only special as the first character.

Examples:
- Match all files with ".txt" extension: "*.txt"
- Match all C files that start with "t" in the VM directory:
  `File.glob("VM/t*.c")` → L("VM/thread.c","VM/typeTable.c")
- `File.glob(*)` is the same as `File.glob("*")` and matches all files in the current directory.
- Directories are indicated with a trailing "/":
  `File.glob(*)` → L("Bin/","Src/","Tests/","testThemAll.log","VM/")
- Windows understands "/" but if you want to use back slashes ("\"), use raw strings: `File.glob(0'|VM\*.c|)` to keep back slash from quoting the next character (in this case, the pattern would become "VM*.c"). Or double quote ("VM*.c") or concatenate (0'|VM\| "*.c").
- glob("/") always produces "/".
- glob does inline expansions. For example,
  `File.glob("[ST]*",0x10)` might produce L("Src/","Tests/","Tmp/")

and `File.glob("[ST]*/T*/*.zkl")` might produce
L("Src/Test/testThemAll.zkl", "Src/Time/date.zkl").

The flags. Flag constants are in zkl.h.zkl. They can be combined.

Flag	Meaning
FILE.GLOB. ONLY_ONE (1)	Return the first match.
FILE.GLOB. NO_PATH (2)	Don't prepend any path information to the matched file name.
FILE.GLOB. NO_TRAILING_SLASH (4)	Don't add a trailing slash to matched directories. "/" still yields "/".
FILE.GLOB. NO_DIRS (8)	Don't match directories.
FILE.GLOB. ONLY_DIRS (0x10)	Only match directories.
FILE.GLOB. IGNORE_CASE (0x20)	Unix only (Windows always ignores case). Case is ignored when doing wild card expansions. ONLY the name segments that contain \, ?, *, [or] case fold. For example, in "Src/foo\\.zkl", "Src" has to be exact but "foo.zkl" folds.

This method uses the "wildmat" pattern matching code written by Rich $alz.
Throws:
Returns: List of file/directory names.

- **glob(**`Data`, `flags=0`**)**: As above, only the Data holds a list of patterns. Concisely: `Data(0, String, "p1", "p2", "p3"…)`, and what matches is (p1 and (p2 or p3 …)).
  First glob(p1) and then one of p2 or p2 … has to glob. P1 matches path and name, p_n just match names.
  So, to get all music files in the current directory:
  ```
  File.glob(Data(0,String,
      "*","*.mp3","*.wma","*.ogg"),0x20)
  ```
- **globular(**`startingDirectory`, `wildCardPattern`, `recurse=True`, `flags=FILE.GLOB.NO_DIRS`, `out=Data(0,String)`**)**: Match file names. Basically a recursive (or not) glob. Starting at *startingDirectory* (which can be a pattern that matches more than one directory), finds all the files that match the pattern and glob flags. As the files are found, they are fed to *out*. See Objects.Sink for what out can be (`Sink.write(out)` is called). *out* is closed.

Examples:
- To get all the zkl files under the Src directory:
  `File.globular("Src","*.zkl")`
  `File.globular("Src","*.zkl").toList()`
- To get the above as a list:
  `File.globular("Src","*.zkl",True,8,L())`
- To find all the directories in, and below, the current directory:
  `File.globular(".","*",1,0x10)`
- A slightly more refined example:
  `File.globular("[LZ]*","*",0,0x10,L())` → L("LZO/Release/",
  "ZeeLib/Debug/", "ZeeLib/Release/") as the starting directories
  evaluate to L("LZO/", "ZeeLib/") (which you can evaluate with
  `File.glob("[LZ]*",0x10)`).
- `File.globular(".","*.c")` writes the names of all C files under the
  current directory to a Data (null terminated) and returns the Data. You
  can look at this with reduce or foreach.
- `pipe:=Thread.Pipe(); givePipeToThread(pipe);`
  `File.globular(".","*.c",True,0,pipe)` each of the matching C
  file names is written to the pipe. This is handy if you want to find files
  in this thread and process them in another thread.
- Post process: `globular(…,fcn(name){ })`. Calls a Fcn/Method for
  each match.
  Eg `File.globular(".","z*h",False,0,`
  `              fcn(nm){ println(nm) })`

  Returns: What `Sink(out).close()` returns
- **info(**fileName**)**: Returns info about a file. See info in the Methods section.
- **isDir(**directoryName**)**: Checks to see if directoryName is the name of a
  directory.
  Returns: Bool
- **len(**fileName**)**: Returns the number of bytes in file. See len in the section
  above.
- **mkdir(**path [,permissions=777 (octal)]**)**: Make a directory.
  Throws: IOError
  Returns: True (directory created), False (path exists, might not be a directory)
- **mkdir_p(**path,verbose=False**)**: Make all directories in path.
  Throws: IOError
  Returns: True
- **mktmp()**: Make a file in a "safe" way. The name starts with "zklTmpFile".
  See Also: `System.popen`
  Throws: IOError

Returns: File

- **pump(**sink[, action ...]**)**:
  Another type of loop, similar to apply but with multiple actions. The calls are
  `r=a₁(readln()); r=a₂(r); r=a₃(r) ...`
  An example: Given a CSV file that looks like:
      02/12/13,11:59 AM,139,75,50,,,
      02/12/13,06:30 PM,133,78,46,,,
  that needs to be read into a list that looks like:
      L(L("02/12/13",11.98,"139","75","50","\n"),
        L("02/12/13",18.50,"133","78","46","\n")
  (a list of lines with the time converted to a float), this works:
  ```
  csv:=File.open("in.csv","r").pump(List,
      fcn(a){a.split(",").filter()},  //line to list
      fcn([(_,t)]v){v.set(1,     //modify time: t:=v[1]
          Time.Date.parseTime(t) : //text to (H,M,S)
          Time.Date.toFloat((_).xplode())) }); // to float
  ```
  If a file to file conversion (ie write results to a file) is desired, use the write
  method as the last action. For example, to uppercase a file:
  ```
  File("in.txt")
      .pump(Void,"toUpper",File("out.txt","w").write)
  ```
- **pump(**Data([N]),sink[,action ...]**)**: Use Data a reusable buffer.
  Does NOT drop nulls.
- **pump(**N, action [, ...]**)**: Create an internal Data buffer of size N.
  If **Data()** is used, it signifies use the **read** method, ie read bytes into a Data
  and pass that to the actions. This can be useful if you are copying lots of files
  and want to minimize allocations.
  Note: The Data is used as buffer and is reused [after running all the actions].
  So, if you store the data, be sure to make a copy.
  Note: .pump(**Data()**, ...) is different from .pump(**Data**, ...)! In the latter
  case, a new Data is created to be used as the sink, ie it is the same as
  .pump(Data().write, ...).
  For example, to copy one file to another, you could use:
  ```
  fin,fout:=File(srcName,"rb"), File(dstName,"wb");
  fin.pump(Data(0d524_287),fout); fin.close(); fout.close();
  ```
  Using the upper case example:
  ```
  File("in.txt").pump(Data(1000),
      File("out.txt","w"),"text","toUpper")
  ```
  Note: If you actually want a Data as the sink, use .pump(Data, ...) or
  d:=Data(); file.pump(d.write, ...)

N is basically the Data example but with a fixed size read (since Data
creation uses the size only as a hint).

howza determines how the file contents are streamed.

See also: Notes on the pump method at the start of this chapter.
Returns: The last calculated value or a list of those values.

- **reduce(** f, *initialValue*=self.readln() [,parameters]**)**: A feedback
  loop which runs f until the end of the file is reached. The calls are:
      p:=*initialValue*;
      p=f(p,self.readln(),parameters);
      p=f(p,self.readln(),parameters);
      ...
  To stop the loop, return(Void.Stop) or return(Void.Stop,result).
  To print a file with line numbers:
      File("data.c","r").reduce(fcn(n,line)
          {print("%d: %s".fmt(n,line)); n+1},1)
      →
  1: /* data.c : the Data object : A container of bytes
  2: * Supports both Stream and Sequence semantics
  3: * Acts as a bunch of strings, lines or just a jumble of bytes.
      ...
  Find the length of the longest line in a file:
      File("foo.txt").reduce(
          fcn(len,line){line.len().max(len)},0)
  howza determines how the file contents are streamed.
  Returns: p

- **rename(** oldPath,newPath **)**: Rename/move a file or directory.
  Throws: IOError
  Returns: True

- **searchFor(** filename, pathList=System.classPath, globIt=False **)**:
  Look for a file (first, see if *fileName* exists), and, if it doesn't, search for it
  along a list of paths (use T for no paths). Optionally, *fileName* can contain
  glob wild cards (if *globIt* is an integer (zero for the default glob)).
  Returns Void if not found, otherwise a name that can be used in open.

  For example, searchFor("compiler.zkl") might return Void because the
  Compiler directory isn't on the classPath but
  searchFor("Compiler/compiler.zkl") would return
  "C:/ZKL/Src/Compiler/compiler.zkl" because "C:/ZKL/Src" is. Likewise,
  searchFor("compiler.zkl",L("C:/ZKL/Src/Compiler")) finds the file.
  If *globIt* is an integer, it turns on wild card matching and *globIt* is used as the
  glob flags (which are ORed with FILE.GLOB.NO_DIRS and

FILE.GLOB.ONLY_ONE). To use just these defaults, use a *globIt* of 0.
`searchFor("C*/Compiler.z*", System.classPath,`
`FILE.GLOB.IGNORE_CASE)` will find "Compiler/compiler.zsc" or
"Compiler/compiler.zkl" since both are on the class path (ignore case is only
needed on Unix systems, Windows always ignores case in file names). A wild
card in a chunk triggers glob matching for that chunk, matching is per file
element (ie the chunk between slashes has to have a wild character).
Returns: String, Void

- **setModTime(**name,time_t**)**: Set the modification time on a file.
  See also: `info`, `Time.Clock.mktime`
  Returns: Bool
- **splitFileName(**fileName**)**: Split a file name into parts:
  Behaves differently on Unix and Windows (Unix doesn't have drive, set to
  "").
  Assumes the file name is valid (eg from `glob`).

[0]	Drive or locator	"", "C:" (Windows), "\\NAS"
[1]	Path	"", "/", "/Dir/"
[2]	File name (exclusive of extension)	"foo", "" (eg "ZKL/")
[3]	Extension	".txt", ""

Examples:
- `"fred.txt"` → `L("","","fred",".txt")`
- `"fred"` → `L("","","fred","")`
- `"foo/fred.txt"` → `L("","foo/","fred",".txt")`
- `"foo/./fred.txt"` → `L("","foo/","fred",".txt")`
- `"foo/."` → `L("","foo/",".","")`
- `"../foo/../fred.txt"`→`L("","../foo/../","fred",".txt")`

Throws: IOError
Returns: List of Strings

Properties
- **eof**: Returns True if the open file is at End of File.
  Throws: IOError
- **fileName**: Returns the name of the file.
  Returns: String
- **stderr**: The standard error file. Usually Console but can be redirected with
  the normal command line controls.
- **stdin**: The standard input file. You can read this but not close or write to it.
  Usually Console but can be redirected with the normal command line
  controls.

Objects

- **stdout**: The standard output file. Usually Console but can be redirected with the normal command line controls.

Discussion

Tricks
If you are given a list of file name patterns (eg "*.[ch]") and want to expand that into a single list of file names, you can use:

```
names.reduce(
    fcn(list,name){ list.extend(File.glob(name)); }, L());
```

For example, names=L("*.[ch]") might expand to L("allocate.c", "memory.h", "void.c").

Since files are closed when they are garbage collected, you usually don't need to manually close them. However, you don't know when that will actually occur. You can ensure a file is closed by using critical. For example:

```
var file=File("foo.txt","r");
critical(file,noop,close){
    while(1) {file.readln().print()}
}
```

will read from foo.txt until the end of the file is reached (which throws TheEnd) and then close the file. OnExitBlock can also do this.

File.DevNull

Full name: [TheVault.]File.DevNull
Inherits from: Stream
See Also: Objects.Thread.DrainPipe

Abstract
A helper class. Use this if you want a "no nothing" file or console stub

Discussion
If you are optionally writing to a stream (such as a log file), you don't want to always test to see if you should or should not write to the stream:

```
var logFile;
if (loggingTurnedOn) logFile=File(name,"w");
if (loggingTurnedOn) logFile.writeln("This is too much work");
```

Instead, you can stub the log file, set it to the real file if you are logging to file and pretend you are always logging to a file:

```
var logFile=File.DevNull();
if (loggingTurnedOn) logFile=File(name,"w");
logfile.writeln("Much better");
```

Float

Inherits from: Object

Abstract
Floating point numbers. Floats are immutable, that is, they don't change. You "change" them by creating new ones (usually indirectly).

The compiler recognizes the following format for float constants (from Microsoft Visual C++ documentation):
> [-] [digits] [.digits] [e | E [-] digits]
> Digits are one or more decimal digits. If no digits appear before the decimal point, at least one must appear after the decimal point. The decimal digits may be followed by an exponent, which consists of an introductory letter (e, or E) and an optionally signed decimal integer.

In additon, "_" can be used as a separator: 1_234.5 == 1234.5

Terms
- *Value* refers to the numeric value of self.

Methods
- **abs()**: Returns the absolute value of *value*.
  Returns: Float(abs(*value*))
- **ceil()**: Returns the smallest integral value not less than *value*.
  Returns: $\lceil value \rceil$
- **clamp(***min, max***)**: Returns the closest value in the range [*min,max*].
  Returns: Float
- **closeTo(***n, tolerence***)**: Returns ((*value-n*).abs() <= *tolerance*). Yes, the sign of *tolerance* matters.
  Returns: Bool
- **copy()**:Returns self. Since Floats are immutable, self is equivalent to a copy.
  Returns: self
- **create(***x=self***)**: Create a Float with *value* set to x.
  Returns: Float
- **floor()**: Returns the largest integral value not greater than *value*.
  Returns: $\lfloor value \rfloor$
- **hypot(***x***)**: Calculate the hypotenuse of a right triangle where the two right angle legs are *value* and x.
  Returns: $\sqrt{value^2 + x^2}$

- **max(**ints or floats**)**: Returns the maximum of self and the parameters.
  Returns: Float
- **max(**list**)**: Returns the maximum of the contents of the list.
  Returns: Float
- **min(**ints or floats**)**: Returns the minimum of self and the parameters.
  Returns: Float
- **min(**list**)**: Returns the minimum of the contents of the list.
  Returns: Float
- **pow(**x**)**: $value^f$
  x is a float (either explicitly or by conversion).
  Error if:
    - $value{=}{=}0.0$ and $x{\le}0$
    - $value{<}0.0$ and x is not an integer value
  Throws: MathError
  Returns: $value^x$
- **random(**top**)**: Returns a uniformly distributed number in [*value*,top) (ie may equal *value* but won't equal top).
  Returns: Float
- **round()**:
  Returns: Float
- **sqrt()**: Square root
  Throws: MathError if *value*<0
  Returns: $\sqrt{value}$
- **toBool()**: Returns True if *value* is non zero, otherwise, False.
  Returns: Bool
- **toFloat()**:
  Returns: self
- **toInt()**: Convert *value* to an integer.
  Returns: Int
- **toString(**precision=6, format="g"**)**: Convert *value* to a string and return it.
  Precision is maximum number of digits after the decimal point.
  Format is one of (you'll recognize these from C's printf):
    - "f":   [-]mmm.ddd
    - "eE": [-]m.dddE±nn
    - "gG": Use "e" or "f" format depending on which "fits" best.
  Examples:
    - (1.23456789).toString()   → 1.23457
    - (1.23456789).toString(2,"f") → 1.23
    - (1234567.89).toString(6,"e") → 1.234568e+006

Throws: ValueError
Returns: String

Degrees/Radians Methods

- **toDeg()**: Convert *value* (expressed in radians) to degrees.
  Returns: $value \times 180.0/\pi$
- **toRad()**: Convert *value* (expressed in degrees) to radians.
  Returns: $value \times \pi/180.0$
- **toPolar(y)**: Convert rectangular coordinates (x,y) to polar coordinates (r,angleInRadians). *Value* is x.
  Returns: $L(r, angle) == L(\ \sqrt{value^2 + y^2}, \tan^{-1}\dfrac{value}{y}\ )$
- **toRectangular(angleInRadians)**: Convert polar coordinates (r,angle) to rectangular coordinates. *Value* is r.
  Returns: $L(x,y) == L(\ value \times \cos(angle), value \times \sin(angle)\ )$

Trig Methods

- **cos()**: Cosine. *Value* is in radians.
  Returns: cos(*value*)
- **acos()**: Arc cosine.
  Returns: cos⁻¹(*value*)
- **sin()**: Sine. *Value* is in radians.
  Returns: sin(*value*)
- **asin()**:
  Returns: sin⁻¹(*value*)
- **tan()**: Tangent. *Value* is in radians.
  Returns: tan(*value*)
- **atan()**: Arc tangent.
  Returns: tan⁻¹(*value*)
- **tan2(x)**: Calculate the principal value of the arc tangent of self/x, using the signs of the two arguments to determine the quadrant of the result.
  Returns: A value in $[-\pi, \pi]$.

- **sinh()**: Hyperbolic sine.
  Returns: sinh(*value*))
- **cosh()**: Hyperbolic cosine.
  Returns: cosh(*value*)
- **tanh()**: Hyperbolic tangent.
  Returns: tanh(*value*)

Other Methods

- **exp()**: e^n, where n is *value*.
  Returns: e^{value}
- **log()**: Natural logarithm of *value* (log base e) for *value* > 0.
  Throws: MathError
  Returns: $\log_e(value)$ aka ln(value)
- **log10()**: $\log_{10}(value)$ for *value* > 0.
  Throws: MathError
  Returns: $\log_{10}(value)$

- **frexp()**: C's frexp.
  Throws:
  Returns: L(normalized fraction, power of 2)
- **modf(**fractionalPartAlwaysPositive=False**)**: Split *value* into two parts: the part left of decimal point (integer part) and the part to the right of the decimal (fractional part).
  Examples:
  ```
  (1.23).modf()       → L(1,0.23)
  (-1.23).modf()      → L(-1,-0.23)
  (-1.23).modf(True)  → L(-1,0.23)
  ```
  Returns: L(integer part, fractional part)

Properties

- **e**: $e \approx 2.71828182845904523536$
- **MIN**:
- **MAX**:
- **pi**: $\pi \approx 3.14159265358979323846264338327950288419716939937510$
- **sign**: Returns -1, 0, or 1 if self is negative, zero or positive.
  Returns: Int

Operators

For binary ops (eg +, <), the second operand is converted to a float (if it isn't already one), the operation is performed and a float result returned. Examples:
```
1.5 + 2      → 3.5
1.0 + 2.5    → 3.5
1.5 + True   → 2.5  because True.toFloat() → 1.0
1.0 + Void   → Error because Void won't convert to a Float
1.5 + "2.3"  → 3.8
```

Operators

- **eq** (==): Returns False if the other operand isn't Int or Float. (`x==y`) is equivalent to (`x==y.toFloat()`).
  Result: Bool
- **neq** (!=): Returns (`not (self==X)`)
  Result: Bool
- **lt** (<): (x < y) returns (`x<y.toFloat()`). Y can be any object that has a toFloat method.
  Result: Bool
- **lte** (<=):
  Result: Bool
- **gt** (>):
  Result: Bool
- **gte** (>=):
  Result: Bool

- **add** (+): (x + y) returns (`x+y.toFloat()`). Y can be any object that has a toFloat method.
  Result: Float
- **sub** (-):
  Result: Float
- **mul** (*):
  Result: Float
- **div** (/):
  Throws: MathError on divide by zero
  Result: Float
- **mod** (%): Modulo
  Result: Float
- **negate** (unary -):
  Result: Float(-*value*)

Discussion

The built in random number generator has a uniform distribution[87], to create a random number generator with a normal (or Gaussian) distribution[88]:

---

87 http://en.wikipedia.org/wiki/Uniform_distribution_(discrete)
88 http://en.wikipedia.org/wiki/Normal_distribution

```
//normally distributed random w/mean & standard deviation
// using the Box-Muller transform89
fcn mkRand(mean,sd){
   pi:=(0.0).pi;
   rz1:=fcn{1.0-(0.0).random(1)}  // from [0,1) to (0,1]
   return('wrap(){((-2.0*rz1().log()).sqrt() *
                  (2.0*pi*rz1()).cos()) *sd + mean })
}
```

var g=mkRand(1,0.5) creates a function that returns normally distributed numbers with a mean of 1 and standard deviation of ½. Eg g() → 0.636199. To test this:

```
// create a list of 1000 Gaussian random numbers
ns:=(0).pump(1000,List,g);
mean:=(ns.sum(0.0)/1000);   //-->1.00379
```

// calc standard deviation of ns: $\sqrt{\dfrac{\sum (x-\bar{x})^2}{n}}$ //-->0.494844

```
(ns.reduce('wrap(p,n){p+(n-mean).pow(2)},0.0) /1000).sqrt()
```

---

89 http://en.wikipedia.org/wiki/Box%E2%80%93Muller_transform

GarbageMan

Full name: [TheVault.]GarbageMan
Inherits from: Object

> *One threads garbage is another threads treasured memory*
> -- Programming proverb

Abstract
The GarbageMan controls garbage collection.

Methods
- **collect(**waitUntilCollected=True**)**: Signals the garbage collector to start a collection cycle. If one is currently running, that counts. If *waitUntilCollected*, collect doesn't return until the current collection cycle has finished.
  Returns: Void
- **stats(**collectThenPrint=True**)**: Prints out some statistics about the objects the garbage collector can see.
  Returns: Void.
- **WeakRef(**object**)**: Create a weak reference to *object*. Allows you to determine if *object* has become garbage.
  A WeakRef has these properties:
    - **isDead**: True if *object* has been collected.
    - **ref**: The object being watched. Void if *object* has been collected.
  Returns: WeakRef or Void if object is not collectible (which Void isn't).

Discussion
Garbage collection is the process of reclaiming objects that are no longer in use. For example:
```
x = "Hello" + " World";
x = Void;
```
At this point, the string "Hello World" is no longer referenced by anyone, thus the memory it uses can be reclaimed. Garbage collection "just happens", it works in the background[90] while your program runs, reclaiming garbage. That said, collection is not a computationally cheap process and can exact a toll on performance.

---

90 Literally, it is a thread.

Weak References

From the Wikipedia:

> A weak reference is a reference that does not protect the referenced object from collection by a garbage collector; unlike a strong reference. An object referenced only by weak references is considered unreachable (or weakly reachable) and so may be collected at any time.[91]

A strong reference can be created with Objects.Ref.
A weak reference will only create for references to objects that are, in fact, collectible. Some objects are immortal and never die, so a weak reference would actually be a strong reference and is not allowed:

```
GarbageMan.WeakRef(True)  → Void
GarbageMan.WeakRef(Void)  → Void
```

A weak reference can be useful for testing the garbage collector:

```
var wr=GarbageMan.WeakRef(String("This is"," a test"))92
wr.isDead  → False
do(5) {GarbageMan.collect()}    // or just wait a while
wr.isDead  → True
```

---

91 http://en.wikipedia.org/wiki/Weak_ref
92 A string, eg s:="test string", may not be collectible if it is embedded in function code. Strings created at run time are collectible (which isn't the case with String("test string")).

Import

Full name: [TheVault.]Import
Inherits from: Class

Abstract
Import a Class or library from the Vault or file system. The file is compiled if need be.

Functions
- **import(**rootClassName, addToVault=False, ignoreVault=False, runConstructor=True**)**: Look around for a class or library and load it. RunConstructor can also be a list of parameters to pass to the constructor (which are flattened when the constructor is called). This is for scripts.
  Throws: LoaderError, ImportError (a child of LoadError), others
  Returns: Class or Native
- **lib(**libraryName, addToVault=False**)**: Look around for a library and load it.
  This is for when you want to only load a library, for example when foo.zkl and foo.dll co-exist; Import.lib("foo") will not find foo.zkl.
  A front end to System.loadLibary.
  Throws: LoaderError, ImportError (a child of LoadError), others
  Returns: Class
- **init(**rootClassName, addToVault=False, ignoreVault=False, runConstructor=True**)**:
  This just calls import, ie Import("foo") calls Import.import("foo").
  Returns: Import.import(rootClassName, addToVault, ignoreVault, runConstructor)

Discussion
Import loads a Class or Library from the Vault or file system. It will compile source code if it can't find a compiled version. If the class will be useful to other programs, it can be added to the Vault (the system start up code does this so things like the compiler are readily available). If you wish to bypass the Vault, you can (you might be developing a new version of a core class). Normally, it is always a good idea to run the constructor (it initializes the class) but, in some cases, this may not be the desired behavior.

Source code is searched for along System.classPath.
Libraries are searched for along System.libPath.

Examples:
```
Date=Import("Time.Date");  // from the Vault
Date=Import("Time/date.zsc");    // Read compiled file
Date=Import("Time/date.zkl");    // Compile source code
Date=Import("Src/Time/date");    // Compile source
println(Date.ctime());

ZLib=Import("zeelib");           // Import library
```

Search Order
1. If searching the Vault: The Vault is searched for the RootClassName, and if found, it is returned. The constructor is not run, it is assumed that, if it is has been loaded into the Vault, it has been constructed. This is not true in the case of scripts so, if it can be determined that the class is a script, the constructor is run (if runConstructor is True or a List).
2. A file name (the name ends with ".zkl", ".zsc" or "."). The file system is searched for the file. System.classPath is used in the search. A ZSC file is just loaded (using System.loadFile2), a ".zkl" file is compiled and if the extension is a dot, first a "*RootClassName*.zsc" file is looked for, then "*RootClassName*.zkl".
3. Now, heuristics are applied. RootClassName is mangled into a ".zsc" file name and searched for in the file system. If that fails, it is mangled into a ".zkl" file name and searched for (if found, the file is compiled).
4. Finally, an attempt is made to load the file as a library.

File System to Vault Mapping
The Vault is laid out like a file system. The idea to make it easy to look at a Class full name and know where it is in the file system, just by replacing dots with slashes. For example, take "TheVault.Compiler.Compiler". Replace the dots to get "TheVault/Compiler/Compiler", then replace "TheVault" with the entries in System.classPath or libPath and you should be able to find the corresponding file. In this example, classPath is L("C:/ZKL","C:/ZKL/Src","C:/ZKL/Built") and indeed,
>   C:\ZKL>ls -l C:/ZKL/Src/Compiler/compiler.*
>   ---a--- 65054 18:24:06 05/21/2007 C:/ZKL/Src/Compiler/compiler.zkl
>   C:\ZKL>ls -l C:/ZKL/Built/Compiler/compiler.*
>   ---a--- 25072 18:43:40 05/21/2007 C:/ZKL/Built/Compiler/compiler.zsc

You might have noticed a small problem on Unix systems: a case mismatch. A common zkl convention is to capitalize class names. This conflicts with another common convention, that of capitalized directory names and lower case file names.

Objects

So, the compromise (on Unix, Windows doesn't care), is to force paths (file and vault) to match case and to ignore case for class and file names.

Importing a Library
Libraries are treated like classes or files, only less so. This means that if a class has the same name as a library, the class will be loaded instead of the library. This is unfortunate but works that way so that the programmer doesn't need to know they are different. You can included the extension in the file name (for example `Import("zeelib.dll")`) but that doesn't work so well if you want your code to work across platforms (the library is named "zeelib.so" on Unix).
To avoid worrying about this possibility, use `Import.lib("zeelib")`.

Scripts
The constructor of a script is the script, which is functionally different from Class constructors. If a script is in the Vault (as is Test.testThemAll) and you import it, you usually want to run it; this is the case when you invoke a script from the command line; you want the script to run the same no matter where it is found – in the Vault or file system. But this is a problem for import because it doesn't know a script from Class (basically because there isn't a difference). So, to help import out, if the RootClass has the isScript flag set, the constructor will be run if the script is in the Vault and runConstructor is True/List. For example:

```
AKA(Test.testThemAll);
Attributes(script);        // flag for Import
```

Int

Inherits from: Object

Abstract
Sixty four bit integers. Integers are immutable, that is, they don't change. You "change" them by creating new ones (usually indirectly).

The compiler recognizes the following as integer constants:
- [-][0-9]+ : A decimal integer. Eg 123, -123, 0123
- [-]0x[0-9a-fA-F]+ : A hexadecimal integer. Eg 0xab, 0xAB, -0x12. 0X12 isn't a hex constant.
- 0b is binary and 0d is decimal.
- "_" can be used as a separator: 1_234 == 1234
- When using 0b, 0d or 0x "|" characters are allowed and ignored. For example, 0b1100|0000 is 0xc0 and 0d1_000 is 1,000.

Terms
- *Value* refers to the numeric value of self.

Methods
- **abs(**[*n*]**)**: Returns the absolute value of *value*. If *n*, returns the absolute value of *n*.
  Returns: Int(abs(*value*)) or Int(abs(*n*))
- **bitAnd(**mask, [mask ...]**)**: Bitwise AND *value* with mask(s).
  Returns: Int(*value* & mask [& mask ...]) in C speak
- **bitNot()**: Bitwise NOT *value*. Also known as one's complement.
  Returns: Int(~*value*) in C speak
- **bitOr(**mask, [mask ...]**)**: Bitwise OR *value* with mask(s).
  Returns: Int(*value* | mask [| mask ...]) in C speak
- **bitXor(**mask, [mask ...]**)**: Bitwise XOR *value* with mask(s).
  Returns: Int(*value* ^ mask [^ mask ...]) in C speak
- **clamp(**min, max**)**: Returns the closest value in the range [*min,max*].
  Returns: Int
- **copy()**: Returns self. Since Ints are immutable, self is equivalent to a copy.
  Returns: self
- **create(**n=self**)**: Create an Int with *value* set to n.
  Throws: OutOfMemory
  Returns: Int

Objects

- **div2(**n**)**: Divides *value* by n retuning ($\lfloor$value/n$\rfloor$, value%n)[93]. Signed parameters may suprise you.
  Eg (3).divr(5) → T(0,3)==$^3/_5$. (13).divr(5) → L(2,3)==$2^3/_5$.
  Returns: T(*self*/n,remainder)
- **filter(**count, [f [,static parameters]]**)**:
  Another way of writing [*value*, *value*+*count*-1].filter(…).
  To skip multiples of three:
      (10).filter(**10**, '%(3)) → L(10,11,13,14,16,17,19)
  Note that there are only 7 results, not 10.
- **filter(**count, T(f, T(f2, static parameters), f3 …)**)**:
  This is useful when you have multiple filters, they act like a big "and" statement.
  For example, to strip out 13,15 and 19 from a list of numbers:
      (10).filter(10, T('!=(13), '!=(15), '!=(19))) →
  L(10,11,12,14,16,17,18)
  Returns: ROList
- **filter1(**count|* [,f [,static parameters]]**)**: Same as filter but stops at first True result.
  Returns: Int|Void
- **len()**: Returns the number of bytes in *value*. (0xffff).len() → 2
- **len(**base**)**: If base is specified, returns the number digits in *value*$_{base}$. Base can be 2, 10 or 16. The absolute value of *value* is used.
  (0xffff).len(2) → 16, (0xffff).len(16) → 4, (-123).len() → 3
  Returns: Int
- **log2(**[n]**)**: Returns log$_2$(*value*). *Value* is treated as unsigned and log2(0) is 0.
  If n, use that instead of value.
  (0xffff).log2() → 15
  Log$_2$ is also the position of the MSB[94] (most significant bit).
  Returns: Int
- **max(**ints or floats**)**: Returns the maximum of self and the parameters.
  To find the max in a list of numbers, use list.reduce(list[0].max)
  Returns: Int
- **max(**list**)**: Returns the maximum of the contents (as ints) of the list.
  Returns: Int
- **min(**ints or floats**)**: Returns the minimum of self and the parameters.
  Returns: Int
- **min(**list**)**: Returns the minimum of the contents (as ints) of the list.
  Returns: Int

---

93 $\lfloor$n$\rfloor$ is n.toInt()
94 http://en.wikipedia.org/wiki/Most_significant_bit

- **minMax(**ints|floats|List**)**: As in min or max but returns both. For example: (13).minMax(5) →L(5,13) (ie a two element sort). Returns: L(min,max)
- **minMaxNs(**List**)**: Returns the index of the min and max elements. For example: (0).minMaxNs(L(4,5,1,2,3)) →L(2,1). Returns: L(index of min,index of max)
- **Property(**name**)**: Same as Object.Property except the instance is an undefined Int. For example: x:=123; x.Property("name").instance → 0 See: Objects.Object.Property Returns: Property
- **pump(**sink[,action …]**)**: The same as (0).pump(self,...)
- **pump(***,sink[,action …]**)**: The same as (0).pump(*,…), ie infinite.
- **pump(***count*,sink[,action …]**)**: Starting at self, run actions *count* times, optionally aggregating the results into a list. The result of (3).pump(2,List,a1,a2) is L(a2(a1(3)),a2(a1(4))). If aggregate is False, the last calculated value is the result. Some examples:
  - To print a boolean math table:
    ```
    println("x   y   and   or");
    (0).pump(2,Void,fcn(a){(0).pump(2,Void,'wrap(b){
        println("%d   %d   %d   %d"
        .fmt(a,b,a and b, a or b))
      })
    });
    ```
    → x y and or
    ```
    0 0  0  0
    0 1  0  1
    1 0  0  1
    1 1  1  1
    ```
  - Five rolls of a die:
    ```
    fcn die{ (0).random(1,7) }
    (0).pump(5,List,die)  → T(3,6,3,1,5)
    ```
  - Four rolls of the dice:
    ```
    (0).pump(4,List,fcn{return(die(),die())})
      → L(L(6,5), L(5,2), L(1,4), L(5,6))
    ```
  - 0 + 1 + 2 + 3 + 4 … :
    ```
    (0).pump(10,List,fcn(n,p){p[0]=p[0]+n}.fp1(L(0)))[95]
    ```
    → L(0,1,3,6,10,15,21,28,36,45)

---

[95] If you were to rewrite this as f:=fcn(n,p){ p[0]=p[0]+n }.fp1(L(0)), then every time you (0).pump(10,List,f), you would get a continuation of the series.

This works by using a list to hold the previous value, thus maintaining state.

See also: reduce, "notes on the pump method" at the start of this chapter.

Returns: last result | List

- **random**: A xor shift random number generator[96] with a period of $2^{128} - 1$. Its properties have not been verified, don't trust it if it matters.
- **random()**: Returns a non-negative random integer.
- **random(*stop*)**: Returns `random(self,stop)`.
- **random(start,stop)**: Return a number in the range [start,stop) (ie it might equal start but it won't equal stop). If start is an integer, the result is integer, otherwise, the result is a floating point number.

Examples:

- `(0).random()` → 2500
- `(0).random(10)` → 5 (an integer between zero and nine)
- `(0).random(0.0,10)` → 1.54759 (a floating point number between zero and nine, can include zero).
- `(0).random(0.0,1)` → 0.249947 (a float between zero and one)
- `(0).random(-10,0)` → -6
- Let's say you need an enumerated list of coin tosses:
  ```
  var coin=[1..].zip((0).random.fp(2));
  coin.walk(3)  ; // → L(L(1,0),L(2,1),L(3,0))
  coin.walk(2)  ; // → L(L(4,0),L(5,0)) , one head in 5 tosses
  ```

All threads share this data, which may skew the "random-ness" for each thread.

A test of the distribution of 0-9 over 10 million trials:
```
dist:=L(0,0,0,0,0,0,0,0,0,0);
do(0d10_000_000){n:=(0).random(10); dist[n]=dist[n]+1}
N:=dist.sum();
dist.apply('wrap(n){"%.2f%%".fmt(n.toFloat()/N*100)});
```
→ 10.02%, 10.00%, 10.00%, 9.99%, 10.00%, 10.00%, 10.00%, 10.01%, 9.99%, 10.00%

Returns: Int or Float

- **reduce(*count*|*,f,initialValue=value* [,parameters])**: A feedback loop which runs *fcn count* times. The calls are:
  ```
  p:=initialValue;
  p=fcn(p,value,  parameters);
  p=fcn(p,value+1,parameters);
  … count times
  ```

To stop the loop, `return(Void.Stop)` or `return(Void.Stop,result)`.

An example:

- The geometric series: $\underline{1 + \frac{1}{2} + \frac{1}{4} + \ldots}$ $(2^0 + 2^{-1} + 2^{-2} + 2^{-3} + \ldots)$[97]:

---

96 Currently and subject to change without notice.
97 http://en.wikipedia.org/wiki/Geometric_progression

```
(0).reduce(19,
    fcn(p,n){(p+=(2.0).pow(-n)).println(); p},0.0)
```
→ 1, 1.5, 1.75, 1.875, 1.9375, 1.96875, 1.98438, 1.99219, 1.99609, 1.99805, 1.99902, 1.99951, 1.99976, 1.99988, 1.99994, 1.99997, 1.99998, 1.99999, 2

and returns 2 (rounded, 1.999996185302734375 actual)

Returns: p

- **shiftLeft(**n**)**: Shift *value* left n bits.
Returns: Int(*value* << n) in C speak
- **shiftRight(**n**)**: Shift *value* right n bits
Returns: Int(*value* >> n) in C speak
- **split(**base=10**)**: Return a list of digits, base is between 2 and 36.
(12).split() → L(1,2), (0xABC).split(16) → L(10,11,12), (0).split() → L()
See also: toLittleEndian, toBigEndian, toString
Returns: List
- **toBigEndian(**numBytes**)**: Convert *value* to *numBytes* of big endian goodness.
For example:
(0x1234567890).toBigEndian(5) → L(0x12,0x34,0x56,0x78,0x90)[98]
If *numBytes* is greater than the number of bytes in *value*, the result is padded with zeros: (0x12).toBigEndian(2) → L(0,0x12)
See also: split, toString, toLittleEndian
Returns: List of *numBytes* Ints.
- **toBool()**: Returns True if *value* is non zero, otherwise, False.
Returns: Bool
- **toChar()**: Converts *value* to a character. If *value* is not in the range [0,255], ValueError is thrown. No character set is assumed, a one character string is created with that character being *value*.
For example: (0x31).toChar() → "1"
See Also: To convert to UTF-8, use toString(-8).
Throws: ValueError
Returns: String
- **toFloat()**: Convert *value* to a floating point value and returns it.
Returns: Float
- **toInt()**: Returns self.
Returns: Int
- **toList()**: Same as *value*.walker().walk() and *value*.pump(List).
Returns: List(0,1,2,..*value*)

---

98 To convert a list of Ints to another radix, use apply:
(0x1234).toBigEndian(2).apply("toString",16) → L("12","34")

- **toList(**stop**)**: Same as `self.walker(stop-`*value*`).walk()`.
  Returns: List(*value*,*value*+1,...stop-1)
- **toLittleEndian(***numBytes***)**: Convert *value* to *numBytes* of little endians.
  For example: `(0x1234567890).toLittleEndian(3)` → L(0x90,0x78,0x56)
  See also: split, toBigEndian, toString
  Returns: List of *numBytes* Ints.
- **toString()**: Convert *value* to a decimal (base 10) string and return it.
- **toString(**B**)**: Convert *value* to a base B, where is B is from 2 to 36.
- **toString(**-8**)**: Convert *value* to UTF-8 where self is the digits of the
  encoded UTF-8 character: `"\u20ac" == "€" == (0x20ac).toString(-8)`.
  To convert from a UTF-8 character to Int:
    `utf_int:=utf.reduce(fcn(s,c){ 0x100*s + c.toAsc() },0)`
  Examples:
      `(5).toString(2)` → "101"
      `(15).toString(16)` → "f"
      `(12).toString()` → "12"
      `(0xC9).toString(-8)` → "É"
  Throws: ValueError
  See also: split, toBigEndian, toLittle
  Returns: String
- **walker()**: Creates a walker from 0 to *value* − 1, ie `(0).walker(`*value*`)`.
- **walker(***count***)**: Creates [*value*..*value*+*count*-1].
- **walker(*******)**: Creates a walker from *value* to infinity (and beyond).
  `(0).walker(*)` makes a good "base" walker which you can tweak to walk
  the walk (see Objects.Walker).
  Returns: Walker

Properties
- **isEven**: Returns True if *value* is even.
- **isOdd**: Returns True if *value* is odd.
- **MAX**: The biggest positive integer.
- **MIN**: The negative integer furthest from zero.
- **nextPowerOf2**: The next power of 2 that is greater or equal to self.
  `(200).nextPowerOf2` → 256, `(256).nextPowerOf2` → 256
- **num1s**: Returns the number of 1 bits in self (treated as unsigned).
  Returns: Int
- **numDigits**: Returns the number of digits in self (treated as signed). Zero has
  no digits, -1 has 1 digit.
  Returns: Int
- **sign**: Returns -1, 0, or 1 if *value* is negative, zero or positive.

- **text**: The same as `self.toChar()`.

Operators
For binary ops (eg +, <), the second operand is converted to an integer (if it isn't already one), the operation is performed and the result returned. Examples:

```
1 + 2     → 3
1 + 2.5   → 3
1 + True  → 2 because True.toInt() → 1
1 + Void  → Error because Void won't convert to an Int
1 + "2"   → 3
```

The OPs
- **eq (==)**: Returns False if the other operand isn't Int or Float. (x==y) is equivalent to (x==y.toInt()) if y is a Float.
  Result: Bool
- **neq (!=)**: Returns (not (*value*==X))
  Result: Bool
- **lt (<)**: (x<y) returns (x<y.toInt()). Y can be any object that has a toInt method.
  Result: Bool
- **lte (<=)**:
  Result: Bool
- **gt (>)**:
  Result: Bool
- **gte (>=)**:
  Result: Bool

- **add (+)**: (x+y) returns (x+y.toInt()). Y can be any object that has a toInt method.
  Result: Int
- **sub (-)**:
  Result: Int
- **mul (*)**:
  Result: Int
- **div (/)**:
  Throws: MathError if divide by zero.
  Result: Int
- **mod (%)**: Modulo
  Result: Int
- **negate (unary -)**:
  Result: Int(*-value*)

Objects

Language

Full name: [TheVault.]Language
Inherits from: Object

Abstract
This object contains information about the zkl Programming Language.

Methods: None

Properties
- **authors**: Returns a list of the people who created and wrote zkl.
  Returns: List of Strings
- **email**: Where to send email about zkl.
  Returns: String
- **license**: The license that governs the zkl executable. As of this writing:
  The license for the zkl Programming Language executable.

  This is basically the zlib license and covers only this program.
  Not covered:
  * - Source code.*
  * - Programs produced by this program (they are yours).*
  * - [Shared] libraries (such as extensions) used by this program.*

  Copyright (c) 2007,2008,2009,2010,2011 Craig Durland

  This program is provided 'as-is', without any express or implied
  warranty. In no event will the author(s) be held liable for any damages
  arising from the use of this program.

  Permission is granted to anyone to use this program for any purpose,
  including commercial applications and redistribute it freely, subject to
  the following restrictions:

  1) The origin of this program must not be misrepresented; you must not
  *   claim that you wrote the original program. If you use this program*
  *   in a product, an acknowledgment in the product documentation would be*
  *   appreciated but is not required.*
  2) You may not distribute an altered version of this program. You may,

Returns: String
- **name:**
  Returns: "zkl"
- **version**: A list of the major and minor version numbers, a mystery number, and the release date.
  Returns: List
- **versionString**: A text version of the version.
  Returns: String
- **webSite**: The url of the zkl website: http://zenkinetic.com/
  Returns: String

Operators: None

Discussion

List

Full name: [TheVault.]List
Inherits from: Object
See Also: Objects.ROList, Objects.Thread.List

Abstract

A list is a mutable linear collection of heterogeneous objects. In other words, a list can contain objects of different types (for example, a list might contain both strings and numbers).

"L" is short hand for "List".
To create a list containing two numbers and one string: `List(1,2,"three")` or `L(1,2,"three")`.

The first item in a list is at *offset* zero.

A List *might* be thread safe or it might not be. If you need a guaranteed thread safe List, use Thread.List or Thread.Pipe. If you want a read only list, use ROList (you can convert any list to read only with the makeReadOnly method).

Terms
- *"items"* refers to the contents of the List
- *"offset"*: See **Rules for *Offset*** (below)
- *"length"*: See **Rules for *Length*** (below)
- *"thread-safe"*: A method or property is marked thread safe if multiple threads can perform that operation (or any other that is also thread safe) at the same time without clobbering each other. This is ONLY true if the list is a thread safe list.

Methods (if marked *thread-safe*, that is only true if self is *thread-safe*)
- **append(**objects**)**: *thread-safe*
  Append each of the objects to the end of *items*.
  Returns: self
- **clear()**: *thread-safe* Removes all items from self.
  Returns: self
- **clear(**objects**)**: The same as `clear().append(objects)`.
  Returns: self
- **concat(**seperator="",prefix="",suffix=""**)**: Not *thread-safe*

Concatenate *items* into a string.
Example: `L(1,"two",3.4).concat(",")` → "1,two,3.4"
  `L(1,"two",3).concat(",", "(", ")")` → "(1,two,3)"
Returns: String

- **copy()**: *thread-safe* Creates a new instance and copies *items* to the new list.
Throws:
Returns: List

- **create([**objects**])**: Create a new List instance and optionally append objects to it. The new list is the same type as self (ie thread safe lists create thread safe lists, unsafe lists create unsafe lists).
Throws:
Returns: List

- **createLong(***size [, fill, runFill=False]***)**: Create a new List and preallocate space for *size* items. The items don't exist, this method just reduces the amount of memory allocation that has to be done if you know the size of the list. This is a regular list in all respects. The new list has the same thread safety as self.
If *fill*, all element are set to *fill*. If *runFill*, each element is set to `fill()`.
For example, `List.createLong(5,Node,True)` is the same as
  `(5).pump(List(),fcn{ Node() })`.
Throws:
Returns: List

- **del(***offset [,length]***)**: *thread-safe*
Remove items from self. `del(-1)` deletes the last item, `del(0,*)` clears the list (see clear).
Throws: IndexError
Returns: self

- **extend(**objects**)**: *thread-safe*
Similar to append, but if one of the objects is a list, that list is "flattened" and its contents are appended. Empty lists are ignored.
Lists are not recursively flattened.
This actually works with circular lists.
Examples:
```
L(1,2).extend(3)          → L(1,2,3)
L(1,2).extend(L(3,4))     → L(1,2,3,4)
x=L(1,2); x.extend(x)     → L(1,2,1,2)
L(1,2).extend(L(3,L(4)))  → L(1,2,3,L(4))
```
See also: flatten
Throws:
Returns: self or a new ROList if self is a ROList

- **find(**x,*offset*=0,*length*=*****) *thread-safe*
  Searches *items* for x and returns the *offset* where it is found or Void if not found.
  Offset and *length* can be used to restrict the breadth of the search.
  X's eq operator method is used for comparison (as in `holds`).
  Returns: Int or Void
- **flatten()**: *thread-safe* A convenience method that "flattens" self by removing empty lists and replacing lists with their contents (one level only).
      `L(L(),1,T(2),L(T(3))).flatten()` → L(1,2,L(3))
  Returns: `ROList.extend(self.xplode())` (an ROList)
- **get(***offset* [,*length*]**)**: *thread-safe* The same thing as __sGet.
  Throws: IndexError
  Returns: Object, List or ROList
- **holds(**x,*offset*=0,*length*=*****): *thread-safe*
  Returns True if x is in *items*.
  X's eq operator method is used for comparison:
      `(x==items[n] and items[n].isType(x))`
  Examples:
  `L("one","two",3).holds(3)`   → True
      `L(1,2,3).holds("3")`   → False
      `L(1).holds(1.0)`   → False
  Throws:
  Returns: Bool
- **index(**x,*offset*=0,*length*=*****): *thread-safe*
  Same as `find` but throws IndexError if not found.
  Throws: IndexError
  Returns: Int
- **insert(***offset*,object(s)**)**: *thread-safe*
  Insert objects before the item at *offset*. If *offset* is equal to length (or *), objects are appended.
      `L(1).insert(0,2)`   → L(2,1)
      `L(1).insert(-1,2)`   → L(2,1), -1 is the last item
      `L(1,2).insert(-1,3)` → L(1,3,2)
      `L(1).insert(*,2)`   → L(1,2)
  Throws: IndexError
  Returns: self
- **len()**: *thread-safe* Returns the number of *items*.
  Returns: Int
- **makeReadOnly()**: *thread-safe* Convert self to a Read Only List. The list can not be converted back.
  Returns: ROList

Objects

- **pad(**n,obj**)**: Append obj to self n times.
  Returns: self
- **pop()**: Remove the last *item*.
- **pop(***offset***)**: Remove an *item* and return it.
- **pop(***offset, length***)**: Remove *items* and return them.
  Thread-safe
  This method behaves the same as:
      result=*items*[offset,length]; *items*.del(offset,length);
  If length is used, a list of items is returned; otherwise, a singleton is returned.
  For example:
      L(1,2,3).pop(0)   → 1 & the list is L(2,3)
      L(1,2,3).pop(0,1) → L(1)
  Throws: IndexError
  Returns: Object or ROList
- **push**: A synonym for append.
- **remove(**object(s)**)**: *thread-safe*
  Search *items* for objects and, if found, remove all of them. Found is defined
  as (*items*[n].isType(*object*) and *object*==*items*[n]).
  Examples:
      L(1,2).remove(1)   → L(2)
      L(1,2).remove(1,2)   → L()
      L(1,1).remove(1)   → L()
      L(1,2,4).remove(1,2,3)   → L(4)
      L(L(1,2),"three") – L(1,2) → L("three")
      L("3").remove(3)   → L("3")
  To remove a string from a list of strings while ignoring case:
      list.filter(fcn(s1,s2){(not s1.matches(s2))} ,s2)
  Throws: whatever == throws
  Returns: self
- **removeEach(**object(s)**)**: *thread-safe*
  The same as remove except, if object is a List, the contents of the list are
  removed. L(1,2,3).removeEach(L(1),2) is the same as
  L(1,2,3).remove(L(1).xplode(),2). Both return L(3).
  Throws: whatever == throws
  Returns: self
- **reverse()**: Reverses *items*, in place. *thread-safe*
      L(1,2,3).reverse()   → L(3,2,1)
      L(4,23,6,1).sort().reverse() → L(23,6,4,1)
  Returns: self
- **set(***offset, newValue***)**: *thread-safe*

238 List

Set the item at *offset* to *newValue*. This is the same as `items[offset]=newValue`.
If self is read only, a new read only list is returned.
Throws: IndexError
Returns: self or new read only list

- **__sGet(***offset* [,*length*]**)**: *thread-safe*
Implements `list[offset [,length]]`.
`list[offset]` returns the item at *offset*.
`list[offset,*]` returns a list of the items after, and including, the one at *offset*.
`list[offset,length]` returns a list of length items (or shorter).
Throws: IndexError
Returns: Object, List or ROList

- **__sSet(***x,offset*[,*length*]**)**: *thread-safe*
Implements `list[offset [,length]]=x`
`list[offset]=x` replaces the item at *offset* with x.
`list[offset,2]=x` replaces the two items at (*offset*, *offset*+1) with x.
Throws: IndexError
Returns: x

- **swap(***offset,offset***)**: *thread-safe*
Swap two items. `swap(0, -1)` swaps the first and last items.
Throws: IndexError
Returns: self

- **tail(n)**: not *thread-safe*
Returns a list of the last n items of self. If n is larger than length, n is set to length.
Returns: read only list

- **toBool()**: *thread-safe* Returns True if there are any items in self.
Returns: Bool

- **toData(**[mode=Int|String]**)**: *thread-safe* Each item in self is added to a Data. If an item is also a list, its contents are added.
If *items* are circular or recursive, this method will dead lock or break.
Throws:
Returns: Data

- **toDictionary()**: *thread-safe* Converts a list of key,value pairs into a Dictionary.
Items are either a list of key/value pairs or a list of lists, where each item is a list of key/value pairs.
Examples:
    L("key","value",1,2).toDictionary() → D(key:value, 1:2)

```
L( L("key","value"),L(1,2) ).toDictionary()
   → D( key:value, 1:2 )
```
Throws: TypeError, ValueError
Returns: Dictionary

- **toList()**: *thread-safe*
Returns: self

- **toString(***numItems=N*, *depth=2***)**: Not entirely thread safe
Returns "L(...)", where "..." is usually replaced by the contents of the list. The number of items printed is controlled by *numItems*; if it is zero, the result is "L()" or "L(...)". If it is *****, the entire contents are printed. The default value is implementation defined. *Depth* (which can be *****) controls how deep objects are traversed. For example, a recursive list:
```
r:=L(1); r.append(r,3); r.toString() → L(1,L(1,L(...),3),3)
r.toString(*,0) → L(1,L(...),3)
```
Throws:
Returns: String

- **xplode(***offset=0*, *length=****)**: *thread-safe*[99]
Replaces self in the parameter list with *items*. This almost the same as pushing list[offset,length] into the parameters, the difference being xplode(offset) pushes the rest of the list (list[offset] returns one item). Examples:
```
f("a",L(1,2,3).xplode(),"b") → f("a",1,2,3,"b")
f(L(1,2,3).xplode(1,1)) → f(2)
f(L(1,2,3).xplode(3))      → IndexError
f(L(1,2,3).xplode(3,1)) → f()
```
Note that this is ONLY useful in a parameter list. In all other cases, xplode just returns Void. Some deviate examples:
  - println("a",L(1,2).xplode().len(),"b") → "a0b". This happens because L(1,2).xplode().len() turns into (x.xplode()).len() → (Void).len(1,2) → 0. One might think it should have been: (1,2).len() → *mystery result* but that's not the way it works.
  - L(1).xplode().append("hoho") → NotFoundError: Void doesn't have append.
See Also: Objects.VM.pasteArgs
Throws: IndexError

---

99 The issue of thread safety is not as silly as it first appears. If there is a global shared resource (for example a dictionary of lists) and multiple threads read and xplode from that resource (at the same time of course), it would not be funny at all if yet another thread was changing the contents of those lists. I'll spare you the details of how painful that was to figure out but it was a vocabulary expanding experience.

Returns: Void
- **walker()**: Returns a iterator for walking the list.
  Example:
      foreach x in (L(1,2,3)){…}   // indirectly creates a Walker
  Thread safety: While the creatation and operation of the walker is thread safe, if *items* are changed by another thread while walking, what gets walked is open to question. However, it won't break.
  Throws:
  Returns: Walker

Stream methods

- **lose()**: *thread-safe* Does nothing.
  Returns: self
- **flush()**: *thread-safe* Does nothing.
  Returns: self
- **write(**objects**)**: *thread-safe* A synonym for append.
  Returns: self
- **writeln(**objects**)**: *thread-safe* A synonym for append.
  Returns: self

Utility Methods

These are **not** thread safe.
- **apply(**Fcn | Method | Op | Class | String | List [,static parameters]**)**: L(1,2).apply(f) → L(f(1),f(2))
  Apply a transformation to each item of the list and return a list of the results. The original list isn't modified.
  Apply can be used to multiply two vectors:
      fcn vecmul(v1,v2,f)
          { v1.apply('wrap(v){ v2.apply(f.fp(v)) }) }
      vecmul(T("a","b","c"), T(1,2), '+)
        → L(L("a1"), L("a2"),
            L("b1"), L("b2"),
            L("c1"), L("c2"))
- **apply(**Fcn [,static parameters]**)**: Fcn is a function that takes one or more parameters, the first of which is an item from the list and the rest are the static parameters, which don't change.
  Examples:
      L(1,2).apply(fcn(x){ x + 10 }) → L(11,12)
      fcn f(x,y){ y*(x + 10) }
      L(1,2).apply(f,10) → L(110,120)

- **apply(**Method [,static parmaters]**)**: This doesn't seem very useful but here is a way to convert each item to a string:
    ```
    L(1,3.4,self).apply("%s".fmt) →  L("1","3.4","Class(RootClass#)")
    ```
- **apply(**Class [,static parmeters]**)**: This also seems to be of dubious value, unless you want to create a bunch of classes:
    ```
    class C{ var n; fcn init(n){ self.n=n; } }
    x:=L(1,2).apply(C) → L(Class(C),Class(C))
    x[0].n==1 and x[1].n==2
    ```
- **apply(***methodName* [,static parmaters]**)**: For each item, call the named method with optional parameters.
    Convert a list of integers to hex strings:
    ```
    L(15,16).apply("toString",16) → L("f","10")
    ```
- **apply(***propertyName***)**: Retrieve the named property for each item.
    ```
    L("one",2,3.4,L(5)).apply("type") → L("String","Int","Float","List")
    ```
- **apply(***varName***)**: If the list contains Classes (for example, if it is the one we created in the "Class" example above), we can query a class variable.
    ```
    class C{ var n; fcn init(n){ self.n=n; } }
    L(1,2).apply(C).apply("n") → L(1,2)
    ```
Note that the three String apply methods (methodName, propertyName and varName) are somewhat dicey; what actually happens is that
item.resolve(name) is called for each item and, depending on what the result is, the following is appended:
  - Method, Property or function: The method, property or function is called with the static parameters.
  - Otherwise, the result is appended.
So, unless you know the contents of the list, this could be a bit of a crap shoot.
See Also: callMethod, callProperty, apply2, filter, reduce, Utils.Helpers.listZipWith.
Throws: Many
Returns: ROList

- **apply2(**Fcn | Method | Op | Class | String | List [,static parmaters]**)**: L(1,2).apply2(f) → f(1); f(2) → Void
A side effects only version of apply, the results are not saved or returned. Another form of a loop or for the pedantic who want to avoid the overhead of creating a list.
See also: reduce
Returns: Void

- **calcChunk(***i,max,*flags=0**)**: This method calculates *offset* and *length* for a vector containing *max* items. *Items* contains the indexing parameters. *i* is the index of the offset parameter in items (usually 0 or 1).

For example, if you are managing array A, containing N items, the validity of A[1] can be calculated with `L(1).calcChunk(0,N)` → L(1,1) (one item at offset one, the first parameter (the zero in the calcChunk call) is where to find the offset into A). For A[1,2], use `L(1,2).calcChunk(0,N)` → L(1,2) (two items, starting at offset one). `L(1,200).calcChunk(0,5)` & `L(1,*).calcChunk(0,5)` → L(1,4).

Useful when implementing __sGet and __sSet for your class; you can call calcChunk on vm.arglist. If C is a class, then `C[3]=4` results in `C.__sSet(4,3)`. You can use `vm.arglist.calcChunk(1,max)` to verify 3 as the offset.

This method throws on errors. For example, `L(1).calcChunk(0,0)` throws an IndexError as 1 is out of bounds for an empty array. Which can be confusing as `L().calcChunk(1,max)` will also generate an IndexError.

See Rules for Offset and Length (below).
Only one dimensional arrays are supported.
Flags control the behavior in boundary cases.
Throws: IndexError, conversion errors.
Returns: L(offset,length)

- **callMethod(**methodName**)**: Call a method on each item and return a list of the results. *Items* are not modified.
  Examples:
  ```
  L("1","22","333").callMethod("len")   → L(1,2,3)
  L("1","22","333").callMethod("toInt") → L(1,22,333)
  L(1,22,333).callMethod("toString",16) → L("1","16","14d")
  ```
  See also: apply
  Throws:
  Returns: List

- **callProperty(**propertyName**)**: Get a property for each item of a list and return the results. *Items* are not modified.
  Example:
  ```
  L("one",2,3.4,L(5)).callProperty("type")
      → L("String","Int","Float","List")
  ```
  See also: apply
  Throws:
  Returns: List

- **filter(**f [,static parameters]**)**: Calls f for each item of the list, converts the result to Bool and, if True, appends it to the result list.

Examples:

- `L(0,1,"2").filter()` → L(1,"2")
- Find all strings in a list:
  `L(1,"two",3.4).filter(fcn(x){ x.isType("") })` → L("two")
- Static parameters are passed unchanged to the function. One use might be to find all strings that match a pattern:
  ```
  x:=names.filter(
          fcn(nameFromList,pattern)
              { nameFromList.matches(pattern) },
                       pattern);
  ```
  Then, if pattern = "*oo*" and names = L("foo","oo","bar","kangaroo")
  x → L("foo","oo","kangaroo")

See also: a"notes on the filter method" at the start of this chapter.

Returns: List

- **filter1(f [,static parameters])**:
  The same as filter but returns False (nothing passed) or `.filter(...)[0]`. Traversal stops when an item "passes".
  For example, a stack trace shows Helpers.__fcn#15_403 and you would like to examine that function. Since you can't directly access it (due to the "#" in the name), you need a sneak attack:
  ```
  Utils.Helpers.fcns.filter1(fcn(f){f.name.matches("*#15*")})
     → Fcn(__fcn#15_403)
  ```
  This filter takes each Fcn in Helpers, extracts the name and string matches against the name.
  See also: a"notes on the filter method" at the start of this chapter.
  Returns: Object or False
- **filter1n(f [,static parameters])**:
  The same as filter1 but returns an index instead of an item. Note the that the index can be zero so use this test:
  ```
  if (False!=list.filter1n(…)) …
  ```
  See also: a"notes on the filter method" at the start of this chapter.
  Returns: Int or False
- **filter22(f [,static parameters])**: Another version of filter, this splits *items* into two lists, one that passed the filter and one that didn't.
  For example, in `left,right=rest.filter22('<,pivot);`, left is a list of the items that are less than pivot and right is the ones that aren't.
  `L(1,2,3,4).filter22('<,3)` → L(L(1,2),L(3,4)).
  Throws: yes
  See also: a"notes on the filter method" at the start of this chapter.
  Returns: ROList(ROList(items that pass),ROList(the other items))

- **filterNs(**f [,static parameters]**)**:
  The same as filter1n but returns indexes all items that pass.
  Returns: List
- **merge(**sorted list|<sorted objects>**)**: Merge list with self using the <
  operator. It is assumed that both lists are sorted. Assumes both self and list
  are sorted in increasing order.
  If < throws, self is in an unknown state.
  Throws: Whatever self[n]<list[m] throws.
  Returns: self
- **pump(**sink[,action ...]**)**: Another type of loop, similar to apply but with
  multiple actions.
  pump(List,x,y,z) returns the same result as
  apply(x).apply(y).apply(z) or apply(T(x,y,z)).
  pump(Void,x,y,z) is equivalent to apply(T(x,y,z))[-1,1].
  See also: apply, reduce, "notes on the pump method" at the start of this
  chapter.
  Returns: The last calculated value or a list of those values.
- **reduce(**f, *initialValue=items*[0] [,static parameters]**)**:
  Reduce the list to a single value or calculate a value from the contents of a
  list. Another form of a feedback loop.
  F is a callable that takes two (or more) parameters, the first parameter is the
  previous value of f(p,i) (or *initialValue*) and the second is an *item*, followed
  by, if any, the static parameters (which won't change).
  Reduce returns the previous value.
  To stop the loop, return(Void.Stop) or return(Void.Stop,result).
  The starting value is *item*[0] or *initialValue*.

  ```
  L().reduce(f)      → Void
  L().reduce(f,i)    → i
  L(x).reduce(f)     → x
  L(x).reduce(f,i)   → f(i,x)
  L(x,y).reduce(f)   → f(x,y)
  L(x,y,z).reduce(f) → p=f(x,y); p=f(p,z)
  L(x,y).reduce(f,i) → p=f(i,x); p=f(p,y)
  ```
  Note that it takes two values before calculations can start.
  Reduce is equivalent to:
  ```
  p:=initialValue;
  foreach i in (items)
      { p=f(p,i,static parameters) }
  ```
  Examples:
    - To calculate the maximum string length of a list of strings:
      ```
      names:=L("Fred","Sam","Theodore");
      ```

```
names.apply("len")    // → L(4,3,8)
    .reduce((0).max) → 8
```
The functions calls are: 0.max(4,3), 0.max(4,8)

- To find the longest name:
  ```
  names.reduce(fcn(x,y){ if (x.len()>y.len()) x else y })
  ```
  → "Theodore"

- To concatenate the names[100]:
  ```
  names.reduce(fcn(x,y){String(x," ",y)},
      "The names are:") → "The names are: Fred Sam Theodore"
  ```

- If the initial value is a data sink, reduce can act as a data pump. To send the names through a pipe:
  ```
  names.reduce(fcn(pipe,name){pipe.write(name)}, pipe);
  ```
  (pipe.write returns the Pipe)

- Sum a list: `L(1,2,3,4,5).reduce('+)` → 15
  To sum as floats: `L(1,2,3,4,5).reduce('+,0.0)` → 15.0

- The static parameters can be used instead of variables. For example, to count the number of times a string occurs in a list of strings:
  ```
  count:=names.reduce(
      fcn(count,nameFromList,name)
          { return(count + (name==nameFromList)) },
      0,name));
  ```
  If names == L("foo","bar") and name == "foo", then the call sequence is:
  ```
  → f(0,"foo","foo") → 0 + 1
  → f(1,"bar","foo") → 1 + 0
  → 1
  ```

This is a very powerful method, once you wrap your brain around its capabilities.

See also: apply2

Returns: object

- **run([*saveResults*=False [,static parameters]]):**
  ```
  L(f,g).run() → f(),g() → Void
  L(f,g).run(True,a)     → L(f(a),g(a))
  ```
  Run the functions, methods and properties in *items* and optionally return a list of results. *SaveResults* must be True if you want the results, otherwise, you only get side effects.
  ```
  T(String.create,Int.create).run(True,123) → L("123",123)
  ```
  Returns Void or ROList

- **runNFilter(*highPass*=True [,0 [,static args]]):**
  ```
  L(f,g).runNFilter()      → (f() or g())
  L(f,g).runNFilter(False) → (not (f() and g()))
  ```

---

[100]Or use the concat method

Run the functions, methods and properties in *items* and return True when one returns True (or what_it_returns.toBool() is True, this stops the traversal). Returns False if all of them do.

If *highpass* is False, the logic is reversed (low pass). Traversal stops when filter.toBool() is False (and the result is True).

For example:

```
b    :=Atomic.Bool();
list:=L(b.isSet, f);
list.runNFilter()           → False if f() returns False
b.set(); list.runNFilter() → True, f is never called
```

See Also: filter, run

Throws: Yes

Returns Bool.

- **runNFilter(**Bool,1 [,static args]**):**
  ```
  L(f,g).runNFilter(True, 1) → if (f() or g()) index else False
  L(f,g).runNFilter(False,1) →
  if (not (f() and g())) index else False
  ```
  Same as runNFilter() but, instead of a True/False result, the index of the first success is returned or False if no pass.

  Throws: Yes

  Returns: False or Int

- **runNFilter(**Bool,2 [,static args]**):**
  ```
  L(f,g).runNFtiler(True, 2) → L(0,5) when f() → 5, g() → ""
  L(f,g).runNFilter(False,2) → L(1,"")
  ```
  Same as runNFilter(Bool,1) but returns the index and result of the item that passes.

  Throws: Yes

  Returns: False or ROList(Int,*items*[n]())

- **shuffle():** Shuffle the list using Knuth's Algorithm P.
  This is an in-place shuffle, so if self is read only, a copy is made and shuffled.
  To shuffle [0..51]: (0).pump(52,List).shuffle() or
  [0..51].walk().shuffle()

  Returns: A shuffled list.

- **sort():** Sort the list. This usually only works for homogeneous lists (all of the items are of the same type).
  Examples:
  ```
  L(4,23,6,1).sort() → L(1,4,6,23)
  L("one","two","3").sort() → L("3","one","two")
  L(1,"two",3).sort() generates an error
  ```
  If the list contains Classes, and those classes implement __opGT, the list can be sorted.

Throws: Mostly conversion errors.

Returns: self or a sorted ROList

- **sort(**cmpFcn='<**)**: Sort the list, using a compare function. This allows the programmer to decide how a list is to be sorted, for example, in reverse. The compare function takes two parameters and returns True if the first parameter is considered smaller than the second (for an ascending sort). Examples:

  L(4,23,6,1).sort('<) → L(1,4,6,23)
  L(4,23,6,1).sort('>) → L(23,6,4,1)
  L("one","two","3").sort('>) → L("two","one","3")
  T(T("two",2),T("one",1)).sort(fcn(a,b){a[0] < b[0]})
  → L(L("one",1),L("two",2))

  Returns: self or a sorted ROList

- **sum(**initialValue=0**)**: Add up all *items*. The initial value determines the type of the value:

  L(1,2,3).sum()   → 6
  L(1,2,3.5).sum()   → 6 but L(1,2,3.5).sum(0.0) → 6.5
  L(1,2,3.5).sum("") → "123.5"

  Throws: Yes, if there are type mismatches

  Returns: self

- **zip(**objects**)**: Creates a new list of lists: Each sublist consists of one item from each of the source lists.

  T(1,2).zip(T(3,4),T(5,6)) → L(L(1,3,5),L(2,4,6))
  T(1,2).zip(T(3,4),"abcd") → L(L(1,3,"a"),L(2,4,"b"))

  Returns: List of lists

- **zipWith(**f,objects**)**: Apply f to slices of each list.

  This is List.apply applied "vertically". A slice is taken through each list and that slice is used as a parameter list for f, which can be anything that is callable. The result is added to a list of results. The shortest list determines the length of the result.

  Names in other languages for similar functionality: map2 and mapcar.

  Examples:

  T(1,2,3).zipWith(List,T(4,5,6),T(7,8,9,10))
      → L(L(1,4,7),L(2,5,8),L(3,6,9))
  T(1,2).zipWith('+,T(3,4),L(5,6,7,8)) → L(9,12)

  Returns: List

Properties

- **isReadOnly**:

  Returns Bool.

- **isThreadSafe**:

Returns Bool.
- **type**:
Returns "List", "ROList" or "TSList".

Operators
- **eq** (**==**): Not *thread-safe*. Returns True if two lists are the same length and contains the same objects (as described in holds). Contained lists are recursively compared. If you just want to know if the two lists are the physically the same, you could use list1.id==list2.id.
- **neq** (**!=**): not eq. Not *thread-safe*.
- **add** (**+**): *thread-safe* Append the second operand to *items*: *items*.append(x)
- **mul** (***): Not *thread-safe*. Make n [shallow] copies of self. If n isn't a number or is less than zero, self is returned. For example, L(5,6)*2 → L(L(5,6),L(5,6))
- **sub** (**-**): *thread-safe* Remove the second operand from *items*: *items*.remove(x) (doesn't throw)

Discussion
Lists are what programmers think of when the word "list" is used. A list can contain any object in any arrangement. It is common for a list to contain objects of two or more types (for example, integers and floats or integers and strings). Lists grow and shrink as needed, they are not fixed in size (fixed lists do exist, see ROList).

More Fun Things You Can Do With Reduce
Reduce is very powerful and generally useful method. Here are a few things it can be used for.
- Summing and concatenating:
  ```
  L(1,2,3).reduce('+) → 6
  L(1,2,3).reduce('+,"") → "123"
  L(1,2,3).reduce('+,"", ",") → "1,2,3,"
  L(1,2,3).reduce('+,"", ",")[0,-1] → "1,2,3"
  ```
- Maximum:
  ```
  L(1,3,2).reduce(fcn(x,y){if (x > y) x else y}) → 3
  L("one","two","three").reduce(fcn(x,y){ x > y and x or y})
      → "two"
  ```
- Longest string:
  ```
  L("one","two","three","four")
      .reduce(fcn(x,y){if (x.len() > y.len()) x else y})
      → "three"
  ```
- Looping: The rolling sum can be used as an index. In this example, we need to process a list while processing another list; ie a nested loop. But we don't

want to use foreach, that would be gauche. An example of our two lists:
L(1,3,5) and L(L(),L(),L()). The result: L(L(1),L(3),L(5)). The how:

```
results:=L(L(),L(),L());
L(1,3,5).reduce(
    fcn(n,x,results){ results[n].append(x); n+1 },
    0,results);
```

Rules for *Offset*
- The first item is zero: [0].
- The last item is [-1].
- If *offset* is < 0, it is added to the length. It is an error if the result is out of bounds.
- *Offset* = * ≈ *offset* = length
- If length isn't present (ie list[offset]), length defaults to 1.
- list[offset] returns one item or throws an error.

Rules for *Length*
- The default for length is 1.
- "*" is short hand for the number of items. [0,*] is the entire list, [n,*] is the rest of the list, starting at the nth item.
- If *length* is < 0, it is recalculated to be the number of items available plus length. It is an error if the result is out of bounds. For example, if there are three items, then [0,-1] ≈ [0,2], [1,-1] ≈ [1,1], [2,-1] ≈ [2,0], [0,-2] ≈ [0,1].
- If *offset* + *length* is greater than the number of available items, *length* is truncated to what is available.
- If offset is out of bounds, the (calculated) range is out of bounds, or length is zero, L() is returned.

Rules for the Sake of Rules
- Methods that do traversals do so in order from smallest *offset* to largest (to preserve order or for the sake of side effects). This can be relaxed if there are no side effects (eg to take advantage of parallelism) but the result is as-if the operation was ordered.

Method

Inherits from: Object
Notes

- You may need to put the object in parenthesis to access the method. For example, to access the "method" method of an integer, `(1).method` works but `1.method` is a error (it looks too much like a floating point number).

Abstract
Method is the Object that wraps "uncalled" methods calls. A Method can be treated like any other object.

Methods

- **defer(**[parameters]**)**: Returns `Deferred(self,parameters)`. For example, `f:=fcn{"Thread"}.future.defer()` delays spawning a thread until f is used (such as `f+1` → "thread1").
  Returns: Deferred
- **future()**: Run this method in a thread.
  Returns: future (a Deferred)
- **toBool()**:
  Returns: True
- **toString()**: Returns "Method(*instanceName.methodName*)".
  For example: `List.append.toString()` → "Method(List.append)".
  The works by back tracing the method in the object. If the object has multiple names for the same method, one of them is used.
  Returns: String
- **unbind()**: Deletes the bound instance. When the Method is called, the new instance must be passed in as the first parameter.
  Examples:
  `"foo".len()` → 3 but `"foo".len.unbind()("hoho")` → 4
  `m:="".translate.unbind().fp1("123","321");`
  `m("a:1 b:2 c:3")` → "a:3 b:2 c:1"
  Returns: new Method

Properties

- **instance**: The instance that this method is bound to. For example,
  `"foo".len.instance` returns "foo",
  `L().Method("append").instance.name` returns "List".
  Returns: Object

Objects

- **methodName**: Returns the name of the method. Eg `"foo".len.methodName` returns "len".
  Returns: String

Discussion

The Method object is what C programmers would call a "pointer to function" with a lot of baggage attached. It can be passed around, stored in other objects, etc, just like any other object. It always remains bound to the instance it was created with and will keep that instance from being recycled by the garbage collector (until itself is collected). So, in the far future, you can call it or, long after you've lost track of the instance, you can use it to regain contact with that lost instance.

Method objects are automatically created upon access. For example,
`method="foo".len;`
creates a Method object wrapping the string "foo" and method "len". Invoking the method via `method()` returns 3.

Methods can also be created explicitly: `"foo".Method("len")` → Method(String.len)

If you want to bind parameters to the Method, you can do so with the "fp" methods. For example,
`    title = Console.println.fpM("101","<title>","</title>")`
 creates a Method that prints a HTML title: `title("Hello")` → "<title>Hello</title>".

MinImport

Full name: [TheVault.]MinImport
Inherits from: Class
See Also: Objects.Import, Objects.System.classPath, Keywords.AKA
Notes
- `MinImport("foo")` is the same as `MinImport.import("foo")`
- Use a class name. This will search the Vault first and save a lot of resources if the class has already been loaded. For example, `MinImport("Compiler.Compiler")`
- If you need to bypass the Vault and only load from the file system, use "*filename*.zsc" instead of the class name. For example, `MinImport("Compiler/compiler.zsc")`

Abstract
A minimal version of Import. It loads a compiled class from the Vault or the file system.

Functions
- **import(**rootClassName, addToVault=False, runConstructor=True**)**
  Throws: LoaderError, others
  Returns: class
- **init(**rootClassName, addToVault=False, runConstructor=True**)**
  Returns: `import(rootClassName,addToVault,runConstructor)`

Discussion:
Find a class in the Vault or, if not there, look in the file system for the compiled class. For example, `MinImport("Compiler.Compiler")` looks in the Vault for Compiler.Compiler and, if found, returns it. If the compiler hasn't been loaded yet, it will root around in the file system, looking in places pointed to by System.classPath for the class, and, if found, load the class with System.loadFile. If addToVault is True, the loaded class will be put into the Vault, using the vault path specified by the AKA keyword.

The conversion from class name to file name is simple: "." is replaced by "/" and ".zsc" is appended. On Unix, the last part of the file name is case folded. Examples:
- "Import" → "Import.zsc". Case is ignored on Windows and Unix.
- "Compiler.Compiler" → "Compiler/Compiler.zsc". On Unix, case is ignored for "Compiler.zsc" only.

Network.TCPClientSocket

Full name: [TheVault.]Network.TCPClientSocket
Inherits from: Object
See Also: Appendix D, A Toy Web Server, zklCurl, a web extension library

Abstract
A TCP/IP client socket. Used to connect to web servers and things like that.

Methods

- **addrInfo(**addr**)**: Get information about something at the other end of a IP address or host name. This method is a utility method and has no effect on, and is not affected by, the current state of the socket.
  Returns a list of three items:
    - Canonical name of the host (String).
    - IP addresses for this host (List of Strings).
  For example: `Network.TCPClientSocket.addrInfo(`"www.google.com"`)` might return:
       L("www.google.com",
          L("173.194.33.113", "173.194.33.112",
            "2607:f8b0:4005:800::1014"))
  `addrInfo(`"localhost"`)`: L("core-shot", L("127.0.0.1"))
  `addrInfo(`"127.0.0.1"`)`: L("localhost", L("127.0.0.1"))
  `addrInfo(`"::1"`)`: L("::1",L("::1"))
  IPv6 ready (usually).
  Returns: List of lists
- **close()**: Closes the socket.
  It is OK to close a closed socket.
  Returns: self
- **len()**: Returns the number of bytes currently sitting in the read buffer. Might not be the number of bytes that a read() will actually return but it should be close.
  Returns: Int
- **connectTo(**serverName, port**)**: Connect to a server socket (such as a web server, port 80). The server name is a address that `addrInfo` might return (or accept).
  Returns: new TCPClientSocket that can write to the server
- **read(**[False]**)**: Not thread-safe. Read the bytes currently in the socket and returns them. If empty, wait for some data to show up.

If the number of bytes returned is zero, that means the socket has been closed.
Throws: IOError
Returns: Data

- **read(**n**)**: Read n bytes from the socket. If more than n bytes are available, only n of them are returned. If less than n are available, waits for the rest to show up.
Throws: IOError, TheEnd. If TheEnd is thrown, it is because the other end of the socket was closed. In this event, consider all data in transit lost.
Returns: Data

- **read(**True**)**: Read until the socket closes. If the number of bytes returned is zero, that means the socket has been closed. In the normal case, you call read(True), get a bunch of data, and call it good.
Throws: IOError
Returns: Data

- **toBool()**: True if the socket is open. This might not reflect the true status (see warnings for why).
Returns: Bool

- **wait(**timeout=block**)**: Waits for activity on the socket.
To poll for activity on a list of sockets:
```
fcn testSocket(s){ s.wait(0)!=False }
while(not (s:=sockets.filter(testSocket)))
    { Atomic.sleep(0.05) }
// s has the sockets with data or have closed
```
Returns: 1 if there is data waiting, False if no data is waiting, Void if there was an IOError (such as the socket is closed).

- **write(**data, ...**)**: Not thread-safe. Write a String, Data, List, or Int object to the socket.
Here are the bytes actually written:

Object	What is written
Data	The bytes in Data
Int	The LSB (Least Significant Byte) $\approx$ int[0] $\approx$ int.bitAnd(0xFF)
List	Recursively writes the contents of the list.
String	The bytes in the string. write("foo") writes three bytes.

Throws: IOError, TheEnd. If TheEnd is thrown, it is because the other end of the socket was closed or the connection has been broken. In this event, consider all data lost.
Returns: Int (the number of bytes written)

Properties
- **`hostAddr`**: The IP address of the host this socket is connected to. For example: "127.0.0.1" or "72.14.253.99".
- **`hostName`**: The canonical name of the host this socket is connected to. For example: "www.google.com".
- **`isClosed`**: Returns True if the socket is not open (ie never opened or has been closed).
  Returns: Bool

Operators: None

Warnings
- You may not be able to tell that the socket has been closed until you attempt to read from, or write to, it. This is because if the other end of the socket is closed, that event might not propagate until access is attempted.

Discussion
These TCP/IP sockets are much higher level than most socket packages but you still have to do a bit fiddling to use them, and it helps to know about sockets. Since they attempt to hide much of the socket details, they are not very general.

TCP/IP sockets are byte streams. You can, for example, serialize a class through a socket: `Compiler.Asm.writeRootClass(self,socket);`

Note: Sockets are for two processes to talk to each other, just like two people talking on a phone. Attempting to use a socket like party line will be just as pleasant, so don't do that. For threads, Pipes will probably work better.

Example: Connect to a Web Server

Talking to web servers requires that you speak HTTP[101], the language of the web. TCP/IP sockets are used to connect to web servers. Some web servers (like Apache) will close the socket after a request, other (like Google's GWS) don't[102].

101http://wikipedia.org/wiki/Http and RFC 2616 (http://tools.ietf.org/html/rfc2616).
102HTTP 1.0 responses are usually all at once, HTTP 1.1 can be chunked

Requesting a web page from an Apache server[103]:

```
hp  :=Network.TCPClientSocket.connectTo("www.hp.com",80);
data:=hp.write("GET / HTTP/1.1\r\nHost: www.hp.com\r\n\r\n")
        .read(True);
println(data);
```

[Note: In the HTTP GET request, the first parameter after "GET" is the page requested, in this case, "/", the "root" page. Your home page is probably something like "/~joe/".]

Prints Data(67893). Who ever thought a web page could be so big?

```
print(data.text);
```

Prints the response header and HTML that makes up the web page:

> HTTP/1.1 200 OK
> Date: Fri, 23 Feb 2007 06:04:59 GMT
> Server: Apache
> Expires: Fri, 23 Feb 2007 08:04:59 GMT
> Connection: close
> Transfer-Encoding: chunked
> Content-Type: text/html
>
> 1000
> <!DOCTYPE HTML PUBLIC "-//W3C//DTD HTML 4.01 Transitional//EN"
> "http://www.w3.or
> g/TR/html4/loose.dtd">
> <HTML lang=en-us>
> <HEAD>
> ...

To get a web page from a server that doesn't close the request socket takes more work. There are two approaches; one is to use an older protocol and the other to parse the output. For this example, www.google.com is used. The GWS server doesn't close the connection after a request with the HTTP 1.1 protocol but does if the request is made with the HTTP 1.0 protocol. Using HTTP 1.0 is easy:

```
google:=Network.TCPClientSocket.connectTo("www.google.com",80);
data  :=google.write(
    "GET / HTTP/1.0\r\nHost: www.google.com\r\n\r\n")
    .read(True);
print(data.text);
```

Response:

> HTTP/1.0 200 OK

103Some web server are picky about the amount of time between the opening of the socket and the receipt of the request (for example Google). So, if you are typing a request in the shell, you might want to do it on one line.

>   Content-Type: text/html
>   Server: GWS/2.1
>   Date: Sat, 24 Feb 2007 21:27:15 GMT
>   Connection: Close
>
>   <html><head>
>   ...

The GWS server returns a different response for HTTP 1.1 requests. To get that page, the response has to be parsed to know when to stop because the connection isn't closed. We'll cheat, based on advanced knowledge, and look for a block length of zero. This is a very simple test and will fail in other cases. An equally lame test is to look for "</html>".

```
serverName:="www.google.com";
server:=Network.TCPClientSocket.connectTo(serverName,80);
server.write("GET / HTTP/1.1\r\nHost: %s\r\n\r\n"
   .fmt(serverName));
while(1){
   text:=server.read().text;
   print(text);
   if (text.find("\r\n0\r\n")) break;   // lame test 1
// if (text.find("</html>")) break;     // lame test 2
};
server.close();
```

Response (comments in **bold**):

>   HTTP/1.1 200 OK
>   Content-Type: text/html
>   Server: GWS/2.1
>   Transfer-Encoding: chunked
>   Date: Sat, 24 Feb 2007 21:38:10 GMT
>
>   f19   ← **block length (in hex)**
>   <html><head>
>   ...
>   <a href=/intl/en/about.html>About Google</a></font><p> ...
>   Google</font></p></center></body></html>**[carriage returrn]**
>   0 **[carriage return][line feed]**   ← **block length**

This is a lame test for a couple of reasons: The Content-Type isn't checked to to see if it is chunked or not, and, most important, there is no way of knowing that read will contain all of the bits we are searching for (they could very well be split across reads). But, then again, we aren't writing a HTTP client either.

Example: The Client Side of a Socket Based Client/Server Application
To connect to programs via the network, sockets are ideal. You need a server (see TCPServerSocket) and one or more clients. The client connects to the server and, once a connect has been made, reads data from, and writes data to, the server. A peer to peer program is one where two or more clients talk to each other but a server is usually required to provide a known point of contact so that clients can connect to each other.

```
const serverAddress="localhost"; // or "127.0.0.1"
const port           =50000; // FreeBSD can be picky
```

Since the client and server are running on the same computer, the server is the "local host". The TCP port is some arbitrarily big number. If the client and server were running different computers, the address would be different and you would probably have to configure your firewall to allow communications.

Now we create the client. Since the server might not be running yet, we'll retry a few times before giving up.

```
reg clientSocket;
println("Connect to server at %s:%s...".fmt(serverAddress,port));
do(3){
    try{ clientSocket=
        Network.TCPClientSocket.connectTo(serverAddress,port); }
    catch(IOError){      // server not available, wait a bit
        println("Waiting for server ...");
        Atomic.sleep(10);
    }
    else{
        println("Connected!");
        break;
    }
}
if (not clientSocket)
    throw(Exception.BadDay("Socket server not available"));
```

Now that a connection has been established with the server, fake up some data to send to the server. Sockets are byte streams, meaning there are no "breaks" in the data, you really do need to treat it as one stream of bytes that start at the first write and end when the socket is closed. Thus, even though you write chunks of data, it is very possible you'll read different sized chunks, you only know that you'll get all the data. So, to make sense of the stream, you need to impose your own order on the stream. To do this, we'll use a very simple text based "packet" protocol: <one byte length><text>.
Here is the function to create a packet.

Objects

```
fcn createPacket(msg){
    p:=Data();
    p.append(msg.len(),msg); // Data.append() returns self
}104
```

Now to write the data to the server. For this very simple example, we'll only encode
the data in one direction. The amount of data read will depend on network latency.
[Note: this example won't work until the example server has been started].
```
packets:=L("one","this is a test");
foreach packet in (packets){
    clientSocket.write(createPacket(packet));
    data:=clientSocket.read();
    println(data.text);  // print what the server sent us
}
clientSocket.close();  // tell server this client is done
```

Now we'll create another client to tell the server to shut down. "STOP" is the magic
keyword.
```
ClientSocket:=
    Network.TCPClientSocket.connectTo(serverAddress,port);
clientSocket.write(createPacket("Should be in another thread"));
clientSocket.write(createPacket("STOP"));
clientSocket.close();
```

All done with this example. One thing we do need to be careful of is when the
program exits to the OS, the OS will clean up the socket. If the server is in the
middle of a read, that read will break. In this example, we won't care.
```
println("Client done");
```

The output looks like:
> Connect to server ...
> Waiting for server ...
> Connected!
> Server received a data packet of length 3   // sent to me from the server
> Server received a data packet of length 14
> Client done

104If you want to be overly clever:
```
    fcn createPacket(msg){ Data(0,0,msg.len(),msg); }
```

Network.TCPServerSocket

Full name: [TheVault.]Network.TCPServerSocket
Inherits from: Object
See Also: Appendix D, A Toy Web Server

Abstract
A TCP/IP server socket. Used to create things that client sockets can connect to.

Methods
- **close()**: Closes the socket. If the socket is listening, it will stop. It is OK to close a closed socket.
  Returns: self
- **listen(**handlerFcn|Pipe|Method**)**: Not thread-safe. Start accepting requests from client sockets that are connecting to this machine and port. When a client socket connects (possibly from a remote machine), the server creates a new (local) client socket and calls handlerFcn(*newClientSocket*, self). The handler should be quick so that the server can get back to listening. A handler might create a thread that connects the two clients sockets. The server continues to listen until it is closed.
  The OS starts queuing requests to a server socket when the socket is opened so a client can actually write before the server socket starts listening and the request won't be missed.
  The the handler is a Pipe/Straw, Pipe.write(0, clientSocket) is called. The handler return value is ignored.
  If the handler throws, the server socket stops listening but remains open and listen can be re-called.
  Throws: IOError
  Returns: self when self is closed.
- **open(**port**)**: Open a TCP/IP server socket on localhost at port. This creates a new server socket that ready to start listening for client sockets. Use listen to actually accept connections.
  Throws: IOError
  Returns: New server socket
- **toBool()**: True if the socket is open.
  Returns: Bool

Objects

Properties

- **hostname**: Returns the name of the server.
  "" if the socket hasn't been opened yet.
  See also: TCPClientSocket.addrInfo, Objects.System.hostname.
  Returns: String
- **isClosed**: Returns True if the socket is not open (ie never opened or has been closed).
  Returns: Bool
- **isListening**: Returns True if the socket is actively listening.
  Returns: Bool
- **port**: Returns the port the server was opened on. Zero if the server hasn't been opened.
  Returns: Int

Operators: None

Discussion
A very simple client/server example:
```
const port=50000;
out:=Thread.Pipe(); ab:=Atomic.Bool();
ss:=Network.TCPServerSocket.open(port);
cs:=Network.TCPClientSocket.connectTo("localhost",port);
    // create thread that listens to server socket
fcn(ss,out,ab){ ss.listen(out,ab) }.launch(ss,out,ab);
ab.wait();
    // kick the server, write 4 bytes to the socket it creates
cs.write("hoho");
ss.close(); // close server socket and stop thread
out.read().read().text.println();  // Pipe(socket(Data(4 bytes)))
```
Running this code snippet will print "hoho"

Example: The Server Side of a Socket Based Client/Server Application
Here is the server side of a very simple TCP/IP based client/server application. This can be running on same machine as the client or on any computer that can be reached by a TCP/IP network (modulo any firewalls). The client and server can even be in the same program but that doesn't make a lot of sense.
Read the client side example first, then this one.

First, create the server socket on some random port.
```
const port=50000;
serverSocket:=Network.TCPServerSocket.open(port);
println("Server started at %s:%d"
    .fmt(serverSocket.hostname,serverSocket.port));
```

Now create the server. Yes, it is this simple:
```
try{ serverSocket.listen(handler); } catch(IOError){}
```
That is because this is a very simple server. It just waits for a client to request a connection, and when one does, it punts the request to a function to do the actual work. And then it goes back to waiting. If the server socket is closed, the server stops. In fact, that is the only way to stop the server, other than throwing an exception at the VM it is running in.

Again, in a real program, we might need to wait a bit to let the threads finish and make sure the client has cleaned up before exiting to the OS.
```
println("Server done");
```

Here is the function that handles a new client connect request. It needs to be very simple so the server can get back to work (since it is running in the same thread as the server). So it just creates a new thread to deal with the client.
```
fcn handler(socket,erver){
    Handler().launch(socket,server);
}
```

Here is where most of the work happens.
This class is a thread that is created each time a new client connects to the server.
Thus, there can be more than one client connected at a time.
The thread is started with the remote client socket and the server socket. It then reads a data packet, prints it out, writes the packet length to the client and repeats until the client closes the socket.
If "STOP" is received, the server socket is closed, telling the server to exit.

Objects

```
class Handler¹⁰⁵{
   fcn liftoff(socket,server){
       println("\n----------------"
               "Socket handler started in ",vm);
       while(1){
          packet,len:=readPacket(socket);
          if (len==0) break;            // client closed socket
          println("Received: ",packet);
          if (packet=="STOP"){ server.close(); break; }
          socket.write(
              "Server received a data packet of length ",
              .fmt(len));
       }
       println("Client closed socket, stopping this thread.");
       socket.close();
   }
   // to be continued …
```

The packet reader/decoder is pretty simple. The first byte of our very simple protocol is the length of the message and is followed by that many characters (bytes). So, first read one byte. If we can't do that, it means the socket has closed. Otherwise, read the rest of the packet and return the text and packet length. This is wrapped in a try block to catch the client closing the socket (TheEnd is thrown by read(n) on an attempt to read from a closed socket). If the socket does close, all data in it is gone, so return an empty packet.

```
   fcn readPacket(socket){
       try{
          data   :=socket.read(1);
          len    :=data.bytes(0);
          packet:=socket.read(len).text;
          return(packet,len);
       }catch(TheEnd){ return("",0); }
   }
} // class Handler
```

Output:

       Server started at core-shot:50000

       Socket handler started in VM#2

       Received: one

       Received: this is a test

       Received:

       Client closed socket, stopping this thread.

---

[105]This could be a declared a static function (actually, the compiler does that for us) as it has no instance data. Which reduces the amount of memory that needs to be allocated.

```
------------------
Socket handler started in VM#6
Received: Should be in another thread
Received: STOP
Client closed socket, stopping this thread.
Server done
```

Talking to a Terminal

Sockets are used to talk to TCP terminal emulators such as HyperTerminal. Here is a tiny telnet server:

```
var terminal;
Network.TCPServerSocket.open(23)// Port 23: default telnet port
     .listen(handler);          // wait for connection
fcn handler(s,server){          // terminal connected
   terminal=s;
   server.close();                 // stop listening so we can talk
}
terminal.write(GREEN,"> ",BLACK);
line:=Data();
while(1){
   char:=terminal.read(1); terminal.write(char);
   if (char.text=="\r"){
      if (line){ println(line.text); line.clear(); }
      terminal.write("\n",GREEN,"> ",BLACK);
   }
   else line.append(char);
}
// ANSI color escape sequences
const ESC     ="\x1b";
const BLACK   =ESC + "[30m";
const RED     =ESC + "[31m";
const GREEN   =ESC + "[32m";
const YELLOW  =ESC + "[33m";
const BLUE    =ESC + "[34m";
const MAGENTA =ESC + "[35m";
const CYAN    =ESC + "[36m";
const WHITE   =ESC + "[37m";
```

Run the server and then connect to it with a TCP terminal such as HyperTerminal. Use a TCP connection to "localhost" (if the running on the same machine as the server), port 23. The server will send a green "> " as prompt and will echo typed characters. This server is way to limited to work with telnet.

Object

Abstract
Object is the object that all other objects are built from. Object's are virtual and don't exist on their own, only as the parent of another object.

Objects that inherit from Object will overwrite one or more of these methods, properties and operators. Look there first for information, and then look here.

Methods
Functions marked *Reserved* means you can't use that name for a function, class or variable.

- **BaseClass(***name***)**: *Reserved*. In the case of a Class, this is equivalent to class.Class.*name*, otherwise, it is equivalent to object.Object.*name* (Method or Proptery), if such syntax existed. In most cases, resolve and BaseClass will return the same value.
  The compiler is kind enough to convert `x.BaseClass.y` to `x.BaseClass("y")`. Thus `x.BaseClass.id` and `x.BaseClass("id")` are the same.
  For example:
    - The Exception class overwrites the toString method. So `Exception.resolve("toString")` returns the Exception Class function "toString" but `Exception.BaseClass("toString")` returns the Class method "toString".

  Who cares? Mostly compiler writers. In general, if you want to be sure you are accessing something in Object or Class and not in the class itself or things it inherits from, or something bad will happen if you need to call an Object method and don't (because it has been overwritten), use BaseClass. One place where this happens frequently is with the name property (because "name" is a popular name). In another case, it is the only way to access the methods of TheVault. Of course, some Objects just can't play nice, for example, Language's name property.
  Throws:
  Returns: Method or property value
- **copy()**: Returns self.
- **create(**parameters**)**: The create method is roughly equivalent to "new" in C++.
  Create is called to create a new object instance. Most objects can create instances of themselves; they can replicate themselves.

For example:

- L(1,2,3) calls List.create(1,2,3) which creates a List with three elements.
- L(1,2,3)(4,5,6) creates two lists; first, one with elements 1, 2 and 3 and second, one with elements 4, 5, and 6.
- x=1; y=x(2); sets variables x to integer 1 and y to integer 2. This is the same as x=1; y=2;

Class creation is a bit more complicated, the compiler and the VM work together to create new class instances. Classes don't implement a create method; if, for some reason you want to create a new class instance outside of the usual channels, use copy.

Throws: NotImplementedError

Returns: Doesn't. Object doesn't implement this method.

- **dir()**: Print interesting information about self.
- **fp(**parameters**)**: Fixes the parameters as the first parameters to self. This is a closure of self over the parameters aka partial function application[106] of the parameters, which is also related to currying[107].
    - p:="".fp("foo") ≈ String.Method("create","foo")[108]
      p("bar") ≈ String.create("foo","bar") → "foobar"
      p("b","a","r") → "foobar"
    - df:=fcn f(x,y){ x/y }.fp(10);
      df(2) → f(10,2) → 10/2 → 5, df(3) → 3
    - df:="%d %d".fmt.fp(1);
      df(2) → "1 2", df(3) → "1 3"

Closures are "stackable" (function composition):
```
fcn f(x,y,z){ "%s%s%s".fmt(x,y,z) }
pf1:=f.fp(1); pf2:=pf1.fp(2); pf3:=pf2.fp(3);
pf3() → "123"
```
Note that composition doesn't always work. If we want to compute f(g(h(x)), then f.fp(g.fp(h))(x) doesn't work as x is passed to f, not h. Use Objects.Utils.Helpers.fcomp or fcn fgh(x){f(g(h(x)))} or f.fp(g.fp(h.fp(x)))() (if x is fixed).

An infinite Fibonacci sequence:
```
var fib=fcn(ab){ ab.append(ab.sum()).pop(0) }.fp(L(0,1))
do(15){ fib().print(",") }
→ 0,1,1,2,3,5,8,13,21,34,55,89,144,233,377,
fib() → 610, Utils.wap(fib).walk(5) → L(987,1597,2584,4181,6765)
```

106http://en.wikipedia.org/wiki/Partial_application
107http://en.wikipedia.org/wiki/Currying
108If Method took fixed parameters, which it doesn't, which is why .fp exists

Returns: Function of reduced arity (a Deferred closure).

- **fp1(***parameters***)**: Fixes all parameters but the first: *parameters* are fixed as the 2nd through N^{th} parameters to self, returning a function of one parameter, the first.

```
fcn f(x,y,z){ x+y+z }
g:=f.fp1(2,3);    // g(x) → f(x,2,3)
g(1) → f(1,2,3) → 6, g("1") → "123"
```

This is useful for wrapping Methods that need more than one parameter.
Returns: Function of one parameter (a Deferred closure).

- **fp2(***parameters***)**: Fixes parameters after the first two: *parameters* are fixed as the 3nd through N^{th} parameters to self, returning a function of two parameters.

Note: Parameter initializers for the first two parameters are ignored.

```
f:=fcn(a,b=4,c=5,d=6,e=7){}.fp2(9);
f("a","b","c","d") → f("a","b",9,"c",7)
f() and f("a") are undefined.
fcn g(a,b,c){ String(a,b,c) }
h:=g.fp2(1); h=h.fp1(2); h=h.fp(3);
h() → "321"
```

but `h:=g.fp(1); h=h.fp1(2); h=h.fp2(3); h()` doesn't work (b isn't defined); it should be written `h:=g.fp(1); h=h.fp(2); h=h.fp(3)` or `h:=g.fp(1).fp(2).fp(3)`
Returns: Function of two parameters (a Deferred closure).

- **fpN(***n***,fixedArgs)**: Fixes parameters after the first *n*. When called, the caller supplies [at least] n parameters. Given f.fp(n,a_0 ... a_i)(p_0 ... p_j), the resulting call is:

$$f(p_0 ... p_{n-1}, a_0 ... a_i, p_n ... p_j)$$

If there are not at least *n* p's, the result is undefined.
If f is itself a closure (of g), then g gets the combined/new parameters. This effectively makes evaluation right to left (right associative)[109].
Returns: Function of *n* parameters (a Deferred closure).

- **fpM(***mask***,fixedArgs)**: Fixes arbitrary parameters to self. This is a generalization of fp. *Mask* is a bit string that consists of "1" (fixed parameter) or "0" (parameter supplied on call) for each parameter that self takes. A "-" says to chop all parameters at that point.

```
fcn f(x,y,z){ "%s%s%s".fmt(x,y,z) }
p:=f.fpM("101",1,3); p(2) → "123"
```

Notes:

- Leading zeros may be required. For example, `f.fpM("001",a)` is very different from `f.fpM("1",a)`.

---

[109]Without fixing parameters by name, chained fp's are largely unmanageable anyway.

- Any *fixedArgs* after *mask*.len() are ignored. Any call parameters after zeros.len() are appended.
- The reason a mask string is used (vs named parameters) is Methods[110]:
  ```
  pf:="%d%d".fmt.fpM("01",123);
  pf(4) → "4123"
  ```
- `f.fpM("0")` → f
- `f.fpM("1",a)` → `f.fp(a)`, `f.fpM("01",a)` → `f.fp1(a)`,
  `f.fpM("001",a)` → `f.fp2(a)`, `f.fpM("0001",a)` → `f.fpN(3,a)`
  and so on.
- `f.fpM("")` and `.fpM("-")` mean that f doesn't want any parameters, no matter what it is called with. For example, readln in a walker or pump.
- `f.fpM("0")` means use only the first passed parameter and ignore the rest (if any). This is useful for passing Methods to things that will call that method with extraneous parameters that would conflict with defaults.

Returns: Function of reduced arity (wrapped in a Deferred closure).
- **isChildOf(**object**)**: Returns False. Class makes this useful.
- **isInstanceOf(***object***)**: Returns *obj*.type(*object*). Class and fcn makes this useful.
- **isType(**object [,object …]**)**: Returns True if self and object are the same type. The parameter is an object, not a name or id. For example:
  ```
  (1).isType(Int) returns True.
  (2).isType(3)   returns True.
  (2).isType("2") returns False.
  ```
  If you want to check for a Class, use `self`; function, use `self.fcn`; Method, use `NullClass.Method`; Property, use `NullClass.Property` (but NOT `self.Property`).
  `x.isType(List)` is slightly more efficient than `x.isType(L())` but are otherwise the same. Since "", 0, and 0.0 are cached, the only difference using these objects vs the Vault names is aesthetic; which do you prefer: `x.isType("")` or `x.isType(String)`? Use that one.
  If there more than one parameter, True is returned if self matches any of them.
  Returns: Bool
- **len()**: Returns 0.
- **Method(***name***)**: Search the methods for Method *name*. If found, returns the Method.

---

[110]Methods don't have a prototype that names the parameter list. Besides, a functions prototype may not reflect all the possible parameter lists.

For example:

"foo".Method("toString") returns Method(String.toString).
    "foo".Method("notfound") throws NotFoundError.
Throws: NotFoundError
Returns: Method

- **method(**name**)**: The same as Method(name). This exists for symmetry with property.
  Throws: NotFoundError
  Returns: Method
- **method(**name, True**)**: Just check to see if there is a method that goes by *name*. Returns True if there is.
  Returns: Bool
- **method(**index, methodIsInstance=False**)**: Returns the name of a method. This is symmetrical with method(name, False):
      "".method("len", False).xplode() : "".method(_) → "len"
  Returns: String ("" if out of range)
- **noop()**: Does nothing and returns self.
- **print(**[parameters]**)**: Shorthand for Console.print(*obj*, parameters).
  Returns: String
- **println(**[parameters]**)**: Shorthand for Console.println(*obj*, parameters).
  Returns: String
- **Property(**name [, var]**)**: Search self for a variable (if self is a class) or property and return a Property object for it. This allows you to treat a variable or property like a method or function. For example:
      p=self.Property("name");
      p();   // same as self.name or self.property("name")
  Parents are not searched.
  The "var" parameter allows you restrict searches when using Property with classes:
  klass.Property(*name*, 0) ≈ klass.Property(*name*)
      klass.Property(*name*, 1): Search only variables
      klass.Property(*name*, 2): Ignore variables
      object.Property(*name*, ?) ≈ object.Property(*name*)
  A class variable exits if klass.Property(*name*, 1) doesn't throw.
  Throws: NotFoundError
  Returns: Property
- **property(**name**)**: Search the properties for a property named *name*. If found, return the value of that property. Unlike Property, it does not look at variables.

`"foo".property("id")` might return 15175936.

Throws: NotFoundError

Returns: object

- **property(**_name_,`True`**)**: Just check to see if there is a property that goes by _name_. Returns True if there is.

  Returns: Bool

- **resolve(**_name_**)**: _Reserved._ Search self for a method or property named _name_ and return it. The name is a string.

  For example:

  `"foo".resolve("id")` might return 22591048

      `"foo".resolve("len")` returns Method(String.len), which is a Method object.

  See also: Objects.Class.resolve

  Throws: TypeError if name is not a String, NotFoundError if _name_ is not found. Also TypeError, IndexError.

  Returns: object

- **resolve(**_name_,`N|*`**)**: This variant checks for methods or properties named _name_ and returns a non-zero result if it found.
  - N==1: Check for method. Result is MethodType.
  - N==2: Check for property. Result is PropertyType.
  - *: All of the above. You can also bit or any of these; to check for a method or property: N=3.
  - MethodType and PropertyType are defined in `vm.h.zkl`; `include(vm.h.zkl)`
  - To just check for existence, use
    `if (`_object_`.resolve(`_name_`,*)) found();`

  Throws:

  Returns: False, non-zero Int

- **__sGet(**`i`**)**: Throws Exception.NotImplementedError

  `object[i]` gets translated into `object.__sGet(i)`.

- **__sSet(**`v,i,len`**)**: Throws Exception.NotImplementedError

  `object[i]    = x` is translated into `object.__sSet(x,i)`.

  `object[i,n] = x` is translated into `object.__sSet(x,i,n)`.

- **toBool()**:   Throws Exception.NotImplementedError
- **toData()**:   Throws Exception.NotImplementedError
- **toFloat()**:   Throws Exception.NotImplementedError
- **toInt()**:   Throws Exception.NotImplementedError
- **toList()**:   Returns ROList(self).
- **toString()**: Returns self.name. See Properites.
- **toType(**_object_**)**: Convert self to the same type as _object_ (if possible). For example: `x.toType(1.0)` $\approx$ `x.toFloat()`, `x.toType(List)` $\approx$

x.toList(). This is *not* guaranteed to work as it has to do some guessing, which goes like this: *x*.toType(*y*) → x.Method("to"+y.type)(x) plus some special casing.
Throws: NotImplementedError, conversion errors.
Returns: object

Properties
- **fullName**: The name and "path" of self. For example, L().fullName returns "TheVault.List" and (1).fullName returns "TheVault.Int". If the object or an instance of the object in in the Vault, a vault path is returned (which always starts with "TheVault."), otherwise, self.name is returned. Classes have a slightly different behavior.
  Returns: String
- **id**: Returns a unique ID for this object. The ID is an int.
- **methods**: Returns a list containing the names of self's methods. For example, (Void).methods returns L("toBool", "toString", "create", , ...).
- **name**: Returns the string self refers to itself as. For example, L().name returns "List" and (1).name "Int".
- **otype**: Object Type. Returns the name of the type. For example, (1).otype returns "Int" and "".otype returns "String".
- **properties**: Returns a list containing the names of self's properties. For example, (Void).properties returns L("id", "name", "fullName", "type", "otype", "properties", "methods").
- **type**: Pretty much the same as otype but defers to object for what it wants to be called. For example, Time.Clock.type returns "Clock" while Time.Clock.otype returns "native".
- **vaultPath**: The place in the vault that this object thinks it should go, if it were to go there.

Operators
- **==**: Returns True if both operands are the same object. There are no conversions, no nothing, they both have to be the same object.
- **!=**: (*obj*!=y) returns not (obj==y)
- **<, <=, >, >=**: Throws Exception.NotImplementedError
- **+, -, *, /**: Throws Exception.NotImplementedError
- **%**:   Throws Exception.NotImplementedError

Discussion
Object is something that doesn't quite exist. It is used to build all other objects but can't be found "in the wild".

Op

Inherits from: Object

Abstract

Op is an Object that wraps operators. An Op can be treated like any other object. The ops are: =, !=, <, <=, >, >=, +, -, *, /, %, "not", "--" (two dashes, negate). As parameters, `'+` is syntactic sugar for `Op("+")`.

Methods

- `call(a)`, `call(a,b)`, `call(a,b,c...)`: Perform the operation.
  `Op("+").call(1,2)` is equivalent to 1+2 and `call("1",2)` → "12".
  Likewise for logical: `Op("<")(a,b,c)` → a<b<c.
  If Op has a **stored operand**, it is used as the second operand for **math** ops:
    `Op("+",1).call(5)` → 5+1 → 6
  For **logical** ops, it repeated: `'>(0)(a,b,c)` → `(a>0)` and `(b>0)` and `(c>0)`.
  For **negate** and **mod**, only the first parameter is used.
  For **not**, only the first parameter is used (n:=Op("not"); n(a,b,c) → n(a)).
  If there is a stored operand (ie `'!(f)`) then `'!(f)(i)` → `(not f(i))`.
  If this ordering doesn't work for you, use one of the **fp** methods to change it; for example, `'+.fp("foo")("bar")` → "foobar".
  There are several variants, see below for more discussion.
  Throws: Unknown
  Returns: Unknown
- `create(opName [,operand])`: Create an Op bound to a op code.

Name:	"=="	"!="	"<"	"<="	">"	">="
Sugar:	'==	'!=	'<	'<=	'>	'>=

Name:	"+"	"-"	"*"	"/"	"%"	"not"	"--" (negate)
Sugar:	'+	'-	'*	'/	'%	'!	N/A

  Once an Op has been created, a subsequent call to create is treated as a call.
    `op:=Op("+"); op(1,2)` → 3
  Which means that only the Op in the Vault can create new Ops but you can store that in a var: `var op=Op; anOp:=op("+");`
  See Syntactic Sugar below.
  Throws: NameError
  Returns: Op
- `toBool()`:
  Returns: True

- **toString()**: Returns "Op(*op*)" or "Op(*op*Operand)", eg "Op(+)", "Op(+1)".
  Returns: String

Discussion
Ops are useful where a fcn is just too heavy weight or verbose.
Some examples:

- `L(1,2,"3").apply(Op("+"),10)` ≈ `L(1,2,"3").apply('+,10)` ≈
  `L(1,2,"3").apply('+(10))` ≈ `L(1,2,"3").apply(fcn(x){ x+10 })`
  → L(11,12,"310")
- Quick sort:
  ```
  fcn qsort(list) {
      if (not list) return(list);      // L() → L()
      reg pivot=list[0], rest=list[1,*];
      left,right:=rest.filter22('<),pivot);
      T.extend(qsort(left),pivot,qsort(right));
  }
  qsort(T(5,3,32,67,2,78,23,542,1))  → L(1,2,3,5,23,32,67,78,542)
  qsort("the quick brown fox".split()) → L("brown","fox","quick","the")
  ```
- `Op("+").call(1,2)` → 3
- `Op("+")(1,2,3)` → 6, `.call` is implicit
- `f:=Op("+"); f(1,2,3)` → 6

So many options …
The call method can apply the op to lots of parameters. Here are the rules:

Op(op).call(a1)   → error (unless op is "--" or "not")
Op(op)(a1,a2)   → (a1 op a2)
Op(op)(a1,a2,a3) → ((a1 op a2) op a3) and so on

Op(op,X)(a1)   → (a1 op X)
Op(op,X)(a1,a2) → ((a1 op X) op a2) and so on

Op "--" ignores X and stops at a1.
Op "not" ignores X and stops at a1.
Op "%" takes at most two parameters (a1,a2 or X & a1).

The logic ops add a little wrinkle in that they stop if False is generated. So, in
```
Op("==")(5,6,launchMissles)
```
missiles are not launched.
The following are equivalent:
```
if(5<x<10)            println(x," is between 5 and 10");
if(Op("<")(5,x,10))println(x," is between 5 and 10");
```

Objects

You can switch the order of the operands by using the fix parameters method. For
example, to calculate the reciprocal of a list:

```
[1..5].apply('/.fp(1.0)) → L(1,0.5,0.333333,0.25,0.2)
```

Revisiting one of the first examples:

```
L(1,2,"3").apply('+.fp(10)) → L(11,12,13)
```

Syntactic Sugar

As a parameter, `'op` is converted to `Op("op")`. See create for the list of sugars.
Thus `.filter('>,3)` is converted to `.filter(Op(">"),3)` and
`L(1,2,3,4,5).filter('>,3)` → L(4,5).
`L(1,2,3).reduce('+)` → 3.
To include parameters to the op, just pass them as usual. A handy increment operator
is `'+(1)`: `T(1,"two",3).apply('+(1))` → L(2,"two1",4)

Property

Inherits from: Object
Notes
- You may need to put the object in parenthesis to access the method. For example, to access the "Property" method of an integer, `(1).Property("name")` works but `1.Property("name")` is a error.

Abstract
Property is a Object that can be used to wrap a object property or class variable. A Property can be treated like any other object.

Methods
- **create()**: Return the value of the Property. For example, the following are equivalent:
  ```
  list     = L();                        list.name;
  property = L().Property("name"); property();
  L().property("name");
  ```
  If the Property wraps a variable, then:
  ```
  class C { var x = 123; } px := C.Property("x");
  C.x ≈ px() → 123
  ```
  Returns: Unknown
- **toString()**: Returns "Property(*instanceName.methodName*)" or "Var(*className.variableName*)".
  For example:
  ```
  List.Property("name").toString() → "Property(List.name)"
      class C { var x; } C.Property("x").toString() → "Var(C.x)"
      class {var x}.Property("x").toString() → "Var(__class#0.x)"
  ```
  Returns: String
- **toBool()**: Returns True

Properties
- **instance**: The instance that this property is bound to. For example, `L().Property("name").instance.name` returns "List".
  Returns: Instance
- **value**: Returns the value of the property or variable.
  Returns: Unknown

Discussion

Property exists so you can "package" a property or variable and pass it around. It is a "pointer to value" that is used to defer dereferencing. It provides method like access to properties and variables. It is created via the "Property" Object method.

Ref

Syntax: Ref(object)
Full name: [TheVault.]Ref
Inherits from: Object
See Also: Objects.Deferred.'wrap

Abstract
A Ref is a strong reference to an object, as opposed to a weak reference (see
Objects.GarbageMan.WeakRef).
A Ref is basically a one element list.
Changes to a Ref are thread safe.

Methods
- **create(**object**)**: Create a Ref container holding object.
  Returns: Ref
- **apply(f)**: `ref.set(f(ref.value))`. `Ref(0).apply('+,1,2,3)` → Ref(6).
  `Ref(0).apply.fp('+)(1,2,3)` → Ref(6).
  Returns: self
- **dec()**: Decrements, and sets, the contents of the Ref as if it were an integer.
  Throw: NotImplementedError if `-1+ref.value` doesn't work.
  Returns: old value
- **inc()**:
  Returns: `incN(1)`
- **incN(**x=1**)**: Increments, and sets, the contents of the Ref as if it were an
  integer.
  Throw: NotImplementedError if `1+ref.value` doesn't work.
  Returns: old value
- **set(**object**)**: Sets the contents of the Ref to object.
  Returns: self
- **toBool()**:
  Returns: `self.value.toBool()`, which might recurse (eg `Ref(Ref(True))`)

Properties
- **ref**: Returns the contents of the Ref.
  Returns: Object
- **value**: Same as ref.

Operators: none

Discussion

A long winded factorial loop:
```
fcn fact(n){
    r:=Ref(1);
    (1).pump(n,Void,'wrap(n){ r.set(n*r.ref) });
    r.ref;
}
fact(5) → 120
```

A Ref can be used for pass by reference (as opposed to pass by value); however, it does not store a reference to a variable but rather the value of that variable.

```
n:=5; r:=Ref(n); n=0; r.ref → 5
```

RegExp

Full name: [TheVault.]RegExp
Inherits from: Object

Abstract
Basic regular expressions.
RegExp is not thread safe.

Remember to double quote "\\" in your expression string if you use "" strings.
Since this can be painful, consider using raw strings.

Methods
- **create(**pattern**)**:
  Throws: ValueError
  Returns: RegExp
- **matches(**text,move=False**)**: Check to see if the string matches the regular expression.
  Clears matched but does not set it. If move is True, the pattern is walked down the string looking for a match, similar to prepending ".*".
  Throws: ValueError
  Returns: Bool
- **pump(**text,sink,…**)**: Pump the chunks of text that match the regular expression.
  ```
  RegExp("79.|3.|7.").pump("139350936979874",List)
    → L("39","35","36","798","74")
  ```
  The default is to extract the entire match but if a group is used, that is extracted. Note that only the first group is used.
  ```
  RegExp("\\$(..)\\$").pump("foo$ab$bar$cd$santa",List)
    → L("ab","cd")
  ```
  To count words in text:
  ```
    RegExp("\\w+").pump(text,Dictionary().incV) → Dictionary
  ```
  Text can be String or Data.
  Returns: Something
- **search(**text,move=False,startAt=0**)**: Search a String or Data for RE matches. Sets matched.
  Throws: ValueError
  Returns: True if matched

Objects

Properties

- **matched** : A list describing the match. Matched[0] is a list of the offset and length of the entire match, the next items are group ("()") matches (strings). Returns: List(List(offset,len) [,Strings])
- **matchedNs** : A list describing the match. Matched[0] is a list of the offset and length of the entire match, the next elements are group ("()") matches, also offset/length pairs.
Returns: List of integer pairs: List(List(offset,len), ...)

Operators: None

Discussion

This object provides a basic regular expression matching/processing for Strings. It is based on the regex package originally written by Ozan S. Yigit.

Examples:

- Parsing time. If you know that the time is formatted as "hh:mm", where there can be one or two of each digit and the time can be anywhere in a string, the following will pluck it out: \D*(\d+):(\d+) This RE breaks down to: zero or more non digits followed by one or more digits followed by a colon followed by one or digits. Oh, and save the digits. To put it into a program:

  ```
  re:=RegExp("\\D*(\\d+):(\\d+)");
  ```

  The backslashes have to be doubled up because String converts "\\" to "\". It is easier to write:

  ```
  re:=RegExp(0'|\D*(\d+):(\d+)|);
  ```

  Now to use it:

  ```
  re.matches("12:4")      → True
  re.matched              → L()
  re.search("12:4")       → True
  re.matched              → L(L(0,4),"12","4")
  re.search("The time is 1:04AM");
  re.matched              → L(L(0,16),"1","04")
  re.matchedNs            → L(L(0,16),L(12,1),L(14,2))
  ```

Syntax

Close to a subset of PCRE (Perl Compatible Regular Expressions) but don't expect compatibility; be happy if it happens.

Expression	Matches
character	A single character. Unless it is one of: . \ [ ] ( ) * + ^ $
. (dot)	Any character
\c	Match a character or type of character.

c	Matches
\d	A digit: Typically [0-9]
\D	Not a digit
\s	Whitespace, including newlines ("\n") and carriage returns ("\r")
\S	Non-whitespace
\t	Tab
\w	Alphanumeric, including "_"
\<	Beginning of word. Word is \w
\>	End of a word.
\c	The character c. eg "\a" matches "a", \\ matches "\" (remember that code for matching a back quote is "\\\\" or 0'"\\". The "normal" back-quoted characters (tab, newline, backspace, etc) work as expected; ie \t matches a tab and doesn't need doubled backslashes.

Expression	Matches
[set] [a-z] [^set]	Match a character in a set

Set	Matches
[abc]	Any of the three characters "a", "b", or "c"
[a-z]	Range of characters between. [0-9A-Fa-f] will match hex digits.
[a-b-c]	Same as [a-c]
[a-a]	"a"
[-abc] [abc-]	"-", "a", "b" or "c"

Expression	Matches	
	z-a	Error
	[^set]	Any character NOT in the set. The caret has to be the first character.
	[^]-]	Any character except "]" and "-". Also "[^]]" and "[^-]"
	[]	"]". Also "[]a]" matches "]" and "a"
	[]-]	"-" or "]". "-" and "]" don't have special meaning if they are the first characters in the set but "]" has to be the first character after the "[" and "-" can be the next or last.
	\	"\". "\" has no special meaning in a set; regular string quoting will handle the character conversion. For example, "[\n]" will put a newline in the set, "[\\]" is a single backslash.
*	Zero or more matches of any of the above expressions. Greedy. Note that "x*" will match "" with a match length of 0 characters.	
+	As "*", but one or more. Greedy.	
\?	As "+" but one or none: "f\\?" matches "foo" and "bar"	
( )	Group: used to hold the results of a match. Numbered 1 to 9	
\1 \2 … \9	Match the nth group For example: (fo.*)[1-3]\1 matches "foo1foo", "foo2foo", "foo3foo" (fo.*)-\1 matches "foo-foo" "fo-fo", "fob-fob", "foobar-foobar", …	
^	Start of string	
$	End of string	
A|B	A or B. If A doesn't match, try to match B. Use as many as you want. You will need to use groups to have multiple sets: .(79.|3.|7.)..(5|6) This is greedy and doesn't back track.	

ROList

Full name: [TheVault.]ROList
Inherits from: Object

Abstract
A Read Only List. This is a List that can not be modified, only read. It is thread safe.
ROList is almost entirely a subset of List, with one addition method: build.
T is shorthand for ROList: T(1,2,3) is the same as ROList(1,2,3).

Modified Methods
- **copy( )**: Create a writable copy of self.
  Returns: List
- **create(**[objects]**)**: Create a new Read Only List instance.
  Returns: ROList
- **makeReadOnly( )**: Does nothing.
  Returns: self
- **reverse( )**: Returns a reversed copy of self.
  Returns: ROList
- **set(***offset*,*newValue***)**:
  Returns: ROList
- **sort( )**: Makes a copy of self and sorts it.
  Returns: ROList

Deleted Methods
- __sSet, clear, createLong, del, insert, pop, remove, replace,
  reverse, swap, write, writeln

Unchanged Methods
- __sGet, append, apply, apply2, calcChunk, callMethod,
  callProperty, cat, close, concat, extend, flatten, filter,
  filter1, filter22, find, flush, holds, index, len, reduce,
  run, runNFilter, sum, toBool, toList, toString, walker, xplode

Modified Properties
- isReadOnly:
  Returns True.
- isThreadSafe:
  Returns True.
- type:
  Returns "ROList"

Modified Operators
- add (+): Returns a new ROList with x appended.

Deleted Operators
- sub (-)

Unchanged Operators
- eq (==), neq (!=)

Sink

Syntax: Sink(object)
Full name: [TheVault.]Sink, the create method
Inherits from: Object
See Also: Objects.Notes on Pump

Abstract
A Sink is something you can use to aggregate data, the same as used by the pump methods.

Methods
- **create(**obj**)**: Create a sink for writing.
  Objects with a write method can be used as a sink, as well as methods and functions. See the list in the Notes on Pump (at the beginning of this chapter). Sink(sinkObj) → sinkObj, ie sinking a sink just returns the source sink.
  Returns: Sink
- **close()**: Close the sink for further writing and return the contents.
  If the sink is an Method, obj.instance.close() (if it exists) is called and the instance is returned.
  Returns: Object
- **toBool()**:
  Returns: True
- **write(**i**)**: Write i (and any other parameters) to the sink. If it needs to, the sink will transform i to the appropriate type.
  Throws: Something if i is incompatible with the sink.
     AccessError if the sink is closed.
  Returns: self

Properties
- **isClosed**:
  Returns: Bool

Operators: none

Discussion
This is the object pump uses as a sink.

Small Dictionary, PolyGraph

Full name: [TheVault.]SD (a create Method)
Full name: [TheVault.]PolyGraph (a create Method)
Inherits from: Object

Abstract
A small dictionary is a immutable Dictionary that has a maximum of 256 string keys.
A polygraph is a small dictionary where all values are True.

Both these objects have the same methods and properties as Dictionary minus the
modify methods.

Discussion
Dictionaries can be large lumbering things that are overkill for things like small
symbol tables. A small dictionary is just a key/value store plus be bit of overhead for
the index and can't be changed. A polygraph is even simpler; it is a set of strings (the
keys) that you query to see if it holds another string.

```
d := SD("one",1, "two",2); d["one"] → 1
p := PolyGraph("one","two"); p["one"] → True, p[3] → False
```

startup

Inherits from: Class

Abstract
The startup script is loaded by the VM to act as the zkl "shell". If you want a customized version of zkl, modify this class[111].

Discussion
After the VM has initialized itself, the last thing it does is load this class and pass control to it (by running the constructor).
The startup described here is the default supplied with zkl, it should be modified if you desire different functionality.

zkl <zkl *file*> ...
If the command line has parameters and the first parameter isn't an option (ie that parameter doesn't start with "-" or "--"), it is assumed that a zkl script is being run.

- **zkl *name*.zkl ...**
  The file is compiled and the constructor is run.
- **zkl *name*.zsc ...**
  The file is loaded and its constructor is run.
- **zkl *path.name* ...**
  Import is called with the pathname. This means that things like "Tests.class", "Test.testThemAll Tests", "Misc.fact" work as expected.

zkl [options] ...
The options are:

- --#! *text*: Write a #! line to object file (use with –out or –Out)
  "--#! ." will examine the first TWO lines of the source file for a #! line
- --compile (-c) fileName: Compile a file
- --Debug (-D) *integer*: Set the compiler debug level
- --debug (-d) : Compile debuggable
- --exit : Exit
- --help (-?) : Print command line options
- --I (-I) *path*: Append to the include path
- --I= *path*: Set the include path
- --load (-l) *fileName.zsc*: Load a compiled file

111Currently, you have to do this with "set zklIgnoreWad=1" or recompiling zkl. An alternative runtime override is to specify your shell on the command line: zkl myshell

- --out (-o) *file or directory*: Write compiled file to file or directory. If a directory is specified, the file name is fileName.zsc.
- --Out (-O) *directoryName*: Write compiled file to *directory*/class.vaultPath/fileName.zsc. If the class you are compiling uses AKA, this is a easy way to have it place itself, *directoryName* being the top of the output tree.
- --parse (-P) *fileName*: Parse a file and print the parse tree.
- --quit : Exit
- --resolve *name*: Find name in class
- --run (-r) : Run the constructor
- --runFcn *name*: Run a named fcn in class
- --tokenize *fileName*: Tokenize a file
- --unasm : Unassmemble class
- --version (-v) : Print the zkl version

After the options are parsed, startup sits in a loop, reading input, evaluating it and printing the result. *Control-C* will terminate the shell.

The Shell

The shell portion of startup handles user interaction – something is typed at the console prompt, startup compiles it and prints the result. Variables, named functions and classes are stored so that they can be referenced later[112]. If a variable, class or function is created with the same name as an existing object, it overwrites it.

```
zkl: 1 + 2
3
zkl: class c { var x = 123 }
zkl: c().x
123
zkl: fcn c { println("Hello from ",self.fcn) }
zkl: c()
Hello from Fcn(c)
```

Variables

In order for variables to be stored[113], they have to be declared with "var" the first time they are set. Registers are never stored.

```
zkl: var x = 123       // create variable and save it
123
```

112It does this with a lame imitation of prototype-based programming. Variables are used for the "slots", stored data is collected into a class and inheritance is used to give the command access to the stored data.

113If you don't use the variable outside of the current line, you can ignore this.

```
zkl: x + 1            // use saved variable
124
```

Miscellaneous
- Blank input lines are ignored.
- "?" prints a infomercial.
- "exit" is a predefined function that will terminate the shell.
- "help" is a predefined function that also prints the infomercial.
- Constants (const) are never stored; they are transient data.

Continuation Lines
While the compiler doesn't support continuation lines, the shell does. If the line ends with "\", the prompt changes and you can continue the line. The first line that doesn't end with "\" signals the end of the line.

```
zkl: fcn f{\
zkl: ...> println("Hello"); \
zkl: ...> }()
Hello
```

All Done
You can exit the shell in several ways:
- *Control-C* (^C) will immediately exit, which is usually the easiest way to exit. The drawback is if you have open files, they may drop data as they are not given the opportunity to close.
- *Control-D* (^D) *Enter* will do a nice controlled exit.
- "exit" and "exit()" will also exit nicely, as long as you haven't overwritten this predefined function.

Command History and Editing
Command history and line editing is handled by the OS shell. For example, on Windows, the CMD shell maintains a history stack that can be accessed with the arrow keys. On Unix, the shell attempts to load the zklEditLine shared library to provide this functionality (unless $zklNoEditLine is set).

Annoyances
Due to the way the shell is implemented, inheriting from classes defined in the shell doesn't work[114]. Thus:

```
zkl: class A {}
zkl: class B(A) {} // "A" is not a class?!?
```

114The shell stores classes in variables and you can't inherit from a variable.

Objects

generates a cryptic error. However, if both classes are defined on the "same" line, or the parent is stored in the Vault, it works:

```
zkl: class A {} class B(A) {}    // OK
zkl: class A {}        \
zkl: ...> class B(A) {}           // OK, used continuation line
zkl: Vault.add(A,"Tmp");          // Add A to the Vault
zkl: class B(Tmp.A) {}            // OK, A is real
```

String

Full name: [TheVault.]String
Inherits from: Object

Abstract

Character strings[115]. While a character set is neither implied nor imposed, each character is 8 bits. Unicode or wide characters are not supported and character zero is unavailable (it is reserved for internal use).

Strings are immutable, that is, they don't change. You "change" them by creating new ones (usually indirectly).

String Constants

> "hoho"
> "foo" "bar"
> Adjacent strings self concatenate: "foo" "bar" → "foobar". (You may need to enclose the strings in ()s: (`"foo" " %s"`).`fmt(x)` → `"foo %s"`.`fmt(x)`).

Strings can't span lines:

> "foo
> bar"

doesn't work but you could rewrite it as:

> "foo\n"
> "bar"

Special Characters	
\\	"\"
\b	Backspace
\e	Escape (\x1b)
\f	Form feed
\n	Newline
\r	Carriage return
\t	Tab
\xAB	Hex: Converts the hex constant AB to a character[116]. "\x09" ≈ "\t", "\x0a" ≈ "\x0A" ≈ "\n"

115For the old timers: An null terminated array of unsigned bytes: unsigned char string[]
116Curiously, "a\x00b" ≈ "ab" as the null is ignored.

Special Characters	
\uABCD	Unicode: Converts a four [hex] digit Unicode character (16 bits) to a UTF-8 character (two to three bytes). For example: "\u00A2,\u20ac" → "¢,€" (six characters: two for "¢", one for "," and three for "€")[117].
\Uxx...;	Multibyte Unicode: takes one to six hex digits and converts them to UTF-8. The digits must be terminated by a semicolon. "\Ua2;" → "¢ ", "\U1F0A1;" → 🂡
	Any other character just quotes itself: "\?" → "?"

Raw String Constants

Sometimes, the special characters get in the way (in regular expressions, for example). The string "AbackslashtBbackslash" can be created with: "A\\tB\\". Which isn't pretty and get down right ugly when you have to double quote a lot of things. For that, you can use raw strings: 0'*Sentinel-Character*Text*Sentinel* (zero single-forward-quote sentinel text sentinel). The sentinel character can be anything except space characters or backslash[118]. The following are all equivalent to the example string:

```
    0'XA\tB\X     0'"A\tB\"     0'|A\tB\|     0'$A\tB\$     0':A\tB\:
```

If you want to mix special character and raw you can use string concatenation:

```
    0'"A\tB is "     "A\tB" → "A\tB is A    B"
```

Terms
- *"value"* refers to the characters in the String.
- *"offset"*: See **Rules for *Offset*** (below)
- *"length"*: See **Rules for *Length*** (below)

Methods
- **append(**str,str...**)**: Creates a new string, the same as String.create(self,str...).
  Returns: new string
- **apply(**f [,*paramters*]**)**: Walks each character in *value*, applying a transform and collecting the results in a String.
  Example: The rot13 function (rotate text by thirteen characters) can be written using apply:

117If you want to view UTF-8 text with an application such as Internet Explorer, WordPad, OpenOffice Writer, etc, write a Unicode BOM (Byte Order Mark, U+FEFF) as the first character of the file. For example: `file.write("\ufeff\u00A2,\u20ac")` → *"BOM¢,€"*

118But be reasonable! For example, # works but whoever reads your code could be easily confused into thinking it is the start of a comment.

```
var letters=
    "ABCDEFGHIJKLMNOPQRSTUVWXYZabcdefghijklmnopqrstuvwxyz";
var rot13Letters=
    "NOPQRSTUVWXYZABCDEFGHIJKLMnopqrstuvwxyzabcdefghijklm";
fcn rot13(c){       // rotate one character
    try{ rot13Letters[letters.index(c)] }
    catch{ c }
}
"Hello World!".apply(rot13) → "Uryyb Jbeyq!"
```
See also: pump,translate
Returns: String.

- **charAt(**_offset,length=1_**)**: Another name for __sGet.
Throws: IndexError
Returns: String

- **close()**: Does nothing. For Stream compatibility.
Returns: self

- **copy()**: Returns self. Since Strings are immutable, self is functionally equivalent to a copy.
Returns: self

- **counts(**[string]**)**: Count the number of each character in self and return a list of those counts. If string, only return the counts for those characters.
Examples:
```
"text".counts()  → L("e",1, "t",2, "x",1)
"text".counts("at") → L("a",0, "t",2)
```
If you want a L(L(c,n), ...), use
```
"text".counts().pump(List,Void.Read,ROList)
  → L(L("e",1),L("t",2),L("x",1))
```
If you want to know the letters used the least and most:
```
ns,cs := "this is a test".counts().filter22((1).isType);
(0).minMaxNs(ns).pump(List,cs.get); -→> L("a"," ")
```
And, since there are several letters that are the "mostest", this will get them:
```
ns,cs := "this is a test".counts().filter22((1).isType);
a,b    := (0).minMax(ns);
ns.enumerate().pump(List,
        'wrap([(e,n)]){ if(n==b) cs[e] else Void.Skip });
  → L(" ","s","t")
```
Returns: List

- **create(**text="" [,_object_ ...]**)**: Create a String with _value_ set to text. If a parameter isn't a string, its toString method is called. Examples:
```
s:="text"; s("foo")  → "foo"
"".create(1,"two",3)      → "1two3"
String("this is ","a test") → "this is a test"
```
Returns: String

Objects

- **del(**offset,length=1**)**: Delete a substring and return the remainder.
  Returns: String
- **filter(**f**)**: Push characters through a filter.
  Returns: String
- **find(***pattern,offset=0,length=****)**: Look for a pattern in *value*. If found,
  returns the offset of where the pattern is, otherwise Void is returned.
  Offset and length determine the characters in self to search.
  Throws:
  Returns: Int or Void
- **fmt(**parameters**)**: Pretty much the same as C's sprintf. See below for a
  discussion of the format string (which is self).
  Throws: ValueError, conversion errors
  Returns: String
- **get(***offset,length=1***)**: Another name for __sGet.
  Throws: IndexError
  Returns: String
- **glob(**text,flags=1**)**: This is match but with self being the wild card
  pattern.
  Returns: True is there is a match, else False.
- **holds(**text [,text …]**)**: Returns True if any of the parameters are in *value*.
  Examples:
  ```
  "this is a test".holds("this")        → True
  "this is a test".holds("foo")         → False
  "this is a test".holds("foo","s a")  → True
  ```
  Returns: Bool
- **inCommon(***text, [,text …]***)**: Returns the characters of text that are in
  value. For example:
  ```
  "123".inCommon("345")   → "3"
  "".inCommon("345")      → ""
  "123".inCommon("")      → ""
  "1,12".inCommon("12")   → "112"
  ```
  To count the occurrences of a character:
  ```
  "1,12,123".inCommon("1").len() → 3
  ```
  Note: This method is basically (*value* - (*value* - *text*)) or
  value.filter(*text*.holds).
  Returns: String
- **insert(**offset,string,...**)**: Concatenate strings and insert them at offset.
  Throws: IndexError
  Returns: new string

- **index(**pattern,*offset*=0,*length*=***)**: Same as find but throws IndexError if not found.
  Offset and length determine the characters in self to search.
  Throws: IndexError
  Returns: Int
- **isSpace()**: Returns True if *value* consists entirely of white space.
  Returns: Bool
- **len()**: Returns the number of characters in *value*.
  Examaple: "123".len() → 3, "".len() → 0
  Returns: Int
- **len(**8**)**: Returns the number of UTF-8 characters in *value*.
  ```
  u:="\ufeff\u00A2,\u20ac";    // "BOM¢,€"
  u.len() → 9, u.len(8) → 4
  ```
  Throw: ValueError if *value* contains an invalid UTF-8 character.
  Returns: Int
- **matches(**wildCardPattern,**flags=1)**: Check to see if *value* matches a Unix shell like wild card (glob) expression.

Text	Matches
\x	Turns off the special meaning of x and matches it directly; this is used mostly before a question mark or asterisk, and has no special meaning inside square brackets. If flags has bit 1 set (ie 0x2), "\" is ignored for all but ? * [ ] This is for Windows files names.
?	Matches any single character.
*	Matches any sequence of zero or more characters.
[x...y] [x-y] [x-y-] [-...] [] []x...y] []-] []x-]	Matches any single character specified by the set x...y, where any character other than dash or close bracket may appear in the set. Exceptions: "]" can be the first character in the set and "-" can be the last, if you use both. Otherwise, either can be first. "[" is not special inside the set, so "[[]" and "[a-z[]" will match "[" A **dash** may be used to indicate a range of characters. That is, [0-5abc] is shorthand for [012345abc]. More than one range may appear inside a character set; [0-9a-zA-Z._] matches almost all of the legal characters for a host name. [-], [x...y-] and [-a-z] all match "-". [[-]], []-a-z] are undefined. [\] matches "\".

Text	Matches
[^x...y] [^]]	This matches any character not in the set x...y, which is interpreted as described above. ^ is only special as the first character.

Flags: A bit pattern that changes the match behavior.

Bit	Effects
0 (0x1)	If 1, case is ignored when matching. Sets are not affected. For example, `"x".matches("X",1)` → True but `"x".matches("[X]",1)` → False.
1 (0x2)	If 1, the quote character ("\") is restricted; it will only escape ?, *, [or]. This is to accommodate Windows use of that character in file names.

Matches provides a simple alternative to regular expressions (see Objects.Regexp). While it quickly becomes cumbersome for non trivial patterns, it is especially good for matching file names.
To check to see if a string is the prefix of another string, use
`s.matches(prefix+"*")`.
This method is based on the "wildmat" pattern matching code written by Rich $alz.
Throws: Conversion errors
Returns: True is there is a match, else False.

- **prefix(***string, . . .***)**: Returns the number of characters in the prefix of self and strings. Examples:
  ```
  "foo".prefix("foobar") → 3
  "foobar".prefix("foo") → 3
  "foo".prefix("barfoo") → 0
  ```
  Returns: Int
- **pump(**sink[, action . . .]**)**: Another type of loop, similar to apply but with multiple actions.
  See also: Notes on the pump method at the start of this chapter.
  Returns: The last calculated value or a string concatenation of those values.
- **reduce(**function, *initialValue*=self[0] [, static parameters]]**)**
  Iterate over *value*, applying function to each character. This is equivalent to:
  ```
  self.split("").reduce(...) // convert to List
  ```
  and (with some hand waving about initialValue and static parameters)
  To reverse a string: `"123".reduce(fcn(s,c){ c + s })` → "321"
  To count the occurrences of a character:

"1,12,123".reduce(fcn(n,c){n + (c=="1")},0) → 3
See also: Notes on the reduce method at the start of this chapter.
Throws: Yes
Returns: Unknown
- **replace(**searchFor, replaceWith**)**: Replace all occurrences of *searchFor* with *replaceWith*. *Value* is unchanged.
Example: "this is a test".replace("t","T")　→ "This is a TesT"
Throws:
Returns: String
- **rfind(**pattern,start=***)**: Same as find but in the reverse direction.
Note: If start is not *, the match may include start. For example:
"..X..".rfind("..",-2) == "..X..".rfind("..",3) → 3
"..".rfind("..",0) and "..".rfind("..",1) → 0
Returns: Int or Void
- **reverse()**: Reverse the characters.
Returns: String
- **set(**offset,length,text**)**: Replace a chunk of value with text.
Returns: new String
- **__sGet**: Perform subscript read operations on *value*.
Zero is the first position in a String.
- **__sGet(**offset**)**: This is string[*offset*]. Returns the character in *value* at *offset*.
- **__sGet(**offset,length**)**: This is string[*offset,length*]. Returns *length* characters of *value*, starting at *offset*. If there aren't length characters available, returns as many as possible (which might be none, ie "").
See below for special values *offset* and *length* can have.
Throws: IndexError
Returns: String
- **sort()**: Sort the string in ascending order, retaining duplicates.
Returns: String
- **span(**openToken,closeToken,matchOuterMostSpan=True**)**: Span a sequence of characters that start with openToken and end with closeToken (which can be more than one character but not the same). The token counts will be the same.
Examples:
"a(b)c".span("(",")")　→ L(1,3)
"/*a/*bc*/d*/".span("/*","*/",True)　→ L(0,12)
"/*a/*bc*/d*/".span("/*","*/",False)　→ L(3,6)
"a((b)c)".span("(",")",True),"a((b)c)()".span("(",")") → L(1,6)
"a((b)c)".span("(",")",False)　→ L(2,3)

```
"abc".span("(",")")  → L()
"abc)".span("(",")"),"a((b)(c)".span("(",")") → Void
```
Returns: L(start of span, length of span), Void (bad count or invalid), L() (not found).

- **split([**separator=Void,maxSplits=***)**: Splits *value* into chunks with the splits occurring at *separator*. A list containing the chunks is returned. If there are more splits than *maxSplits* allows, the remainder of *value* is appended to the list. The list will not contain more than maxSplits + 1 chunks.
- **split()**, **split(**Void,n**)**: Split *value* at white space
- **split(**separator[,n]**)**: Split *value* at separator.
- **split(""**[,n]**)**: Split *value* at each character, with a maximum list length of n.

This is different from the other forms of split in that it doesn't return a remainder, it just explodes the string into a list.

Examples:
```
"1 2   4  5 ".split()      → L("1","2","4","5")
"1 2   4  5 ".split(" ")  → L("1","2","","","","4","","5","")
"1 2 3 4 5".split(Void,2)  → L("1","2","3 4 5")
".1.2.3..4.5".split(".")   → L("","1","2","3","","4","5")
".".split(".")             → L("","")
"".split(".")              → L("")
"123".split(".")           → L("123")
"123".split("")            → L("1","2",3")
```
Returns: List

- **strip(**whichSide=0**)**: Remove white space characters.

-1	Strip from left side
0	Both sides
1	From right side

Example: `"    foo bar      ".strip()` → "foo bar"
          `"  foo bar \n".strip(1)` → " foo bar"

Returns: String

- **tail(**n**)**:
  Returns the last n characters of self. If n is larger than length, n is set to length.
  Returns: String
- **toAsc()**: Converts the first character of *value* to a integer.
  For example: `"123".toAsc()` → 0x31, `"".toAsc()` → 0
  To convert a string: `"123".toData().bytes()` → L(49,50,51)
  Returns: Int
- **toBool()**: Returns True if *value* isn't empty, otherwise, False.
  Returns: Bool

- **toData(**[mode=Int]**):**
  Returns: Data
- **toFloat():** Converts *value* to a floating point number and returns it.
  See Objects.Float for format specification.
  Throws:
  Returns: Float
- **toInt(**B=10**):** Convert *value* from base B (where B is in [2,36]) to a integer.
  Examples:
  ```
  "123".toInt()   → 123
  "ab".toInt(16) → 171
  "101".toInt(2) → 5
  "a".toInt()     → ValueError
  "".toInt()      → ValueError
  ```
  "" can be a pain, since you might like it to convert to zero. Here is a work around: (digits or 0).toInt() If there are no digits to be had, 0 is substituted (or the default value of your choice) and that is converted to an Int. Another example:(digits[a,b] or 123).toInt()

  Throws: ValueError if a character isn't valid or string is ""
  Returns: Int
- **toLower():** Return a lower case version of self. Only letters in "A-Z" are converted.
  Returns: String
- **toString():** Returns self.
  Returns: String
- **toUpper():** Return a upper case version of self. Only letters in "a-z" are converted.
  Returns: String
- **translate(**srcTable,dstTable**):** Translate characters in srcTable to the corresponding characters in dstTable. That is, if self is "a" and srcTable is "a" and dstTable is "b", the result is "b". This is a character by character translation of self through the tables.
  Example: The rot13 function (rotate text by thirteen characters) can be written using translate:
  ```
  cs:=["a".."z"].pump(String);   // "abcd…z"
  srcTable:=String(cs,cs.toUpper()); // "ab…zAB…Z"
  dstTable:=String(cs[13,*],cs[0,13]);
  dstTable =String(dstTable,dstTable.toUpper());
  a,b:="Hello World!",a.translate(srcTable,dstTable);
  println("\"%s\"-->\"%s\"-->\"%s\""
          .fmt(a,b,b.translate(srcTable,dstTable)));
  ```
  "Hello World!"-->"Uryyb Jbeyq!"-->"Hello World!"

Returns: String
- **unique()**: Remove redundant characters from value and return what's left. The resulting set remains ordered.
Returns: String
- **walker([n=3])**: Returns a Walker that iterates over *value*. Normally, this is called by foreach but you can call it too. N has the same semantics as Data.

n	walker.next() returns
0	Int (one byte of *value*)
1	String, one line at a time
2	String, *value*
3	String, one character at a time using __sGet.

Examples:
```
"123".walker().walk()        → L("1","2","3")
"123".walker(0).walk()       → L(49,50,51)
"123\nabc".walker(1).walk()  → L("123\n","abc")
"123\nabc".walker(2).walk()  → L("123\nabc")
"123".walker(3).walk()       → L("1","2","3")
```
Returns: Walker
See also: Objects.Walker, Keywords.foreach
- **zip(objects)**: Creates a new list of strings: Each sublist consists of one item from each of the source strings.
```
135".zip("24678") → L("12","34","56")
```
Returns: List of strings
- **zipWith(f,objects)**:
```
"135".zipWith('*',T(2,4,6,7,8)) → L("11","3333","555555")
```
Returns: List of strings

Properties:
- **text**: returns self

Operators
For most binary ops (eg +, <), the second operand is converted to a string (if it isn't already one), the operation is performed and a string result returned.
Examples:
```
"1" + "2"   → "12"
"1" + 2     → "12"
"1" + True → "1True" because True.toString() → "True"
"1" + Void → "1Void"
"1" < "2" ≈ "1" < 2     → True
"12" < "2" ≈ "12" < 2 → True
```

The OPs

- **eq** (==): If the other operand isn't a String, returns False. Otherwise, returns True if the two strings hold identical characters (and the same number of them in the same order).
  Result: Bool
- **neq** (!=): If the other operand isn't a String, returns True. Otherwise, returns not eq.
  Result: Bool
- **lt** (<): Returns True if *value* is lexically less than the second string.
  Result: Bool
- **lte** (<=): Returns True if *value* is lexically less than, or equal to, the second string.
  Result: Bool
- **gt** (>): Returns True if *value* is lexically greater than the second string.
  Result: Bool
- **gte** (>=): Returns True if *value* is lexically greater than, or equal to, the second string.
  Result: Bool
- **add** (+): Create a new string by concatenating the second string to value and returning the result.
  Result: String
- **sub** (-): Create a new string by removing all occurrences of the characters in the second string from *value*.
  Examples:
  `"1232" - "2"` ≈ `"1232" - 2` → "13"
  `"This is a test" - "te"` → "This is a s"
  Remove all whitespace: `string - " \t"`
  Result: String
- **mul** (*): The second operand is a integer. Concatenates n copies of *value* and returns it.
  Example: `"abc" * 3` → "abcabcabc"
  Result: String

Discussion

Often[119], you'll want (or need) to treat a string as a list of characters (as C programmers do). When the string methods just don't work, you might have to deal the string on a character by character basis. You can do this with string[*n*], foreach, reduce, or by exploding the string into a list. As an example, how would you find all

---

119Especially if you are an old timer who thinks of a string as a byte stream

the unique characters in a string (or, put another way, remove all the redundant characters from a string)? One way would be to look a character, and if it hasn't been seen yet, put it into another pile. When you have examined all the characters in the string, the pile contains the unique characters. Here are three ways of doing that:

```
reg s="This is a test";
reg result="";                              // #1
foreach c in (s){ i(not result.holds(c)) result+=c }
result=                                     // #2
    s.reduce( fcn(r,c){ if(not r.holds(c)) r+=c; r });
result=s.split("")                          // #3
    .reduce( fcn(r,c){ if(not r.holds(c)) r+=c; r },"");
→ "This ate"
```

Pick your your favorite style. Both are side effect free (outside of the function they are used in), #1 will appeal to the imperative crowd and the functional people will like the second and third. #2 and #3 are completely side effect free. #3 also shows how easy it is for a string to morph into a list.

You might be asking yourself "who cares about side effects anyway"? Nobody, until they have to use threads. There is more discussion about this in Class.threading.

Rules for *Offset* (in order):
- The first element is zero: [0].
- The last element is [-1] or [length – 1].
- If *offset* is < 0, it is added to the length.
- If offset < 0 or offset ≥ length, IndexError is thrown.

Rules for [*Offset,Length*] (in order):
- If the string is empty, the result is "".
- The *Offset* rules are applied, but, instead of an error, "" is returned.
- The default for length is 1.
- "*" is short hand for the number of elements. [0,*] is the entire list.
- If *length* is < 0, it is reset to (*value*.len() – *offset* + *length*). If still < 0, "" is the result. Thus [0,-n] is everything but the last n characters.
- If *offset* + *length* is greater than the number of available characters, *length* is truncated to what is available. Thus "123"[2,100] yields "3".

Formatting

Strings support formatting very similar to that of C's printf and sprintf. The "fmt" method takes parameters that are then formatted according to the codes in *value*. Examples:
- `"%s %s %s".fmt(self,self.fcn,123)` →
    "Class(RootClass#) Fcn(__constructor) 123"

- `"%02d:%02d:%02d".fmt(2,3,4)` → "02:03:04"

Format: [text][%[<flags>]<tag>][text]

- %% → %
- %<non-tag>: unchanged. For example, "%*" → "%*"
- flags: [+- 0,][W][.P]
- tags: bBcdfeEgGsx
- For each tag, there needs to be a corresponding parameter.

Flag	Action
+	For numbers, always prefix a "+" or "-" (%d, %f, %e, %g) Ignored by strings (%s, %c).
space	If the number is non-negative (not "" for %s), prefix a blank. Ignored by %c.
-	Left justify in the field
0	Pad the field with leading zeros.
,	Use commas every three digits for %d, %f: `"%,d".fmt(1234)` → "1,234" For %x, bytes are separated by "|": `"%,x".fmt(0x1234)` → "12|34" Binary: Nibbles: `"%,.2B".fmt(0x1234)` → "1|0010|0011|0100"
W	Minimum field width. The tag can overflow this field without being truncated (however, see Precision below). Right justified and blank padded unless overridden by "0" or "-". For floating point, width includes dot and fractional part. In other words, if you want three digits dot two digits, W is 6 ("%6.2f")
P	Precision (width)

Tag	Action performed on the corresponding parameter
Base conversion (%B)	Specifies the base used for conversion (eg 2 is binary, 8 is octal). The base range is 2 to 36.
Float (%e %E %f)	The number of digits after the decimal point.
Float (%g %G)	The number of significant digits.
Integer (%d %b %x) character (%c)	Ignored.
String (%s)	Defines the maximum number of characters that will be

Flag	Action	
		used.
		• If the string length is less than P, no padding is done (unless width is used). Use W = P for fixed field size.
		• If W < P, W is expanded to P.

Tag	Action performed on the corresponding tag parameter (v):
B	Convert v to an integer of the base specified by the precision (2 to 36). Binary: `"%.2B"`: 5 → "101", 3.4 → "11", "7" → "111"5 Octal: `"%.8B"`: 8 → "10" Hex: Use %x (although "%.16B" works just as well). If the base isn't specified ("%B"), the base is undefined.
b	Convert to Boolean `"%b,%b,%b,%b".fmt(3,L(),L(1),Void)` → "True,False,True,False"
c	Character
e E	"Scientific": [±]m.fffE±nnn, where the number of f's is specified by the precision. A precision of zero suppresses the fractional part and decimal point. The default precision is six.
d	Decimal
f	Floating point: [±]mmm.fff, where the f count is specified by the precision. A precision of zero suppresses the fractional part and decimal point. The default precision is six.
g G	"Best" floating point representation. Uses %e or %f. The decimal point and any trailing zeros are suppressed.
I	Ignore this parameter. `"%d%I%d".fmt(1,2,3)` → "13"
s	String: Call method v.toString and use that.
x	Hexadecimal (unsigned). `"%x".fmt(-1)` → "ffffffffffffffff"

Notes:
- The significant digits of a number are never truncated (those digits left of the decimal point). A field will expand to hold them all. The fractional part of a floating point number may be truncated.
- Strings may be truncated (by the field precision).
- If you combine flags "+" and " ", you'll get one of the actions but which one is undefined. Eg "%+ d".fmt(1) could generate "+1" or " 1".

- If the flags or tags are incomplete or malformed, the result is undefined.

System

Full name: [TheVault.]System
Inherits from: Object

Abstract
The System object provides access to the operating system.

Methods
- **chdir(**directory**)**: Change directories.
  Throws: IOError
  Returns: The previous directory
- **cmd(**cmd**)**: Tells the OS shell to run a command. The exit code is returned.
  There is no provision to capture the output of the command.
  For example: System.cmd("ls");
  See also: popen
  Returns: Int
- **exit()**: Stop zkl and exit to the OS. The default exit code is 0.
- **exit(**n**)**: Do the above and set the exit code to n.
- **exit(**msg**)**: Halt the VM, display a message and exit with exit code 2.
  On Unix, if the environment variable zklDumpCore is defined to 1, a core
  dump is produced. For example:
      ulimit -c unlimited   # allow a core file to be saved
      zklDumpCore=1 zkl   # set $zklDumpCore and run zkl
      zkl: System.exit("goodbye world")
      goodbye world
      Aborted (core dumped)   # file core is now exists (and it is big)
  See the Makefile for how to look at the core file with gdb.
  Returns: Doesn't
- **getenv(**name,default=Void**)**: Look up name in the environment variables,
  and, if it is there, return it. Otherwise, return the default.
- **getenv()**: Returns all of the environment variables as a Dictionary of keys
  and values.
  Throws:
  Returns: String, Dictionary or Void
- **loadFile(**fileName,runConstructor=True**)**: Attempt to load a ZSC or
  wad file. System.classPath is searched for *fileName*. If the file is a ZSC
  (.zsc), it is not added to the Vault but, if it is a wad, the classes in the wad are

added to the Vault. Also, the case of a wad, it is undefined which class is returned.

If *runConstructor* is True or List, the Class constructor is run, otherwise, it isn't. If *runConstructor* is a list, the constructor is run with the list as the parameter list. This second case is for scripts (where the constructor is the script). One reason you might *not* want to run a constructor is if the file is a script and you don't want to run the script, just load it. Or the constructor might throw LoaderError, which could confuse your error handler.

Wads

- Constructors are run in the same order as the classes were added to the wad.
- The wad builder decides which constructors will be run and which classes will get parameters.
- Every class in the wad that has its "run constructor with parameters" flag set gets the same parameters (from *runConstructor*), which the class is free to ignore.
- All classes are added to the Vault before any constructors are run[120].
- Put your "main" as the last file in the wad, then, when its constructor is run, all of the objects will have been constructed[121].
- Wad can contain Wads.

Unix: If there is a backslash in *fileName*, case folding and globbing is done.
See Also: Keywords.pimport, Utils.Wad
Throws: LoaderError, NotFoundError, whatever the constructor throws
Returns: Class

- **loadFile2(**fileName, searchTheVault=False, vaultPath=False, runConstructor=True**)**
This is loadFile with 2 many options.

120This is so wad classes that import other wad classes won't hit the file system.
121This will avoid "unresolved externals".

Parameter	Action
fileName	As in loadFile. System.classPath is searched.
searchTheVault	If String, TheVault.find(string) is called, and, if found, that Object is returned. Else the Vault is ignored.
vaultPath	If String, the loaded Class will be stored in the Vault as: *path*.<Class.name> If True, the class is stored in as: <Class.vaultPath>.<Class.name> If False, the class is not added to the Vault. If the file is a wad, this is ignored and the wad contents are added to the Vault.
runConstructor	As in loadFile

Throws: LoaderError, NotFoundError, whatever the constructor throws
Returns: Class

- **loadLibrary(**fileName**)**: Load a shared library that contains a native Object. System.libPath is searched for the library.
Throws: LoaderError, NotFoundError
Returns: The result of running the library constructor. A library constructor is different from a Class constructor so the result won't be a Class but is usually the Object the library implants. Refer to the library documentation to make sure.
- **popen(**cmd,mode**)**: Tells the OS to fork a shell and run a command. The mode determines whether you can read ("r") from or write to ("w") the cmd.
For example:
```
p:=System.popen("ls","r"); p.read().text.println();
p.close();
```
See also: cmd
Throws: IOError
Returns: File
- **toBool()**: Returns True.

Properties
- **argv** : Returns the command line parameters.
For example: L("C:\zkl\VM\Release\zkl.exe","-c","Src\walker.zkl")
Returns: ROList
- **classPath**: This is getenv("zklClassPath") or a default value (see Environment Variables) converted to a list.

This is a normal list so it can be augmented if need be.
For example: L("C:/zkl","C:/zkl/Src","C:/zkl/Built")
Returns: List

- **cwd**: Returns the current working directory.
  Throws: IOError
  Returns: String
- **hostname**: Returns the host name.
  Returns: String
- **includePath**: This is getenv("zklIncludePath") or a default value (see Environment Variables) converted to a list.
  This is a normal list so it can be augmented if need be.
  For example: L("C:/zkl/Include")
  Returns: List
- **isUnix**: Returns True if the OS is a Unix variant (such as Linux).
  Returns: Bool
- **isWindows**: Returns True if the OS is a Windows variant (such as Windows XP).
  Returns: Bool
- **libPath**: This is getenv("zklLibPath") or a default value (see Environment Variables) converted to a list.
  This is a normal list so it can be augmented if need be.
  For example: L("C:/zkl/Lib")
  Returns: List
- **OS**: Returns the name of the operating system.
  For example: "Windows" or "Unix"
  Returns: String

Operators: None

Discussion

A ZSC is a ZKL Serialized Class, which is a Class that has been serialized to a byte stream (like a File or Data). Asm.writeRootClass is used to do this. Another way to think of them: they are basically the same thing as a compiled class written to a byte stream (file). The extension for a ZSC file is ".zsc".

A wad is a collection of ZSCs. Wads are typically built with Utils.Wad

Shared libraries are used to add Objects to the zkl system without having to recompile zkl itself. On windows, the extension is ".dll". On Unix/Linux/FreeBSD, ".so" or ".so.*n*".

Objects

Import is usually used to wrap the loader methods and hide the ugly details.

The Test Classes
The Test classes are for automated/regression testing

> *Experience is the name everyone gives to their mistakes.*
> -- Oscar Wilde

Testing is important. Not anybodies idea of fun and nobody wants to do it but it is still important. The test classes are part of the system so you'll have one less excuse to avoid this chore. It is hoped that they provide a testing framework that has minimal impact on your productivity while giving you some CYA as you make future changes. It goes without saying (but I'll do it anyway) that "one off" scripts don't need a test suite but than again, everybody is probably using "throw away" code written long ago.

Test.testThemAll

Full name: [TheVault.]Test.testThemAll
Inherits from: Class

> *I've written some perfectly wonderful code. But this isn't it.*
> *-- Groucho Marx, muttered during a 3am bug hunt*

Abstract
A script for running Unit Tests in Parallel

This class is actually a "script", that is, a class that is meant to be run from the command line as a standalone program. It is used to run collections of unit tests. Unit tests are typically collected into files and one or more of those make up a test suite. TestThemAll allows you to test the entire suite as easily as testing a single file of unit tests.

From the zkl shell:
```
zkl: Test.testThemAll           // test the current directory
zkl: Test.testThemAll directory
zkl: Test.testThemAll directories
zkl: Test.testThemAll – file(s)
zkl: Test.testThemAll directories -- files
```

You can also call testThemAll within a program:
```
Test.testThemAll(".");
Test.testThemAll();          // same as above
Test.testThemAll(directory);
Test.testThemAll("--","file");
Test.testThemAll("-n10","--","test*.zkl");
Test.testThemAll("-n10 -- test*.zkl".split().xplode());
```

The tests can be interrupted by pressing the escape (**ESC**) key; when the current group of tests is finished, testing stops and stats are printed.

Discussion

If you have a directory filled with files that contain unit tests, you can use testThemAll to run all those tests in parallel. For example:
```
>ls Tests
const.zkl      fence.zkl   number.zkl  var.zkl
dataref.zkl    iso8601.zkl Object/     vault.zkl
date.zkl       logical.zkl thread.zkl  xnotUsed.zkl
```
All these files are unit testers (see Test.UnitTester, especially "returnClass(tester)". The directory "Object" and file xnotUsed.zkl are not tests and will be ignored (any files that start with x or X and directories are ignored).

TestThemAll takes all of the test files and gives each one to a thread that then runs the tests in that file. This can save time over running each set of tests sequentially (depending on the number of cores and how much time a test spends navel gazing). Each test file returns a UnitTester[122], these are collected and, after all the tests have been run, the results for all tests are printed.

Options

The options are the same if run from the command line or called:
- *directory*: "/[^Xx]*.zkl" is appended and the result is run through File.glob. In example above, "." → "./[^Xx]*.zkl" → const.h ... vault.zkl
- "--": All names after this option are considered file names (not directory names). They are expanded with File.glob. In the example above:
  -- const.zkl fence v* → const.zkl, fence.zkl, var.zkl, vault.zkl
  (source files are searched if there is no extension)
- --cho *minutes-to-run-tests* : Repeatedly run all of the tests, until time has elapsed; the tests are run as a group, the time is checked after each group has run so there may be some over shoot of the time.

122or else!

- --forever: Run the tests until ESC is pressed.
- --log : Log the test results to "testThemAll.log"
- --logTo *file* : Write the test results to *file*.
- -n *N* : Run all the tests N times. "--n" works the same.
- -R: Recurses in the directories. "--R" works the same.

If called within a program, each option needs to be a separate parameter:
    zkl Test.testThemAll tests -- foo/bar ≈
    `Test.testThemAll("tests","--","foo/bar")`

Here is an example of a test run:
    C:\zkl>zkl Test.testThemAll -R Tests

        ...
        =================== Unit Test 90 ===================
        Syntax error: A name can't start with a number: 123
        Close to
        <text>:Line 1:var R;R=123.toInt();
        Test 90 passed!
        =================== Unit Test 91 ===================
        Test 70 passed!
        =================== Unit Test 71 ===================
        Test 91 passed!
        =================== Unit Test 92 ===================
        Test 71 passed!
        =================== Unit Test 72 ===================
        Test 16 passed!
        ...
Notice that the sequence numbers are out of order, showing that the tests are actually running in parallel.

At the end of the run, stats are printed out:
        ...
        Tests/Object/class.zkl
        443 tests completed.
        Passed test(s): 443 (of 443)

        Tests/Object/list.zkl
        356 tests completed.
        Passed test(s): 356 (of 356)

    Tests/Object/data.zkl
    436 tests completed.
    Passed test(s): 436 (of 436)

    Executive summary: 1 pass in 00:00:23
      4,414 tests completed (42 files)
      Passed test(s): 4,414 (of 4,414)
      Failed test(s): 0
      Flawed test(s): 0
      Failed files(s): 0

Avoid cloudy code, it will just rain bugs.
-- Zander Kale, Zen programmer

Test.UnitTester

Full name: [TheVault.]Test.UnitTester
Inherits from: Class

I really do not know that anything has ever been more exciting than diagramming test cases.
-- Gertrude Stein, programmer

Abstract
The UnitTester class provides a framework for running small, targeted tests. The tests can be in the form of source code or compiled code.

Contained classes: UnitTester
The UnitTester class contains a single class of interest: UnitTester. The base class init function returns an instance of UnitTester.UnitTester. Pass in the name of the test source (usually the name of a file).
Thus, the following are all equivalent:

- `TheVault.Test.UnitTester.UnitTester(__FILE__)`
- `TheVault.Test.UnitTester(__FILE__))`
- `Test.UnitTester(__FILE__))`   `// UnitTester is part of the core`
- `Import("Test.UnitTester")(__FILE__))`

Class Variables (UnitTester.UnitTester)

- **numnFailed**: The number of tests that failed. A failed test is one that didn't provide the expected result.
- **failedList**: A list of all the tests that failed in this run. For example: L(3,6,12).
- **numFlawed**: The number of tests that are flawed. A flawed test is one that doesn't have a "R" class variable.
- **flawedList**: The list of flawed tests. For example: L()
- **N**: The number of tests.
- **numPassed**: The number of tests that passed.
- **payload**: A list of tests with problems. For example: L(5,"Result and expected result are different: c d").

Functions

- **stats(**out=Console**)**: Prints the stats for this test run.
- **testRun(**f,expectedException,expectedResult,atLine=Void**)**: Run some compiled code and examine the results. F is called with no parameters (f()) and the result is compared to expectedResult. If f throws an exception, that exceptions name is compared to expectedException. A failure occurs if the result is not the expected result or an unexpected exception was thrown or the wrong exception was thrown. If expectedException is Void, no exception is expected.
  The test is run in the environment of the test file, ie as if it was a normal function of that file.
- **testSrc(**srcCode,expectedCompileException=Void, expectedRunException=Void,expectedResult=Void,atLine=Void**)**: Compile and run a test.
  The source code is a string that contains code that will be compiled and run in a isolated "sandbox" – the code will not be able to access the class variables and other resources contained in the test file.
  The exceptions can be Void, a string (the name of expected exception) or a list of exception names.
  - The test code must have a class variable named "R", which is used by the UnitTester to compare to the expected result. If the test code throws an exception, R is not needed.
  - If an exception is thrown during compilation, that exception is compared to expectedCompileException and a failure is logged if it is not the same, or was/wasn't expected. ExpectedCompileException equal to Void means that no compiler exceptions are expected.

Examples:
- Passes because of invalid code:
  `testSrc("print","SyntaxError");`
- Fails because code compiles:
  `testSrc("print(5);","SyntaxError");`

- If an exception is thrown when the code is run, that exception is likewise compared to expectedRunException.

Examples:
- Passes because runtime error was expected:
  `testSrc("var R; R.bar;",Void,"NotFoundError");`
- Fails, unexpected TypeError was thrown:
  `testSrc("var R; R.bar=1;",Void,Void,1);`
- An example of a test that runs to completion:
  `testSrc("var R=\"hoho\";",Void,Void,"hoho");`
- A flawed test:
  `testSrc("1+2",Void,Void,3);    // no var R`

If atLine isn't Void, it is the line number of the test. This makes is easier to locate a failed test:

```
tester.testSrc("var R; x",Void,Void,123,__LINE__);
```

Didn't expect an exception but got: SyntaxError : Can't find "x" (in x)
  Close to
<text>:Line 1:var R; x
Test 77 failed. I hate it when that happens (line 155).

Discussion
This class has nothing in common with other unit testers (such as Java's JUnit).

Small, simple tests are quick and easy to write. When you find an error in your code, it is often easy to write a test case that exposes the error. These tests can be collected into a bunch tests that can be used to repeatedly run "regression" tests. Iteratively developing such a test suite takes much of the drudgery out of testing, and, once you fix a bug, you can be assured that if it attempts to resurrect itself and bite you, you'll find it when it does. The UnitTester class provides a class to easily manage a collection of these tests. It can verify that the code compiles as well as runs and gives the expected results. While it is targeted at short snippets of source code, it can also run large chunks of code and examine the results.

At the end of your test file, return the tester so that Test.testThemAll can use this group of tests as part of a greater suite of tests.

In my opinion, an "ideal" unit test is less than one line of code. But, sometimes, a test just isn't that easy and can be down right ugly. Such are the "joys" of testing. In such cases, it is usually easier to use testRun.

Example

```
tester:=TheVault.Test.UnitTester(__FILE__);

tester.testSrc("var R=1+2;",Void,Void,3,__LINE__);
tester.testSrc("var R=5;",Void,Void,3,__LINE__);

fcn test{ return(123); }
tester.testRun(test,Void,123,__LINE__);

tester.stats();
returnClass(tester);     // ← DO THIS! (see Test.testThemAll)
```

```
>zkl test.zkl
======== Unit Test 1 =====test.zkl==3========
Test 1 passed!
======== Unit Test 2 =====test.zkl==4========
Result and expected result are different: 5 3
Test 2 failed. I hate it when that happens (line 4).
======== Unit Test 3 =====test.zkl==7========
Test 3 passed!
3 tests completed.
Passed test(s): 2 (of 3)
Failed test(s): 1, tests L(2)
```

I write great code. Sometimes.
-- Zander Kale, muttered during a [different] 3am bug hunt

The Thread Support Classes
Full name: [TheVault.]Thread
See Also: Objects.Atomic, Keywords.critical

Abstract
Thread is a collection of Objects and Classes that support threading.
The Atomic object has the "lower" level thread objects (locks, etc), these classes build on those to provide higher level "utility" objects.

Contained Objects and Classes:

`HeartBeat`	Do something repeatedly.
`Pipe`	Communicate between multiple threads.
`Semaphore`	Control access to a resource.
`Straw`	A one element Pipe.
`StrawBoss`	Recruit a bunch of threads to work on a problem.
`Timer`	Run something after a set amount of time.

Thread.DrainPipe

Full name: [TheVault.]Thread.DrainPipe
Inherits from: Stream
See Also: Objects.File.DevNull

Abstract
A helper class. Use this if you want a "do nothing" Pipe

Discussion
If you call something that needs a Pipe but don't want to create one, use this.

Thread.Heartbeat

Full name: [TheVault.]Thread.Heartbeat
Inherits from: Thread.Timer
See Also: Thread.Timer

Abstract
A repeating timer, a pulse train.

Class variables
- **funcToRun**: The function that will be run.
- **interval**: The number of seconds between ticks.
- **nthTick**: The current tick count.

Functions
- **cancel()**: Call this if, having started a timer, you want to stop the train.
- **go()**: Start the timer.
- **init(**funcToRun,intervalInSeconds**)**:
- **init(**funcToRun,intervalInSeconds,count**)**:
  Get ready to run a function every tick. FuncToRun is anything that is runnable, such as Fcns, Methods, etc. If count is present, it is the number of times to run the function.

Discussion
A heartbeat timer is a timer that ticks at regular intervals. At each tick, it runs a function. Applications could include moving the hands of a clock every seconds (although thread latency might make this too variable), blinking a LED, updating a displayed image, checking the status of hardware, etc.

The function is passed the Heartbeat in case it wants to query or change something. The called function can dynamically modify the interval and the next function called but might be more pain that it is worth, consider just copying and modifying the code (it is only 20 lines).

Examples
- Print "Thump" once per second for ten seconds, starting one second from now:
  ```
  Thread.HeartBeat(fcn{ println("Thump") },1,10).go();
  ```
- Do the same thing but let the called function decide when to stop:
  ```
  fcn thumper(heartBeat){
      println("Thump");
      if (heartBeat.nthTick==10){
          heartBeat.cancel();
          println("OK, enough banging, stop");
      }
  }
  Thread.HeartBeat(thumper,1).go();
  ```

Warning
Time is a pretty casual concept so don't expect any kind of accuracy.

Thread.List

Full name: [TheVault.]Thread.List
Inherits from: Object

Abstract
A thread safe List. This is the same as Object.List with the addition of thread safe [write] locks on all operations. Use one of these if more one or more threads can access the list.

Modified Properties
- `isReadOnly`:
  Returns True
- `isThreadSafe`:
  Returns True
- `type`:
  Returns "TSList"

Thread.Pipe

Full name: [TheVault.]Thread.Pipe
Inherits from: Stream, Object

Abstract
A pipe is a object stream between two threads. Pipes are unidirectional and may be of fixed length.

Pipes are object streams (as opposed to bytes streams like files): data exits in the same form as it entered the pipe.

These pipes are not related to Unix pipes, other than conceptually.

Pipes are multi-producer and multi-consumer; any number of threads can write to a pipe and any number can read from a pipe.

Methods

- **breakIt(**exception=Void**)**: Break the pipe and shut it down. The pipe is closed. The data that is in the pipe remains in the pipe but can't be read. The pipe can't be written to. If you need the data that is in the pipe, use open(). If you want others to to be able to discern why the pipe was broken, you can add an exception. This exception will be thrown by read or write if either attempts to access a broken pipe.
  Breakit is mechanism for producers or consumers to signal other users of the pipe that something bad has happened; it need not have anything to do with the integrity of pipe itself. It is roughly equivalent to pipe.throw(exception), if such a thing existed.
  Returns: self
- **clear()**: Closes and removes all data from the pipe. Due to the nature of threads, if somebody is writing to the pipe at the same time, the new data may or may not be erased.
  Returns: self
- **close()**: Close the pipe and rebuff all further attempts to write data. Existing data remains in the pipe, you can continue to read (until the pipe is empty) .
  Returns: self
- **create()**: Create a new Pipe.
  Returns: Pipe
- **filter(**f**)**: Filter the contents of the Pipe.
  Returns: List
- **flush()**: Attempts to optimize the Pipe. Not particularly useful.
  Returns: self
- **len()**: Returns the number of objects in the pipe, which might be changing as you are asking this question.
  Returns: Int
- **open()**: Reopens the pipe if it has been closed or broken. Any data that was in the pipe (if and when it was closed or broken) is still there. Use clear if you need to.
  The break exception is set to Void.
  Opening an already open pipe does nothing.
  Returns: self
- **pump(**sink[, action ...]**)**: Another type of loop, similar to apply but with multiple actions. The calls are r=a$_1$(read()); r=a$_2$(r); r=a$_3$(r) ...
  To read five items from pipe *p* into a list:
      (0).pump(5, List, *p*.read.fp(True)) // force timeout to True, not n
  To read from a Pipe into a Data:

```
pipe.pump(Data(0,String))
```
See also: Notes on the pump method at the start of this chapter.
Returns: The last calculated value or a list of those values.

- **read**(timeout=True): Read one object from the pipe.
  - With no timeout, read returns the first item in the pipe or waits (blocks) until something is written to the pipe or the pipe is closed or broken.
  - Timeout. If no data is available in that number of seconds, a PipeError is thrown.
  - If the pipe was broken with an exception, that exception is thrown; otherwise, a PipeError is thrown.
  - If the pipe is closed, TheEnd is thrown.

  Throws: PipeError, TheEnd, other
  Returns: Object

- **readln**(timeout=True): Same as read.
- **reduce**(f,*initialValue*=self.read() [,parameters]): A feedback loop which runs f until the pipe is closed. The calls are:
  ```
  p:=initialValue;
  p=f(p,self.read(),parameters);
  p=f(p,self.read(),parameters);
  ...
  ```
  To stop the loop, return(Void.Stop) or return(Void.Stop,result).
  Returns: p

- **toBool()**: Returns True if there is data in the pipe.
  To check collection of pipes for available data:
  ```
  pipes=L(pipe1,pipe2,... ); p=pipes.filter("toBool");
  ```
  Returns: Bool

- **wait**(timeout=True,waitForClosed=False,throw=False): Wait for activity.
  - If waitForClosed is True, wait will block until the pipe is closed (or times out).
  - If wait times out, False is returned.
  - If the pipe has closed, True is returned. There might be data in the pipe.
  - If the pipe has data, and waitForClosed is False, 1 is returned. There might *not* be data in the pipe, if there are multiple readers.

  One use of wait to check for activity on a collection of pipes.
  ```
  pipes=L(pipe1,pipe2,... ); p:=pipes.filter("wait",0);
  ```
  p is a list of pipes that have data or have closed. To poll until activity:
  ```
  while(not (p:=pipes.filter("wait",0)))
      {Atomic.sleep(0.05)}
  ```

If you want to wait for the pipe to become empty, use
```
Atomic.waitFor(pipe.Property("isEmpty"))
```
See also: Objects.Atomic.wait

Throws: Timeout (if throw is True)

Returns: False (timeout), True (closed), 1 (data).
- **walker()**: Returns a walker so you can read the pipe from within a foreach loop.
  Returns: Walker
- **write(**x,timeout=True**)**: Write an object to a pipe.
  - Any object can be written.
  - If the pipe is broken, an exception is thrown. If the pipe was broken with an exception, that exception is thrown; otherwise, a PipeError is thrown.
  - If the pipe is closed, TheEnd is thrown.
  - If the pipe is full[123], write will block (but not longer than timeout) until there is room.

  Throws: PipeError, TheEnd, other

  Returns: Bool
- **writeln(**x,timeout=True**)**: Same as write.
  Returns: x

Properties
- **hasData**: Returns True if the pipe can be read without blocking. Might be a lie if there are multiple readers.
  Returns: Bool
- **isBroken**: Returns True if the pipe has been broken.
  Returns: Bool
- **isClosed**: Returns True if the pipe has been closed. Note that since breaking a pipe also closes it, isClosed will also return True if the pipe has been broken.
  Returns: Bool
- **isEmpty**: Returns True if the pipe is empty at the moment. Due to the nature of threads, something might be entering the pipe as you are asking this question; in which case, as soon as empty returns True, it is actually False.
  Returns: Bool
- **isOpen**:
  Returns: Bool, (not isClosed)
- **whyBroken**: Returns the exception that was passed to breakIt.
  Returns: Class or Void

123Whatever that means – implementation dependent.

Discussion

Pipes are a commonly used thread object; they make it easy to connect one (or more) thread(s) to other thread(s). Pipes can be used in non-threaded applications but it doesn't make a lot of sense to add all the overhead where a simple list would suffice.

Pipes are created open.
Data flows into a pipe and stays there until it is read or cleared.

If a Pipe is blocked, it can be interrupted by an Exception thrown at the blocked thread.

Timeouts

The timeouts are considered to be hints and are intended to avoid infinite waiting. About the only guarantee is that the method won't give up before the time out has expired (ie, it will wait at least that long). Successful reads and writes can take longer than the time out, depending on contention.

Timeout Value	Blocks
None	Yes
True or Void	Yes
False or <= 0	No; the operation succeeds immediately or fails
N (Int or Float)	Not more than N seconds

Multi-Producer, Multi-Consumer

Multiple producers (threads) can write data to pipes, and multiple consumers can suck data out of a pipe. Multiples of either are unusual, but when you need it, you really need it.

Object Stream are Typeless

Pipes are object streams, that is, data flows out of the pipe in the same format and size that it enters the pipe. If a number goes into the pipe, followed by a list, that number flows out, followed by the list. A really twisted example would be to write a pipe into a pipe, you could even write a pipe into itself (a Klein pipe?) but please don't! (a different pipe is OK and they can both be active). Lists are also object streams.

Note that that Streams like File, Data and ZeeLib are byte Streams, where the data is "flattened" to bytes as it enters the stream. This means you can't use Pipes in programs that want byte streams, such as Compiler.Asm.writeRootClass.

Closure
One thread closing a pipe is a signal to another thread that the thread is done, finished, kaput. Usually, the producer closes the pipe when it has produced as much as it is going to and closing the pipe lets the consumer know it has all the data it is going to get. But the consumer could also shut the pipe to tell the producer to shut up and go away. In a nice way of course.

Breakage
Pipes can be broken. Pipes don't usually suffer from internal breakage, usually one of the users runs into problems and breaks the pipe to let the other users know a problem has occurred. Here are a couple of examples:
- If the Tokenizer finds a unterminated string, it will break the token output pipe to signal the Parser that there is a syntax error.
- If the Parser sees an invalid token, it will break the token input pipe to tell the Tokenizer, if it is still running, that there is no need to do any more work.

Activity
If you want to wait until the pipe is written to, use wait:
```
Atomic.wait(True,pipe);
```
This will sleep until the pipe has data in it (or is closed). Of course, if there is more than one reader, the data might be gone when wait returns.

If you want to read the contents of a pipe (eg to keep it from clogging or to pass the data as a lump): `pipe.close(); pipe.walker().walk()` → List

Examples
Here is very simple example of a program talking to itself:
```
pipe:=Thread.Pipe(); pipe.write("Hello World!");
println(pipe.read());
```
The output is (drum roll): "Hello World!"

Objects

This example creates a producer thread that writes to a pipe that is read by the main thread.

```
fcn producer(pipe){
    pipe.write("one");
    pipe.write("two");
    pipe.close();
}
pipe:=Thread.Pipe();
producer.launch(pipe);      // create the producer thread
        // the consumer reads the pipe until closed:
foreach x in (pipe){ println(x); }
```

The output is:

   "one"
   "two"

A slight variation, with multiple producers.

```
fcn producer(pipe){ pipe.write("one"); pipe.write(2); }
p:=Thread.Pipe();
    // create three producers
producer.launch(p); producer.launch(p); producer.launch(p);
while (x:=p.read(5)){ print(x); }
```

Output:

   one2one2one2
   VM#46 caught this unhandled exception: PipeError : Timeout waiting for data

Observations:

1. Three producer threads are created.
2. Objects of different types are written to the pipe.
3. One pipe is created and passed to each producer thread.
4. The Producer no longer closes the pipe. It can't because doing so would cause one of the other threads to write to a closed pipe and error.
5. Since the pipe is never closed, foreach would hang after the last object is read from the pipe. It left as an exercise to the reader to learn about thread control and figure out the proper way to close the pipe. Hint: An Atomic.Int plus an Atomic.wait would do the trick. And, if you want to see it in action, look the source code for Test.testThemAll.
6. As a cheap work around, a timeout is used to avoid blocking forever. A try/catch could be used to handle the exception. It is a bad idea to rely on timing in cases like this – time is a weak concept where threads are concerned.

Now let's look two threads that talk to each other.

```
fcn A(inputPipe, outputPipe){
    outputPipe.write("Hello");
    reply:=inputPipe.read();
    println(reply);
}
fcn B(inputPipe, outputPipe){
    text:=inputPipe.read();
    outputPipe.write(text + " World");
}
p1:=Thread.Pipe(); p2:=Thread.Pipe();
A.launch(p1,p2); B.launch(p2,p1);
```

The output is: "Hello world"

A picture might help show the information flow:

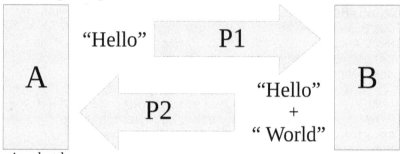

Here is what happens:
- Two pipes are created, one for passing information from A to B and vice versa. Remember that pipes are unidirectional so two are needed.
- Threads A and B are created, with the pipes crossed. This is because what is output for A is input for B.
- A writes "Hello" to its output pipe and waits for a reply from B. B waits for a message from A.
- B gets "Hello" from A, appends " World" to it and sends it back to A.
- A receives "Hello World" from B and prints it.

Other fun examples:
- Ping Pong: Bounce data between threads until somebody decides enough is enough and closes a pipe.
- Data Pump: Pass data around a chain of threads, back to the beginning.

Objects

Advanced Example: The Easy Bake Cookie Machine and Multi-Producer Pipes
Cookie Monster likes cookies. Lots of cookies. But making them takes too long. So,
after a Internet search, CM decides to buy some EasyBake Cookie Machines. The
EasyBake Cookie Company makes sophisticated automated industrial cookie baking
machines that feature user selectable recipes and allow multiple machines to be
controlled by a single start switch. The machines all feed a single conveyor belt that
feed a single cookie packaging machine (or, this case, a Cookie Monster).

Now, let's build a EasyBake Cookie Machine. When the buyer receives their
machine, they need to do some simple configuring: Select the cookie recipe, connect
it up to the conveyor belt and wire the "master" start switch. When the start switch is
pressed, all the machines will start baking cookies and send them to the conveyor
when baked.

```
var cookieRecipes=
   T("peanut butter", "chocolate chip", "ginger snap");
class EasyBakeCookieMachine{
   const MAX_COOKIES     = 2;
   const NO_MORE_COOKIES = Void;
   fcn init(cookieName,  conveyor, startSwitch){
      launch(cookieName, conveyor, startSwitch);
   }
   fcn liftoff(cookieName, conveyor, startSwitch){ // thread
      println("The ",self.name," is ready to start baking ",
            cookieName," cookies.");
      startSwitch.wait();
      do(MAX_COOKIES){
         Atomic.sleep(0.001);         // bake the cookie
         conveyor.write(cookieName); // cookie ready to eat!
      }
      conveyor.write(NO_MORE_COOKIES);
   }
}
```

Here is what a conveyor belt looks like:
```
   var conveyor=Thread.Pipe();
```
It is simply a Pipe that, very important!, can be written to by **multiple producers**.
That is, many threads can write to the pipe without the data being scrambled.

And, finally, the Cookie Monster:
```
class CookieMonster{
   fcn init{
      startSwitch:=Atomic.Bool();
      // Install and configure each machine
      foreach cookie in (cookieRecipes)
      { EasyBakeCookieMachine(cookie,conveyor,startSwitch); }
      numMachines:=cookieRecipes.len();

      cookiesEaten:=0; numEmptyMachines:=0;
      startSwitch.set();        // start making cookies!
      While(1){            // eat cookies until I burst
         // get the next available cookie
         cookie:=conveyor.read();
         if (not cookie){
            // one of the machines is out of cookie dough
            numEmptyMachines+=1;
            // stop eating when all machines are empty
            if (numEmptyMachines==numMachines) break;
         }
         else{
            cookiesEaten+=1;
            println("Yum, a tasty %s cookie!".fmt(cookie));
         }
      }
      println(cookiesEaten, " cookies eaten (burp).");
   }
}
```

Now, let's start eating!
```
CookieMonster();
      The EasyBakeCookieMachine is ready to start baking chocolate chip cookies.
      The EasyBakeCookieMachine is ready to start baking ginger snap cookies.
      The EasyBakeCookieMachine is ready to start baking peanut butter cookies.
      Yum, a tasty peanut butter cookie!
      Yum, a tasty ginger snap cookie!
      Yum, a tasty chocolate chip cookie!
      Yum, a tasty ginger snap cookie!
      Yum, a tasty chocolate chip cookie!
      Yum, a tasty peanut butter cookie!
      6 cookies eaten (burp).
```

The important takeaway here (from the programming point of view anyway) is that
Pipes can be multi-producer.

Multi-Consumer Pipes
An exercise for the interested reader is to extend the cookie machine to add Bert to the mix (so to speak) and have Cookie Monster and Bert engage in a cookie eating contest.

Another interesting bit of trivia about Pipes is that threads can pass a pipe amongst themselves and not worry about contention.

Thread.Semaphore

Full name: [TheVault.]Thread.Semaphore
Inherits from: Class.

Abstract
The classic counting semaphore, an atomic object that guards a fixed number of shared resources

Functions
- `init(availableResources=1)`:
  Returns: Semaphore
- `value()`: Returns the number of threads holding a semaphore.
  Returns: Int
- `available()`: Returns the number of available resources at this moment.
  Returns: Int
- `acquire(block=True)`:
  Returns:
- `release()`: Returns a resource. Any thread can do this, not just a semaphore owner.
  Returns: Int

Discussion
Semaphores are typically used to restrict access to a limited shared resource. An example would be a database object that has five access connections. If there are ten threads who want to access the database, only five can at any one time. A semaphore of five can be used to "nicely" control access. The code might look something like:

```
class DB{
   var semaphore;
   fcn init{ semaphore=Thread.Semaphore(5); }
   fcn gimiAccess{ semaphore.acquire(); }
   fcn imOuttaHere{ semaphore.release(); }
   fcn read …
   fcn write …
}
db=DB();
db.gimiAccess(); // when this returns, I can access database
db.write …
db.release();    // let another thread have access
```

Thread.Straw

Full name: [TheVault.]Thread.Straw
Inherits from: Stream, Object

Abstract
A Straw is a one element Pipe.
See: Objects.Thread.Pipe

Thread.StrawBoss

Full name: [TheVault.]Thread.StrawBoss
Inherits from: Class

Abstract
Useful when one set of threads is pumping out objects that can be processed by an independent set of threads. The two sets of threads are connected by a pipe (straw), though which the objects are pushed.

Class variables
- **pipe**: The pipe the class was created with.

Functions
- **abortMission(**e=Exception.BadDay**)**: Stop and die. The contract has been terminated, and the reason is in e.
- **done()**: Tell the workers to go home (exit), there is no more work coming down the pipe.

Objects

- **init(**`f,n,thePipe=Thread.Pipe()`**)**: Start n worker threads, each of which will read something from the pipe and send it to function or method f. You can think of this as "`f(pipe.read())`". F has to do something with the result, nobody else will touch it. Also, it is common to send a list of parameters down the pipe so you may need to decant them; consider using f as an intermediate function to explode the parameters and call the "real" worker function or use the Object.fp method to bind the parameters to f. Call write to get work started.
  Returns: StrawBoss
- **lendAHand()**: Throw some spare cycles at the problem. Instead of calling stopAndWait, do this: `done(); lendAHand(); wait();`. This will effectively add you to the worker pool.
- **stillRunning()**: Returns a list of vmIDs of the the worker threads still running.
  Returns: List
- **stopAndWait(**`timeout=Void`**)**: Same as calling `done(); wait();`
- **wait(**`timeout=Void`**)**: After done has been called, you can call this to wait for the workers to finish what they are doing.
- **write(**`x,timeout=Void`**)**: Same as `pipe.write(x,timeout);`

Discussion

A StrawBoss is useful when one set of threads is pumping out objects that can be processed by other threads without repercussions. One example of this is a compiler that parses chunks of code that can then be compiled to code. These chunks need to be free of interdependencies in order to avoid having to "lock step", which can kill parallelism. Read only dependencies are fine.

Example: Two simple examples:
```
// The worker function
// doesn't get much simpler than this
fcn f(x){ println(x, " ", vm); }

boss:=Thread.StrawBoss(f,5); // create 5 worker threads
foreach n in ("testing 123"){ boss.write(n); }
println("Waiting ....");
boss.stopAndWait(); // or boss.done();
                    //    boss.lendAHand(); boss.wait();
// Do something with the results
```
Output:
```
        t  VM#11
        e  VM#11
        s  VM#9
```

```
Waiting ....
t VM#11
i VM#9
n VM#8
1 VM#8
2 VM#8
3 VM#8
g VM#11
  VM#9
```

From this you can see that only three of the five threads go to do any work; there was so little to do that they were able to hog it all. Also because the processing was so simple, the output is essentially serial. This changes with more complex processing.

More realistic code might include something like:
```
strawBoss.write(vm.arglist);      // (x,y,z)
fcn f(x){ theRealF(x.xplode); } // f(L(x,y,z))→ theRealF(x,y,z)
```

Thread.Timer

Full name: [TheVault.]Thread.Timer
Inherits from: Class
See Also: Thread.Heartbeat

Abstract
Wait for while and then run a function. Analogous to a kitchen egg timer; you set the timeout and go off and cook something else. The timer dings when the egg is done.

Functions
- **cancel()**: Call this if, having started a timer, you want to cancel the action (ie don't run the function).
- **go()**: Start waiting
  Returns: Timer, ie self
- **init(**funcToRun, secondsToWait**)**: Get ready to run a function after a number of seconds has lapsed. FuncToRun is anything that is runnable, such as Fcns, Methods, etc.

Discussion
A timer starts a thread and, basically, goes away and vegetates until time is up and then runs the function and exits. Thus, the program that starts the Timer ticking can go do other things and forget about the Timer. At the appointed time, the function

Objects

starts running in the other thread and does whatever it does. Since it is in another thread, it won't be able to talk to you unless you have set up some sort of communications channel.

Example: run f after 10 seconds:
```
t:=Thread.Timer(f,10);
t.go();
```
or, the "just do it" method:
```
Thread.Timer(f,10).go();
```

Example: Print "Ding" after 10 seconds:
```
Thread.Timer(fcn{println("Ding")},10).go();
```

Example: Let's set up an alarm that will go off in one hour if not turned off. Basically, we arm the alarm and, if we are not proactive, it will go off.
```
fcn soundTheAlarm{ screamingSiren(); }
alarm:=Thread.Timer(soundTheAlarm,3600).go(); // armed and ready
doStuff();
alarm.cancel();
```
If doStuff doesn't take more than one hour (3600 seconds), the alarm will be canceled before it goes off. Otherwise, while stuff is happening, a big racket will occur.

Time and Date Objects

Abstract:
The Time section of the Vault holds objects and classes related to time and date manipulation. This section covers some basic date calculations. For more elaborate date manipulation, check out ISO8601.

Time.Clock

Full Name: [TheVault.]Time.Clock
Inherits from: Object
See Also: Objects.Time.Date, Objects.Time.ISO8601

Abstract
The Time object provides some minimal information about time.

Methods
- `mktime(`y,m,d=1,h=0,m=0,s=0`)`: Convert to time_t.
  Returns: time_t (seconds from some starting point)
- `tickToTock(`time_t,local=True`)`: Convert a time_t into a localTime or UTC time (if local is False). A time_t is what time or File.info() returns; `Time.Clock.tickToTock(Time.Clock.time)` is the same as `Time.Clock.localTime`.
  Returns: List.
- `toBool()`: Returns True.

Properties
- `localTime`: Return the time in the current time zone in a List.
  The list elements are:
  0: Year: eg 2006
  1: Month: 1 (January) … 12
  2: Day of the month: 1 … 28,29,30,31
  3: Hour: 0 … 23
  4: Minute: 0 … 59
  5: Seconds: 0 … 59
  6: Possibly undefined elements

Examples:
- To get the current date:
  `year,month,day = Time.Clock.localTime;`
- To get the current year: `year = Time.Clock.localTime[0];` or
  `year,_ = Time.Clock.localTime;`
- The current time: `_,_,_,hh,mm,ss = Time.Clock.localTime;`

Returns: List
- **runTime**: Return the number of seconds that have occurred since zkl started running. The value is a floating point number.
  Returns: Float
- **time**: Returns an integer number of seconds from some starting point.
  Returns: Int
- **timef**: Returns `time` + fractional seconds.
  Returns: Float
- **timeZone**: Returns information about the current time zone and day light savings time. The information is returned in a List:
  - Offset from UTC in seconds. For example, Pacific Standard Time trails UTC by eight hours so the offset is 28800 seconds.
  - The name of the current time zone (probably in English) or "". For example: "Pacific Standard Time".
  - True if this time zone is currently in Daylight Savings Time.
  - The name used for DST (probably in English) or "". For example: "Pacific Daylight Time".

  Returns: List(Int,String,Bool,String)
- **UTC**: Returns the current Coordinated Universal Time (aka GMT) as a List. See localTime for the list elements.
  Returns: List

Operators: None

Discussion

The Clock object relays information about time obtained from the operating system. It is a minimal set and is dependent on the OS for accuracy. The Time.Date and Time.ISO8601 classes build on this information to provide more complete time and date information.

Time.Date

Full name: [TheVault.]Time.Date
Inherits from: Class
See Also: Time.Clock, Time.ISO8601 (non core)

Abstract
A class that provides a collection of date related utilities. Uses ISO8601 format where applicable.

Class variables
- The months:
  January, February, March, April, May, June, July, August, September, October, November, December
  Symbolic constants that can help make your code a little cleaner. January is 1, December is 12.
- The days in a week:
  Monday, Tuesday, Wednesday, Thursday, Friday, Saturday, Sunday
  Symbolic constants, in ISO8601 order: Monday is 1, Sunday is 7.
- **dayNames**: A list of day names (in English): L("Sunday","Monday", …"Sunday").
  These can be indexed by the day variables.
  `Date.dayNames[Date.Monday]` → "Monday". Note that the names work for both ISO8601 and for calendars that use Sunday as the first day of the week (Sunday = 0).
- **monthNames**: A list of month names (in English): L("","January", …, "December"). These can be indexed by the month variables.
  `Date.monthNames[Date.April]` → "April"

Functions
- **addHMS(**L(Y,M,D,h,m,s), hr,mn=0,sec=0**)**: Add time to a date.
  Returns: L(Y,M,D, h,m,s)
- **addYMD(**L(Y,M,D), y,m,d**)**: Add an offset to a date. When adding months and years, the day tries to remain the same, in the same month, modulo the number of days in the resulting month.
  The input is not validated.
  `Time.Date.addYMD(T(2010,12,2), 0,1,2)` → L(2011,1,4)
  Throws: ValueError
  Returns: L(Y,M,D)

Objects

- **ctime(**[time_t]**)**: A clone of the C routine of the same name. Returns a time stamp using the current [local] time and date, for example "Mon Jan 8 02:00:51 2007". If a time_t is passed in (for example from File.info()), that time is used; ctime() and ctime(Time.Clock.time) are equivalent.
  Returns: String
- **dayName(**weekday**)**: Returns the English name for a day. 0 is "Sunday", 1 is "Monday" and 7 is again "Sunday", which works for calendar weeks that start with Monday (ISO8601) or Sunday.
  Returns: String
- **daysInMonth(**year,month**)**: Calculates the number of days in a particular month, taking into account leap years. Example:
  daysInMonth(2006,Date.February) ≈ daysInMonth(2006,2) → 28
  Returns: Int
- **daysInYear(**year**)**: Calculates the number of days in a year, taking into account leap years. Examples
  Date.daysInYear(2006) → 365
  Date.daysInYear(2000) → 366
  Returns: Int
- **httpDate()**: Returns the current date in HTTP 1.1 [header] format. For example: "Sun, 06 Nov 1994 08:49:37 GMT"
  Returns: String
- **isLeapYear(**year**)**: Evaluates if year is a leap year.
  Returns: Bool
- **monthName(**month**)**: Returns the English name for a month. 1 is "January", 12 is "December".
  Returns: String
- **monthRange(**year,month**)**:
  Calculates the number of days in a month and the week day that month starts on. Useful for creating calendars. The week is Monday based, and starts at one. For example, January 2007 has 31 days and starts on a Monday. So
  monthRange(2007,1) ≈ monthRange(2007,Date.January) → L(1,31)
  Returns: L(*first_day_of_the_month*, *days_in_month*)
- **nthDayInYear(**year,month,day**)**: Calculates the nth day of the year a date falls on.
  Examples:
  - The first day in 2006: nthDayInYear(2006,1,1) → 1
  - In 2006 there were 365 days so 2006-12-31 was day 365
    Time.Date.nthDayInYear(2006,12,31) → 365
  Returns: Int

- **parseDate(**dateString**)**: Parse a date string of the form "yyyy-mm-dd" where the three fields are one or more digits. If the year is less than 1,000, 2,000 is added. The month and day are verified.
  Time.Date.parseDate("11-8-1")   → L(2011,8,1)
  Time.Date.parseDate("2011-2-29") → ValueError, 2011 is not a leap year
  Leading and trailing space is OK.
  Blank entries are auto filled with the current date: "--" is now, "--1" is the first day of the current month/year.
  Throws: ValueError
  Returns: List(year,month,day) (as integers)
- **parseTime(**timeString, *limitHours*=True**)**: Parse a time string of the form "hh:mm:ss" where the three fields are zero or more digits. If *limitHours* is True, time is restricted to one day and "AM"/"PM" is parsed (case independent).
  Time.Date.parseTime("1:2pm") → L(13,2,0)
  Time.Date.parseDate("::3")   → L(0,0,3)
  Throws: ValueError
  Returns: List(hours,minutes,seconds) (as integers)
- **prettyDay(**[year,month,day]**)**: Pretty print a date, defaulting to the current date. Algorithm by Tamminen Eero. Examples:
  prettyDay(1995,3,9) → "Thursday, the 9th of March 1995"
  prettyDay()   → "Monday, the 8th of January 2007"
  Returns: String
- **subYMD(**L(Y,M,D), y,m,d**)**: Subtract an offset from a date. When subtracting months and years, the day tries to remain the same, in the same month, modulo the number of days in the resulting month.
  The input is not validated.
  Time.Date.subYMD(T(2011,1,2), 0,1,2) → L(2010,11,30)
  Time.Date.subYMD(T(2000,2,29),1,0,0) → L(1999,2,28) // leap year
  Throws: ValueError
  Returns: L(Y,M,D)
- **to24HString()**: Return the local time as a 24 hour clock string.
  Returns: String "13:45"
- **toAMPMtring()**: Return the local time as a 12 hour clock string.
- **toAMPMString(**h,m**)**: Use the passed in time.
  Returns: String "01:23AM"
- **toFloat(**h,m,s=0**)**: Convert hh:mm.ss to a fractional number representing the time. For example, toFloat(4,15) → 4.25 (since 15 minutes is one quarter of an hour).
  Returns: Float
- **toHMSString(**h,m,s**)**: Convert hours, minutes and seconds to a string.

`Time.Date.toHMSString(0,0,5025)` → "01:23:45"
Returns: String "HH:MM:SS"

- **toHour(**`fractionalTime`**)**: Convert a fractional time to hours, minutes and seconds. For example, `toHour(4.255)` → L(4,15,18)
Returns: L(h,m,s), list of integers
- **toYMDString(**`y,m,d`**)**: Format a date, four digits for the year, two digits for the month and day.
Returns: "yyyy-mm-dd"
- **week01(**`year`**)**: Returns the Monday of the first week in year, which actually might be in the previous year. Uses the ISO8601 rules. Examples:
  - The first week of 2006 started Monday, January 2nd. `week01(2006)` → L(2006,1,2)
  - The first week of 1987 started on Monday, the 29th of December 1986 (1986-12-29): `week01(1987)` → L(1986,12,29)
Returns: L(year,month,day)
- **weekDay(**`[year,month,day]`**)**: Returns the day in the week for a date using the ISO8601 notation (1 = Monday, 7 = Sunday). Defaults to the current day. For example: `weekDay(2007,February,6)` → 2 (Tuesday)
Returns: Int
- **weeksInYear(**`year`**)**: Calculates the number of weeks in a year, according to the ISO8601 spec. A year has 52 weeks (364 days) or 53 weeks (371 days) in it.
Returns: Number of weeks
- **zeller(**`y,m,d`**)**: Returns the day in the week for a date using Sunday centric notation (0 = Sunday, 1 = Monday, 6 = Saturday). This is a version of Christian Zeller's algorithm as modified by Tomohiko Sakamoto.
Returns: Int

Discussion

The Date class provides a collection of functions that can tell you some basic things about dates. It is ISO8601 (an international standard for date and time representation) centric, mostly in that Monday starts the week, rather than Sunday. However, if you want to work in a Sunday centric calendar, there is usually a parallel routine or easy work arounds. A much more extensive set of date manipulations can be found in Time.ISO8601.

Utilities

Abstract
The utilities are a collection of small, useful functions and classes.

Utils.Argh

Full name: [TheVault.]Utils.Argh
Inherits from: Class

Abstract
A Class to parse a Unix-like command line.

A data structure is built that describes the available options which is then used to parse a command line (a list of words). It can also be used to print a usage line. Two parsing options are provided: A "traditional" loop through the options or callback functions.

Class variables
- **leftOvers**: Holds the parameters that occur after a "--". For example, in "-f foo --gui -- bar", leftOvers → L("bar").
- **loners**: Holds the non option parameters. In "-f foo --gui bar", loners → L("bar").

Functions
- **init**(L([+]*option_long_name*,*short_name*,*doc_string*),…): Create a option template. Each option is described by a three item list:
  - The long name, that is, the option that is prefixed by a "--". If the name starts with a "+", the option requires a parameter. For example: "compile" (--compile) or "+file" (for --file *file_name*).
  - The single character name for the same option. For example: "c" (-c) or "f" (-f). If there is no short name, use "".
  - A doc string. A very short (one line) option description. This is used printing a usage message. For example: "Compile a file" or "File to compile".

  Using the above examples, the call to init would be:
  ```
  Argh(T("compile","c","Compile a file"),
       T("+file","f","File to compile"));
  ```

- **init(**L(*[+]option_long_name, short_name, doc_string, fcn*),…**)**: Same as above, except provides a callback function for each option. Can be intermixed with the above form (ie it is OK to have both types of options). Returns: Argh Class
- **parse(**list, complain=True**)**: Parse a command line against options. The command line is any list that looks like argv, a list of strings. For example:
  ```
  parse(vm.arglist); // the part of argv passed to scripts
  parse(L("-c","—file","foo.bar"));
  cmdLine="-c —file foo.bar"; parse(cmdLine.split());
  ```
  The line is parsed left to right, call backs are called as they are encountered.
  Throws: NameError, ValueError if the list has errors in it.
  Returns: List of (*option_long_name, value*) pairs.
- **usage(**[text[, …]]**)**: Print a usage message to stderr. If called with parameters, they are printed first, one per line. For example:
  - usage();
    Options:
      --compile (-c) : Compile a file
      --file (-f) <arg>: File to compile
  - usage("The compiler program");
    The compiler program
    Options:
      --compile (-c) : Compile a file
      --file (-f) <arg>: File to compile
  Returns: Unknown

Example (Looping)

```
argh:=Import("Utils.Argh")(
   T("compile","c","Compile something"), // --compile, no arg
   T("+file","f","File name"));          // --file <arg>

foreach option,arg in (argh.parse(vm.arglist)){
   switch(option){
      case("compile"){ … }
      case("file")   { … }
   }
}
klass(argh.loners.xplode());
```

Example (Callbacks)

```
var file;
argh:=Import("Utils.Argh")(
   T("compile","c","Compile something",   // --compile, no arg
      fcn{ Compiler.Compiler(file) } ),
   T("+file","f","File name",             // --file <arg>
      fcn(arg){ file=arg; }),
);
argh.parse(vm.arglist);
```

You can mix and match callbacks or no callbacks as you please. But remember that callbacks will be called before you get a chance to use looping.

These examples are examined in detail below.

Discussion

The Argh class provides a convent way to parse Unix command line options. Or any list of strings that looks like a Unix command line. Using the class consists of three phases: creating the possible options, parsing the command line, and finally, acting on the command line.

Format

A command line can contain several things:

- A word, such as "foo.c"
- A single character option, prefixed by a dash: "-c"
- A single character option that takes a parameter: "-f foo.c"
- Multiple single character options, the last of which can take a parameter: "-cf foo.c"
- Note: the space between the option letter and parameter is optional.
- A option word (one or more characters), prefixed by two dashes: "--compile"
- A long option with parameter: "--file foo.c"
- Notes:
    - Space between the long option name and parameter is required
    - Long and short options can't be mixed together
    - Options are case sensitive.
- Non options are words that don't start with a dash and are not parameters to options. These are collected separately.
- "--" signals the end of commands and the rest of the line is to be handled verbatim. These are collected separately.

Class Creation

To create a class that handles "-c", "--compile", "-f" and "--file", do the following:

Objects

```
argh=Utils.Argh(
     T("compile","c","Compile something"),
     T("+file","f","File name"));
```

The Argh initializer takes a list of options: The long name of the option, prefixed by "+" if a parameter is required, the short name of the option (or "") and a short description that is used for a "help" or usage message.
You can also attach a callback function to each option. In this case, the callback will be called as each option is parsed (and will be passed the arg associated with the option).

Parsing
Unlike many command line handlers, Argh parses the command line at once, rather than parse option, dispatch, repeat. The input is left unchanged. To parse the command line for f, file, c or compile:
```
parsedArgs=argh.parse(vm.arglist);
```
For scripts, startup passes the script constructor a "pruned" argv, so the script can work the same in a named function, ie the script doesn't care if the arglist originated at the command line or from a function call. Parse will throw NameError or ValueError if it encounters an unknown option or if an option is missing a parameter. It will also print a usage message to stderr (if the complain flag is True):
>zkl foo -f
    Option "f" is missing an arg
    Options:
     --compile (-c) : Compile something
     --file (-f) <arg>: File name
    ValueError : Option "f" is missing an arg

  >zkl foo –-foo
    Unknown option: foo
    Options:
     --compile (-c) : Compile something
     --file (-f) <arg>: File name
    NameError : Unknown option: foo

Parse returns a list of options found and their values:
  >zkl foo -f foo.bar --compile
   → L(L("file","foo.bar"),L("compile",False))

Processing
Now that the command line has been parsed, it can be processed.

Looping:
```
foreach option,arg in (vm.arglist){
    switch(option){
      case("compile"){ … }
      case("file")   { … }
    }
}
```
Callbacks: `argh.parse(vm.arglist)`

And if you want to be terse, the example can be written:
```
var file;
Import("Utils.Argh")( … ).parse(vm.arglist);
```

Here we do whatever it is we need to do if told to compile and what file it is we are to compile. Let's add to the example and assume we want to run the compiled object with some parameters that are also passed in. For example:

> foo –ffoo.zkl –c one two

We have seen what most of this parses to as but what about "one" and "two"? The argh class puts the parameters that are not options into a "loners" list. In this case:

```
L("one","two")    // argh.loners
```
So, to run something with these parameters:
```
something(argh.loners.xplode());
```
will call something with two parameters, rather than a list.

Yet another thing Unix command lines handle is the "--" option, which signals end of normal parsing. In this case, argh bundles this into "leftOvers":

> foo –ffoo.zkl –c one two -- sam

```
argh.leftOvers → L("sam")
```

Utils.BlackHole

Full name: [TheVault.]Utils.BlackHole
Inherits from: Class

Abstract
An object that has only Class methods and properties but has all methods and properties. Like File.DevNull, only more so.

Discussion
A useful data sink. It needs to be in a variable to be a sink:
```
bh:=Utils.BlackHole; bh.eatTheGalaxy() → BlackHole
bh.galaxy → BlackHole
```

Objects

A BlackHole will eat most non-Object methods and properties and return itself. Use it as a stub for a not yet defined class.

Utils.Generator

Full name: [TheVault.]Utils.Generator
Inherits from: Class
See Also: The Illustrated Examples Appendix for a discussion of how generators are implemented.

Abstract
Create a Generator that can be used to iterate over a collection. Generators are implemented with fibers, which means the (user supplied) generator function needs to use vm.yield to "generate" data.
Note: Pay special attention to when you can call yield (see Objects.VM.yield).

Functions
- **init(**f [,parameters]**)**: Create a Generator. f is a function that uses vm.yield to return values. Parameters are passed to f on the first call. Returns: Walker

Discussion
Generators are useful when you want to create a recursive walker. Ordinary Walkers can't be implemented recursively, which is really painful for things like tree traversals. Using a generator, you can write a recursive traversal, wrap it in a Generator and get all the benefits of a Walker. That sounds more painful than it actually is. For example, consider the depth first traversal of a binary tree. Here is a code snippet:

```
class Tree{
    var root;
    ...
    fcn walker{ Utils.Generator(walk,root); }
    fcn walk(node){
        if (node){
            vm.yield(node);
            self.fcn(node.left);
            self.fcn(node.right);
        }
    }
}
```

The walk function traverses the tree and uses vm.yield to pass the node it is visiting back to the walker. When it is done, it just exists. This a natural way to write the traversal. The Tree walker function packages walk into a Generator. Thus

```
tree:=Tree();
foreach node in (tree){ println(node.payload); }
```

behaves as expected. You can also use the generator directly:

```
g:=Utils.Generator(tree.walk,tree.root);
println(g.next().payload);
```

See Objects.VM for more about this example.

Coroutines

Generators can also be used to implement the classic producer/consumer coroutine algorithm:

```
fcn producer(resource)
    { foreach x in (resource){ vm.yield(x) }}
fcn consumer(producer){
    result:=L();
    foreach x in (producer){ result.append(x); }
    result;
}
```

Given a resource (such as a file, string, list, database, etc), the producer reads something and yields it. The consumer reads from the producer, does something with what it read, and tells the producer to do it again until there is nothing left to read. The consumer then returns the result of its calculations.

```
consumer(Utils.Generator(producer,"This is a test"));
```
→ L("T","h","i","s"," ","i","s"," ", "a"," ","t","e","s","t")

```
consumer(Utils.Generator(producer,File("helloWorld.txt")));
```
→ L("Hello World\n")

To do the same thing with threads requires a thread safe[124] way of passing data between the producer and consumer. With fibers, there is only one process so no locking is needed.

The consumer can also be written as:

```
fcn consumer(producer){ producer.walk(); }
```

124Such as a Pipe, which does the locking needed to be thread safe.

Utils.Helpers

Abstract
A collection of utility functions.

- **blowChunks**(walkable,sz,sync=List): Consumes the source in chunks of
  size sz.
  Utils.Helpers.blowChunks("12345",2).walk() →
  L(L("1","2"),L("3","4"),L("5"))
  Utils.Helpers.blowChunks("12345",2,String).walk() →
  L("12","34","5")
  Throws: TheEnd (source is empty)
  See also: pump with Void.Read
  Returns: Walker
- **fcomp**(f,g ...): Function composition
      f:=Op("+",1); g:=Op("*",2); h:=Op("-",3);
      fgh:=Utils.Helpers.fcomp(f,g,h);
      fgh(10) → 15 as f(g(h(10))) → f(g(7)) → f(14) → 15
  The same thing:
      fcn f(x){ x+1 } fcn g(x){ x*2 } fcn h(x){ x-3 }
      fgh:=Utils.Helpers.fcomp(f,g,h);
    or
      T(10).pump(Void,h,g,f)
  Note that fgh:=f.fp(g.fp(h)) doesn't work. In this case fgh(10) would
  pass 10 to f, not h.
  Returns: Deferred closure
- **gerber**(action,T(collection,filters)$_1$,...,T(c,fs)$_N$) → List
- **gerber**(True, action,T(collection,filters),...) → Walker
  Where action is a runnable that will be called with N parameters, collection is
  a Walker or something that has a walker method[125] and the filters (with
  collection$_x$) are runnables that will be called with x parameters.
  List comprehensions[126], nested loops with conditions or guards.
  The first collection (or walker) is iterated over and, if an item passes all
  filters, the next collection/filter list is examined, repeat all the way down. A
  collection of items (length N) that makes it to the end is passed, as a
  parameter list, to action.

125All but the first walker need to be able to be restarted (eg List but not File or Pipe).
126http://en.wikipedia.org/wiki/List_comprehension

Examples:
```
Utils.Helpers.gerber( fcn{vm.arglist}, // filtered results
    T( T(1,2) ),               // a simple collection
    T( [7..9] ), '!=(8) ), // everything but 8
    T( ["a".."a"] ) )          // just "a"
 → T( T(1,7,"a"), T(1,9,"a"), T(2,7,"a"), T(2,9,"a") )
Utils.Helpers.gerber(True, fcn{vm.arglist}, // → Walker
    T( [1..] ),                // an infinite collection
    T( [7..9], '!=(8) ),
    T( ["a".."a"] ) ) : w:=_; // w=Walker
    w.walk(5) → T( T(1,7,"a"), T(1,9,"a"), T(2,7,"a"), T(2,9,"a") , T(3,7,"a") )
Utils.Helpers.gerber( '*(2),
    T( [0..8], fcn(n){n*n > 20} ) ) → L(10,12,14,16)
```
which is the same as:
```
[0..8].filter(fcn(n){ n*n>20 }).pump(List,'*(2))
```
If there is only one finite collection and you don't need a walker, it is usually easier to use filter and pump, as shown in the last example.

If creating a Walker and gerber doesn't generate any results, TheEnd is thrown:
```
Utils.Helpers.gerber(True,fcn{},
    T([1..10],fcn{False})).walk() → TheEnd
gerber(True,fcn{},T([1..0])).walk() → TheEnd
```
If you don't like that, use pump instead of walk:
```
gerber(True,fcn{},T([1..0])).pump(List) → L()
```
Returns: List or Walker

- **listUnzip(**listOfLists**)**: Create a new list of lists, each sublist is made from one item from each of the source sublists.
  ```
  Utils.Helpers.listUnzip(T(T(1,2),T(3,4),T(5,6)))
      → L(L(1,3,5),L(2,4,6))
  ```
  Note: `listUnzip(listUnzip(a))` → a
  Returns: List of lists, very much like List.zip

Utils.MD5

Full name: [TheVault.]Utils.MD5
Inherits from: Method
References: RFC 1321 (http://www.ietf.org/rfc/rfc1321.txt)
See Also: MsgHash library for other hashes.

Abstract
Calculate the MD5 hash of a String or Data object.
Utils.MD5 is a method.

Utils.MD5(String | Data**)**: Calculate the MD5 hash.
Throws: TypeError
Returns: String

Discussion
From the RFC (Request For Comment):

> *This document describes the MD5 message-digest algorithm. The algorithm takes as input a message of arbitrary length and produces as output a 128-bit "fingerprint" or "message digest" of the input. It is conjectured that it is computationally infeasible to produce two messages having the same message digest, or to produce any message having a given prespecified target message digest. The MD5 algorithm is intended for digital signature applications, where a large file must be "compressed" in a secure manner before being encrypted with a private (secret) key under a public-key cryptosystem such as RSA.*

Examples
- `Utils.MD5("message digest")` → "f96b697d7cb7938d525a2f31aaf161d0"
- Calculate the MD5 hash of a file: `Utils.MD5(File("foo","rb").read())`

Utils.range

Full name: [TheVault.]Utils.range
Inherits from: Fcn
Syntax: **range(**count**)**, **range(**start,stop,step=1**)**
Returns: Walker
See Also: Keywords.Range, Objects.Int.Walker, Objects.Walker, Keywords.foreach

Abstract
Range creates a Walker that provides the functionality of the "traditional" for loop: iterating in discrete steps. Ranges are over Ints, Floats or characters.

Functions
- **range(**n**)**: Returns `range(0,n,1)`
- **range(**start,stop,step=1**)**: Count up or down by step.
  If stop is "*", the sequence is infinite (unless it is a character range).
  Throws: ValueError

Returns: Walker

Discussion

Range provides more information than a do() loop; mainly control of the step size and an index variable at the expense of verbosity and overhead. Range is intended to provide similar functionality to C's for loops. A range Walker has all the functionality of a Walker.

zkl	C equivalent (int i; float f;)
`foreach i in (Utils.range(10))`	for (i = 0; i < 10; i++)
`foreach i in (Utils.range(3,10))`	for (i = 3; i < 10; i++)
`foreach i in (Utils.range(10,0,-1))`	for (i = 10; 0 < i; i--)
`foreach f in (Utils.range(0.0,1,0.1))`	for (f = 0.0; f < 1.0; f += 0.1)
`foreach i in (Utils.range(3,*))`	for (i = 3; 1; i++)
`do(10)`	for (i = 10; --i;)

<u>Special Cases</u>
- Character ranges: `Utils.range("a","d")` → "a", "b", "c", "d"
  `*` isn't special: `Utils.range((40).toChar(),*)` → "(",")", "*", thus
  `Utils.range("a",*)` → [] as "a" > "*".
  Only the first character is used. `range("efg","abc",-2]` → "e", "c", "a"
  This is restricted to ASCII characters.
- The terminal value of a range might be excluded:
  `range(0.5,3)` → 0.5, 1.5, 2.5
  `range(1,6,2)` → 1, 3, 5

Utils.Wad

Full name: [TheVault.]Utils.Wad
Inherits from: Class

Abstract

A wad is a bunch of ZSCs (ZKL Serialized Class) "wadded" into a byte stream that can then be packaged into a file. This is somewhat analogous to a [extremely limited] TAR (Tape ARchive) or JAR (Java ARchive) file.

Functions
- `buildWad(manifest)`: Convert the items listed in the manifest into a wad. The manifest is a list of items that describe each wad entry. Each item is one of:

- A class name (that can be consumed by Import) or a class.
- A L(*name,run*) pair. The name is as above and *run* controls the running of the constructor at load time:
    - 1/True if the constructor should be run when the wad is loaded. This is the normal case. An empty parameter list is a passed to the constructor (which is normal for constructors).
    - 0/False/Void: Don't run the constructor. This is for scripts that will be run later. For example, a library of scripts.
    - 2 if the class is a script that should be run with parameters[127] when loaded. f Import(*don't run constructor*) is used to load the wad, this is treated as if it were 0 (when loaded by Import).
- A L(Data,*vault path*) pair. This can be used to stuff arbitrary [binary] data into the Vault. The path is used verbatim to create the vault path, no sanity checking is done.
    - If you want to store a text file in a wad, append a zero[128].
      `text=File("text.txt","r").read().append(0);`

For example:
```
manifest=
   // Get helpers from the Vault, run constructor
   T("Utils.helpers",
      "Compiler/compiler.zsc", // get class from file system
      L("script.zsc",0),  //load file, don't run constructor
      L(File("jj.jpg","rb").read(),    // Data
     "Pictures.jpg"),
);
```
If the run constructor field is missing, it is filled in based on the isScript property (scripts are not run).
See Also: Objects.System.loadFile
Throws: LoaderError, others
Returns: Wad

- **verifyWad(**wad**)**: Basically does a dummy load of the wad to verify its correctness. Prints out some information.
- **wadToC(**wad, stream=Console, wadName="wad"**)**: The wad is converted into a C data structure that can be loaded at runtime (see wad.c). It is basically a huge unsigned array of chars.

Discussion

---

[127]The parameters are passed in from System.loadFile, Import, the command line, etc.

[128]Once a Data enters a wad, it becomes a ConstData and, unlike a Data, can't grow to include the trailing zero that strings need.

Wads are a convenient way to package Classes for inclusion in C code or for binary distribution. zkl itself uses a giant wad to store the classes that are considered part of the "core" language. A program might consist of several files, making distribution "messy"; packaging them in a wad enables the end user to consider them a single unit.

Import, MinImport, System.loadFile, and System.loadFile2 will all load a wad file, although the importers want the file to have a ".zsc" extension.

All the Classes in the wad are stored into the vault, which means they need to use the AKA keyword.

Examples
Here is how the zkl wad is built (lots of files are missing for brevity):
```
Var Wad=Import("Utils.Wad");
var manifest=T(
   "exception.zsc", "minimport.zsc", …,
   L("Compiler/compiler.zsc",666),…,L("startup.zsc",0)  );
wad:=Wad.buildWad(manifest);
Wad.verifyWad(wad);
Wad.wadToC(wad,File("wad.c","wb"));
```

The output looks like:
```
Building wad: ................ 124,831 bytes
Wad header
   Protocol:       1.0
   Infomercial:    zkl Wad
   Time Stamp:     Mon Feb 18 11:19:40 2008
   Number of ZSCs: 13
   Data size:      154,280 bytes
   Run list:       1111101101110
   Flags:
```

Class Name	Offset	Size	Run
Exception	0	7,307	1
MinImport	7,307	476	1
Utils.Helpers	7,783	10,859	1
…			
startup	148,096	6,184	0

Note: startup was explicitly set to not run the constructor, testThemAll was set implicitly based on the fact it is a script.

Objects

wad.c looks like:
```
/* This file is machine generated (by Wad.wadToC)
 * Don't mess with it, your efforts will be in vain.
 * Generated Mon Feb 18 11:19:40 2008
 */
    // Number of ZSCs: 13
    // Exception              MinImport
    // Utils.Helpers          Thread
    // Utils.Argh             Nested Wad(Compiler/compiler.zsc)
    // Import                 Test.UnitTester
unsigned char wad[154666] = {
0x20,0x20,0x77,0x5f,0x8a,0x00,0x01,0xda,0x31,0x2e,0x30,
...
}
```
In this example, the file order is very important because of the interdependencies[129].
For example, the constructors of the compiler components will try to load the other
components, so those need to be added to the Vault first.

Script Example

The next example is very simple. We would like a script to print the current time and
date. The code looks like:
```
    AKA(nowIsTheTime);          // needed by buildWad
    d:=Import("Time.ISO8601");
    println("It is now ", d.DateTime().pretty());
```

The problem is that the ISO8601 class isn't part of the core, so this code won't run
unless the zkl tree is around (we'll ignore details like Date would work just as well
and other irritating facts). What we can do is package ISO8601 and the above code:
```
    Wad:=Import("Utils.Wad");
    wad =Wad.buildWad(L("Time.ISO8601","nowIsTheTime.zkl"));
    Wad.verifyWad(wad);         // verify wad
    f:=File("nowIsTheTime.zsc","wb"); f.write(wad); f.close();
```
Build the wad:
```
Building wad: ..
Wad header
  Protocol:       1.0
  Infomercial:    zkl Wad
  Time Stamp:     Tue Apr 17 22:16:21 2007
  Number of ZSCs: 2
  Data size:      9765 bytes
  Run list:       10
  Flags:
```

129The loader processes the wad serially, a class is read, constructor run (if it should be) and stuffed
  into the Vault. Then the next class is processed.

```
Class Name                     Offset   Size
----- ----                     ------   ----
  Time.ISO8601                      0    9571
  nowIsTheTime                   9571     194
Checking: ..
```
And run it:

```
>zkl nowIsTheTime
It is now 22:24:05 Tuesday, the 17th of April 2007
```

Utils.wap

Full name: [TheVault.]Utils.wap
Inherits from: Fcn
Syntax: **wap(f)**, where f is something that throws TheEnd or IndexError
Returns: Walker
See Also: Objects.Walker

Abstract
Create a Walker using a callable that throws TheEnd (eg another Walker or
Data.readln) or IndexError (eg List.__sGet).
A wap'd callable gets called with one parameter: 0,1,2,3, … Use .fp* to change this.

Discussion
Very useful for creating Walkers from scratch.
Examples:

- Walkers typically start at the beginning of an object. What if you'd rather start
  in the middle? Using Data as an example:
  ```
  d:=Data(0,String,"This","is","a","test");
  d.seek(8);                     // start at character 8
  w:=Utils.wap(d.readln.fpM("")); // NO parameters
  w.walk() → L("a","test")
  ```
  This creates a Walker that using d.readln() calls. Since readln(n) means
  something, by using .fpM("") we ensure readln gets no parameters.
- Given a Walker, how to enumerate it? (Enumerators, for this discussion,
  transform each *i* into L(*n,i*), where *n* is 0,1,2, …). Using "w" from the
  previous example:

```
        w2:=Utils.wap('wrap(n){return(n,w.next())}');
        w2.walk() → L( L(0,"a"), L(1,"test") )
```
- `fcn w2(w){ w=w.walker();`
  ```
        Utils.wap('wrap(){T(w.next(),w.peek())}').walk()
  }
  ```
  ```
  w2("1234") → L(L("1","2"),L("2","3"),L("3","4"))
  p:=Thread.Pipe(); p.write(1).write(2).write(3).close();
  w2(p) → L(L(1,2),L(2,3))
  ```

Utils.zip

Full name: [TheVault.]Utils.zip
Inherits from: Fcn
Syntax: `zip(object,…)` → L(L(obj$_0$[0],obj$_1$[0],…), L(obj$_0$[1],…),…)
Returns: List of lists

Abstract
The same as `zipWith(ROList.create,obj,obj,…)` except the objects have to
support a "get" method, not a "walker" method.

Utils.zipWith

Full name: [TheVault.]Utils.zipWith
Inherits from: Fcn
Syntax: `zipWith(f,walkable,…)` → L(f(w$_0$[0],w$_1$[0],…), f(w$_0$[1],…),…)
                   `zipWith(False,f,walkable,…)` → f(w$_0$[n],…,w$_m$[n])
                   `zipWith(Void,…)` → `zipWith(idFcn,…)`
Returns: List or last result

Abstract
Stack a group of collections and pass vertical slices to a function.

Discussion
Runs f with parameters from each walkable until any one of the walkers is
exhausted. If the first parameter is False, the results are not aggregated.
```
Utils.zipWith('+,T(1,2,3,99),T(4,5,6)) → L(5,7,9)
Utils.zipWith(False,fcn(n,line){"%3d: %s".fmt(n,line).print()},
     [1..],File("foo.txt"))
```
   → **1:** file foo
     2: line two of foo

```
Utils.zipWith(Void,[0..],["a".."c"])
  → L( L(0,"a"),L(1,"b"),L(2,"c") )
```
You can write enumerate like so[130]:
```
var enumerate=Utils.zipWith.fp(Void,[0..]);[131]
enumerate("abc") → L(L(0,"a"),L(1,"b"),L(2,"c"))
enumerate("abc","hoho") → L(L(4,"a","h"),L(5,"b","o"),L(6,"c","h"))
```

How about file enumeration in parallel?
```
pipe:=Thread.Pipe();
fcn{File("foo.txt").pump(Void,pipe.write); pipe.close()}
    .launch();  // create thread
Utils.zipWith(False,
    fcn(n,line){"%2d: %s".fmt(n,line).print()},
    [1..],pipe);
```
This creates a thread that reads a file line by line and writes it to a pipe. When done, it closes the pipe (which is very important as it tells zipWith when to stop). zipWith then combines a counter with the lines.

130Note: since the function is a partial (ie the counter is closed over), it does not reset across calls.
131Note that enumerate() is an infinite list

Vault and TheVault

Full name: [TheVault.]TheVault, [TheVault.]Vault
Inherits from: Object
Notes: **TheVault** is a reserved word, **Vault** is not.

Abstract
The Vault provides a global store for "native" objects and classes.

Use `TheVault.BaseClass` or `Vault` to access the methods and properties.

Methods
- **add(**class | native [,path]**)**: Add something to the vault. If path is present, and is a string, it is used to specify the location of the object. If not present, the vaultPath property is used (for classes, vaultPath is set with the AKA keyword).
  If the path doesn't exist, it is created.
  Throws: ValueError
  Returns: True
- **addAs(**object,path**)**: Add something to the vault. Path is used to specify the location of the object.
  If the path doesn't exist, it is created.
  Returns: True
- **bestFit(**path**)**: Returns the longest number of characters that match the name of something in the Vault.
  Examples:
  ```
  TheVault.BaseClass.bestFit("Walker")        → 6
  TheVault.BaseClass.bestFit("Walker.range") → 6
  ```
  To get the object that has the best fit, use find. For example:
  ```
  path:="Walker.range";
  n:=TheVault.BaseClass.bestFit(path);
  Vault.find(path[0,n]);        → Walker
  ```
  Returns: n (0 if no match)
- **cache()**: The Vault contains a cache of commonly used objects that the VM requires. This method returns the contents of that cache. Used by the compiler as an optimization in conjunction with the opVCache instruction.
  Returns: List of objects
- **cache(**object**)**: Searches the cache for object and returns its cache index. For example: `Vault.cache(List)` or `Vault.cache(TheVault.List)`. The match has to be exact; this doesn't work: `Vault.cache(List())`.

Returns: Int or Void
- **cache(**Void, *name***)**: Search the cache for an object named *name*. If found, return the cache index. This is shorthand for: `Vault.cache(TheVault.name)` or `Vault.cache(Vault.find("name"))`. For example: `Vault.cache(Void,"List")`.
Returns: Int or Void (if name not found).
- **cache(**Void, *n***)**: Returns the nth entry in the cache.
Throws: ValueError if *n* is out of range.
Returns: Object
- **chase(**path**)**: Follow path, using resolve, starting at the top of the Vault. This is an "extended" resolve.
Examples:
```
    TheVault.BaseClass.chase("Walker")  → Walker
    Vault.chase("Walker.range")         → Fcn(range)
```
Throws: NotFoundError
Returns: Object
- **dir(**outputClass=Console**)**: Writes a sorted, formatted list of the Vault contents to the output class. For example:
```
    Atomic
    Compiler
        Asm
        Compiler
        Parser
    Console
```
To write the list to a file:
```
    TheVault.BaseClass.dir(File("foo.txt","w"));
```
Throws:
Returns: Unknown
- **find(**name**)**: Search the vault for name. Basically resolve. If not found, returns Void.
For example: `TheVault.BaseClass.find("Time.Clock")` → Clock
"" matches TheVault.
Note: Void isn't in the Vault so you don't have to worry about find("Void") being ambiguous. Of course, that creates its own set of problems.
Returns: Object | Void
- **holds(**class | native**)**:
Examples:
```
    TheVault.BaseClass.find(Atomic)        → True
    TheVault.BaseClass.find(Atomic.Lock)   → False
```
Returns: Bool
- **path(**class | native**)**: If the object is in the Vault, return its vault path.

Objects

Examples:
```
TheVault.BaseClass.path(Atomic)  → "TheVault.Atomic"
TheVault.BaseClass.path("")      → "TheVault.String"
```
Returns: String or Void
- **resolve(**name**)**: Search the vault for name. If found, returns the object, otherwise, throws NotFoundError.
  For example:
```
TheVault.BaseClass.resolve("Time.Clock") → Clock
TheVault.BaseClass.resolve("Time")        → NotFoundError
```
  Throws: NotFoundError
  Returns: Object

Properties
- **contents**: Returns the current contents of the Vault. For example:
  L("TheVault", "Compiler.Compiler", "Compiler.Parser", "Compiler.Toknizer", "Import", "Test.UnitTester")
  Returns: List of names

Operators: None

Discussion
The Vault is somewhat like a file system for objects; it is used to hold "global" objects, that is, those objects that are considered to be useful enough to be stored in place is visible to every other object. The compiler will look here when it tries to resolve references. The "core" objects (such as List, String and Compiler) are stored here. The Vault acts like a Dictionary where the key is a "directory" entry; for convenience, the key usually has a direct mapping to the actual file system (see Objects.Import). The "dir" method displays a listing of the objects in the Vault.

A "native" object is one that is written in C. These are created by the VM itself or by a C library.

Typically, Import is used to add things to the vault.

Why is BaseClass required to access things in the Vault?!?
Blame it on the compiler; when it sees TheVault.*anything*, it treats that as a reference to something in the Vault. This is what makes code like
```
Clock=TheVault.Time.Clock;
```
work. If it didn't work like this, the above code would have to be
```
Clock=TheVault.BaseClass.resolve("Time.Clock");
```

which isn't any fun either. The compiler had to make a choice. Which is why "Vault" exists, so you can have it *your* way.

Why TheVault and Vault?

Because using BaseClass becomes so annoying, especially when interacting with the Vault in the shell, the Vault object exists. It is the same object as TheVault, minus the "resolve" method, so it behaves like other objects. Thus, things like `Vault.dir()` work as expected. Note, however, that "Vault", unlike "TheVault", is not a reserved word. "Vault" exists as a convenience object, not an essential one.

Quirks

The concept of a "directory" is a bit ambiguous, which can be useful or just confusing. Consider:

```
TheVault.BaseClass.add(Compiler.Compiler,"");
TheVault.BaseClass.dir();
```

will yield:

```
        ...
    Compiler
    Compiler
        Compiler
        Parser
    Console
```

Now the key "Compiler" is two things: a Class and a directory that holds the compiler Classes. It is definitely confusing but also reduces typing if you use the compiler a lot:

```
Compiler.compileFile
```

is equivalent to

```
Compiler.Compiler.compileFile
```

The Thread Class and the Thread.Pipe Object use the same trick to mix objects and classes. This will work as long as the vaultPaths are not the same; if they are, the objects won't coexist.

VM

Full name:　　[TheVault.]VM
Inherits from: Object
See also:　　Keywords.Class

Abstract
A Virtual Machine object, which might be a thread or fiber (created by another object) running some code.
VM threads can be created with the `launch` Class and Function methods, fibers by `createFiber`.

Methods
- **argsMatch(**matchParameters**)**: This method attempts to provide parameter pattern matching, similar to that found in C++[132] and other languages. The args-to-be-matched are vm.arglist.
Here is an example:

```
class Line{
    fcn intersect{
        if (vm.argsMatch(Line))
            return(intersectLine(vm.pasteArgs()));
        if (vm.argsMatch(Circle))
            return(intersectCircle(vm.pasteArgs()));
        throw(Exception.ValueError("Line.intersect:
            (%s)???".fmt(vm.pasteArgs())));
    fcn intersectLine(line)    { ... }
    fcn intersectCircle(circle){ ... }
}
```

Parameter	Matches Parameter *P*
None	Matches only if vm.arglist is empty (ie L())
*	Match anything
NullClass	Any class
Class	*P*.isInstanceOf(*Class*)
nullFcn	Any function
fcn	*P*.isInstanceOf(*fcn*)
0	Int
1	Int or Float

132Function/Method overloading. For example, with two function f(int x){} and f(char *s){}, f(1) and f("foo") call different functions. Also multiple dispatch or multimethods.

Parameter	Matches Parameter *P*
""	String
"name"	*name*==*P*.name. Eg argsMatch("RegExp")
List, ROList	List or ROList
other	Match same type (*P*.isType(*other*))

If there are fewer *matchParameters* than in vm.arglist, the extras in vm.arglist are ignored. In other words, `fcn{ vm.argsMatch(0) }(1,"ignored")` → True. This is different from the the special case `fcn f{ vm.argsMatch() }` where `f()` → True and `f(1)` → False.

See also: Keywords.switch

Returns: Bool

- **createFiber(**f [,parameters]**)**: Create a fiber wrapped around function f. A VM is created and f is run in that VM. The calling VM is stalled until the fiber yields or f returns (if it returns before it yields).

  Fibers can create fibers.

  To see the state of the fibers, you can use:
  ```
  println(vm.vms,vm.vms.apply(fcn(v){ v.isFiber }));
  ```
  which might print something like "L(VM#4369,VM#33)L(2,0)", which means there are two VMs, one of which is a running fiber.

  Throws: yes

  Returns: The result of the first yield or f(parameters).

- **kick(**targetVM [,*instance (or child) of Exception.HeyYou*]**)**: Throw a HeyYou exception at a VM. This is useful if you want to kick another thread or fiber.

  Notes:
  - If the target isn't running, it doesn't take kindly to being kicked, even if it is dead.
  - You can't throw at self.
  - If a thread is blocked (for example, waiting for a OS operation to finish or in a driver) it might ignore the exception until it becomes unblocked. Most Atomic objects and waits are interruptible.

  Warnings:
  - If multiple threads throw exceptions at another thread or one thread throws several exceptions at another thread, the receiving thread's catch block might catch all of them or only one (depending on the timing). If it catches more than one, it will ignore all but one of them. And it is entirely unknown which one that will be.
  - You are expected to go out of your way to avoid using this mechanism.

Throws: ValueError, TypeError

Returns: Bool. False if VM is not excepting exceptions or already has a pending exception, True if the exception is now pending.

- **nthArg(n)**: Returns the nth parameter to the currently running function.
  Throws: IndexError if n is out of range.
  Returns: Object
- **pasteArgs(_offset_=0)**: Take the parameter list of the running function and paste it into the parameter list of the object being called. This is useful for "trampoline" functions that just want to pass their parameters to another function. For example
  ```
  fcn f(args){ println(vm.pasteArgs()) }
  fcn{ g(1,vm.pasteArgs(),2) }
  ```
  This is equivalent to vm.arglist.xplode(_offset_,*) without the overhead of creating a list. Default parameters have been expanded and if parameters have changed, pasteArgs uses the current values[133].
  Throws:
  Returns: Void
- **resume()**: Restart a stalled fiber. Not thread safe!
  If self is a stalled fiber, it resumes running. The calling VM stalls until the fiber yields or exits. Note that the VM calling resume doesn't have to be the VM that created the fiber, but it will be the VM that stalls waiting on the fiber.
  Throws: AssertionError
  Returns: The result of the next yield or the terminal result of the fiber
- **stackTrace()**: Dumps a stack trace to the Console.
  Throws: AssertionError
  Returns: Void
- **toString()**: Returns "_self.name_" or "DeadVM".
  Returns: String
- **yield([result,...])**:
  If self is a running fiber, the fiber is stalled and control returns to the VM that resumed or created it. Result is returned to the createFiber/resume call that started the fiber running.
  Only the running fiber can tell itself to yield; telling a fiber to yield from another thread is an error. There are some other restrictions to ensure that a fiber only yields at a "safe point", one that can be resumed. This does NOT work:
  ```
  fcn f(g){ g(1) } f(vm.yield);
  ```
  because the "vm.yield" method is bound to the wrong VM. While

---

[133]`fcn(x){ x=3; println(vm.pasteArgs()) }(1,2)` → "32"

```
    fcn g(v){ v.yield(1) } vm.createFiber(fcn{ g(vm) });
```
does work, it is poor form because the fiber can't be reclaimed (as it is self referencing: g's parameter list holds the fiber)[134].

Throws: AssertionError if the vm/fiber can't yield.

Returns: Result, ROList, or Void (same as return)

Properties

- **arglist**[135]: Returns a copy of the list of parameters that was used to call the currently running function. Default parameters have been expanded. If there are no parameters, a read only list might be returned (either way, the list is empty). Since it is a copy, changing the list has no effect on the actual parameters.
  Returns: List or ROList
- **isDead**: Returns True if the VM is kaput. Pretty much (not isRunning).
  See Also: isRunning
  Returns: Bool
- **isFiber**: Returns the following:
  0: Not a fiber
  1: Is a fiber and it is stalled
  2: Is a fiber and it is running
  It should be obvious that vm.isFiber returns 0 or 2.
  Returns: Int
- **isRunning**:
  Returns: True if the VM is running. False means the VM has stopped and is in the process of being garbage collected. This is THE test for VM "health". However, a VM that that answers "yes" may be in the process of saying "no". It should be obvious that vm.isRunning returns True.
  See Also: isDead
  Returns: Bool
- **isThread**: Returns True if this VM is a thread. This value will remain unchanged until the VM is reused. Be aware that the answer might change by the time you get it.
  Returns: Bool
- **libraries**: A list of the names and authors of the libraries used by the VM.

134VMs are "root" objects; all root contents are marked by the garbage collector. If a fiber is stalled and not marked, it can be reclaimed. Thus a fiber that contains a reference to itself can never be reclaimed.

135It would seem to make more sense for arglist to have been a function property (ie self.fcn.arglist) but indirect references to arglists in dead VMs are a potential problem (circuitous but easy to do). And, yes, arglists do live in the VM, functions just receive a reference to them.

Returns: List of Strings
- **name**: Returns "VM#*n*" where n is a positive integer. For example "VM#1", "VM#45". VMs are recycled so you may see the same name arise from the ashes. No two VMs will have the same name. A VM awaiting resurrection will return "DeadVM".
Returns: String
- **numArgs**: Returns the number items in self.arglist without actually making a copy of the arglist.
Returns: Int
- **numThreads**: Returns the number of currently running threads. Which may be changing as you make this call.
Returns: Int
- **registers**: A VM contains at least two registers: R, X and a set of zero or more dynamic registers. This returns a list of the values in the register file (which are object instances). The number of dynamic registers change as the program runs. R is the result register (which holds function return values, among other things), X is the temp register and the register file holds block local values (for example, variables created with the "reg" keyword).
Throws: AssertionError
Returns: L(R,X,reg0,...)
- **regX**: The X register. When the compiler creates a constructor, it stores the result of the constructor in X and self in R as the last bit of constructor code. Thus, if you care, you can get both the new instance and a result when creating a new instance.
Example:
```
fcn eval(text){
   TheVault.Compiler.Compiler.compileText(text)
      .__constructor();
   return(vm.regX);
}
eval("1+2");  // compile and run "1+2", returning 3
```
Notes:
- If the constructor uses returnClass, this won't be of much use.
- If the running VM is the one looking at the X register (for example, the eval function above), you could be looking at a Heisenbug – the act of looking at regX could cause it to change. If X isn't making sense, you may need to look at the asm code to see if your code is changing regX.
Throws: AssertionError
Returns: Object

- **vms**: No, not a VAX. This returns a list of the all the VMs running at this moment in time. By the time you get this list, it may no longer be valid as threads can be created and may exit at any time.
  Returns: List of VM instances
- **xxception**: While a onExit function is running, xxception is set to the exception that caused the onExcit function to run. True means that an uncatchable exception was thrown. Void means an uneventful exit, no exception thrown.
  Returns: Void, Exception or True.

Operators
- **==**: Returns True if both operands are the same [live] VM.
- **!=**: Returns Bool.

Discussion
A VM is an instance of a running program or code. The most obvious ones are threads. But Objects can also create VMs to run "helper" programs; zkl programs that an Object calls from C code. A VM is an Object just like any other, although it is more dynamic and can expire while you are looking at it. In fact, they are very dynamic: the test suite causes hundreds of thousands of VM life cycles.

You should treat a VM instance as a "weak reference"; while the instance exists, it may not be valid. It could be a thread or fiber that has died or is undergoing some type of transformation.

Threads

Typically, you'll see only one VM. However, there can a lot of them, depending what is running. For example, the test suite can have over one hundred threads running; the compiler, four or more.
To find all the running threads at a point in time:
```
vm.vms.filter(fcn(v){ v.isThread })
```
example output: L(VM#3)
It is important to note that by the time this has run, it could well be out of date.

Fibers

Fibers are basic non-preemptive threads that behave like functions, continuations, generators or coroutines. A fiber is a VM that can be called like a function and can suspend itself, returning control, and a result, to the calling VM. You treat fiber VMs like any other object. The is no particular reason to use a fiber over a thread; they do, however, allow you to easily write recursive walkers (aka generators) and avoid locking issues when used like threads. Since they are not preemptive, if you call a fiber and it stalls, you will stall. They consume about same amount of resources as a thread[136]. The VM makes extensive use of fibers to run "helper" code.

Warnings

- References to threads or fibers won't stop them from dieing. For example:
  ```
  fiber:=vm.createFiber(fcn{ vm.yield(vm) });
  fiber.resume();
  ```
  fiber is now a reference to a dead VM. The VM is still a valid object but it won't do anything useful. A reference to a stalled fiber (one that has yielded) will keep the fiber from being recycled.
- It is a really bad idea to have more than one thread controlling fibers. Two threads calling resume will probably crash the VM (this is difficult for the VM to protect against). It is reasonable for one thread to manage a bunch fibers or pass a fiber amongst threads.
- Fibers are restricted as to when they can yield. They won't yield from within a method. You'll run into this when, for example, you try to yield inside a function called from filter/apply[137], etc.

Exceptions

- If a fiber throws an exception (and doesn't catch it), the exception propagates to the calling VM. The fiber dies.
- Throwing an exception at a stalled fiber will delay the handling of the exception until the fiber is resumed.

Creation

Fibers are created with the "createFiber" method, which creates a fiber running a function. The "yield" and "resume" methods stall and resume a fiber.

Results

Yield causes a fiber to stall and return a value but it is createFiber and resume that actually see the value.

- ```
  r=vm.createFiber(f);
  ```
  R is the result returned by the first yield or the result of f(), if f returns (or exits) rather than yields. One handy thing a fiber can do is yield its vm when starting so that it can be controlled:

136Threads, being creatures of the OS, use OS resources, such as additional stack space. Which can be considerable; on my MS Windows box, I can create about 2,000 threads before I run out of memory but 20,000 fibers are a "mere" blip (or, more correctly, a blimp, but it works).

137Which are List methods that create a fiber to run the function.
  ```

```
        fiber=vm.createFiber(f);
        fcn f{ vm.yield(vm); resumesHere(); }
```
● r=fiber.resume();
Once a stalled fiber has restarted, resume will get the result of the next yield or return value (if the fiber terminates).

● If the fiber throws an exception and doesn't catch it, the exception will kill the fiber and fly past by resume or createFiber (ie they won't get a result)[138].

Generator Example[139]

One of the clearest reasons to use a fiber is the ease in which you write can certain types of walkers; if the walker is best written recursively, it is an exercise in masochism to try and write a "flat" version. Tree traversal is a prime example. Generators are used to return values from the middle of the recursive walker function.

Here is a simple binary tree structure:

```
class Node{  // a three element list would also work nicely
    var left,right,value;
    fcn init(value){ self.value=value; }
}
class Tree{
    var root;
    fcn add(value){
        if(not root){ root=Node(value); return(self); }
        fcn(node,value){
            if(not node) return(Node(value));
            if(value!=node.value){  // don't add duplicate values
                if(value<node.value)
                        node.left =self.fcn(node.left, value);
                else node.right=self.fcn(node.right,value);
            }
            node
        }(root,value);
        return(self);
    }
    fcn traverseInOrder(node=root){
        if(node){
            self.fcn(node.left);
            println(node.value);
            self.fcn(node.right);
        }
    }
}
```

138Assuming that createFiber or resume aren't wrapped in try
139Another example would be an random number generator

Objects

```
    fcn walker{ CarpetCrawler(self) }
} // end Tree
```

Now build a tree:
```
tree:=Tree().add("D").add("A").add("C").add("B");
        C
       / \
      A   D
     / \
        B
       / \
```

```
tree.traverseInOrder();
A
B
C
D
```

Notice how simple it is to write an in order first traversal. But how can we create a walker so that it is just as easy to traverse the tree with, for example, a foreach loop? You could use a callback to spit out nodes from inside the recursion but that is awkward and removing the recursion is even worse. Instead, we can use a generator to suspend the traversal, return a node and then resume traversing. We implement generators with fibers.

We already have our walker template in place, now let's implement it.
```
class CarpetCrawler{
    fcn init(tree){
        var [const] fiber=vm.createFiber(start,tree.root);
        returnClass(Walker.tweak(fiber.resume));
    }
    fcn start(root){   // running in the fiber
        vm.yield(vm);     // stall until Walker wants a node
        walkNode(root);    // yield the first node
        return(Void.Stop); // signal all done
    }
    fcn [private] walkNode(node){  // the fiber
        if(node){
            self.fcn(node.left);     // recurse left branch
            fiber.yield(node.value);  // yield a node's value and stall
            self.fcn(node.right);     // recurse right branch
        }
    }
} // end CarpetCrawler
```

This isn't as pleasant as it should be but we have to do some prep work before we can actually traverse. But notice that walkNode (which actually does the traversal) is basically identical to traverseInOrder.

Here it is in use:
```
foreach node in (tree){ print(node," "); }
println();
→ A B C D
```
And this code knows nothing about the Tree internals, which is how it should be.
Another use:
```
    tree.walker().walk().println(); → L("A","B","C","D")
```
OK, how does this magic work? We'll look at two levels; the generator point of view
and the implementation point of view. Generators/fibers know about yield; the code
runs until it has a result and then it yields that result to somebody else and stalls.
When that somebody is ready for more, it tells the generator to resume and produce
another result. When there are no more results to yield, the generator returns
Void.Stop to signal that. The generator is wrapped by a Walker[140], who will call
fiber.resume each time it wants a value. And the Walker provides the support that
foreach needs.

A simple idea, and walkNode shows that, in the cold harsh light of reality, it can be
that simple. walkNode produces a result and yields it, when there are no more results,
it returns to start, which in turn tells the Walker to stop.

Under the covers, there is lots and lots of state that has to be maintained but that is
not our problem, the VM does the heavy lifting.

Generators are useful enough to have been added as the Utils.Generator class. Using
that we can make the following changes to Tree:
```
class Tree{
    ...
    fcn walker{ Utils.Generator(walk,root); }
    fcn walk(node){
       if(node){
          self.fcn(node.left);
          vm.yield(node.value);
          self.fcn(node.right);
       }
    }
}
```

140We use a Walker template (the default) of zero to infinity. It passes resume an int, which resume
    ignores.

Void

Full name: [TheVault.]Void
Inherits from: Object

Abstract
The Void object is used to indicate an absence of anything, but, since it is an object like any other, that is a convention. It is analogous to C's NULL, Python's None or LISP's nil. There is only one Void object.

Methods
- `create()`:   Returns Void.
- `toBool()`:   Returns False
- `toString()`: Returns "Void"

Properties:
The following values are sentinels for state machines such as pump (see Notes on Pump at the start of this chapter).
- `Again`, `Drop`, `Filter`, `Read`, `Recurse`, `Skip`, `Stop`, `Void`, `Write`, `Xplode`

These markers identical to Void and are difficult differentiate outside of a method. The toString method is one of those. User defined code won't find these of much use outside of passing them to methods.

Operators
- `==` : Returns False unless the other operand is also Void, in which case it returns True. (`Void==y`) is equivalent to (`y.isType(Void)`).
- `!=` : Opposite of ==.

The operators == and != do not try to do a type conversion of the second operand, they just check to see if it is Void or not Void. Thus, operand order can be important:
- `if (Void)` is the same as `if (False)`
- `if (Void == False)` is the same as `if (False)`
- `if (False == Void)` is equivalent `if (not Void)` is equivalent to `if (True)`, which is what you would expect in this case but is not in this case:

```
fcn f{
   if(error) return Void;
   return(result.toBool());
}
if (not f()) println("Error");
```
which can generate erroneous results (because when f returns Void on some errors, if(not f()) becomes if(not Void)). What you probably want is:
```
if (Void==f()) println("Error");
```

Discussion

Walker

Full name: [TheVault]Walker
Inherits from: Object
Sell Also: Keywords.range, Objects.Utils.wap

Abstract
Walkers are the zkl iterator. They walk over sequences, streams, do stepwise iteration, and can be extended to iterate over just about anything. They can also "moon walk": look ahead and push back objects. They can be infinite in length.

Most objects implement a Walker. For example, Strings. `"foo".walker()` returns a Walker that returns "f", "o", "o".

`[a..b]`, `[a .. b]` and `[a..b,step]` are syntactic sugar for range Walkers.

Note: Walker() is syntactic sugar for Walker.zero().

Methods
Notes:
If there is a count, that is the number of results that will be returned.
If there not enough items to fulfill a request, the result will be short. Eg
`T(1).walk(10)` → L(1).

- **apply(**f [,*paramters*]**)**: Walks, applying a transform and collecting the results.
  See also: pump
  Returns: List.
- **chain(**walkables**)**: Returns a Walker that cycles through the walkables as if they were one Walker.
  For example: `Walker.chain("foo",2,["a".."c"]).walk()` →
      L("f","o","o",0,1,"a","b","c")
  `[1..3].chain([7..10,2]).walk()` → L(1,2,3,7,9)
  Returns: Walker
- **chunk(**chunkSize,sink=List**)**: Returns a Walker that consumes source in chunks.
  Examples:
  - `""abcdefghij".walker().chunk(3,String).walk()` →
    L("abc","def","ghi","j")
  - `foreach x,y,z in ([1..9].chunk(3)){}`
    x,y,z → (1,2,3), (4,5,6), (7,8,9)

- "abcdef".walker().chunk(2,String).chunk(2).walk() →
  L(L("ab","cd"),L("ef"))
  Returns: Walker
- **cproduct**(walkables): A lazy cross product.
  Walker.cproduct(["a".."c"],2).walk() →
  L(L("a",0),L("a",1),
     L("b",0),L("b",1),
     L("c",0),L("c",1))
  Which is the same as foreach a,b in (["a".."c"],2){}
  If you use an infinite list, make it the first parameter.
  Returns: Walker
- **create()**: Returns a Walker that counts from zero to zero.
- **create**(transform[,terminus[,peeker]]):
  Walker.create(…) (aka Walker(…)) tweaks Walker.zero() (don't pass
  parameters to the transform).
  Another useful walker to transform is (0).walker(*) (ie walk from zero to
  infinity (and beyond) and pass those numbers to the transform).
  See tweak.
  Returns: Walker
- **cycle**(): Returns a Walker that cycles through its contents.
  For example: [1..3].cycle().walk(6) → L(1,2,3,1,2,3)
  Returns: new Walker, modifies self
- **cycle**(a,b,c): Returns a Walker that cycles through the parameter list.
  For example: Walker.cycle(1,2,3).walk(6) → L(1,2,3,1,2,3)
  If there only one parameter (eg **cycle("abc")**), a.walker().cycle() is
  returned.
  Thus:
  ```
   Walker.cycle("abc").walk(4)          → L("a","b","c","a")
   Walker.cycle(T(1,2,3)).walk(4)       → L(1,2,3,1)
   Walker.cycle(2).walk(4)              → L(0,1,0,1)
   Walker.cycle(T(2)).walk(4)           → L(2,2,2,2)
   Walker.cycle(2,Void.Skip).walk(4)    → L(2,2,2,2)
  ```
  Returns: new Walker
- **drop**(n): The same as do(n){ self.next() } return(self);.
  drop(*) drops everything, drop() and drop(-1) are no-ops.
  Throws: TheEnd
  Returns: self
- **filter**([count,] f=Void [,static args]): Send each item through f
  and, if f returns True, add the item to a list. If f is Void (or doesn't exist), the
  identity function is used (f(x) → x).
  If count, filter attempts to return that many results.

Examples:

- To generate a list of even multiples of 3:
  `[0..12,3].filter(fcn(n){ n.isEven }) → L(0,6,12)`
- To gather all lines in a file that have "foo" in them:
  ```
  File("foo.txt").walker().filter(
      fcn(line){ Void!=line.find("foo") })
  ```
- If you wish to create a lazy [infinite] filter, you can use something like
  `fltr:=[0..].filter.fp1(f)`. Then you can call `fltr(5)` to get the
  next 5 results.

Retruns: List or what aggregate was set to

- **filter**(`Walker,f=Void [,static args]`): This form, for all filters,
  creates a lazy filter.
  Returns: Walker
- **filter1**(`[count,] f=Void [,static args]`): Filter until an item passes.
  If count, it is ignored.
  Returns: Item that passed or False.
- **filter22**(`[count,] f=Void [,static args]`): Filter into two lists.
  If count, filter22 attempts to return that many results.
  Returns: List(items that passed, the ones that didn't)
- **_next**(): Returns True if could read an item. The item is in `.value`.
  Returns: Bool
- **next**(): Returns the next item in the sequence. You can call this anytime to
  walk on and the Walker will track.
  Throws: TheEnd if try to read past the end of the sequence (eg
  `T.walker().next()`) or there is nothing to return (eg
  `T(1,2,3).walker().tweak(fcn{ Void.Stop }).next() )`.
  If you don't like that behavior, use _next, pump or tweak the walker:
  `walker.tweak(Void,Void)` will return Void (forever) instead of throwing
  TheEnd.
  Returns: Object
- **pump**(`[n,] sink [,action, action, …]`): Run the action(s) for each item
  in the walker (the result of an action is passed as the parameter to the next
  action).
  Examples:
  - Take the length of each item in a list:
    `L("1","22","333").walker().pump(List,"len") → L(1,2,3)`
  - Calculate the first 3 factorials from a list:
    ```
    L(3,5,7,10,11).walker()
        .pump(3,List,fcn(x){ x and x*self.fcn(x-1) or 1 })
    → L(6,120,5040)
    ```

- To read a file into a list, stripping leading and trailing white space from each line: `File("foo.txt").walker().pump(List,"strip")`
See also: Notes on the pump method at the start of this chapter.
Throws: If an action does. Does not throw TheEnd (which walk() does).
Returns: List (or what aggregate was set to) or result of last action
- **read()**: The same as `next`.
- **reduce(**[n,] f,*initialValue***)**: The same as List.reduce with an optional count.
Six factorial: `[2..6].reduce('*',1)` → 720
Returns: Object
- **reset()**: Attempt to reset self so the next read will be the first item in the source.
Returns: self
- **sink(***sink***)**: Set the type of data that `apply`, `filter`, `pump` and `walk` return.
T or L: (ROList or List): A list of results
String: String
Data: Data as Data, use `sink(Data,String)` for Data of strings.
Void: Don't aggregate, just save last result.
For example, URL decode[141]can be written as:
```
fcn urlDecode(text){
    w:=text.walker();
    w.tweak(fcn(c,w){
        if(c=="%") w.walk(2).toInt(16).toChar()
        else c
    }.fp1(w))
    .sink(String).walk();
}
urlDecode("http%3A%2F%2Ffoo.com%2Fbar") → "http://foo.com/bar"
```
Throws: ValueError if invalid sink
Returns: self
- **tweak(***transform*[,*terminus*[,*peeker*]]**)**: Modify an existing Walker. If any one of the parameters is **Void.Void** (or Void for transform or peeker), it is ignored.
  - Transform: A function (or Partial) of the form fcn(i) where i is what the walker would normally return.
  Returning **Void.Skip** will skip that value, **Void.Stop** is the same as hitting the end of the stream, return(**Void.Stop**,v) ends the stream with v.
  Void.Read is the same as Void.skip, return(**Void.Read**,n) reads n more items and re-calls the tweak with them as parameters.

141http://en.wikipedia.org/wiki/Url_encode

> `return(`**`Void.Again`**`,`x`)` is retry, passing x as the second parameter.
> **Note**: If transform throws, it is not caught. For eample,
> `Walker(`**`[1..20].next`**`).walk()` throws theEnd because `[1..20]`
> throws under Walker.

- Terminus: What to return when the end of the stream is reached. If you need an infinite stream where Void is always returned when the stream is exhausted, use Void.

  Transform is not called for these values.

  If terminus is a Fcn, it is called (with self as the parameter) and that result is returned. If the Fcn returns **`Void.Again`**, an attempt is made to read another value from the source (you probably want to call reset).

  You can use .atEnd to check for end of stream.

- Peeker: A function (or Partial) of the form `fcn(i,EoS)` where i is the transformed item and EoS is False. If EoS (end of stream) is True, i is Void.

  This is for the case where peek needs to return values that differ from `next` (which won't return peeked values).

You can tweak a tweaked walker. When next is called, the first walker gets a value, transforms it and hands it to the next walker to be transformed and so on. The peeker is ignored until the most recent walker. Note that the base Walker is consumed.

Examples:

Two enumerators:
```
fcn f(i,n){ return(n,i) }
T("a","b","c").walker().tweak(f).walk()
["a".."c"].tweak(f).walk()
  → L(L(0,"a"), L(1,"b"), L(2,"c"))
```

The second is interesting because it shows tweaking a tweaked walker.

Tweaked times 2:
```
w1:="abc".walker();
w2:=w1.tweak(fcn(c){ return(c,c.toAsc()) });
w2.walk() → L(L("a",97),L("b",98),L("c",99))
w1.walk() → TheEnd as w2 consumed w1
```

Returns: self or a new Walker

- **`walk(`**`[n]`**`)`**: Walk self and returns a list of the results.

  Examples:
  ```
  (0).walker(5).walk()=[0..4].walk() → L(0,1,2,3,4)
  "foobar".walker().walk(3)  → L("f","o","o")
  "f".walker().walk(3)    → L("f")
  ```

Throws: TheEnd, same as next. Pump doesn't throw.
Returns: List

- **walker()**: Returns self. This is so that things like
    ```
    foreach x in (foo.walker())
    ```
  work.
  Returns: self (Walker)
- **zero()**: Creates a Walker that always returns zero. More importantly, it doesn't pass any parameters to its transforms (in the case of Walker.zero.tweak).
  Walker() is syntactic sugar for Walker.zero().
  Walker(f) is syntactic sugar for Walker.zero.tweak(f).
  Returns: Walker
- **zip(**sequence, **...)**: A lazy Utils.Helpers.zip.
    ```
    [1..].zip("This is a test".split(" ")).walk() →
      L(L(1,"This"),L(2,"is"),L(3,"a"),L(4,"test"))
    ```
  A list of (n,fib(n)):
    ```
    var nfib=[1..].zip(
        fcn(ab){ ab.append(ab.sum(0.0)).pop(0) }.fp(L(1,1)))
    nfib.drop(3); nfib.walk(5) → L(L(4,3),L(5,5),L(6,8),L(7,13),L(8,21))
    ```
  Enumeration:
    ```
    foreach n,s in ([1..].zip("This is a test".split()))
      { "%2d: %s".fmt(n,s).println(); }
    ```
  → 1: This
    2: is
    3: a
    4: test
    ```
    Walker.zip([0..],(100).random.fp(109)).walk(5)
    ```
  → L(L(0,105),L(1,108),L(2,107),L(3,107),L(4,100))
  Returns: Walker
- **zipWith(**f, sequence, **...)**: A lazy Utils.zipWith.
    ```
    [1..].zipWith('+,[10..]).walk(5) → L(11,13,15,17,19)
    ```
  Returns: Walker

Look Ahead

- **peek()**: Returns the next item in the walk but doesn't remove it. Multiple peeks will return the same value.
  Throws: TheEnd
  Returns: Object
- **peekN(**n**)**: Looks ahead n items and returns that item but doesn't remove it or change the walk order.
  Throws: TheEnd
  Returns: Object

Objects

- **push(**x, ...**)**: Sticks x at the front of the walk such the next call to next or peek will return it.
  Returns: self.

Note: Look ahead affects the n and value properties.

Properties
- **atEnd**: True if the last value has been read. If haven't read, returns True, even if there isn't anything to read.
  w:=L().walker(); w.atEnd → False, w._next(); w.atEnd → True
  Returns: Bool
- **idx**: Index into the source stream. It starts at zero, remains at zero for the first next() and increments thereafter (ie it is the index of the current object).
  Returns: Int
- **n**: The number of objects produced. If look ahead is used, n will be out of sync with the underling stream (idx).
  Returns: Int
- **value**: The current value. Void before the first read.
  Returns: Object|Void

Variables
- **_nameWalker**: This isn't a Walker variable; it is created by foreach loops so you can access the loop walker. For example:
  ```
  foreach c in ("foo"){
     println("character %d is %s".fmt(__cWalker.n,c));
  }
  ```
  Prints:
  character 0 is f
  character 1 is o
  character 2 is o

Discussion
Walkers are the zkl iterators and maintain state as they walk. If you want to access a object in a linear fashion, Walkers will do it. Foreach is implemented with Walkers. Many objects support walkers so you can loop over them "out of the box". In addition, it is easy to implement walker functionality for your favorite class or code. Filter/pump/reduce also iterate over collections but do it in one shot and have limited access to the lexical environment. Walkers offer more flexibility and "iterative" style.

In Use

Walkers are the object foreach uses for iteration, which is very convenient as most objects have walkers (if iteration is possible). Examples:
- To iterate over each character in a String: `foreach c in ("foo"){ … }` will walk "f", "o" and "o". Which is same result as `"foo".walker().walk()`.
- To iterate over every line in a text file:
  `foreach line in (File("text.txt")){ … }`

Looping Without foreach

While a common use of a walker is [invisibly] in a foreach loop, they are also very useful when you want to apply a transform to a sequence (defined by its walker). The filter, next, pump, reduce and walk functions can all do this.

<u>next</u>

Next allows you "unroll" a foreach loop and give you a finer grained control of looping.

For example, the following reads from a file, skipping over lines until it sees a line with "GO!" in it. It then prints the rest of the file.

```
walker=File("test.txt").walker();
while(Void==walker.next().find("GO!")){} // or filter1
// instead of: foreach line in (walker){ print(line); }
// use
walker.pump(Console.print);  // print the rest of the file
```

<u>filter</u>

The search in the above example could also be written as:
```
walker.filter1(fcn(line){ Void!=line.find("GO!") });
```

<u>walk</u>

Walk can be used to generate a range of numbers:
```
[0..12,3].walk()          → L(0,3,6,9,12)
```
If you have an infinite sequence, you can walk parts of it:
```
var s=[0..*]; s.walk(5);  → L(0,1,2,3,4)
s.walk(3);                → L(5,6,7)
```

<u>pump, reduce</u>

The pump and reduce functions are basically loops. Say you want to print a file with line numbers. Here is a simple function that does that:
```
File("foo.zkl").walker().pump(Void,
    fcn(line,rn){ print("%4d: %s".fmt(rn.inc(),line)) }.fp1(Ref(1)));
```

Objects

Running this on the preceding file produces:
```
1: File("foo.zkl").walker().pump(Void,
2:   fcn(line,rn){ print("%4d: %s".fmt(rn.inc(),line)) }.fp1(Ref(1)));
```
It would be simpler to use a global variable for the line count, this method avoids external state.

And, of course, you can change "File" to any object that supports a walker and get a numbered list. Let's show another way to avoid global state:
```
Utils.Helpers.fcns.walker().reduce(
    fcn(n,line){ println("%d: %s".fmt(n,line)); n+1 },1);
```
1: Fcn(__constructor)
2: Fcn(objectDir)
3: Fcn(commaize)
...
And finally, zip is really good for things like this.

Creating new Walkers: the tweak

- To repeat 5 forever: `(0).walker(*).tweak(fcn{5})` or `Walker(fcn{5})`
- Methods can work tweak as well as functions:
  ```
  (0).walker(*).tweak("").walk(10)  →  "0", "1", ...
  (0).walker(*).tweak(1.0).walk(10) →  1.0, 2.0, ...
  (5).walker(*).tweak(T).walk(10)   →  L(5), L(6), ...
  ```
- Consider the Collatz conjecture[142], which is that the sequence

  $$f(x) = \begin{cases} n/2 \text{ if } n \text{ is even} \\ 3n+1 \text{ if } n \text{ is odd} \end{cases} \text{ for } n>0 \quad \text{will always end in 1 [and is finite]. How}$$

  would we write a walker that generates these sequences? First, code the formula:
  ```
  fcn collatz(n,cs=L()){ cs.append(n);
     if(n==1) return(cs);   // stop the recursion
     if(n.isEven) return(self.fcn(n/2,cs));
     return(self.fcn(3*n+1,cs));    // odd
  }
  ```
  which is tail recursion all the way down (a while loop would work just as well). Note that we assume the conjecture is true, otherwise we would have a run away program (and a lot of fame for disproving the conjecture).
  ```
  collatz(10)  →  L(10,5,16,8,4,2,1)
  ```

  Now for the walker: `var cs=[1..].tweak(collatz)`. This is an infinite sequence that generates the Collatz sequences for all natural numbers. How about the first four?

142http://en.wikipedia.org/wiki/Collatz_sequences

cs.walk(4) → L(L(1), L(2,1), L(3,10,5,16,8,4,2,1), L(4,2,1))
The fifth? cs.walk(1) → L(L(5,16,8,4,2,1))
The tenth? cs.pump(5,Void) → L(10,5,16,8,4,2,1)

Now, for extra credit: Of the first 100 sequences, how many are longer than 25?

```
[1..100].tweak(collatz)
    .reduce(fcn(n,cs){ if(cs.len()>25) n+1 else n },0) → 32[143]
```

Creating a Walker for a Class

If a class can be thought of in a "linear" manner, it is often useful to have a walker attached to it. For this example, we'll create a deck of cards, which is sequence of fifty two individual cards:

```
class Deck{
    var deck;
    fcn init{ deck=[1..52].walk().copy(); shuffle(); }
    fcn shuffle{ deck.shuffle() }
    fcn __sGet(n){ return(deck[n]); }
    // Several possibilities here: deck.walker() or:
    fcn walker{ return(Utils.wap(__sGet)); }
}
```

Now, when we create a new deck of cards: deck=Deck() we get 52 shuffled cards. On to walkers; the __sGet function implements Deck[n], which also works as a Walker access method. So, in this case, the walker function is easy, it is small wrapper on __sGet (to convert IndexError exceptions to return(Void.Stop)). Even easier would be to use deck.walker(). In both cases, calling deck.walker().next() is equivalent to both deck[n] and deck.__sGet(n). And,

```
    foreach card in (deck){ println(card); }
```

is the same as calling deck.walker().next() 52 times, at which point __sGet throws an IndexError and stops the walker.

What if we wanted the walker to deal five card hands instead? And, we want to keep dealing until the deck is empty. In this case, the deck needs to store some state because a Walker won't. This chunk of code will do the trick:

```
var n=0;
fcn dealHand(numCards=5){
    if(n + numCards >52) return(Void.Stop);
    hand:=deck[n,numCards]; n+=numCards;
    return(hand);
}
fcn walker{ return(Walker(dealHand.fp(5))) }
```

---

[143]Also [1..100].pump(List,collatz,"len").filter('>(25)).len()

In this case it is important that the walker function is NOT passed the index, so we hardcode the parameter in the call to dealHand. Now, to deal the entire deck in hands of five cards, we use the same foreach loop as above and change "card" to "hand":

```
foreach hand in (Deck()){ println(hand); }
```

This will result in something like this:

```
L(26,40,34,4,27)
L(32,35,33,14,44)
...
```

After 50 cards are dealt, there is no longer enough cards to make a complete hand, so the loop stops.

Inheriting From Walker

The short version is you can't. But you can fake it. The miserable part is creating a method "shadow" layer.

```
class C{
   var [const mixin=Walker] walker=?.walker().tweak(?);
   var [const]
       next=walker.next,
       peek=walker.peek,
       ...              // as many Walker methods as you need
```

Then C.next() becomes C.walker.next().

We want C.walker to have a mixin value so that if we make a typo (eg peek=walker.peak) the compiler will point out that Walker doesn't contain a "peak".

Appendix A: zkl Grammar

Ah yes, the dreaded Grammar. Watch the eyes start to glaze over, like the goo on a hot-out-of-the-oven Krispy Krème.
-- Zander Kale

The following grammar is quite loose, it is not formal nor complete; it is intended to be a "how to" guide to combining elements into a program. Many things are undefined or incompletely defined here, look for complete definitions in the relevant sections of the manual.

Fonts: keyword, **code literals**, *defined somewhere in here*, **concept definition**

Concepts

program := *block* (the enclosing brackets are usually implicit)

object := The turtle that the rest of the world resides on. A virtual concept, as only instances of objects exist.

instance := An instance of a o*bject*. Examples: *number, string, class.*
instance := *class | fcn | method | …*
instance := *instance*([*parameters*]); Instance creation: call the objects "create" method or creates a new copy of a class and call the constructor and init functions.
instance := object *name* (such as List, L, Atomic, etc)

attributes := **[** attribute-name [,name …] **]** Attributes are placed between a type and name and apply to all the following names.
- For example: var [const] v;

- A comma between attributes is optional; var [private, const] is the same as var [private const].

block := **{** *block* | *expression* | *keyword* | *object* | *assignment* | *listAssigment* | *mathSet* **}**

expression := *stuff* | **(** *stuff* **)** | **(** *stuff* **)** .*dataRef* [more *stuff*]
stuff := *instance* | if | *dataRef* | try | *assignment* | *mathSet* | *call* | *math* | *logic* | throw | *listAssigment* | *number* | *string* | switch | fcn | : | (|)
- A something can be forced/cast to an expression by enclosing something in ()s. For example, if(x) y; isn't an expression[144] but (if(x) y;) is.
- (stuff1)(stuff2) *should* evaluate to a call to stuff1 with parameters stuff2 but doesn't.
- (stuff1)space(stuff2) is the same as (stuff1);(stuff2).
- ((stuff1)space(stuff2)) doesn't work.

control := **(** if | *dataRef* | try | *assignment* | *mathSet* | *call* | *math* | *logic* | *control* | switch | (|) | : **)**
- A mini **(***expression***)**
- if((sideEffects) (control)) *should* work but doesn't.

call := fcn | class | *method* | *instance* | *constName* **(**[*parameter* [, *parameter* ...]]**)** *terminator*
- No space between object and (
- Any object that has a create method (and most do) can be called, to create a new instance or run the instance.
parameter := if | *dataRef* | *assignment* | *mathSet* | *call* | *math* | *logic* | switch | try | (|) | : | *fcn* | *classDefinition*
- A mini *expression* plus functions and classes
- f((sideEffects) (arg)) *should* work but doesn't.

callable := Any instance that is referenced by a *call*.

name := [0-9a-zA-Z_]+ No more than 80 characters.
- It is a bad idea to use a single "_" as a name, as it is often used as a "replace me" symbol.

144Yes, this contradicts *stuff*. What happens is that single a object doesn't (usually) need the expression wrapper so the wrapper is thrown away when parsing.

- The compiler will use two leading underscores and a trailing "#" for "private" symbols (eg "__fcn#1").

Class := The Class *object*, a virtual concept. A container for variables and functions.
class := An instance of a *Class*
class := *class([parameters])*. Class creation: create a copy and call the class constructor and init functions (in that order). This can be overridden in various ways.
- class {…}(x) both defines and creates a new instance of the class.
- class {…}.M defines a class and resolves M against that class.

RootClass := The class that encloses all classes (except itself), eg a source code file.
RunMeClass := A *class* with a runMe function, which overrides class creation.

comment := # rest of line ignored
comment := // rest of line ignored
comment := /* comment */, can be nested: /* /* */ */
comment := **#if** 0|1|*name* \n comment \n **#endif**, can be nested, see below
comment := **#ifdef** *name* → #if 1 if name has been defined, else #if 0
comment := **#define** *name* 0|1   For use with #ifdef
comment := **#fcn** *name* { *body* } For use with #tokenize.
comment := **#text** *name text*   For use with #tokenize
comment := **#tokenize** *name|f|f(parameters)* Evaluate name or function and tokenize the result as a string (as if it were part of the source at that point).
#cmd comments can't be proceeded by anything but space, otherwise they are treated as a comment.

Delimiter := ; , : ( ) { } = ! + - * / % < > " # *whitespace newline*

dataRef := Data Reference. A data description. Data is any object.
dataRef := root.next.next...
dataRef := *dataRef2 | dataRef3*
dataRef2 := variable*Name* | constant*Name terminator*
dateRef2 := *instance.instance | instance.dataRef2 terminator*
dataRef2 := *instance.property terminator*
dataRef2 := *dataRef2([parameters]) terminator*
dataRef2 := *dataRef.dataRef2 terminator*
dataRef3 := *(stuff).dataRef2 | (stuff)(parameters)[.dataRef2] terminator*
- Whitespace (including newline) is OK in front of a dot. Not OK after a dot. For example: foo.bar is the same as foo   .bar

Appendix A: zkl Grammar

assignment := variable = *fcnDefinition* | *classDefinition* | *expression* | *block terminator*
multiple assignment := variable = variable … *assignment*
list assignment := variable, variable [, …] = *expression terminator*
list assignment := *variable, variable [, …]* := *expression terminator*
- Expression must evaluate to an object that supports [] (List being the most popular).
- The destinations must exist (as registers, variables or some combination), unless it is "_".
- If := is used, registers are created (if they don't exist in the enclosing block).
- If "_" is one of the destinations, it is thrown away.

= := reg/var = *expression*. See assignment. The destination must be an existing variable or register (although it may be defined after the assignment).
:= := reg := *expression*
- := is assignment and is the same as = except that it is restricted to registers. If *reg* doesn't exist, it is created in this block. x:=5; acts like reg x:=5; If *reg* does exist, := is the same as = (reg r; r:=5; is the same as reg r=5; or reg r; r=5;).
- r1:=r2:=e; is the same as r1:=e; r2:=e; (e evaluated only once).
- R1:= v= r2:=e is the same as r1:=e; v=e; r2:=e;
- List assignment: r1,r2,_:=e; creates/reuses registers r1, r2 and ignores e[2].

fcn := A function object, a code container. Often contained in a class. A static function can be homeless. All functions are first class objects.
lambda := fcn { … }, an anonymous function
- fcn {…}(x) both defines and calls the function.
- fcn {…}.M defines a function and resolves M against that function.

method := The object equivalent of a function.
property := Passive read-only data attached to a object, roughly equivalent to a read-only class variable.

number := integer | 0x[0-9a-zA-Z]+ | float (123.0 | 1.23 | 0.123 | 1e*N* | 1E*N*)
string := "text" | "one" "two" … Adjacent string constants are concatenated.
    "\\ \b \f \n \r \t" convert to backslash, backspace, formfeed, newline, return, tab
    "\xHH" converts two hex digits into one ASCII character.
    "\uHHHH" converts a four [hex] digit Unicode character to a two to three byte UTF-8 character.

string := 0' *sentinel text sentinel* Raw string. Examples: 0'|text|, 0'"text"

terminator := ; | { | }

logic := and | or | not

mathSet := object *op= expression terminator*
- a += 1 → a = a+1
- The object has to be a singleton, a.b += 1 is illegal.

math := [-] object [*op math*]

op := + | - | * | / | %

[] := *dataref*[...]   → *dataref*.__sGet(...)
    dataref[...]=x → *dataref*.__sSet(x,...)

Keywords

keyword : =
    AKA | Attributes | break | catch | class | const | continue | critical |
    debug | do | fcn | foreach | if | include | onExit | onExitBlock | reg |
    return | returnClass | self | switch | throw | try | var | while

class := class [*attributes*] [*name*][(*parent(s)*)] *block*
attributes := noChildren | private | public | static
- A static class never has more than one instance (the reference or Eve instance).
- Nobody can inherit from a noChildren class.
- A private class is not visible outside of the file it is defined in (ie is only source code can see it). It can be seen with reflection.

: (*compose*) := *expression* with one or more colons in it.
Compose works like so: Given an expression E = E$_1$:E$_2$:...:E$_n$ and pseudo variable X, the result of the composition is X = E$_1$; X = E$_2$(X); ... X = E$_n$(X);
The position of X in E$_n$ is marked by a underscore. E$_{n>1}$ has the following constraints:
- It must have a call (eg function or method). Unless:
- The only time _ isn't a parameter is when assigned (:(x=_)) or :(_).*name*.
- Can't be too complex (whatever that means).
See Keywords.: (compose)

const := Parse time constant, must evaluate to a "simple" constant
const := const *name* = *expression* | *fcnDefinition* | *block*
const := const *nameSpace* { *const* }
- Blocks and expressions are evaluated at parse time (after tokenizing and before compilation), as are calls to const functions

False := A boolean value. There is only one.

fcn := fcn [*attributes*] [*name*][(*prototype*)] *block*
- Define an instance of a Function object.
prototype := *name* | *name=parameter* ...
attributes := private | public
- A private function will not be visible when in a class (but can be found with reflection).
- A static function is one that doesn't reference any instance data. The compiler determines this attribute.

if := if(*control*) *expression terminator*
if := if(*control*) *block*
if := if ... else *expression* | *block* [*terminator*]
if := if ... else if(*control*) *expression* | *block* [else if ...]
if := if ... else if ... else ...
- If an if is part of an expression, such as 5 + if(a<b) b-a else a-b, you will often have to terminate both the if and the expression, depending where the if falls in the expression.
  ```
  5 + if(a<b) b-a else a-b;;   a+b
  5 + if(a<b) b-a else {a-b}; a+b
  ```

switch := switch(*control*) *block*
switch := switch(*control*) { case(...) *block* ... else *defaultBlock* }
switch := switch(*control*) { case(...) [fallthrough] *block* ... }

loop := while (*control*) *block* [fallthrough *block*]
loop := do *block* while(*control*)
loop := do(*n*) *block*
- *block* can contain break and/or continue
loop := foreach *n* in (*object*) *block* [fallthrough *block*]
loop := foreach *a,b,c* in (*x*) *block* [fallthrough *block*]
loop := foreach *a,b,c* in (*x, y, z*) *block*

- *n* is is the name of the control register and is created local to block.
- *Object* needs to have a function or method (named `walk`) that returns a Walker, which most objects do (lists, files, strings, numbers, etc). Since all Walkers have a walk function (which returns the Walker), you can explicitly create a Walker.
- "*_n*Walker" is a register created for access to the walker.
- List assignment works: `foreach a,b,c in (…)`
- A cascading foreach (`foreach a,b,c in (x,y,z)`) is the same as `foreach a in (x){ foreach b in (y){ foreach c in (z) { block }}}`

return := Exit fcn with value. Optional (fcn result is then the result of the last calculation).

```
return() | return(value) | return(value, value, …)
return() → return(Void)
return(value, value, …) → return(List(value, value, …))
```
()'s are required and no space between return and (

returnClass := `returnClass(object)`
- The same as return except that returnClass can be used in a constructor or init function. One, and only one, parameter is required. Of course, that object can be a list.

try := `try` *block* `catch` *block* [`else` *block*]
try := `try` *block* `catch` *block* `catch` *block* … [`fallthrough` *block*]
catch := `catch` | `catch`(*exceptionName* [*,name* …])
catch := `catch(+trace, -trace)` | `catch`(*name*,`+trace`) | `catch(+trace,`*name*`)`

critical := `critical` *block*
critical := `critical`(*lockName*) *block*
critical := `critical`(*lockName, acquireName, releaseName*) *block*
- Restrict execution of block to a single thread. A lock is allocated if need be, otherwise, *lockName* is the name of a var that holds a locking object (such as Atomic.Lock or Atomic.WriteLock).
critical := `critical`(*object, name1, name2*) *block*
- Expand to *object.name1(); block object.name2();* No locking or thread safeing is done.

onExit := `onExit(f` [`,parameters`]`)` ≈ `Deferred.once(f,parameters)`
- When the enclosing function returns, run exit code, equivalent to a "finally" block for a function. The code is always run.

onExitBlock := onExitBlock(f [,parameters])
- When the enclosing block exits, run exit code, equivalent to a "finally" block for a block. The code is always run.

Tailcalls can change *when* you think the exit code will run.

reg := A var in the current scope (block) and are not part of the instance. See :=.

True := A boolean value. There is only one.

var := var [*attributes*] *name*
var := var *name* [, *name* ...]
var := var *name* = *value* ...
var := var *name* = (*expression*) ...
var := var *name* = fcn *block* ...
var := var *name* = class *block* ...
attributes := const | mixin[= class or Vault object] | private | protected | proxy, separated by commas or spaces.
- Constant variables can only be set during declaration.
  For example: var [const] v=5;
- var [mixin] m=List; is the same as var [mixin=L] m; This allows mixin checking to used where the type can't be determined at compile time:
  var [mixin=Op] op=Op("+");

Void := An object that doesn't do much. Like a nil or null, only more so. There is only one.

Comments

There are three types of comment: to end of line, block and a combination of the two. Comment characters in strings are ignored and the characters that start a comment must be preceded by white space (or the start of a line or other delimiter). Comments are recognized by the tokenizer and never reach the parse stage.

- C++ "//" ignore to end of line type: // text
- Shell "#" ignore to end of line type: # text
- C type "/* */" block type: /* text */
  Text can span multiple lines. Single line comments are active and can preempt the closing comment /* // */ and /* # */ are errors but
  /* // */ two

line comment */ is OK. Strings are also active so /* "*/" */ is valid as is /* "//" */. The "*/" does not need to be preceded by white space (/**/, /***********/ and /*foo*/ are valid).

Block comments can be nested.

The text in a block comment is tokenized so it must be syntactically valid (or just enough so that the tokenizer can recognize the end of the comment).

- C preprocessor type: #if *value*|*name* #else #endif

  This type overloads shell comments to become block comments. This style is only valid if the cmd word is at the start of a line (optionally preceded by white space) and all the characters are in a single word (ie #if and not # if). Otherwise, this is just another line comment and, as such, interacts the in same way with the above comments (specifically, /* can hide #endif).

  Value must be zero (0), one (1) or something previously created by #define. It is an error if *name* hasn't been defined.

- #ifdef *name* #else #endif

  Name is something that may have been created by #define. If it was, the #ifdef becomes "#if 1", otherwise, "#if 0".

- #define *name* 0|1: Associate a name with zero or one for use with #if. #define doesn't span compilation units (eg files) and thus isn't seen in included files and vice versa. *Name* must be a valid name (valid is defined elsewhere).

- See the concepts section for #fcn, #text and #tokenize.

Data Reference Resolution

The compiler resolves references to data (objects) using a "look up, look down" algorithm:

A. Search upwards for the "root". The root is the object in the class hierarchy that matches the first element of the data reference.

    1. First, is the first element:
- a const, number, string, expression
- self: The root is the enclosing class definition
- self.fcn: The root is the enclosing function definition
- TheVault: The search starts in the Vault
- If any of the above, goto B

    2. The block is examined for:
- A parameter (if started in a fcn and still in that fcn).

  In fcn f(a){a.len()}, the root of a.len() is parameter a.
- A function, class, register, variable, parent, call:
  - If a call, the result of the call replaces the stuff up to that point.

`"foo".len().type` becomes `3.type` → "Int"

- The value replaces name:
  `class C{var v="foo";} C.v.len()` → 3
  Name "v" is replaced with value "foo": `"foo".len()`
- If match, goto B

3. If the top of this class definition is reached (the class that encloses the data reference):
   - The parents are searched in a breadth first search for [class] instance data (parent, class, function or variable).
   - The methods and properties are searched[145]
     `dir()` → `self.dir()`
     A match here might not be the end of the line: `name.len()`
   - If match, goto B
   - the search moves to the enclosing block
   - goto 2

4. If the root class (ie the source code file) is reached:
   - The Vault is checked (eg File, Test.UnitTester)
   - Syntactic sugar is checked (println, ask, etc)
   - If not found, it is a syntax error
   - goto B

5. The search moves to the enclosing block, goto 2

B. Resolve down:
The next item is resolved relative to the previous item.

    Call, class, function, variable, parent, method, property

References are statically bound to the point where it becomes ambiguous[146] and late bound from that point on.

Attributes: const, private, protected, proxy

- If a variable has attribute **const**, it acts like a read-only variable with the restriction that it can only be set once, and that once has to be in the var statement. If not set, it will forever be Void. There is an exception to this rule: const variables in functions (such as init), are always set when the function is run.
- **Private** variables, functions and classes are visible in the compilation unit (usually file) they are defined in. Class.resolve won't find them, thus they are invisible outside of the compilation unit although they can be seen with

---

[145]But print, println and ask are ignored as they can be both Object methods and sugar. Sugar wins here.

[146]The definition of ambiguous is somewhat ambiguous.

reflection (eg class.fcns). This is analogous to static functions in C. In C++, this is between protected and private.

- Anonymous functions and classes are private.
- Private variables are anonymous; they share the attributes of private functions but can't be found with reflection.
- If a class inherits from a compiled class, the new class won't be able to reference the private objects in the parent.

- A **protected** variable can only be set if it is the first word in a data reference or if the reference is to a protected parent variable.

```
var [protected] v; v = 3;                        // OK
class C { var [protected] v; } C.v = 3; // error
class D(C) { C.v = 3; }                           // OK
```

This effectively restricts writing to the class they are defined in, containing classes and parents. These variables are visible to everybody (unless marked private).

- A **proxy** variable is an active or trampoline variable; referencing it causes an action to happen. For example

```
var [proxy] pv = fcn {"test"};   pv; → "test"
```

The action is always pv(), where pv is the proxy variable.

Expressions

An expression is a group of operations that return a result. Expressions can do many things besides math; data references, function calls, try/catch, etc. Sometimes an expression needs to be wrapped in parentheses "()" to avoid ambiguity. Here is the algorithm:

1. Keep track of opening "(" and closing ")" parentheses
2. Check for (*).*. For example ("1"+"2").len() → ("12").len() → 2
3. Check for "if". Example: x:=(if (a==3) 56 else 65);
4. Check for "try". Example:
   x=try{a/0}catch{"division by zero throws"}[147]
5. Check for "break" and "continue": while(1){if (x==3) break}
6. Check for the different types of assignment: a=2; a+=2; a,b,c=f();
7. Check for a data reference
8. Check for a call (function, method, creation, etc)
9. Evaluate the "normal" math stuff: +,-,*,/,%, ==,!=, <,<=,>,>=, not, and, or, unary minus. There is nothing special here, and objects can overload. The precedence rules are almost the same as C, with the exception that evaluation is always left to right.

147An interesting thing about this example is what happens if the try succeeds. For example, if a == 2 and the try is { a/1 }, then x is set to 2.

Operators (precedence: high to low)	C Equivalent
() (function call) .(dot, resolve) [] ( ) (grouping)	() . -> [] ()
not, unary minus	! -
* / % (modulo)	* / %
+ -	+ -
< <= > >=	< <= > >=
== !=	== !=
and or (differs from C)	&& ||

"or" and "and" evaluate their result as a boolean but don't produce a boolean. For example, (1 and 2) evaluates to 2 but behaves as if it were True (since (2).toBool() returns True). They also "short circuit", which means they only evaluate as much of an expression as they need to. For example, (a and 0 and b) can be reduced to (a and 0) (which is (0) unless a blows) and (a or 0 or b) can be reduced to (a). You can take advantage of this in calculations.

- To access a list only if it has elements: (list and list[0]). This returns the empty list if list is L() (since L().toBool() is False) and the first item if list isn't empty[148].
- Code crunch: f() or throw(Exception.BadDay) throws an exception if f() doesn't return a "positive" value. This is the same as <br> if (not f()) throw(Exception.BadDay)

And factorial can be written: fcn(x){ x and x*self.fcn(x-1) or 1 }

Assignment (=, +=, -=, *=, /=) precedence is lower than grouping but is otherwise somewhat ambiguous. If you use "=", etc in a mixed expression, you almost always want to wrap it in (): if ((n=f()) != 4) doSomething(n)
Without the parentheses, this would evaluate as if(n=(f()!=4)), which is a Bool, not a number (assuming f always returns a number).
In n=3+4, n→7; (n=3)+4, n→3; 3+n=4, n→4; the sum is always 7. *When* n is set is not specified.

Compose (:) "chunks" an expression; each chunk is evaluated and rolled into the next chunk, forming a new chunk.

148An even easier way to do this: list[0,1]

Ambiguities, or, what are you trying to express?

If the parser see a "(", it tries to evaluate an expression. Otherwise, it looks for a statement. Failing that, an expression (which, in turn, will look for some statements). Now, what does `if(X) 1 else 2; +5` mean? "If" is a statement, + 5 is an expression. But you can't add a statement and expression so it means an error message. By adding ()s, it can be forced/cast to an expression:

`(if(X) 1 else 2; +5)` or `(if(X) 1 else 2) +5`

In the first case, a ";" is needed to terminate the if statement.

This doesn't need ()s (it doesn't start with "(", it isn't a statement, maybe an expression): `5 + if(X) 1 else 2;; println("ick")` but it does need two semis, one to terminate the if and the second to terminate the expression. So you may prefer ()s and a single semi. Unless you have something like: `5 + if(X) 1 else 2; +6; println("12 or 13")` which really looks better with ()s:

`5 + (if(X) 1 else 2) +6;` If you are writing code you'll have to read later, it will probably make your life easier to use ()s if in doubt.

Chained Compares

Comparison operators (==, !=, <, <=, >, >=) can be chained. For example,
`A==B==C` → `A==B` and `B==C`, where B is evaluated only once. Here are the rules:

- Only three terms (A,B,C) per chain.
- Terms can be anything that is legal in the expression.
  Eg `A == try { B } catch { C } != f(5); A<=(f(5)+1)>B`
- Precedence can't be mixed. Eg `A==B<C` is not legal.
- Evaluation is left to right.
- and/or terminate a chain: `A==B==C and E==F==G` is two chains.
- ()s scope. Not very useful. `(A==B)==C` → `Bool==C`

Scoping

zkl is block (lexically) scoped; if something is created in a block, it stays there, unless explicitly moved to a enclosing block. Classes, functions and variables are scoped to the class or function they are created in. On occasion, something created outside a block will be moved into a block. For example, the loop variable in a foreach statement is moved into the loop block. And, vice versa, a variable is will migrate to nearest enclosing class scope, while a register sticks to its block.

> *It's all very complicated and would take a scientist to explain it.*
> -- Mystery Science Theater 3000

Appendix A: zkl Grammar

Libraries, Objects and Scripts that are not part of the Core

In addition to the "Core" objects, there are zkl components that not distributed with the executable. These include shared libraries (Objects) and scripts that can downloaded from http://zenkinetic.com/.

How to Access
You can use Import to load and access any of these objects, assuming they exist where zkl can find them. See the **Environment Variables** section for where those places are. For example, to load the iso8601 class from it normal location (.../Time/iso8601.zsc or .../Time.iso8601.zkl), use
`ISO8601:=Import("Time.iso8601");` Loading a shared library works the same way: To load zeelib from .../Lib/zeelib.dll, use `ZeeLib:=Import("zeelib");`

Libraries
Libraries include zklBigNum (infinite precision numbers), zklCInvoke (call C code in libraries), zklLZO (LZO compression), and zeelib (Zlib compression, including zip).

Scripts
There is a small set of scrips available for download. They include md5 (a md5 calculator for files), hexDump (see the examples appendix), find (a very simple version of Unix find), zgrep (a simple find/fgrep).

Utils.Compression.LZO

Inherits from: Object

Notes:
- Not part of the zkl Core
- Load this object like so: var LZO = Import("zklLZO");

Notes and References:
1. This library uses the miniLZO (v2.02) compression code, copyright Markus Franz Xaver Johannes Oberhumer.
2. Very fast compression and very faster decompression.
3. Visit the LZO home page at http://www.oberhumer.com/opensource/lzo/
4. The LZO code is GPL'd.
5. See README.LZO, which is included (fun and informative but it won't help you use this library).
6. See ZeeLib for another way of looking at compression or if you need zlib (gzip/.gz) compatibility.
7. This library is thread safe.
8. Triva: The LZO compression code underlies the UPX (Ultimate Packer for eXecutables) utility, which is pretty cool.

Test Suite: testLZO.zkl

Abstract

The LZO library provides a very simple way to compress and decompress data very quickly.

Methods

- **adler32(**data**)**: Compute the Adler-32 (of zlib fame) check sum of data. This is a CRC like value that can be computed quickly.
- **compress(**data**)**: Compresses the data and returns the compressed data and information about it. The original data is not changed.
  Throws: IOError
  Returns: L(size of the uncompressed data, compressed check sum, compressed data)
- **decompress(**size of the uncompressed data, compressed checksum, compressed data**)**: Restore the compressed data to its original uncompressed state. The extraneous data provides the underlying code with a "header" so it can verify that the compressed data is valid. The compressed data is not changed.
  Throws: IOError, ValueError
  Returns: Data

Properties

- **authors**: The people who wrote the code.
  Returns: List of Strings
- **libraries**: A list of the names and authors of the libraries used.
  Returns: List of Strings
- **version** : Returns the version number of the miniLZO library. This number makes sense in hex.
  `LZO.version.toString(16)` → 2020 (= 02.02)
- **versionDate** : Returns the date code of the miniLZO library.
- **versionString** : Returns version string of the miniLZO library.

Discussion

LZO provides low overhead, very quick compression and decompression (visit the web page for stats). If you just want to compress a block of data and then decompress it with a minimum of fuss, this is for you. The compressor has low overhead, especially compared to compressors like GZIP and BZ2. On the flip side, you have to keep track of the information the decompresser needs, you don't get a Stream interface and you don't get a common format (ie, you can't give out compressed data and expect anyone else to be able to decompress it, as you can with gzip'd data).

If you want to store your compressed data in a file or pass the compressed data over a socket, you'll need to invent your own file format (so you can save the header information). At that point, zeelib might be more convent (as it generates gzip headers).

Example:
```
var LZO = Import("zklLZO");
testFile := Data();
   // create a bunch of data by writing a big class to bytes
Compiler.Asm.writeRootClass(Compiler.Parser,testFile);
   // compress the data
len,checksum,data := LZO.compress(testFile);
println("Compressed %s to %s".fmt(testFile,data));
   // decompress the data
d := LZO.decompress(len,checksum,data);
   // verify no data was lost
testFile == d;          // → True
```
Output: Compressed Data(44639) to Data(25833)
Compressed to almost half size, not bad.

Utils.Compression.ZeeLib

Objects: ZeeLib.Compressor, ZeeLib.Inflator
Inherits from: Stream, Object
Notes
- Not part of the zkl Core
- Load this object like so: `var ZeeLib=Import("zeelib");`

References
1. A Massively Spiffy Yet Delicately Unobtrusive Compression Library, http://www.zlib.net/
2. RFC 1950-2, http://www.ietf.org/rfc/rfc1950.txt, http://www.ietf.org/rfc/rfc1951.txt, http://www.ietf.org/rfc/rfc1952.txt
3. The gzip compression utility, http://www.gzip.org/

Test Suite: testZeeLib.zkl
See Also: zipper.zkl, which compresses files into a gzip/pkzip/winRAR compatible file (located in the distribution packages, which is creates).

Abstract
The zeelib library provides a interface to the zlib compression library. The resulting compressed data is compatible with compression programs such as gzip and WinRAR. The objects can be used as parts of a stream. Compressors are thread safe (for example, multiple threads can stream compressed data packets using one compressor).

Compressors and Inflators have the same methods (although the parameters may differ) and properties.

Methods (for ZeeLib)
- `calcAdler32(data)`: Compute the Adler-32 check sum of data.
  Returns: Int
- `calcCRC32(data)`: Compute the CRC-32 check sum of data.
  Returns: Int
- `Compressor(gzip_wrapper=False)`: If gzip_wrapper is True, the compressed data can be read by programs such as gzip or WinRAR.
  Returns: Compressor
- `Inflator()`:
  Throws: OutOfMemory, IOError (zlib error)
  Returns: Inflator

Methods (for both `Compressor` and `Inflator`)

- `calcAdler32(`data`)`: Compute the Adler-32 check sum of data.
  Returns: Int
- `calcCRC32(`data`)`: Compute the CRC-32 check sum of data.
  Returns: Int
- `close()`: Close flushs all zlib data to the object and prohibits any future writes.
  Returns: self
- `create()`: Create a new Compressor or Inflator. Once created, you can write data to compress or inflate it.
    - `Compressor(`gzip_wrapper=False`)`: If gzip_wrapper is True, the compressed data can be read by programs such as gzip or WinRAR.
    - `Inflator()`:
  Throws: OutOfMemory, IOError (zlib error)
  Returns: Compressor or Inflator
- `drain(`[timeout]`)`: Drain is useful if you want to get all of the data contained in a Compressor or Inflator without using a read loop. Drain waits until the object is closed, reads all data (if any) and returns it.
  If a timeout is used and the object isn't closed before time is up, Void is returned.
  Returns: Data (might be empty), Void
- `flush()`: Does nothing. For compatibly with Stream.
- `len()`: Returns the number of bytes received from zlib. Unless closed, this is probably <u>NOT</u> the number of bytes that have been compressed or inflated. Once the object has been closed, len() will return the number of bytes that can be read. Between the time close is called and the first read call, this is the size of compressed or inflated data (eg the size of a file after compression). Read will decrement the length.
  Returns: Int
- `open()`: Same as create. A closed Compressor or inflator can't be reopened – calling open() creates a new object.
  See create.
- `pump(`sink, action, action, ...`)`: Read from self, until closed, pumping data through the actions.
  This can be useful to pump compressed data between threads:
  ```
  var ZLib=Import("zeelib");
  var compressor=ZLib.Compressor(), inflator=ZLib.Inflator();
  ```

Single thread:
```
compressor.write("This is a test"); compressor.close();
d:=compressor.pump(inflator.write)  // → inflator
    .pump(Void);
d.text  → "This is a test"
```
Multi-threaded:
```
fcn{compressor.pump(inflator.write)}.launch(); // Thread1
fcn{inflator.pump(
    fcn(d){println("-->",d.text)} )}.launch(); // Thread2
compressor.write("This is a test");   // not a thread
compressor.close();
    → "-->This is a test"
```

Thread1 moves compressed data from the compressor to the inflater. Thread2 pulls inflated data from the inflator and prints it. If large amounts of data are compressed, it will dribble out in chunks[149]. You can test this using `compressor.write(File("bigFile").read())` multiple times.

When the compressor is closed, it flushes its data and thread1 ends. The inflator sees the this-data-has-been-compressed marker, auto closes, flushes, prints and exists.

Returns: Last action

- **read(**[timeout]**)**: Read waits until the Compressor or Inflator has a chunk of data or is closed and then returns that data. The data is removed from the data queue. If the optional timeout (seconds, interger or float) is used and if data is not ready in that time, Void is returned.
  Throws: TheEnd if closed and empty.
  Returns: Data (might be empty) or Void.
- **walker()**: Returns a Walker that uses read().
  Returns: Walker
- **write**
  - **Compressor: write(**String | Data**)**: Compress some data.
  - **Inflator: write(**Data**)**: Inflate compressed data. Gzip format is automatically detected and handled.
  Throws: IOError (data is not compressed data)
  Throws: OutOfMemory, IOError (object not open)
  Returns: self

Properties (for both objects)
- **adler32**: Returns the rolling check sum, usually Adler32 but might be CRC-32.
  Returns: Int

149You may need to aggregate the chunks to re-form the original data.

- **authors**: The people who wrote the code.
  Returns: List of Strings
- **chunkSize** : Returns the size of the internal buffers used to hold zlib data chunks.
- **isClosed**: Returns True if not open (ie if never opened or has been closed).
- **libraries**: A list of the names and authors of the libraries used.
  Returns: List of Strings
- **version** : Returns the version of the zlib library.

Warning
- Compressors: Multiple producers are supported; for example, threads writing packets to a Compressor (see the test suite for an example). Multiple consumers doesn't make sense and aren't supported. In other words, only ONE thread can read from a Compressor. Also, if one thread is writing and another thread closes that object, it won't be pretty.
- Inflater: Multiple producers doesn't make sense (the compressed data needs to be fed in the same order it was produced). Multiple consumers also don't make sense because Zlib output is chunked (that is, even if packets were compressed, you can't read the uncompressed data a packet at a time from an Inflator).

Discussion
The zeelib library creates a ZeeLib object, which contains two objects (ZLib.Compressor and ZLib.Inflator). Importing the library returns the ZeeLib object; access that to create a Compressor or Inflator.

```
var ZeeLib=Import("zeelib");    // load the zeelib library
Compressor=ZeeLib.Compressor(); // create a new instance
```

The following code will compress a file into gzip format:
```
data:=              // read entire file into Data
   File(textFile,"rb").read();
compressor:=ZeeLib.Compressor(True); // use gzip format
compressor.write(data);              // compress the file
compressor.close();
compressedData:=compressor.drain();
File("x.gz","wb").write(compressedData).close();
```

To read a gzipped file, you could do the following:
```
gz:=ZeeLib.Inflator()
        .write(File("x.gz","rb").read()).close().drain();
```

The following code demonstrates compressing and inflating across two threads. This example is a bit contrived (because it both compresses and inflates) but is small and works. An obvious change would be to add a pipe to feed the compressing (or inflating) thread.

```
    // Multiprocess test, streaming data through a
    // Compressor to a Inflator.
var data=self.unasm(Data());  // generate some text
data.seek(0);                 // start at the beginning

var ZeeLib=Import("zeelib");
var source=ZeeLib.Compressor();
var sink  =ZeeLib.Inflator();

fcn squeeze(data,src) {   // Compression thread
   println("Compressing %d bytes".fmt(data.len()));
   // dribble data into the compressor
   try { while (True) { src.write(data.read(10)); } }
   catch(TheEnd) {}
   src.close();     // will cause the Sink to stop
   // exercise: why is println(source.len())
   // unreliable here?
}
fcn inflate(src,sink) {     // Inflation thread
   size:=src.reduce('wrap(size,z){sink.write(z); size+z.len()},0);
   sink.close();  // sink now has a copy of the original data
   println("Inflated %d bytes to %d bytes".fmt(size,sink.len()));
}
squeeze.launch(data,source);   // create the threads
inflate.launch(source,sink);
sink.drain();  // wait for sink to close (ie inflate thread to end)
   // Both threads are done (exercise: why?)
println("Done");
```

Example output:

```
Compressing 6353 bytes
Inflated 1391 bytes to 6353 bytes
Done
```

Appendix C: Illustrated zkl Code Examples

Hex Dump

For programmers, a hexadecimal dump usually represents the back up against the wall: "What the *&%^ is this program *doing*?!?" and is like looking at chicken entrails. Unpleasant, yes, but none the less, you'll usually have to do it at some point.

```
>zkl hexDump Built/exception.zsc
    0: 20 20 7a 6b 48 00 00 24 | 31 2e 30 00 5a 4b 4c 20    zkH..$1.0.ZKL
   16: 53 65 72 69 61 6c 69 7a | 65 64 20 43 6c 61 73 73   Serialized Class
   32: 00 45 78 63 65 70 74 69 | 6f 6e 00 00 02 00 00 45   .Exception.....E
   48: 2b 61 74 74 72 69 62 75 | 74 65 73 3a 73 74 61 74   +attributes:stat
   ...
```

The above dump is an excerpt of a ZSC file dump. From this, you could verify that Asm.WriteRootClass is working correctly.

Code
```
fcn hexDump(in, out=File.stdout){
   format1 :="%02.x ";
   format16:=format1 * 8 + "| " + format1 * 8;
   NFmt    :="%4d: ";
```

```
reg bytes,text, N=0, d=Data();
try{
   while(1){    // repeat until end of file
      bytes=in.read(16).bytes();
      text =bytes.reduce(fcn(d,c){
         d.append(if(0x20<=c<=0x7E) c.toChar() else "." )
      }, d.clear() ).text;
      out.writeln(NFmt.fmt(N),
            format16.fmt(bytes.xplode()),"  ",text);
      N+=16;
   }
}
catch(MissingArg){    // not a full line
   n:=bytes.len();
   if(n<=8)
      out.write(NFmt.fmt(N),(format1*n)
                  .fmt(bytes.xplode()),"  ");
   else
      out.write(NFmt.fmt(N),
         (format1*8 + "| " +
          format1*(n-8)).fmt(bytes.xplode()));
   out.writeln("   "*(16-n), "  ",text);
}
catch(TheEnd){}
}
```

Discussion
The code is dense.

The first thing to note is the prototype: hexDump(in, out=File.stdout)
Hex dump reads from an input stream (such as a File or Data) and writes to an output
stream, which defaults to the console (or whatever the console has been redirected
to). Thus, it is simple to create a script that dumps a file:

```
Attributes(script);
f:=File(vm.arglist[0],"rb");
hexDump(f);
```

This opens the file in binary mode and lets hexDump have at it. It would be even
easier to do this:

```
hexDump(File.stdin);
```

But, on windows, if there is a control-Z in the file (common in a binary file),
windows will treat that as an End of File marker and close the file, which is not what
we want.

Read Bytes

First, we read sixteen bytes at a time from the input stream:

```
in.read(16).bytes();  →  Data(16) to List of 16 integers
```

The thing to note here is, if there are less than sixteen bytes available, read will read what is available. When there are no bytes available, read will throw TheEnd, which we catch. Thus, we process all bytes, even if the file doesn't contain a multiple of sixteen.

Print Bytes

Each line of sixteen bytes is written as two hex characters, a space, the next byte, etc, followed by the the bytes as text (printable characters only). The line is split into two groups of eight bytes for ease of readability. The text format for a byte is "%02x " or "%02.16B "; two hex digits (with leading zero if only one digit). By multiplying this string by eight, it is repeated eight times to give one group. Using this resulting string as a format, we explode the list of bytes so they become parameters to .fmt. For example: if bytes is L(8,9,10) and format is "%02x %02x | %02x", then

```
format.fmt(bytes.xplode())
→ "%02x %02x | %02x".fmt(L(8,9,10).xplode())
→ "%02x %02x | %02x".fmt(8,9,10)
→ "08 09 | 0a"
```

Print Text

Next, we need to write the bytes as text. We'll define a printable character as one that is between space (0x20) and tilde (~, 0x7E). If the byte isn't printable, substitute a dot. The problem is how to convert a list of bytes or bunch of bytes to printable characters. The idea is to examine each byte and build a string with the printable representation of that byte. We can do this using List.reduce as a data pump; each byte is converted to printable (by a function) and then appended to the previous characters. Any of a number of objects can be used; String, Data, Pipe, etc. We'll use Data out of a (probably misguided) sense of efficiency. Here are the steps:

1. ```
   fcn toPrintable(c)
        { if(0x20<=c<=0x7E) c.toChar() else "." }
   ```
   This function takes an integer and returns a printable character. Note that we can do the comparison without using "and".
2. ```
   fcn append(data,c){ data.append(toPrintable(c)); }
   ```
   This will append the printable character to a Data.
3. ```
   d=Data(); text=bytes.reduce(append, d.clear() );
   ```
   Here we walk each byte, convert it and append it to a Data. The Data is returned. D is cleared each time so we can reuse it.
4. ```
   text=text.text;
   ```
   And finally!, the printable text is extracted from the Data.

And to show that we are really cool programmers, all these steps are packed into one very long statement.

If you prefer to work with Strings, lines 2 and 3 would become:

```
fcn append(str,c){ str + toPrintable(data,c); }
text=bytes.reduce(append,"");
```

and line 4 is eliminated.

Partial Lines

And lastly, we have to handle partial lines (those will less than 16 bytes). We know when that happens because fmt will throw a MissingArg if it doesn't have sixteen bytes to format. We catch that and deal with one of two cases: eight bytes or less (one group) or two groups. Since we know that fmt threw the error, we also know that bytes and text are valid (as they were calculated before the error occurred).

Factorial

The classic recursive factorial program can be written in a clever way. We'll actually look at cleverness inside of clever, just to to be clever. A factorial program is written four ways.

Code

```
1. fcn fact(n){ return(n and n*fact(n-1) or 1); }
2. fcn fact(n){ n and n*self.fcn(n-1) or 1 }
```

Compare to:

```
3. fcn fact(n){     // the recursive part.  input: x   output: x!
     if(0==n) return(1);      // 0! = 1
     return( n*fact(n-1) );  // n! = n*(n-1)!
     }
4. fcn fact(n){
        if(0==n) 1;
        else n*fact(n-1);
   }
5. fcn fact(n){ (1).reduce(n,fcn(N,n){ N*n },1) }
   or fcn fact(n){ (1).reduce(n,'*),1 }
```

Discussion

The first thing to note is that (1) and (2) are exactly the same. (2) is just lazy since it knows that last calculation is the block result so it doesn't have to explicitly "return". (3) is almost the same as (4), (4) is actually a tiny bit bigger (two bytes) but the compiled code is essentially the same. (5) is just a loop using a lambda function.

So, how does it work? First, both programs are only valid for non-negative integers and the results get huge very fast so there is a fairly low limit on those integers before overflow occurs. With that out of the way, we can perform an examination. We'll do this the old fashioned way: plug and grind.

1. `fact(0)` → `return(0 and 0*fact(0-1) or 1)` → `return(False or 1)` → `return(1)`

   The key here is and/or. 0 is equivalent to False (`0.toBool()` is False) and (`False and X`) is False, so `0*fact(0-1)` is never evaluated and the "or" clause is the winner.

2. `fact(1)` → `return(1 and 1*fact(1-1) or 1)` → `return(True and fact(0))` → `return(fact(0))` → `return(1)`

   Here, 1 is equivalent to True and (`True and X`) is X so the "or" clause is ignored (assuming that X is non-zero, which we know to be true in this case).

3. `fact(2)` → `return(2 and 2*fact(2-1) or 1)` → `return(True and 2*fact(1))` → `return(2*fact(1))` → `return(2*1)` (substituting 2) → `return(2)`

   Basically the same as 2, noting that `2.toBool()` is True and using the result obtained in 2. The program performs steps 3, then 2, then 1 (which is why it is recursive) but we've wave our hands here and save some brain cells.

4. And so on for other integers.

What does the compiler think of this cleverness? Not much, the compiled code is all of two bytes smaller than the more legible code.

But Wait! There's More

```
fcn factTail(x,N=1) {
    if(0==x) return(N);
    return(self.fcn(x - 1,x*N));
}
factTail(7) → 5040
```

The code is longer and isn't as "pretty". But! it doesn't recurse. That's right, the compiler converts this into an iterative function though the magic of tail recursion. The generated code becomes something like this:

```
fcn factTail(x,N=1) {
    if(0==x) return(N);
    x-=1; N*=x;
    goto factTail;
}
```

What about integer overflow? `factTail(100)` → 0 so something is clearly wrong. Let's use infinite precision integers to avoid this problem:

```
var [const] BigNum=Import("zklBigNum");
factTail(BigNum(100))
```
→ 93326215443944152681699238856266700490715968264381621
    4685929638952175999932299156089414639761565182862536979
    208272237582511852109168640000000000000000000000000000

Processing Text Files with Scripts and Pipes

zkl can be used to process text files in a manner somewhat analogous to Perl but not as concisely and with a different "flow".

In this this example, the goal is to convert a look up table written in C to a gperf hash table. The command line will look like:

```
>zkl extractTable < list.c | gperf | zkl gperf -i list
```

There are two zkl scripts (extractTable.zkl and gperf.zkl) that are used; one to extract the table from C code and prep it for gperf and the other to post process the gperf output. gperf (http://www.gnu.org/software/gperf/) is the GNU perfect hash table generator. gperf hash tables are used by the zkl VM but gperf produces C code that needs to be modified so that it can be compiled into the VM.

Examples of Text

From list.c (over 4,000 lines of C with five tables):

```
static Instance *
List_makeReadOnly(Instance *self, pArglist arglist, pVM vm) {
    return convertToROList(self);
}
static const MethodTable listMethods[] =
{
    "create",             List_create,
    "toString",           List_toString,
         // utility methods
    "makeReadOnly",       List_makeReadOnly,
    0,                    0
};
```

What gperf wants to see the above transformed into:

```
MethodTable
%struct-type
%language=ANSI-C
%readonly-tables
%delimiters=,
%enum
%omit-struct-type
%%
"create",       List_create,
"toString",     List_toString,
"makeReadOnly", List_makeReadOnly,
```

We'll skip the two gperfs; their output is copious and extraneous for this example.

Code

```
/* extractTable.zkl: Extract a Method or Property table
 * from a C file and convert it to gperf format
 */
Attributes(script);                    // (1)

var structname="MethodTable";
var name        ="";


Import("Utils.Argh")(                  // (2)
L("propertyTable","p","Extract a property table",
            fcn{ structname="PropertyTable" }),
L("methodTable",  "m","Extract a method table (default)", fcn{}),
L("+name",    "n","The name of the table", fcn(arg){ name=arg }),
).parse(vm.arglist);


walker:=File.stdin.walker();  // (3)
//cFile :=File.stdin.readln(*);    // (4)
//walker:=cFile.walker();

   // Match "MethodTable ???[] = " or
   //   "MethodTable methodTable[] = "
tableName:="*%s*%s\\[]*=*".fmt(structname,name);  // (5)


try{  // look for: MethodTable methodTable[] =      // (6)
   while (not walker.next().matches(tableName)){}
   walker.next();
}
catch(TheEnd){
   File.stderr.writeln("Extract: Didn't find ",name);
   System.exit(1);
}
```

```
println(                                                    // (7)
structname,"\n",
"%struct-type\n",
"%language=ANSI-C\n",
"%readonly-tables\n",
"%delimiters=,\n",
"%enum\n",
"%omit-struct-type\n",
"%%");
```

```
while (not (line:=walker.next().strip()).matches("0,*0")){ // (8)
    if(not line or line.matches("//*")) continue;
    println(line);
}
```

Discussion
This code is very linear:
1. Make it clear to everybody (from the user to the compiler) that this is a script.
2. Parse the command line options to find out what table to look for.
3. Create a way to read the file a line at a time.
4. Another way to read the file: read the entire C file into a list and read from that list.
5. Create a search pattern
6. Find the table.
7. Write the gperf header.
8. Read the table, modify it to gperf format and write it.

You might be wondering why ".zkl" isn't specified on the command line
```
>zkl extractTable < list.c | gperf | zkl gperf -i list
```
for extractTable.zkl or gperf.zkl. This isn't a typo, the zkl shell will look for ".zkl" and ".zsc" files and also search the vault.

In Depth:
1. The script attribute isn't necessary in this case but it does make it clear what the intent of this code is.
2. Use the Argh class to parse the command line. Standard stuff. If an option is found (--propertyTable, --methodTable, or --name), a function is called to deal with it. If there is an error, Argh throws an exception and VM exits with a non-zero value, which breaks the pipe line.
```
>zkl extractTable -X  < list.c | gperf | zkl gperf
Unknown option: X
Options:
  --methodTable (-m) : Extract a method table (default)
```

```
    --name (-n) <arg>: The name of the table
    --propertyTable (-p) : Extract a property table
VM#32 caught this unhandled exception:
    NameError : Unknown option: X
Stack trace for VM#32
    ...
(standard input): The input file is empty!
```

Import("Utils.Argh")(*optionParameters*).parse(*cmdLineArgs*)
Import searches for the named class (Argh), creates a copy and calls the init
function with parameters. The parse method/function of the new Argh
instance is then called with the command line args. How is the command line
converted into the arglist? Since a script is basically a class constructor and
constructors don't have a named parameter list, the relevant parts of argv are
copied to vm.arglist.
The option parameters describe each possible command line option. Each is a
list: long name (with a "+" if a argument is required), short name, description
and optional function.

3. This line is the key to this script. We explicitly create a Walker so we can
   process the file at our pace (rather than implicitly via foreach). Doing this
   allows us to structure our look at the file in way better suited to our needs.

4. (2) isn't the only way to do this, it isn't even the only other way. If we needed
   to edit the file (delete, add and modify lines, as gperf.zkl does), reading the
   entire file into a list of lines and using a walker on that works well; the
   walker also acts as a "cursor" into the file.

5. Since the table name isn't hard coded, we have to create the search pattern on
   the fly. We want to be a bit clever about this and not require a table name be
   specified. If we are looking for a method table (the default), structname is
   "MethodTable". Our two patterns are:

   ```
   "*MethodTable*\[]*=*"
   ```

   Or, if a name is specified (eg "listMethods"):

   ```
   "*MethodTable*listMethods\[]*=*"
   ```

   Both these patterns will match

   ```
   "static const MethodTable listMethods[] ="
   ```

6. Here we step through the file. We look at each line until one matches the
   pattern we are looking for. If we find it, we skip the next line ("{") and go to
   the next step. If we search the entire file and don't find a matching line,
   walker throws TheEnd. We could leave it at that but the user would probably
   be at a loss to figure what the hell went wrong. So we catch the exception and
   print a more meaningful error to standard error:

   ```
   >zkl extractTable -n fooMethods < list.c | gperf | zkl gperf
       Extract: Didn't find fooMethods
   ```

```
(standard input): The input file is empty!
```
7. Nothing special here, just print a gperf header to standard out. Each gperf declaration needs to be on a separate line, so "\n" (newline) is used in println to specify that.
8. Walk the rest of the table, until the end of the table is reached.
   The end of the table is marked by a line that is "0,0", so we can stop when we find it. There is a lot going on in the while line. First, the line is read, leading and trailing space is stripped from it and it is stored in the "line" register. If line is "0,[*space*]0", it is the end of the table and the string *matches* method will return True. Note, if the line is "0,0," (trailing comma, a valid terminator for a C array initializer), this will miss it.

   We don't want to send blank or comment lines to gperf (it doesn't like them) so we skip them. Since we stripped out white space, a blank line is "" (which has zero length, which is what not tests for in strings). A comment line is a C++ style comment on a blank line (" // comment") (a convention I force for tables, comments at the end of a non-blank line is fine). If the line matches either of these conditions, skip that line.

   Otherwise, just print the table line.

Roman Numbers

Ever consider how cool it would be to write
```
Roman.CCXX + Roman.XLII → CCLXII(262)
```
Well, you can! If you can solve this problem: how to do you get a class to meaningfully deal with a method/fcn/etc that is unknown at compile time? In this case, it makes absolutely no sense to have a fcn/variable for every possible roman numeral, so there needs to be another way for the Roman class to accept an arbitrary roman number. The normal way would be to write Roman("CCXX") but, for this example, we want to write Roman.CCXX. The solution is use late binding to redirect the unknown method references. Most dynamic languages offer support for this in some way, shape or form. For example, Ruby has the "method_missing" method. This idea for this example came from Ruby Quiz #22, "Roman Numerals".

Code
```
    var Roman=RomanNumber;
```
Yes, that's it. Aside from the RomanNumber class, which is a run of the mill boring class. In use:
```
    var Roman=RomanNumber;          // Force late binding
    println(Roman.CCXX);                    → "CCXX(220)"
```

```
r:=Roman.XLII; println(r);              → "XLII(42)"
println(Roman.CCXX + Roman.XLII);  → "CCLXII(262)"
println(Roman.XL + 2);              → XLII(42)
Roman.IA;                           → ValueError
println(RomanNumber.toRoman(42));  → "XLII"
```

How It Works

Just what is the man behind the curtain doing to make this work? First, we can't let the compiler statically bind to the RomanNumber class, so we store it in a variable, which will force the compiler to use late binding. Next, we link into the "method not found" method, which the VM uses to resolve something that can't be found. When we write `Roman.CCXX`, the compiler turns this into `RomanNumber.resolve("CCXX")`, which isn't in RomanNumber, so the VM calls `RomanNumber.__notFound("CCXX")`.

For extra credit, what does `Roman.CCXX("II")` do? How about `Roman.CCXX.II`? If you answered 2 and 2, you are correct. If you know why, pat yourself on the back.

More Code

Here is the code for the RomanNumber class. It is a quick hack in every sense of the word, written solely to explore, so tread carefully if you want to use it for more than that. It is basically a port, with garnish, of Jason Bailey's solution to the Ruby Quiz #22.

```
var romans=L(       // a list of lists
   L("M", 1000), L("CM", 900), L("D",  500), L("CD", 400),
   L("C",  100), L("XC",  90), L("L",   50), L("XL",  40),
   L("X",   10), L("IX",   9), L("V",    5), L("IV",   4),
   L("I",    1));

class RomanNumber{
   var value, text;
        // create a new instance so we can add two Roman numbers
   fcn __notFound(name){ return(self(name)); }
   fcn init(text){
      self.text=text;
      value     =toArabic(text);
   }
```

```
       // romanNumber needs to be upper case
    fcn toArabic(romanNumber){
        if(not RegExp("^[CDILMVX]+$").matches(romanNumber))
           throw(Exception.ValueError("Not a Roman number: %s"
                                        .fmt(romanNumber)));
        reg value=0;
        foreach R,N in (romans){        // eg "C",100
           while(0==romanNumber.find(R)){
              value+=N;
              romanNumber=romanNumber[R.len(),*];
           }
        }
        return(value);
    }

    fcn toRoman(i){                 // convert int to a roman number
        reg text="";
        foreach R,N in (romans)
           { z:=i/N; text+=R*z; i=i%N; }
        return(text);
    }
    fcn toString  { return("%s(%s)".fmt(text,value)); }
    fcn toInt     { return(value); }
    fcn __opAdd(R){ self(toRoman(value + R.toInt())) }
}
```

Since toArabic and toRoman are probably not obvious, here are some hints.
```
toArabic("XLII"):
        R = "M",  N = 1000, value =  0, romanNumber = "XLII"
        R = "CM", N =  900, value =  0, romanNumber = "XLII"

        ...
        R = "XL", N =   40, value =  0, romanNumber = "XLII"
        R = "X",  N =   10, value = 40, romanNumber = "II",

        ...
        R = "I",  N =    1, value = 40, romanNumber = "II"
        R = "I",  N =    1, value = 41, romanNumber = "I"
        R = "I",  N =    1, value = 42, romanNumber = ""

toRoman(42):
        R = "M",  N = 1000, z = 0, text = "",      i = 42

        ...
        R = "L",  N =   50, z = 0, text = "",      i = 42
        R = "XL", N =   40, z = 1, text = "XL",    i =  2
        R = "X",  N =   10, z = 0, text = "XL",    i =  2

        ...
        R = "IV", N =    4, z = 0, text = "XL",    i =  2
```

```
R = "I",  N =    1, z = 2, text = "XLII", i =  0
```

Device Drivers

Device drivers. Ugh. They are always changing and you hate recompiling your code to add a new driver. If you write to a "virtual" driver, one that every "real" device driver has to conform to, you load can drivers at run time and not touch your "main" code.

Here is a (very simple) virtual driver:

```
class VirtualDriver{
    var name="VirtualDriver";
    fcn read(n) { println("Reading from ",name); }
    fcn write(x){ println("Writing to ",name); }
    fcn open    { println("Opening ",name); }
    fcn close   { println("Closing ",name); }
}
```

And now, our code that writes to the hardware driver, plus a proxy class that insulates us from the actual driver[150]:

```
class Hardware{
    var [mixin] driver=VirtualDriver;
    fcn installDriver(driver){ self.driver=driver; }
    fcn doCoolThings{
        driver.open();
        driver.write("This is a test");
        driver.read(10);
        driver.close();
    }
}
```

When we tell the hardware to do cool things, we get:

```
hardware:=Hardware();
hardware.doCoolThings();
```

→ Opening VirtualDriver
    Writing to VirtualDriver
    Reading from VirtualDriver
    Closing VirtualDriver

OK, now that we have the stub of our hardware controller, let's write a driver for the Gizmo 56 hardware, install and test it. We'll cheat and create the simplest driver possible:

```
class GizmoDriver(VirtualDriver){
    fcn init{ name="Gizmo56 driver"; }
}
```

150As we can't have dynamic parents.

Install a new instance of the driver in the existing Hardware instance and run another test:

```
hardware.installDriver(GizmoDriver());
hardware.doCoolThings();
```
→ Opening Gizmo56 driver
    Writing to Gizmo56 driver
    Reading from Gizmo56 driver
    Closing Gizmo56 driver

This example shows that we can write our high level device controller and install device drivers at run time. There are no recompiles, no relinking, no touching the controller. There is no need to have any drivers resident at run time, once the device is queried or a configuration file is read, the appropriate driver can be loaded and easily installed. You can even swap between drivers on the fly.
The advantage to using a mixin var (vs a normal var) is that the compiler can check for invalid method calls. For example, if the Hardware class were to call "driver.foo()", the compiler would flag this as a syntax error because foo isn't in VirtualDriver. If it wasn't a mixin, this check would be punted to runtime.

Generators

Generators allow you to create iterators that rely on a continuing series of calculations or recursion. For example, consider the following function to calculate prime numbers[151].

```
fcn findPrimes{
    println(2);     // vm.yield(2);
    n:=3; primes:=L(2);
    while(True){
        if(not primes.filter1(fcn(p,n){ n%p==0 },n))
        {     // a new prime number has been found
            println(n);     // vm.yield(n);
            primes.append(n);
        }
        n+=2;     // Prime numbers (>2) are odd
    }
}
```

This will print an infinite list of primes:
    2 3 5 7 11 13 17 19 23 29 31 37 41 43 47 53 59 ...
Which is nice but what if we want to use the primes for calculations? Enter Generators. zkl Generators are built with fibers (co-operative threads) and fibers use

---

151findPrimes was modified from the Wikipedia article on Generators

the VM `yield` method to yield a value, so if we replace the `println` lines (above) with `vm.yield`, we have written a Generator. All that is left to do is to package it:

```
g:=Utils.Generator(findPrimes);
println(g.next());
   → 2
```

Or, to repeat the "print the infinite list" example:

```
foreach prime in (Utils.Generator(findPrimes)){ prime.println();}
   → 2 3 5 7 11 13 17 19 23 29 31 37 41 43 47 53 59 ...
```

In this example, foreach asks the Generator to return a Walker, which it does, then foreach uses that Walker to iterate.

To get the next twenty primes: `g.walk(20)`

The important thing to note about findPrimes is that finding the next prime number requires all of the previously found primes. It is expensive to ask for `primes[n]`, `primes[n+1]`, etc, which a Walker would typically do.

Code
```
class Generator{ // → Walker
   fcn init(f,args){
      var [const] fiber = vm.createFiber(start,vm.pasteArgs());
      returnClass(walker());
   }
   fcn walker{ (0).walker(*).tweak(next); }
   fcn [private] start(f,args){
      vm.yield(vm);
      f(vm.pasteArgs(1));      // f(args), only called once
      return(Void.Stop); // all done, stop walking
   }
   fcn [private] next{ fiber.resume() }
}
```

In this case, fibers are used as a continuation. A prime is computed, returned, the fiber stalls, and the VM state is frozen. When another prime is requested, the VM is thawed, the fiber resumes as if nothing had happened and calculates the next prime.

Let's walk through the code and see how fibers are used. First, "init" creates a fiber running the "start" function with whatever parameters where passed in. The first thing the fiber does is to yield the "continuation" (the VM running the fiber). The fiber is now stalled but is ready to start calculating primes. A Walker is created and returned to put a nice wrapper on the Generator. Nothing happens until somebody calls "next" (via `walker.next()`). When it is called, the fiber resumes. Now start has to repackage the parameters. Init didn't know what parameters were actually passed in, if any, so it just punts whatever it is given over the fence. Now we have to deal with them. We know the function is the first item, and that the rest of the list needs to be converted into parameters to the function:

- `Generator(findPrimes) → start(findPrimes) → findPrimes()`
- `Generator(findPrimes,1,2,3) → start(findPrimes,1,2,3) →`
  `findPrimes(1,2,3)`

Now, program execution will stay in findPrimes, until findPrimes is done (which it never is). Once you find all the primes you want, you can abandon the generator and let the garbage collector "take care" of it. If findPrimes had a built in limit and exited once it reached that limit, the Generator would `return(Void.Stop))`, which would signal the Walker that it is finished and the foreach loop would end.

A much more efficient prime finder is this sieve, which also uses Generators. It is modification of a Python program posed to StackOverflow[152]

```
fcn postponed_sieve(){            # postponed sieve, by Will Ness
    vm.yield(2); vm.yield(3);     # original code David Eppstein,
    vm.yield(5); vm.yield(7);
    D:=Dictionary();              #          ActiveState Recipe 2002
    ps:=Utils.Generator(postponed_sieve); # a separate Primes Supply
    p:=ps.pump(2,Void);           # (3) a Prime to add to dict
    q:=p*p;                       # (9) when its sQuare is
    c:=9;                         # the next Candidate
    while(1){
        if(not D.holds(c)){       # not a multiple of previous
primes
            if(c < q) vm.yield(c);  #    a prime, or
            else{   # (c==q):       #    the next prime's square:
                add(D,c + 2*p,2*p); #    (9+6,6 : 15,21,27,33,...)
                p=ps.next();        #    (5)
                q=p*p;              #    (25)
            }
        }else{                    # 'c' is a composite:
            s:=D.pop(c);          #    step of increment
            add(D,c + s,s);       #    next multiple, same step
        }
        c+=2;                     # next odd candidate
    }
}
fcn add(D,x,s){                   # make no multiple keys in Dict
    while(D.holds(x)){ x+=s }     # increment by the given step
    D[x]=s;
}
```

_____

152//http://stackoverflow.com/questions/2211990/how-to-implement-an-efficient-infinite-generator-of-prime-numbers-in-python/10733621#10733621

To generate the first 200,000 primes:
```
primes:=Utils.Generator(postponed_sieve);
N:=0d200_000;
primes.pump(N,Void,Console.println);
println("The first %,d primes.".fmt(N));
```

Sequence/List Comprehension

List comprehension is used in functional programming to express, in a concise manner, building lists with nested loops. The resulting lists can be infinitely long. Consider this line of Haskell:
```
    take 10 [ 2*x*y | x<-[0..],x^2>3, y<-[1,3..x],y^2<100-x^2 ]
      → [4,6,18,8,24,10,30,50,12,36]
```
which means take the first 10 items from the [infinite] list created by the stuff in []s, which is an expression (2xy) and two loops with guards. The first loop has x going from zero to forever where x squared is greater than three and the second has y as 1 to x counting by two as long as y matches some calculation. Or
```
foreach x in ([0..]){
    if(x*x > 3){
        foreach y in ([1..x,2]){
            if(y*y < 100-x*x) yield(2*x*y);
        }
    }
}
```
So, how to write a function that does comprehension? How about some recursion: Given: an action, parameters and a list of sequences and filters:
   If the list is empty, run action(parameters) and return the result
   else
      Get the first sequence/filter combo from the list
         If sequence is a function, call it to get the sequence
      Get an item (from the sequence) and add it to the parameters
      Run each filter with those parameters.
      If all the filters pass, recurse (with the reduced list)

The Haskell equivalent becomes:
```
gerber¹⁵³(fcn(x,y){2*x*y},
    T( [0..], fcn(x){x*x>3} ),
    T( fcn(x){[1..x,2]}, fcn(x,y){y*y<100-x*x} ) )
    .walk(10) → L(4,6,18,8,24,10,30,50,12,36)
```
Not as pretty as Haskell but it works.

153Because it purées and strains data.

Appendix C: Illustrated zkl Code Examples

And here is the code:

```
4: grind:=fcn(action,[T]args,[T]sfs){
5:    if(not sfs){  // at the bottom, do action
6:        r:=action(args.xplode());
7:        vm.yield(r);
8:        return();  // back out of recursion
9:    }
```

sfs is the list (of lists) containing sequences and filters (with a mixin to indicate it is expected to be a list).

Since the parameters are packaged in a list, they need to be unpackaged when calling action; .xplode() does that. This is going to be packaged in a Generator (so infinite lists aren't a problem), so we yield the result.

```
10:    sf:=sfs[0];    // seq & filters, T(fCreateWalker,...)
11:    sequence:=sf[0];
12:    if(self.fcn.isType(sequence))
13:        sequence=sequence(args.xplode());
14:    else if(Walker.isType(sequence))
15:        sequence.reset();
```

This bit of code is a bit funny. If sequence is a Walker, we need to reset it because we iterate over it multiple times. (If it is a collection, such as "abc", a [new] Walker will be created automagically). If it is a function, that function encodes the sequence, eg fcn(x){[1..x,2]}. The function is passed the parameters that are in play at that point.

```
16:    foreach arg in (sequence){ // create or reuse Walker
17:        arglist:=args.append(arg);
18:        r:=sf[1,*].runNFilter(False,0,arglist.xplode());
19:        if(not r) self.fcn(action,arglist,sfs[1,*]);
20:    }
21: };
```

And this is the meat. runNFilter runs each filter, and, if a filter returns False, runNFilter stops and returns True (strangely enough). If all the filters return True, False if returned (ie no failures) and we have a good set of values. Trim the list of sequences and filters and recurse.

And now, the finishing touch: add a wrapper to simplify the call and return a Generator (see the previous example):

```
3: fcn gerber(action,sequencesAndFilters){
<the grind function, see above>
22:    return(Utils.Generator(
23:        grind,action,T,T(vm.pasteArgs(1)))));
24: }
```

The nice thing about this code is that it works not just for numbers but for any collection that has a walker.[154]

154Note: For the "do it now" case, there is a more concise solution using recursive pumps.

Appendix D: A Toy Web Server

Abstract

This example is of a web server. It is a toy but illustrates using multiple threads to process requests, TCP sockets and how to write difficult to read code. All the web pages are included in the source code to make this a self contained example. A CGI example is included. The server takes about 60 lines of code, the rest is the web pages.

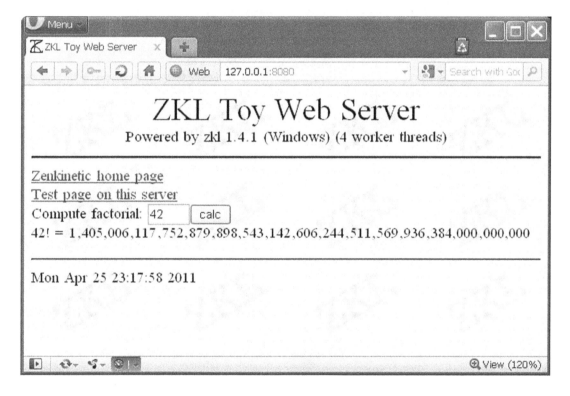

To Run

C:\ZKL>zkl **Src\httpServer.zkl**

The server prints a start up message: HTTP server started at core-shot:8080

Then point your brower at **http://127.0.0.1:8080** (or the address of the machine running the server) and start clicking.

```
//-*-c-*-
```

```
//<pre>
// httpServer.zkl: A toy web server.
// All the web site pages are here, including a CGI one.
// The server is threaded.
// Point your browser at http://127.0.0.1:8080
// http://www.w3.org/Protocols/rfc2616/rfc2616.html

const PORT=8080, SERVLET_THREADS=4;

var [const] BigNum=Import("zklBigNum");

    /* ********************************************************* */
    /* ******************** The Server ********************* */
    /* ********************************************************* */

    // A class to process requests from clients (eg browsers)
    // in a thread. Requests are received via a pipe, which feeds
    // all Servlet threads.
class Servlet{
   fcn init(jobPipe){ self.launch(jobPipe); }
   fcn liftoff(jobPipe){
      while(1){    // read request, write response, repeat
         socket:=jobPipe.read();
         if(socket.wait(60)!=1)      // what is Chrome doing?
            { socket.close(); continue; }
         if(request:=socket.read())
           try{ processRequest(request,socket); }catch{}
      }
   }
   fcn splashdown(h,e){ println("Servlet died before its time"); }
}

    // map requested page to fcn
var getMap=Dictionary("/",homePage, "/favicon.ico",favicon,
    "/testPage",testPage);

fcn processRequest(request,socket){
   println("vvvvvvvvv ",vm,"\n",request.text,"\n^^^^^^^^^^^");

   response:="";

   req:=request.text.split("\r\n");
   method,page:=req[0].split();

   switch(method){       // GET, HEAD, POST, etc
```

```
      case("GET"){
         response=
            ( if(n:=page.find("?")) cgi(page[n+1,*]) else
                                    getMap.find(page,homePage)() );
      }
      case("HEAD"){ response=responseHeader(); }
//       else do something
   }
   socket.write(response); socket.close();    // no Keep-Alive
}


      ////////////////// Start the server //////////////////////

var jobPipe=Thread.Pipe();    // a queue of requests
do(SERVLET_THREADS){ Servlet(jobPipe) }  // start threads

   // Create the HTTP server listen socket
   // Sits here forever passing client HTTP connects to Servlets
serverSocket:=Network.TCPServerSocket.open(PORT);
println("HTTP server started at http://",
   serverSocket.hostname, ":", serverSocket.port);
serverSocket.listen(fcn(socket){ jobPipe.write(socket); });



  /* ********************************************************* */
  /* ******************* The Web Site ******************** */
  /* ********************************************************* */

fcn responseHeader(status=200,reason="OK",other=""){
String(
"HTTP/1.0 ",status," ",reason,"\r\n"
,Time.Date.httpDate(),"\r\n"
"Server: ZTWS (zkl)\r\n"
"Connection: close\r\n"
"Content-Type: text/html; charset=UTF-8\r\n"
,other,
"\r\n")}


const BG="http://www.zenkinetic.com/Images/zklbg3.jpg";

      ///////////////////////// Home page ////////////////////////
fcn homePage(x=5,answer=120){    // GET / HTTP/1.1
String(
responseHeader(),
"<HTML>\n"
"<HEAD>\n"
```

```
   "<title>ZKL Toy Web Server</title>\n"
   0'|<link rel="shortcut icon"
href="http://www.zenkinetic.com/favicon.ico"/>|
"\n</HEAD>\n"
   0'|<BODY background="| + BG + 0'|">| "\n"
   "<font size=+3>\n"
      "<center>ZKL Toy Web Server</center>\n"
   "</font>\n",
   "<center>Powered by zkl %s (%s) (%s worker threads)"

.fmt(Language.version[0,3].concat("."),System.OS,vm.numThreads),
   "</center><hr/>\n"
   0'|<a href="http://www.zenkinetic.com/">Zenkinetic home
page</a></br>|
   0'|<a href=testPage>Test page on this server</a></br>|
   "<form>"
      "Compute factorial: "
      0'|<input type=input name=value maxlength="4" size="4"|
         0'|value="|,x,0'|"/>|,
      0'|<input type=submit name="fact" value="calc"/>|
      ,"<br/>",x,"! = ",answer,
   "</form>"
   ,"<hr/>",Time.Date.ctime(),
"</BODY>\n"
"</HTML>")}


   ////////////////// Test page //////////////////////
fcn testPage{     // GET /page HTTP/1.1
String(
responseHeader(),
"<HTML>\n"
"<HEAD>\n"
   "<title>ZTWS test page</title>\n"
"\n</HEAD>\n"
0'|<BODY background="| + BG + 0'|">| "\n"
   "Test page: Does the browser request the favicon?<br/>\n"
   0'|<a href=/>Go home</a></br>|
"</BODY></HTML>")}


   ////////////////// favicon /////////////////////////
fcn favicon{    // "GET /favicon.ico HTTP/1.1", Chrome/Opera do this
   responseHeader(303,"See Other",
      "Location: http://www.zenkinetic.com/favicon.ico");
}


   ////////////////// CGI: calc factorial //////////////////
```

```
fcn factTail(n,N=1){
   if(n==0) return(N);
   return(self.fcn(n - 1,n*N));
}

fcn cgi(queryString){    // GET /?value=8&fact=calc HTTP/1.1
   args:=queryString.replace("+"," ");
   args=args.split("&").apply("split","=").toDictionary();
   try{
      x:=BigNum(args["value"].toInt());
      if(x>0) return(homePage(x,"%,d".fmt(factTail(x))));
   }catch{}
   return(homePage());
}
```

Appendix D: A Toy Web Server

Index

www.ingramcontent.com/pod-product-compliance
Lightning Source LLC
Chambersburg PA
CBHW080142060326
40689CB00018B/3818